# OpenVPN

## Building and Integrating Virtual Private Networks

Learn how to build secure VPNs using this powerful Open Source application

**Markus Feilner**

BIRMINGHAM - MUMBAI

# OpenVPN

**Building and Integrating Virtual Private Networks**



First published: April 2006

Production Reference: 1170406

Published by Packt Publishing Ltd.
32 Lincoln Road
Olton
Birmingham, B27 6PA, UK.

ISBN 1-904811-85-X

www.packtpub.com

Cover Design by www.visionwt.com

# Credits

**Author**
Markus Feilner

**Reviewers**
Arne Bäumler
Norbert Graf
Markus Heller

**Technical Editor**
Jimmy Karumalil

**Editorial Manager**
Dipali Chittar

**Development Editor**
Louay Fatoohi

**Indexer**
Ashutosh Pande

**Proofreader**
Chris Smith

**Production Coordinator**
Manjiri Nadkarni

**Cover Designer**
Helen Wood

# About the Author

**Markus Feilner** is a Linux author, trainer, and consultant from Regensburg, Germany, and has been working with open-source software since the mid 1990s. His first contact with UNIX was a SUN cluster and SPARC workstations at Regensburg University (during his studies of geography). Since the year 2000, he has published several documents used in Linux training all over Germany. In 2001, he founded his own Linux consulting and training company, Feilner IT (`http://www.feilner-it.net`). Furthermore, he is an author, currently working as a trainer, consultant, and systems engineer at Millenux, Munich, where he focuses on groupware, collaboration, and virtualization with Linux-based systems and networks.

He is interested in anything about geography, traveling, photography, philosophy (especially that of open-source software), global politics, and literature, but always has too little time for these hobbies.

---

I'd like to thank all the people from the OpenVPN project and mailing list, all developers from all related projects (you are doing a great job, thank you!), and especially James Yonan for his contribution, everyone at Packt (especially Louay and Jimmy), Martin Kluge for BSD and networking know-how, Daniel Falkner for Mac screenshots, Sebastian Steinhauer for help on OpenWRT and embedded Linux, Ralf Hildebrandt for help on scripting OpenVPN, Sylvia Eisenreich for help in language matters, and everyone whom I might have forgotten now. A very big thank-you goes to my reviewers Arne, Norbert, and Markus—without your help this would not have been possible. Thank you Arne, for spending so much time in research!

---

*For Agnes.*

# About the Reviewers

**Arne Bäumler** studies information technologies at the University of Applied Sciences in Regensburg, Germany. He is interested in IT-security and network technologies. During his first practical semester at Feilner-IT, he was concerned with research, programming, testing, and rolling out Linux solutions.

**Norbert Graf** is a professional IT specialist in Munich with many years of experience in network security and groupware (both on Windows and Linux). His special fields of interest include Linux Firewalls, Windows-Linux cooperation for groupware, and Samba.

**Markus Heller** has many years of industrial working experience in open source, security, and network engineering. As an author and reviewer he has contributed to many publications and articles. He regularly teaches classes on scripting languages and computational linguistics at Munich University, where he is working on his doctorate.

# Table of Contents

# Preface

OpenVPN is an outstanding piece of software that was invented by James Yonan in the year 2001 and has steadily been improved since then. No other VPN solution offers a comparable mixture of enterprise-level security, usability, and feature richness. We have been working with OpenVPN for many years now, and it has always proven to be the best solution.

This book is intended to introduce OpenVPN Software to network specialists and VPN newbies alike. OpenVPN works where most other solutions fail and exists on almost any platform; thus it is an ideal solution for problematic setups and an easy approach for the inexperienced.

On the other hand, the complexity of classic VPN solutions, especially IPsec, gives the impression that VPN technology in general is difficult and a topic only for very experienced (network and security) specialists. OpenVPN proves that this can be different, and this book is aimed to document that.

I want to provide both a concise description of OpenVPN's features and an easy-to-understand introduction for the inexperienced. Though there may be many other possible ways to success in the scenarios described, the ones presented have been tested in many setups and have been selected for simplicity reasons.

## What This Book Covers

This book provides in-depth information on OpenVPN. After three introductory chapters about VPNs, security, and OpenVPN, some chapters focus on basic OpenVPN issues like installation and configuration on various platforms. Then a block of chapters dealing with advanced configurations and security follows, and the book closes with a chapter on troubleshooting and an appendix full of Internet links.

*Chapter 1: VPN—Virtual Private Network* gives a brief introduction to Virtual Private Networks and discusses in brief networking concepts.

*Chapter 2: VPN Security* introduces basic security concepts necessary to understand VPNs—OpenVPN in particular. We will have a look at encryption matters, symmetric and asymmetric keying, and certificates.

*Chapter 3: OpenVPN* discusses OpenVPN, its development, features, resources, and advantages and disadvantages compared to other VPN solutions, especially IPsec.

*Chapter 4: Installing OpenVPN* covers installing OpenVPN on Windows, Mac, Linux, and FreeBSD. It covers the installation on Linux from the source code and RPM packages. Installation on SuSE and Debian is also covered in detail.

*Chapter 5: Configuring OpenVPN—The First Tunnel* is where we will set up our first VPN tunnel based on a pre-shared encryption key. This chapter also covers tunnels and file exchange between Linux and Windows.

*Chapter 6: Setting Up OpenVPN with X509 Certificates* explains how to use OpenVPN's `easy-rsa` tool to create and manage certificates for secure VPN servers.

*Chapter 7: The Command openvpn and its Configuration File* covers the syntax and options of OpenVPN in detail, including many examples.

*Chapter 8: Securing OpenVPN Tunnels and Servers* introduces safe and secure configurations and explains how to set up basic firewalls for a VPN Server, using `iptables`, Shorewall, Webmin, and both the SuSE and the Windows firewall systems.

*Chapter 9: Advanced Certificate Management*, describes two very useful tools to manage certificates and revocation lists: xca for Windows and TinyCA for Linux. This chapter also explains installation and use of these tools.

*Chapter 10: Advanced OpenVPN Configuration* focuses on advanced OpenVPN configurations, including tunneling through a proxy server, pushing routing commands to clients, pushing and setting the default route through a tunnel, distributed compilation through VPN tunnels with `distcc`, OpenVPN scripting, and much else.

*Chapter 11: Troubleshooting and Monitoring* is what you should refer if you need help when something does not work. Here standard networking tools are covered that can be used for scanning and testing the connectivity of a VPN server.

*Appendix A: Internet Resources:* Though the Internet changes rapidly, many of the links provided have proven very helpful to me during the writing of this book.

# What You Need for This Book

For learning VPN technologies, it may be helpful to have at least two or four PCs. Virtualization tools like XEN or VMware are very helpful here; especially if you want to test with different operating systems and switch between varying configurations easily. However, one PC is completely enough to follow the course of this book.

Two separate networks (connected by the Internet) can provide a useful setup if you want to test firewall and advanced OpenVPN setup.

# Conventions

In this book, you will find a number of styles of text that distinguish between different kinds of information. Here are some examples of these styles, and an explanation of their meaning.

There are three styles for code. Code words in text are shown as follows: "We can include other contexts through the use of the `include` directive."

A block of code will be set as follows:

```
root=/usr/share/webmin
mimetypes=/etc/mime.types
port=10000
host=debian03.feilner-it.home
addtype_cgi=internal/cgi
realm=Webmin Server
logfile=/var/log/webmin/miniserv.log
pidfile=/var/run/webmin.pid
logtime=168
ssl=1
```

When we wish to draw your attention to a particular part of a code block, the relevant lines or items will be made bold:

```
root=/usr/share/webmin
mimetypes=/etc/mime.types
port=10000
host=debian03.feilner-it.home
addtype_cgi=internal/cgi
realm=Webmin Server
logfile=/var/log/webmin/miniserv.log
pidfile=/var/run/webmin.pid
logtime=168
ssl=1
```

Any command-line input and output is written as follows:

**`cd "C:\\Program Files\ OpenVPN\easy-rsa\"`**

**New terms** and **important words** are introduced in a bold-type font. Words that you see on the screen, in menus or dialog boxes for example, appear in our text like this: "clicking the Next button moves you to the next screen".

> Warnings or important notes appear in a box like this.

> Tips and tricks appear like this.

# Reader Feedback

Feedback from our readers is always welcome. Let us know what you think about this book, what you liked or may have disliked. Reader feedback is important for us to develop titles that you really get the most out of.

To send us general feedback, simply drop an email to `feedback@packtpub.com`, making sure to mention the book title in the subject of your message.

If there is a book that you need and would like to see us publish, please send us a note in the SUGGEST A TITLE form on `www.packtpub.com` or email `suggest@packtpub.com`.

If there is a topic that you have expertise in and you are interested in either writing or contributing to a book, see our author guide on `www.packtpub.com/authors`.

# Customer Support

Now that you are the proud owner of a Packt book, we have a number of things to help you to get the most from your purchase.

## Errata

Although we have taken every care to ensure the accuracy of our contents, mistakes do happen. If you find a mistake in one of our books—maybe a mistake in text or code—we would be grateful if you would report this to us. By doing this you can save other readers from frustration, and help to improve subsequent versions of this book. If you find any errata, report them by visiting `http://www.packtpub.com/support`, selecting your book, clicking on the **Submit Errata** link, and entering the details of your errata. Once your errata have been verified, your submission will be accepted and the errata added to the list of existing errata. The existing errata can be viewed by selecting your title from `http://www.packtpub.com/support`.

## Questions

You can contact us at `questions@packtpub.com` if you are having a problem with some aspect of the book, and we will do our best to address it.

# 1

# VPN—Virtual Private Network

This chapter will start with networking solutions used in the past for connecting several branches of a company. Technological advances like broadband Internet access brought about new possibilities and new concepts for this issue, one of them being the **Virtual Private Network (VPN)**. In this chapter, you will learn what the term VPN means, how it evolved during the last decade, why it is necessary to modern enterprises, and how typical VPNs work. Basic networking concepts are necessary to understand the variety of VPN solutions discussed in this chapter.

## Branches Connected by Dedicated Lines

In former times, information exchange between branches of a company was mainly done by mail, telephone, and later by fax. But today there are four main challenges for modern companies:

- The general acceleration of business processes and the rising need for fast, flexible information exchange between all branches of a company has made "old-fashioned" mail and even fax services appear too slow for modern requirements.
- Technologies like Groupware, Customer Relationship Management (CRM), and Enterprise Resource Planning (ERP) are used to ensure productive teamwork and every employee is expected to cooperate.
- Almost every enterprise has several branches in different locations and often field and home workers. All of these must be enabled to participate in the internal information exchange without delays.
- All computer networks have to fulfill security standards to high levels to ensure data integrity, authenticity, and stability.

These four factors have led to the need of sophisticated networking solutions between a company's offices all over the world. With computer networks connecting all desktops within a single location, the need for connections between the sites has become more and more urgent.

In the very beginning, you could only buy dedicated lines between your sites and these lines were expensive, and thus only large companies could afford to connect their branches to enable world-wide teamwork. To reach this goal, fast and expensive connections had to be installed in every site, costing much more than normal enterprise Internet access.

The concept behind this network design was based on a real network between the branches of the company. A provider was needed to connect every location, and a real cable connection between all branches was established. Like the telephone network, a single line connecting two partners was used for communication.

Security for this line was achieved by providing a dedicated network—every connection between branches had to be installed with a leased line. For a company with four branches (A, B, C, and D), six dedicated lines would then become necessary:

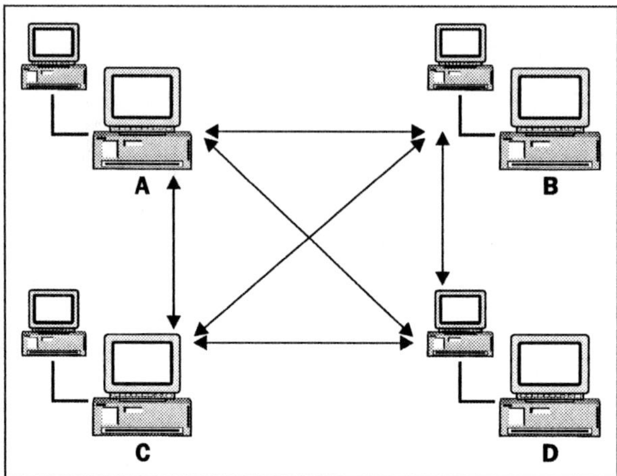


Furthermore, **Remote Access Servers (RAS)** were used for field or home workers who would only connect temporarily to the company's network. These people had to use special dial-in connections (with a modem or an ISDN line), and the company acted like an Internet provider. For every remote worker a dial-in account had to be configured and field workers could only connect over this line. The telephone company provided one dedicated line for every dial-up, and the central branch had to make sure that enough telephone lines were always available.

By protecting the cables and the dial-in server, a real private network was installed at very high costs. Privacy within the company's network spanning multiple branches was achieved by securing the lines and providing services only to hard-wired connection points. Almost all security and availability tasks were handed over to the service provider at very high costs. But by connecting sites directly, a higher data transfer speed could be achieved than with "normal" Internet connections at that time.

Until the middle of the 1990s, expensive dedicated lines and dial-in access servers were used to ensure team work between different branches and field workers of large companies.

## Broadband Internet Access and VPNs

In mid 1990s, the rise of the Internet and the increase of speed for cheap Internet connections paved the way for new technologies. Many developers, administrators, and, last but not the least, managers had discovered that there might be better solutions than spending several hundreds of dollars, if not thousands of dollars, on dedicated and dial-up access lines.

The idea was to use the Internet for communication between branches and at the same time ensure safety and secrecy of the data transferred. In short: providing secure connections between enterprise branches via low-cost lines using the Internet. This is a very basic description of what VPNs are all about.

A VPN is:

- **Virtual**, because there is no real direct network connection between the two (or more) communication partners, but only a virtual connection provided by **VPN Software**, realized normally over public Internet connections.
- **Private**, because only the members of the company connected by the VPN Software are allowed to read the data transferred.

With a VPN, your staff in Sydney can work with the London office as if both were in the same location. The VPN Software provides a virtual network between those sites by using a low-cost Internet connection. This network is only virtual because no real, dedicated network connection to the partner is established.

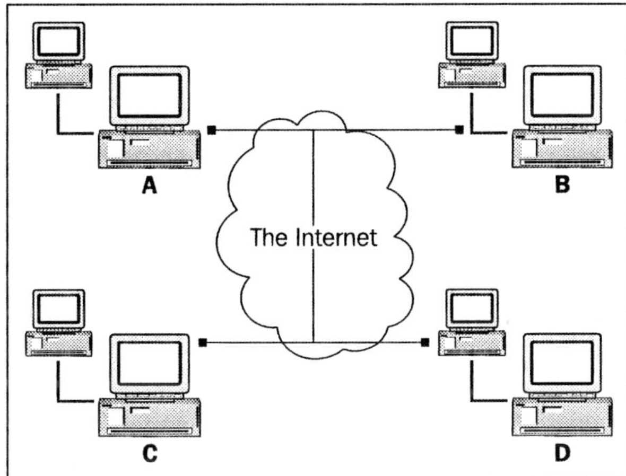


A VPN can also be described as a set of logical connections secured by special software that establishes privacy by safeguarding the connection endpoints. Today the Internet is the network medium used, and privacy is achieved by modern cryptographic methods.

# How Does a VPN Work?

Let's use an example to explain how VPNs work. The **Virtual Entity Networks Inc. (VEN Inc.)** has two branches, London and Sydney. If the Australian branch in Sydney decides to contract a supplier, then the London office might need to know that immediately. The main part of the IT infrastructure is set up in London. In Sydney there are twenty people whose work depends on the availability of the data hosted on London servers.

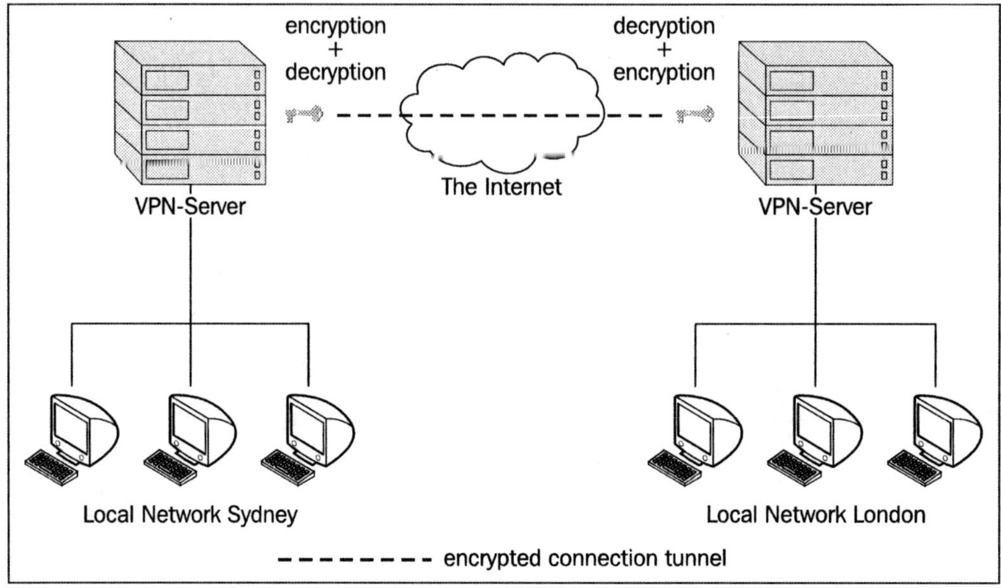


Both sites are equipped with a permanent Internet line. An Internet gateway router is set up to provide Internet access for the staff. This router is configured to protect the local network of the site from unauthorized access from the other side, which is the "evil" Internet. Such a router set up to block special traffic can be called a **firewall** and must be found in every branch that is supposed to take part in the VPN.

The VPN Software must be installed on this firewall (or a device or server protected by it). Many modern firewall appliances from manufacturers like Cisco or BinTec include this feature, and there is VPN Software for all hardware and software platforms.

In the next step, the VPN Software has to be configured to establish the connection to the other side: e.g. the London VPN server has to accept connections from the Sydney server, and the Sydney server must connect to London (or vice versa).

If this step is successfully completed, the company has a working Virtual Network. The two branches are connected via the Internet and can work together like in a real network. Here, we have a VPN without privacy, because any Internet router between London and Sydney can read the data exchanged. A competitor gaining control over an Internet router could read all relevant business data going through the virtual network.

So how do we make this Virtual Network private? The solution is encryption. The VPN traffic between two branches is *locked* with special keys, and only computers or persons owning this key can open this lock and look at the data sent.

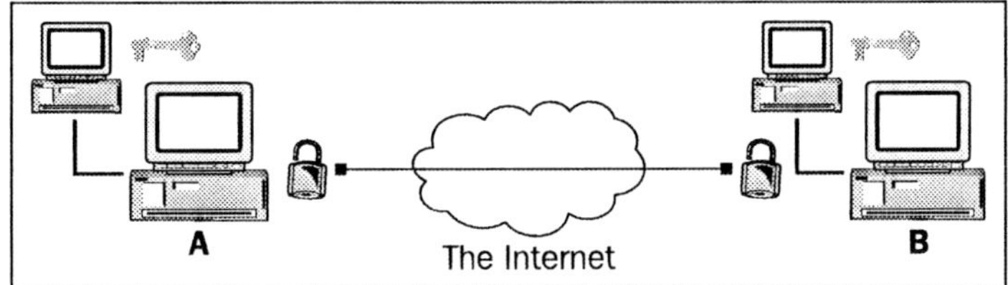


All data sent from Sydney to London or from London to Sydney must be encrypted before and decrypted after transmission. The encryption safeguards the data in the connection like the walls of a tunnel protect the train from the mountain around it. This explains why Virtual Private Networks are often simply known as tunnels or VPN tunnels, and the technology is often called **tunneling**—even if there is no quantum mechanics or other magic involved.

The exact method of encryption and providing the keys to all parties involved makes one of the main distinguishing factors between different VPN solutions.

A VPN connection normally is built between two Internet access routers equipped with a firewall and VPN software. The software must be set up to connect to the VPN partner, the firewall must be set up to allow access, and the data exchanged between VPN partners must be secured (by encryption). The encryption key must be provided to all VPN partners, so that the data exchanged can only be read by authorized VPN partners.

## What are VPNs Used For?

In the earlier examples, we have discussed several possible scenarios for the use of VPN technology. But one typical VPN solution must be added here: More and more enterprises offer their customers or business partners a protected access to relevant data for their business relations, like ordering formulas or stocking data. Thus, we have three typical scenarios for VPN solutions in modern enterprises:

- An intranet spanning over several locations of a company
- A dial-up access for home or field workers with changing IPs
- An extranet for customers or business partners

Each of these typical scenarios requires special security considerations and setups. The external home workers will need different access to servers in the company than the customers and business partners. In fact, access for business partners and customers must be restricted severely.

Now that we have seen how a VPN can securely connect a company in different ways, we will have a closer look at the way VPNs work. To understand the functionality, some basic network concepts need to be understood.

All data exchange in computer networks is based on protocols. Protocols are like languages or rituals that must be used between communication partners in networks. Without the correct use of the correct protocol, communication fails.

# Networking Concepts—Protocols and Layers

There is a huge number of protocols involved in any action you take when you access the Internet or a PC in your local network. Your **Network Interface Card** (**NIC**) will communicate with a hub, a switch, or a router; your application will communicate with its pendant or a server on the other PC, and many more protocol-based communication procedures are necessary to exchange data.

Because of this the **Open Systems Interconnection** (**OSI**) specification was created. Every protocol used in today's networks can be classified by this scheme.

The OSI specification defines seven numbered layers of data exchange, which start at Layer 1 (the physical layer) of the underlying network media (electrical, optical, or radio signals) and span up to Layer 7 (the application layer), where applications on PCs communicate with each other.

The layers of the OSI model are:

1. Physical Layer: Sending and receiving through the hardware.
2. Data Link Layer: Direct communication between network devices within the same medium.
3. Network Layer: Routing, addressing, error handling, etc.
4. Transport Layer: End-to-end error recovery and flow control.
5. Session Layer: Establishing connections and sessions between applications.
6. Presentation Layer: Translating between application data formats and network formats.
7. Application Layer: Application-specific protocols.

This set of layers is hierarchical and every layer is serving the layer above and the layer below. If the protocols of the physical layer could communicate successfully, then the control is handed to the next layer, the Data Link Layer. Only if all layers, 1 through 6, can communicate successfully, can data exchange between applications (on Layer 7) be achieved.

In the Internet, however, a slightly different approach is used.

The Internet is mainly based on the **Internet Protocol** (**IP**).

The layers of the IP model are:

1. Link Layer: A concatenation of OSI Layers 1 and 2 (Physical and Data Link Layers).
2. Network Layer: Comprises the Network Layer of the OSI model.
3. Transport Layer: Comprises protocols like **Transmission Control Protocol** (**TCP**) and **User Datagram Protocol** (**UDP**), which are the basis for protocols of the Application Layer.
4. Application Layer: Concatenation of OSI Layers 5 through 7 (Session, Presentation, and Application Layers). The protocols in the Transport Layer are the basis for protocols of the Application Layer (Layer 5 through Layer 7) like HTTP, FTP, or others.

A network packet consists of two parts: header and data. The header is a sort of label containing metadata on sender, recipient, and administrative information for the transfer. On the networking level of an Ethernet network, these packets are called *frames*. In the context of the Internet Protocol these packets are called datagrams, Internet datagrams, IP datagrams, or simply packets.

So what do VPNs do? VPN Software takes IP packets or Ethernet frames and **wraps** them into another packet. This may sound complicated, but it is a very simple trick, as the following examples will show:

**Example 1**: Sending a (not really) anonymous parcel

You want to send a parcel to a friend who lives in a community with strange people, whom you don't trust. Your parcel has the address label with sender and recipient data (like an Internet packet). If you do not want the commune to know that you sent your friend a parcel, but at the same time you want your friend to realize this before he opens it, what would you do? Just wrap the whole parcel in another packet with a different address label (e.g. without your sender information) and no one in the commune will know that this parcel is from you. But your friend will unpack the first layer and see a parcel still unpacked, and with an address label from you.

**Example 2**: Sending a locked parcel

OK, now let's distrust the commune still more. Somebody might want to open the parcel in order to find out what's inside. To prevent this, you will use a locked case. There are only two keys to the lock, one for you and one for your friend. Only you and your friend can unlock the case and look inside the packet.

VPN Software uses a combination of the earlier two examples:

- Whole Network packets (frames, datagrams) consisting of header and data are wrapped into new packets.
- All data including metadata like recipient and sender are encrypted.
- The new packets are labeled with new headers containing meta-information about the VPN and are addressed to the VPN partner.

All VPN Software systems differ only in the special way of wrapping and locking the data.

> Protocols define the method of data exchange in computer networks. The OSI model classifies protocols in seven layers spanning from network layers to application layers. IP Packets consist of headers with meta-information and data. VPNs wrap and encrypt whole network packets in new network packets, adding new headers including address data.

## Tunneling and Overhead

We have learned already that VPN technology often is called tunneling, because the data in a VPN connection is protected from the Internet as the walls of the a road or rail tunnel protect the traffic in the tunnel from the masses of stone of the mountain above. Let's now have a closer look at how VPN Software does this:

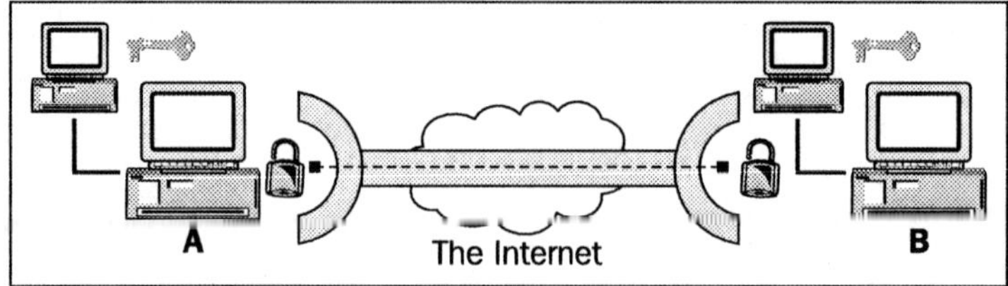


The VPN software in the locations A and B encrypts (lock) and decrypts (unlock) the data and sends it through the tunnel. Like cars or trains in a tunnel, the data cannot go anywhere else but the other tunnel endpoint.

The following are put together and wrapped into one new package:

- Tunnel information (like the address of the other endpoint)
- Encryption data and methods
- The original IP packet (or network frame)

The new package is then sent to the other tunnel endpoint. The payload of this package now holds the complete IP packet (or network frame), but in encrypted form and thus not readable for anyone not possessing the right key. The new header of the packet simply contains the addresses of sender and recipient and other metadata necessary for and provided by the VPN software used.

Perhaps you have noticed that the amount of data sent grows during the process of "wrapping". Depending on the VPN software used, this so called *overhead* can become a very important factor. The overhead is the difference between net data sent to the tunnel software and gross data sent through the tunnel by the VPN software. If a file of 1 MB is sent from user A to user B, and this file causes 1.5 MB traffic in the tunnel, then the overhead would be 50%, a very high level. (Please note that every protocol used causes overhead, so not all of that 50% might be the fault of the VPN solution.) The overhead caused by the VPN Software depends on the amount of organizational data and the encryption used. Whereas the first depends only on the VPN Software used, the latter is simply a matter of choice between security and speed. In other words, the better the encryption you use, the more overhead you will produce. Speed versus security is your choice.

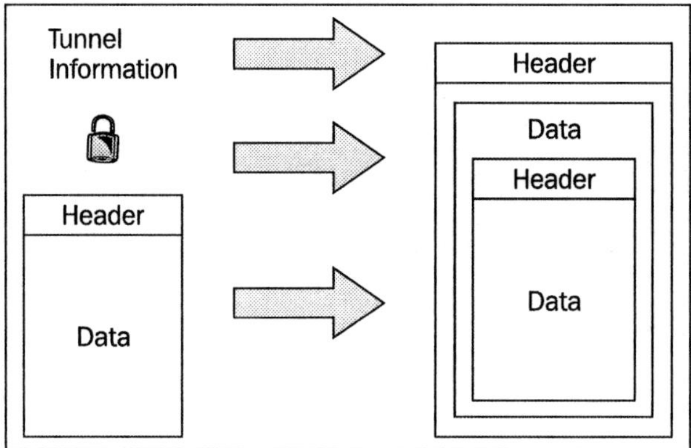

## VPN Concepts—Overview

During the last ten years, many different VPN concepts have evolved. You may have noticed that I always added "network frames" in brackets when I spoke of tunneling IP packets. This became necessary, because in principle, tunneling can be done on almost all layers of the OSI model.

## A Proposed Standard for Tunneling

The **General Routing Encapsulation (GRE)** provides a standard for tunneling data, which was defined in 1994 in **Request for Comments (RFCs)** 1701 and 1702. Perhaps, because this definition is not a protocol definition, but more or less a standard proposal on how to tunnel data, this implementation has found its way into many devices and become the basis for other protocols.

The concept of GRE is pretty simple. A protocol header and a delivery header are added to the original packet and its payload is encapsulated in the new packet. No encryption is done. The advantage of this model are almost obvious—the simplicity offers many possibilities, the transparency enables administrators and routers to look inside the packets and pass decisions based on the type of payload sent. By doing so, special applications can be privileged.

There are many implementations for GRE tunneling software under Linux; only kernel support is necessary, which is fulfilled by most modern distributions.

## Protocols Implemented on OSI Layer 2

Encapsulating packages on the OSI Layer 2 has a significant advantage: the tunnel is able to transfer non-IP protocols. IP is a standard used widely in the Internet and in Ethernet networks. However, there are different standards too. Netware Systems, for example, uses the **Internetwork Packet Exchange (IPX)** protocol to communicate. VPN technologies residing in Layer 2 can theoretically tunnel any kind of packet. In most cases, a virtual **Point-to-Point Protocol (PPP)** device is established which is used to connect to the other tunnel endpoint. (A PPP device is normally used for modem or DSL connections.)

Four well-known Layer 2 VPN technologies, which are defined by RFCs, use encryption methods and provide user authentication:

- The **Point to Point Tunneling Protocol (PPTP)**, which was developed with the help of Microsoft, is an expansion of the PPP and is integrated in all newer Microsoft Operating Systems. PPTP uses GRE for encapsulation and can tunnel IP, IPX, and other packages over the Internet. The main disadvantage is the restriction that there can only be one tunnel at a time between communication partners.
- The **Layer 2 Forwarding (L2F)** was developed almost at the same time by companies like Cisco and others and offers more possibilities than PPTP, especially regarding tunneling of network frames and multiple simultaneous tunnels.
- The **Layer 2 Tunneling Protocol (L2TP)** is accepted as an industry standard and is being used widely by Cisco and other manufacturers. Its success is based on the fact that it combines the advantages of L2F and PPTP without suffering from their

disadvantages. Even though it provides no own security mechanisms, it can be combined with technologies offering such mechanisms like **IPsec** (see the section *Protocols Implemented on OSI Layer 3*).

- The **Layer 2 Security Protocol** (**L2Sec**) was developed to provide a solution to the security flaws of IPsec. Even though its overhead is rather big, the security mechanisms used are secure, because mainly SSL/TLS is used.

Other distinguishing factors between the mentioned systems and protocols are:

- Availability of authentication mechanisms
- Support for advanced networking features like **Network Address Translation (NAT)**
- Dynamic allocation of IP addresses for tunnel partners in dial-up mode
- Support for **Public Key Infrastructures (PKI)**

These features will be discussed in later chapters.

## Protocols Implemented on OSI Layer 3

IPsec is probably the most wide-spread tunneling technology. In fact, it is rather a set of protocols, standards, and mechanisms than a single technology. The wide range of definitions, specifications, and protocols are already the main disadvantages about IPsec. It is a complex technology with many different implementations and many security loopholes. IPsec was a compromise accepted by a commission and therefore is something like a least common denominator agreed upon. This means that IPsec can be used in many different setups and environments, ensuring compatibility, but almost no aspect of it offers the best possible solution.

IPsec was developed as an Internet Security Standard on Layer 3, and has been standardized by the **Internet Engineering Task Force** (**IETF**) since 1995. IPsec can be used to encapsulate any traffic of application layers, but no traffic of lower network layers. Neither network frames, IPX packets, nor broadcast messages can be transferred, and network address translation is only possible with restrictions.

Nevertheless, IPsec can use a variety of encryption mechanisms, authentication protocols, and other security associations. IPsec software exists for almost every platform, and compatibility with the implementation of other manufacturers is secured in most cases even though there are significant problems resulting from proprietary extensions.

The main advantage of IPsec is the fact that it is being used everywhere. An administrator can choose from an abundant number of hardware devices and software implementations to provide his or her networks with a secure tunnel.

Basically there are two relevant methods that IPsec uses:

- **Tunnel Mode**: The tunnel mode works like the examples listed above; the whole IP packets are encapsulated in a new packet and sent to the other tunnel endpoint, where the VPN software unpacks them and forwards them to the recipient. In this way the IP addresses of sender and recipient, and all other metadata are protected as well.

- **Transport Mode**: In transport mode, only the payload of the data section is encrypted and encapsulated. By doing so, the overhead is significantly smaller than in tunnel mode, but an attacker can easily read the metadata and find out who is communicating with whom. However, the data is encrypted and therefore protected, which makes IPsec a real "private" VPN solution.

IPsec's security model is probably the most complex of all existing VPN solutions and will be discussed in brief in the next chapter.

## Protocols Implemented on OSI Layer 4

It is also possible to establish VPN tunnels only on the application layer. **Secure Sockets Layer (SSL)** and **Transport Layer Security (TLS)** solutions follow this approach. The user can access the VPN network of a company through a browser connection between his or her client and the VPN server in the enterprise. A connection is simply started by logging into an HTTPS-secured website with a browser. Meanwhile, there are several promising products available, like SSL-Explorer from `http://3sp.com/showSslExplorer.do`, and products like these offer great flexibility combined with strong security and easy setup. Using the secure connection the browser offers, users can connect network drives and access services in the remote network. Security is achieved by encrypting traffic using SSL/TLS mechanisms, which have proven to be very reliable and are permanently improved and tested.

## OpenVPN—An SSL/TLS-Based Solution

OpenVPN is a newer and an outstanding VPN solution. It implements Layer 2 or Layer 3 connections, uses the industry standard SSL/TLS for encryption, and combines almost all features of the mentioned VPN solutions. Its main disadvantage is the fact that there are still few hardware manufacturers integrating it in their solutions.

# Summary

In this chapter, you have learned about techniques that have been and are used in companies that have computer networks spanning over several branches. You have learned network basics like protocols, networking layers, the OSI reference model, and which VPN solutions work on which layer. You have read what tunneling is, how it works, and how different VPN solutions implement it.

# 2
# VPN Security

In this chapter, we will discuss goals and techniques concerning VPN security. These two terms are linked together very closely. Without security, a VPN is not private anymore.

Therefore, we will first have a look at basic security issues and guiding measures to be taken in a company. Information on symmetric and asymmetric keying methods, key exchange techniques, and the problem of security versus simplicity pave the way for SSL/TLS security and a closer look at SSL certificates. After having read this chapter, you will be prepared to understand the underlying security concerns of OpenVPN (and any other VPN solution).

## VPN Security

IT security and hence also VPN security is best described by three goals that have to be attained:

- **Privacy (Confidentiality)**: The data transferred should only be available to the authorized.
- **Reliability (Integrity)**: The data transferred must not be changed between sender and receiver.
- **Availability**: The data transferred must be available when needed.

All of these goals have to be achieved by using reliable software, hardware, Internet service providers, and security policies. A security policy defines responsibilities, standard procedures, and disaster management and recovery scenarios to be prepared for the worst. Understanding maximum damage and the costs of the worst possible catastrophe can give an idea of how much effort has to be spent in security issues. Security policies should also define organizational questions like:

- Who has the key to the server room when the administrator is on holiday?
- Who is allowed to bring a private laptop?
- How are the cables protected?
- How is a **wireless LAN (WLAN)** protected?

However, discussing all these questions would go far beyond the scope of this book. There are a number of excellent documents online where you can read more about basic security issues that should also be discussed in your company. I only want to mention two of them here: the *IT*

*Baseline Protection* as published by the German BSI and the *IT-Sec Handbook* containing concise security hints and are often quoted as the reference material for all security issues in modern enterprises. You can find them here:

`http://www.bsi.bund.de/english/gshb/index.htm`

`http://www.cccure.org/Documents/HISM/ewtoc.html`

VPN security itself is achieved by protecting the traffic with modern, strong encryption methods, secure authentication techniques, and firewalls controlling the traffic into and from the tunnels. And simply encrypting the traffic is not enough; there are huge differences in security depending on the methods used. The following sections will deal with issues concerning confidentiality and integrity, whereas the approach to ensure availability is discussed in the next chapter.

# Privacy—Encrypting the Traffic

Often passwords or encryption keys are used to encrypt data. If both sides use the same key to encrypt and decrypt data, this is called **symmetric encryption**. The encryption key has to be put on all machines that are supposed to take part in the VPN connection.

## Symmetric Encryption and Pre-Shared Keys

Anybody who has this key can decrypt the traffic. If an attacker gets hold of this key, he or she can decrypt all traffic and compromise all systems taking part in the VPN, until all systems are supplied with another key. Furthermore, such a static, pre-shared key can be guessed, deciphered, or hacked by brute-force attacks. It is merely a matter of time for an attacker to find out the key and to read, or even worse, change the data.

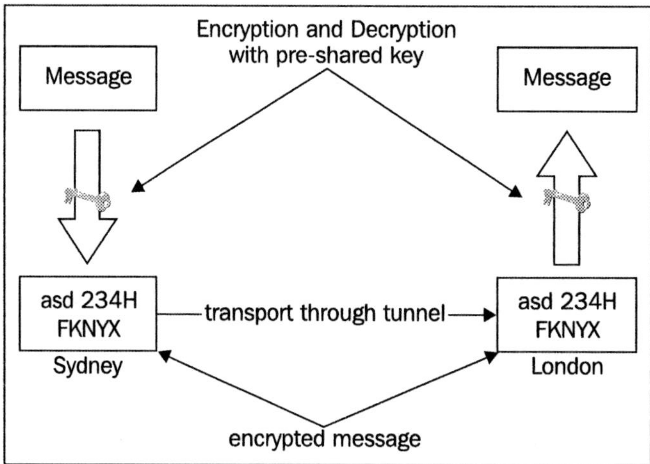


Therefore, VPN software like IPsec changes keys in defined intervals. Every key is only valid for a certain period of time, called *key lifetime*. A good combination of key lifetime and key length ensures that an attacker cannot decrypt the key while it is valid. If the VPN Software is changing keys, then the attacker must be quick, or the acquired key is worthless.

Nevertheless, if the VPN software is permanently changing keys, a method of key exchange between the communication partners has to be used so that both sides use the same encryption key at the same time. This key exchange has to be secured again, following the same principles mentioned earlier. During the last decade many key exchange methods have been invented, some very sophisticated, and lots of them have proven insecure in the meantime. Basically, this key exchange adds a layer of complexity to the VPN software, which is prone to failure or being compromised.

IPsec, the most frequently used VPN technology brings its own protocol for exchanging the encryption keys. This protocol is called **Internet Key Exchange (IKE)** Protocol and has been under development since the mid-nineties and is still not finished. Many discussions about the security of this protocol can be found on the Internet and even though IKE seems to have some security issues, it is used (with IPsec) in many companies.

## Reliability and Authentication

Another danger are so-called **man-in-the-middle** attacks, also know as *eavesdropping*. In this scenario, a hacker intercepts all data traffic between sender and receiver, copies it and forwards it to its true destination. Neither sender nor receiver would notice that the data is being intercepted. The man-in-the-middle can store, copy, analyze, and perhaps even modify the captured traffic. This is possible if the attacker can intercept and decrypt the keys while they are being used for encryption.

## The Problem of Complexity in Classic VPNs

With classical VPNs that use symmetric keying, there are several layers of authentication, exchange of encryption keys, and encryption/decryption. The following are the first three steps of VPNs with symmetric encryption:

1. The partners have to authenticate each other.
2. They have to agree on the encryption methods.
3. Then they have to agree on the key exchange methods used.

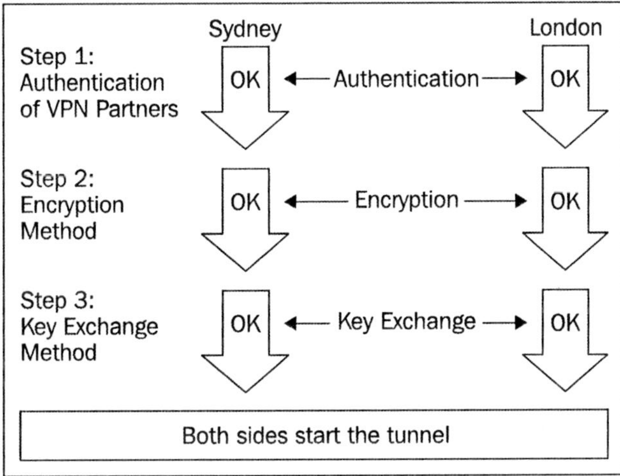

This is why VPN technology is often known as complex and difficult. The last paragraphs have described more or less the basic way in which many modern VPN solutions work. In a nutshell, the different approaches to keying, key exchange, and authentication of VPN partners make the main part of the differences between the VPN Solutions.

## Asymmetric Encryption with SSL/TLS

SSL/TLS uses one of the best encryption technologies called **asymmetric encryption** to ensure the identity of the VPN partner. Both encryption partners own two keys each: one public and the other, private. The public key is handed over to the communication partners, who encrypt the data with it. Because of the selected mathematical algorithm used to create the public/private key pair, only the recipient's private key can decrypt data encoded by his public key.

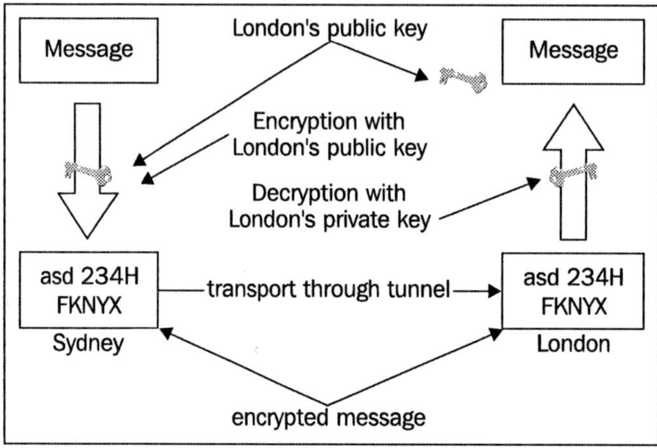


The private keys have to be kept secret and the public keys have to be exchanged.

In the example above, a text message is encrypted in Sydney with the public key of London. The scrambled code is sent to London, where it can be deciphered using London's private key. This can be done vice versa for data from London to Sydney, which is encrypted by the Sydney public key in London and can only be decrypted by the Sydney private key in Sydney.

A similar procedure can also be used for authentication purposes: London sends a large random number to Sydney, where this number is encoded with the private key and sent back. In London, the Sydney public key can decode the number. If the numbers sent and decrypted match, then the sender must be the holder of the Sydney private key. This is called **digital signature**.

# SSL/TLS Security

The SSL/TLS library can be used for authentication and encryption purposes. This library is part of the **OpenSSL Software** that is installed on any modern operating system. If available, SSL/TLS certificate-based authentication and encryption should always be first choice for any tunnel you create.

SSL, also known as TLS, is a protocol originally designed by Netscape Communications Corporation to ensure easy-to-use data integrity and authenticity for the fast growing Internet in the 1990s. Everybody using a modern browser can participate in encrypted communication. SSL/TLS is an outstanding technology that is being used all over the Web for banking, e-commerce, or any other application where privacy and security are needed. It is being steadily controlled, debugged, tested, and improved by both open source and proprietary developers and many corporations.

As SSL/TLS resides beneath application protocols, it can be used for almost any application. Every surfer has noticed URLs beginning with `https://` instead of `http://`, which signifies an encrypted connection. Point your browser to a website encrypted with `https://`, like `https://packtpub.com`.

Whenever you point your browser to such a page for the first time, you have to validate an SSL certificate. Usually, your browser does this for you when the certificate is trustworthy. The screenshot above shows Mozilla's pop-up window, which you receive when there are errors in validating the certificate. Usually, this is just one of these OK buttons most people press during surfing without further attention.

## Understanding SSL/TLS Certificates

By accepting a certificate (pressing OK), the browser is told to trust the issuer (the website that provided the certificate) and you agree to use this certificate for encryption of the communication with this server. When you're using Mozilla, Firefox, or Konqueror, you are prompted if you want to accept the certificate. Click on the button View Certificate, and you will see a screen like that shown in screenshot overleaf in the section on *Trusted Certificates*.

## Trusted Certificates

In the following screenshot, you can see the information contained in the SSL certificate. The information in the fields Issued To and Issued By is probably the most important. If you find a trustworthy organization here, it should be safe to trust this certificate. Trustworthy means one of several organizations who *sign certificates*, thereby guaranteeing the identity of the owner of the certificate.

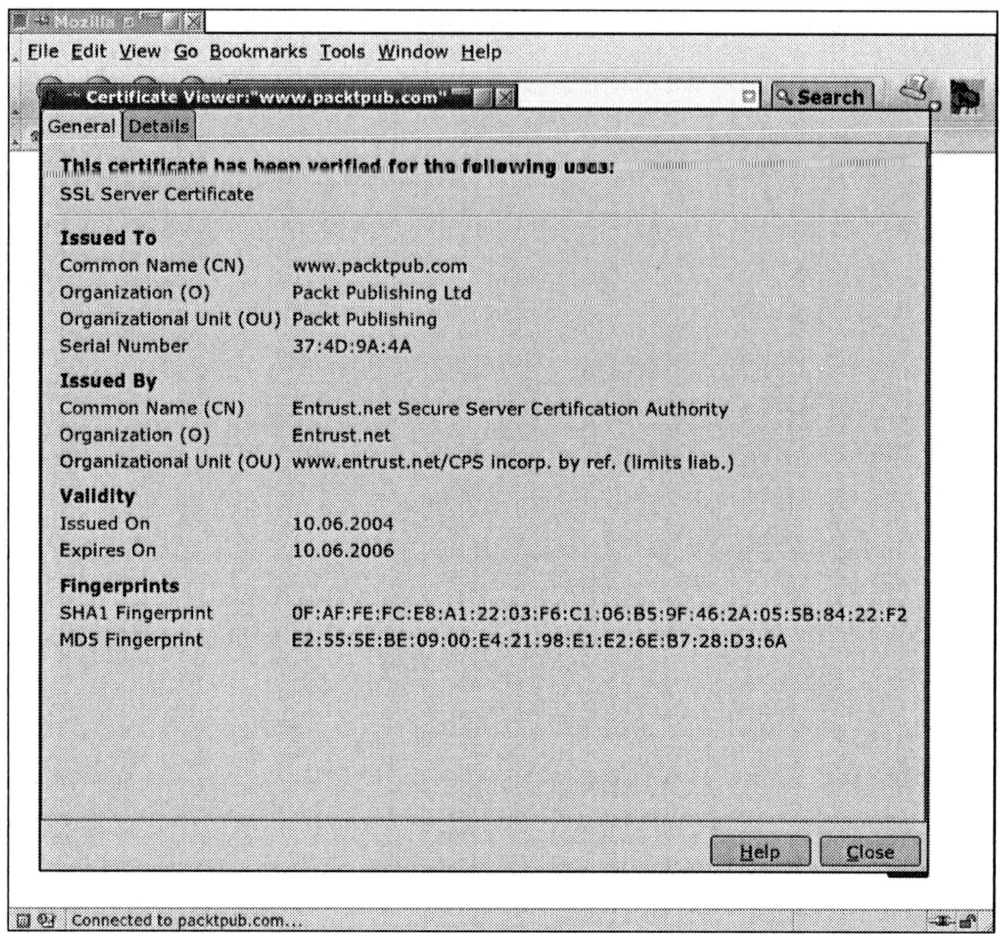


With a signed certificate the owner of the certificate can prove that he or she is who he or she claims to be, to anybody who trusts the certificate authority.

Every TLS-enabled browser contains a list of trustworthy organizations that are entitled to sign certificates and the keys necessary to confirm this.

Click the Close button and have another look at the first window—Security Error. It is in fact a warning. The certificate was originally issued for `www.packtpub.com` and not for `packtpub.com`, from where it was received, and the Mozilla SSL client simply warns about this fact. `www.packtpub.com` is a subdomain of `packtpub.com`, so this difference should not be crucial. However, if you receive a warning that the certificate for domain A was originally issued for domain B, you should become suspicious.

This so-called third-party-authentication scheme is pretty common today. The ID cards and passports we use today work the same way—the government of the state you live in guarantees that you are who you claim to be. This information is only valid for a certain time and could be traced back to the issuer. Almost every other person, company, or organization relies on this information. These principles are also implemented in many modern authentication mechanisms like Kerberos or SSL/TLS.

## Self-Signed Certificates

It is also possible to use certificates that are not signed by authorities mentioned above, but by a local **Certificate Authority (CA)**.

In real life, if a good friend introduces us to a reliable friend of his, we tend to trust him too simply because of the recommendation. But we would not trust somebody we do not know. If you point Mozilla to a site with a certificate that is signed *only* by a local CA, you will receive the following warning:

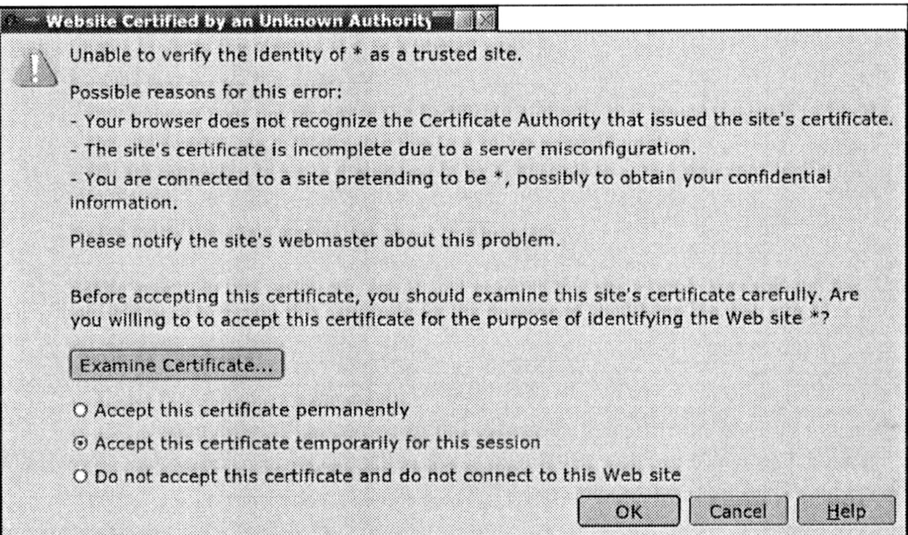


This warning means: "Watch out, I do not know the issuer of this certificate, nor do I know someone who guarantees the identity of the issuer."

Every SSL/TLS client gives you a warning when a client wants to establish an encrypted connection with an unsigned private certificate. Mozilla opens the Window Website Certified by an Unknown Authority.

Click on the button Examine Certificate to view the details of a self-signed certificate in Mozilla:

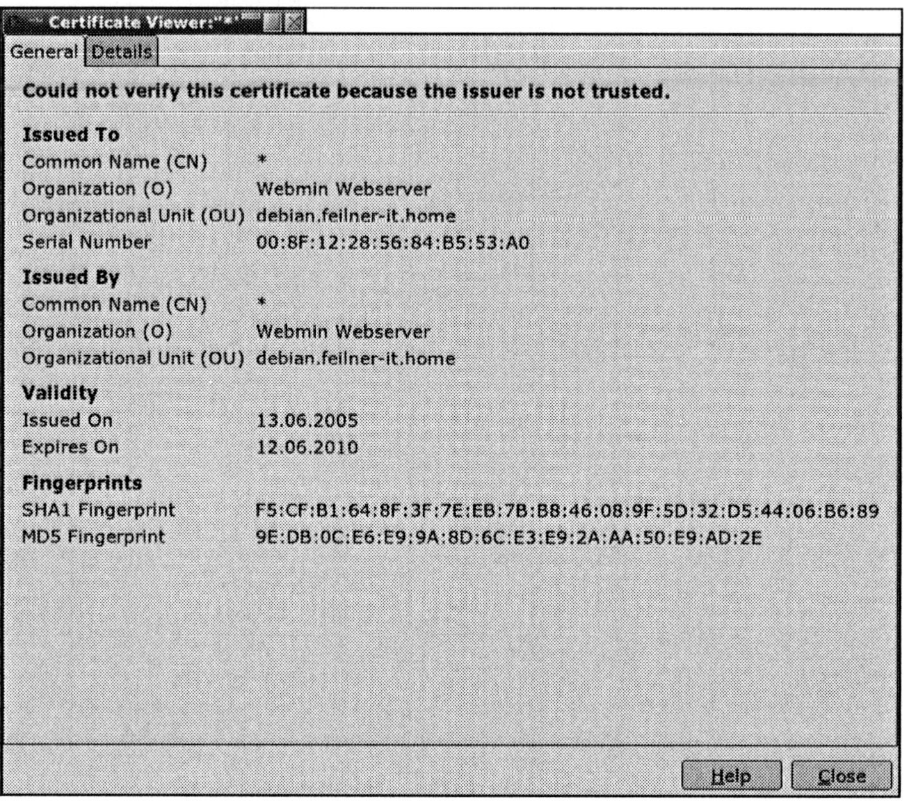


In this screenshot you see a certificate that was built to secure the Webmin administration interface on a local system. Mozilla reports: Could not verify this certificate because the issuer is not trusted. Where does this certificate come from?

The solution is simple: The OpenSSL software package, which contains the encryption software, also provides programs to create certificates and to sign them. Such certificates are called **self-signed certificates**, and can only be considered trustworthy when the issuer or the CA is known to and trusted by the client. Later in this book, you will learn how to create, sign, and manage such certificates.

Self-signed certificates are often used for testing purposes or in local networks because registering (signing) certificates at certificate authorities is expensive and not necessary in many scenarios. However, the security policy of a company should contain definitions about the use of signed and unsigned certificates on servers.

## SSL/TLS Certificates and VPNs

SSL/TLS certificates work exactly the same way with VPNs—a certificate authority is defined or created and all valid certificates issued by this authority are accepted for the VPN. Every client must have a valid certificate issued by this CA and is therefore allowed to establish a connection to the VPN.

A **Certificate Revocation List** (**CRL**) can be used to revoke certificates that belong to clients that must not be allowed to connect to the VPN any longer. This can be done without configuration on any client, simply by creating an appropriate revocation list on the server. This is very useful when a laptop is stolen or compromised.

An organization using a pre-shared key must put this key on every system that connects to the VPN server. The key must be changed on all systems if one single system or key is lost. But if you are using certificates with revocation lists, you only have to put the certificate of the stolen laptop on the server's CRL. When this client tries to connect to the server, access will be denied. There is no need for interaction on with any client.

Connections are refused if:

- No certificate is presented
- A certificate from a wrong CA is presented
- A revoked certificate is presented

Such certificates can be used for many purposes. HTTPS and OpenVPN are only two applications of an abundant variety of possibilities. Other VPN Systems (like IPsec), web servers, mail servers, and almost every other server application can use these certificates to authenticate clients. If you have understood and applied this technology correctly, you have achieved a very high degree of security.

# Summary

In this chapter, you have learned basic security concepts necessary for VPN technologies. There are several websites with excellent material on IT security issues. You have received an overview of basic security and encryption issues and know why complexity is always an enemy of security. With symmetric keying, both encryption partners use the same key, but when asymmetric keying is used, the encryption key is different from the one used for decrypting the data. The SSL/TLS library uses asymmetric keying and provides certificates used by millions of websites. The certificates can be signed by official authorities like our passports or ID cards, or self-signed by a local authority. This is called third-party authentication because a certificate signed by third party is trusted.

# 3
# OpenVPN

In this chapter we will discuss the nature of OpenVPN. We will start with its features and its release history, followed by its basic networking concepts, and a first brief look at the configuration. At the end of this chapter, OpenVPN is compared to IPsec, the quasi-standard in VPN technology.

## Advantages of OpenVPN

With OpenVPN, a new generation VPN entered the scene. While other VPN solutions often use proprietary or non-standard mechanisms, OpenVPN has a modular concept both for underlying security and networking. OpenVPN uses the secure, stable, and lauded SSL/TLS mechanisms for authentication and encryption, and does not suffer from the complexity that characterizes other VPN implementations like market leader IPsec. At the same time, it offers possibilities that go beyond every other VPN implementation's scope:

- **Layer 2 and Layer 3 VPN**: OpenVPN offers two basic modes, which run either as Layer 2 or Layer 3 VPN. Thus OpenVPN tunnels can also transport Ethernet Frames, IPX packets, and Windows Network Browsing packets (NETBIOS), all of which are problems in most other VPN solutions.
- **Protecting field workers with the internal firewall**: A field worker connected to the central branch of his or her company with a VPN tunnel can change the network setup on his or her laptop, so that all of his or her network traffic is sent through the tunnel. Once OpenVPN has established a tunnel, the central firewall in the company's central branch can protect the laptop, even though it is not a local machine. Only one network port must be opened to the local (e.g. customers') network by the field worker. The employee is protected by the central firewall whenever he or she is connected to the VPN.
- **OpenVPN connections can be tunneled through almost every firewall**: If you have Internet access and if you can access HTTPS websites, OpenVPN tunnels should work.
- **Proxy support and configurations**: OpenVPN has proxy support and can be configured to run as a **TCP** or **UDP** service, and as server or client. As a server, OpenVPN simply waits until a client requests a connection, whereas as a client, it tries to establish a connection according to its configuration.

- **Only one Port in the firewall must be opened to allow incoming connections**: Since **OpenVPN 2.0,** the special server mode allows multiple incoming connections on the same TCP or UDP port, while still using different configurations for every single connection.
- **Virtual Interfaces allow very specific networking and firewall rules**: All rules, restrictions, forwarding mechanisms, and concepts like NAT can be used with OpenVPN tunnels.
- **High flexibility with extensive scripting possibilities**: OpenVPN offers numerous points during connection set up to start individual scripts. These scripts can be used for a great variety of purposes from authentication to failover and more.
- **Transparent, high-performance support for dynamic IPs**: By using OpenVPN, there is no need anymore to use static IPs on either side of the tunnel. Both tunnel endpoints can have cheap DSL access with dynamic IPs and the users will rarely notice a change of IP on either side. Both Windows Terminal server sessions and **Secure Shell (SSH)** sessions will only seem to *hang* for some seconds, but will not terminate and will carry on with the action requested after a short pause.
- **No problems with NAT**: Both OpenVPN server and clients can be within a network using only private IP addresses. Every firewall can be used to send the tunnel traffic to the other tunnel endpoint.
- **Simple Installation on any platform**: Both installation and use are incredibly simple. Especially, if you have tried to set up IPsec connections with different implementations, you will find OpenVPN appealing.
- **Modular Design**: The modular design with a high degree of simplicity both in security and networking is outstanding. No other VPN solution can offer the same range of possibilities at this level of security.

# History of OpenVPN

According to an interview on `http://linuxsecurity.com` published in 2003, James Yonan was traveling in Central Asia in days prior to 9/11, 2001 and connecting to his office over Asian or Russian Internet Providers.

The fact that these connections were established over servers in countries with very doubtable security situations made him more and more aware of and concerned about security issues. His research brought the insight that there were two main streams in VPN technology, one promoting security and the other, usability. None of the solutions available at that time offered an ideal blend of both objectives. IPsec and all of its implementations were difficult to set up, but offered acceptable security. But its complex structure made it vulnerable to attacks, bugs, and security flaws. Therefore, the networking approach Yonan found in some of the usability camp's solutions seemed to make more sense to him, leading him to a modular networking model using the **TUN/TAP** virtual networking devices provided by the Linux kernel.

"After some study of the open source VPN field, my conclusion was that the "usability first" camp had the right ideas about networking and inter-network tunneling, and the SSH, SSL/TLS, and IPSec camps had the appropriate level of seriousness toward the deep crypto issues. This was the basic conceptual starting point for my work on OpenVPN."

James Yonan in a `linuxsecurity.com` interview, November 10, 2003. (`http://www.linuxsecurity.com/content/view/117363/49/`)

Choosing the TUN/TAP devices as networking model immediately offered flexibility that other VPN solutions could not offer. While other SSL/TLS-based VPN solutions needed a browser to establish connections, OpenVPN would prepare almost real (but still virtual) network devices, on which almost all networking activities can be done.

Yonan then chose the name OpenVPN with respect to the libraries and programs of the **OpenSSL** project and because of the clear message *this is open source and free software.*

## OpenVPN Version 1

OpenVPN entered the scene of VPN solutions only on May 13, 2001 with an initial release that could barely tunnel IP packets over UDP and only encrypt with Blowfish cipher and SHA HMAC signatures (rather secure encryption and signing methods). This version was already numbered 0.90—which seems ambitious, since only one version (0.91) followed in 2001, offering extended encryption support. For SSL/TLS support, users would have to wait almost one year after the first release. Version 1.0 was released in March 2002 and provided SSL/TLS-based authentication and key exchange. This version was also the first to contain documentation in form of a manpage.

Then, OpenVPN development picked up speed. Only five days later, version 1.0.2 was released, which was the first version with adaptations for **Redhat Package Manager** (**RPM**)-based systems. From this version on, releases were published almost regularly every four to eight weeks.

The following table gives an overview of the releases and lists the dates and versions when certain selected features were added to the 1.x version of OpenVPN. More details can be found in the Changelog sections of the OpenVPN website at `http://openvpn.net/changelog.html` and release notes at `http://openvpn.net/relnotes.html`.

| Date | Version | Important features/changes |
|---|---|---|
| 2001-5-13 | 0.90 | The initial release, with only a few functions like IP over UDP, and only one encryption mechanism |
| 2001-12-26 | 0.91 | More encryption mechanisms added |
| 2002-3-23 | 1.0 | TLS-based authentication and key exchange added<br>First manual page |
| 2002-3-28 | 1.0.2 | Bugfixes and improvements, especially for rpm-based systems like Redhat |
| 2002-4-9 | 1.1.0 | Extended support for TLS/SSL<br>Traffic shaping added<br>First OpenBSD port<br>Extended replay protection makes OpenVPN more secure<br>Further improvement of Documentation (manpage) |
| 2002-4-22 | 1.1.1 | Options for automatic configuration of a OpenVPN network<br>Inactivity control features |
| 2002-5-22 | 1.2.0 | Configuration file support added<br>SSL/TLS as background process—longer keys are possible<br>Various ports added/improved (Solaris, OpenBSD, Mac OSX, x64)<br>Website improved, including "howto"<br>Installation without automake possible |
| 2002-6-12 | 1.2.1 | Binary RPM files for installation on Redhat-based systems provided<br>Intensive improvements on signal handling and key management on restart<br>Support for dynamical changes in incoming packages (like dynamic IPs)<br>Added support for identity downgrade after installation—OpenVPN can be run as non-privileged user |
| 2002-7-10<br>2002-7-10 | 1.3.0<br>1.3.1 | "Housekeeping Releases": Bugfixes, minor improvements, and new features; works now with OpenSSL 0.9.7 Beta 2 |
| 2002-10-23 | 1.3.2 | NetBSD port<br>Support for inetd/xinetd instantiation under Linux<br>Simple building of SSL/TLS certificates added (easy-rsa script)<br>Support for IPv6 over TUN added |
| 2003-5-07 | 1.4.0 | Improvement of replay protection (security)<br>Numerous bugfixes, improvements, and additions |
| 2003-5-15 | 1.4.1 | Improved support for kernel 2.4 |
| 2003-7-15 | 1.4.2 | First beginnings of Windows port (but still missing Windows kernel driver)<br>Gentoo init script |
| 2003-8-4 | 1.4.3 | Bugfix release |

| Date | Version | Important features/changes |
|---|---|---|
| 2003-11-20 | 1.5.0 (and 14 beta versions before that) | Certificate revocation lists<br>TCP support<br>Port to Windows 2000 and XP, including Win32 installer<br>Increased sanity checks in configuration parameters<br>Proxy support added<br>Extended routing functions (like redirect gateway)<br>Improved TLS support, extended key and cipher features |
| 2004-5-9 | 1.6.0 (including 4 release candidates and 7 beta versions) | SOCKS proxy support<br>Various improvements on Windows networking behavior—**Dynamic Host Configuration Protocol** (**DHCP**)<br>Various bugfixes |

## OpenVPN Version 2

Parallel to the improvement and development of OpenVPN version 1, the test bed for OpenVPN version 2 was made in November 2003, and in February 2004, version 2.0-test3 initially prepared the goal of a multi-client server for OpenVPN. This multi-client server is one of the most outstanding features of OpenVPN today; several clients can connect to the VPN server on the same port. On February 22, 2004, the two development branches 1.6-beta7 and 2.0-test3 were merged and further development was continued in version 2's branch.

There were fewer than 29 versions labeled as "test" versions, 20 beta versions, and 21 release candidates, until on April 17, 2005, OpenVPN version 2.0 could be released. This was only possible because of the great number of developers contributing to the project, fixing bugs, and improving performance and stability permanently.

The following list will give a brief overview of the new features added to OpenVPN version 2:

- **Multi-client support**: OpenVPN offers a special connection mode, where TLS-authenticated clients (that are not blacklisted on the CRL) are provided in DHCP-style with IPs and networking (tunnel) data. This way, several tunnels (up to 128) can communicate over the same TCP or UDP port. Obviously, a mode control switch for activating server mode became necessary.
- **Push/pull options**: The Network setup of clients can be controlled by the server. After successful setup of a tunnel, the server can tell the client (both Windows and Linux) to use a different network setup instantaneously.
- A **management interface** (Telnet) is added.
- The Windows driver and software have been improved widely.

# Networking with OpenVPN

The modular structure of OpenVPN can not only be found in its security model, but also in the networking scheme. James Yonan chose the Universal TUN/TAP driver for the networking layer of OpenVPN.

The TUN/TAP driver is an open-source project that is included in all modern Linux/UNIX distributions as well as Windows and Mac OS X. Like SSL/TLS it is used in many projects, and therefore it is steadily being improved and new features are being added. Using the TUN/TAP devices takes away a lot of complexity from OpenVPN's structure. Its simple structure brings increased security compared to other VPN solutions. Complexity is always the main enemy of security. For example, IPsec has a complex structure with complex modifications in the kernel and the IP stack, thereby creating many possible security loopholes.

The Universal TUN/TAP driver was developed to provide Linux kernel support for tunneling IP traffic. It is a virtual network interface, which appears as authentic to all applications and users; only the name tunX or tapX distinguishes it from other devices. Every application that is capable of using a network interface can use the tunnel interface. Every technology you are running in your network can be run on a TUN or TAP interface too.

This driver is one of the main factors that make OpenVPN so easy to understand, easy to configure, and at the same time so secure.

The following figure depicts OpenVPN using standard interfaces:

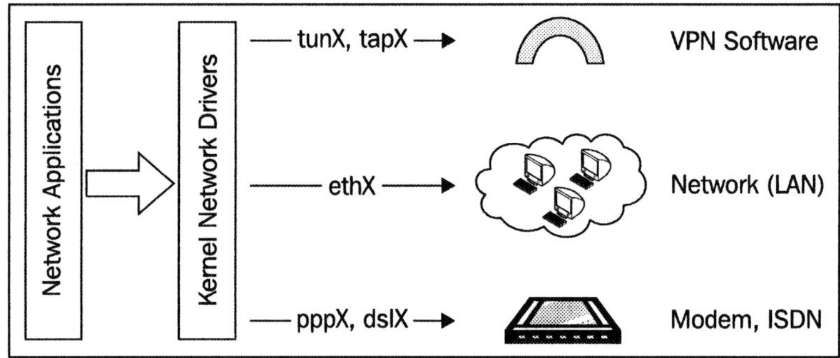


A TUN device can be used like a virtual point-to-point interface, like a modem or DSL link. This is called routed mode, because routes are set up to the VPN partner.

A TAP device, however, can be used like a virtual Ethernet adapter. This enables the daemon listening on the interface to capture Ethernet frames, which is not possible with TUN devices. This mode is called bridging mode because the networks are connected as if over a hardware bridge.

Applications can read/write to this interface; software (the tunnel driver) will take all data and use the cryptographic libraries of SSL/TLS to encrypt them. The data is packaged and sent to the other end of the tunnel. This *packaging* is done with standardized UDP or optional TCP packets. UDP should be first choice, but TCP can be helpful in some cases. You are almost completely free to choose the configuration parameters like protocol or port numbers, as long as both tunnel ends agree on the same figures.

> OpenVPN listens on TUN/TAP devices, takes the traffic, encrypts it, and sends it to the other VPN partner, where another OpenVPN process receives the data, decrypts it, and hands it over to the virtual network device, where the application might already be waiting for the data.

As far as I know, there is no other VPN Software that enables VPN partners to transmit. This concept offers overwhelming possibilities:

- Broadcasts needed for browsing Windows networks or for LAN Games
- Non-IP packets like IPX and almost anything possible in your LAN sent over the VPN to the other side

And since OpenVPN uses standard network packets, NAT is no problem either. A host in the local net in Sydney with a local IP can start a tunnel to another host in the local net in London; which also is equipped with a local IP only.

But there's more. Because the network interface is standardized Linux network interface (either TUN or TAP), anything possible on an Ethernet NIC can be done on VPN Tunnels:

- Firewalls can restrict and control the traffic.
- Traffic shaping is not only possible, but it is also a feature that OpenVPN brings with it.

Also, if you want to use DSL lines with frequent reconnects and dynamically assigned IPs, OpenVPN will be your first choice. The reconnect is much faster than that of any other VPN software we have tested; a Windows terminal server or SSH session does not terminate while one of the VPN partners changes its IP; the session just freezes for some seconds and then you can continue. Can your VPN accomplish that?

## OpenVPN and Firewalls

OpenVPN works perfectly with firewalls. There are a few VPN solutions that can claim to have a similar firewall support, but none can offer the same level of security.

What is a firewall? There is a famous and simple definition: A firewall is a router that does not route. If you consider this not very helpful, here is a more refined definition:

A firewall is a router that routes only selected Internet data. Firewall rules define how to handle specific data and traffic.

Firewalls can be devices or software on PCs, servers, or on other devices. A firewall takes care of the data received and has a closer look on it. Modern firewalls are so-called packet filtering, stateful inspection firewalls. Depending on the OSI layer it is operating in, the firewall can pass decisions based on the data found in the headers of the packets or application data. Packet filtering firewalls usually operate by reading the IP data header; stateful inspection is a mechanism to remember connection states. In this way, internal networks can be protected from external networks, and while Internet connections initiated from the inside can be allowed, all unwanted, unauthorized connections from outside can be rejected. At the same time, incoming data requested by a member of the local net is passed through (because the firewall remembers the *state* of the request).

Under Linux, most firewalls are based on the program **iptables**. This is a user-space interface to the Linux kernel's netfilter firewall functionality, and offers everything modern firewalls should. Probably the best way to protect your LAN is by writing a set of iptables rules with a shell script. However, the usability of such a script is not perfect. Most administrators want a **Graphical User Interface (GUI)** for firewall control, and all hardware firewalls offer this. An outstanding project for this purpose and Linux (iptables) firewalls is the **Shorewall (Shoreline Firewall)** project. It integrates into the Webmin suite—a web-based front end to administer Linux systems from a browser. The Shorewall project has written a guideline about integration of OpenVPN tunnels into Shorewall and more at `http://www.shorewall.net/OPENVPN.html`.

**IPCop** is a promising standalone, easy-to-configure Linux firewall system also equipped with a professional GUI. Standardized installation, simple structures, and modular add-ons make this a fast-growing project. Several companies are developing hardware devices based on IPCop, and the open-source project **Zerina** deals with the integration of OpenVPN: `http://home.arcor.de/u.altinkaynak/openvpn.html`.

## Configuring OpenVPN

Up to now you have seen that OpenVPN has a secure and easy-to-use security approach and a flexible networking model. Consequently, a very simple configuration syntax and good documentation characterize OpenVPN's user interface. Configuration is done by editing a simple text file; the syntax is the same on every operation system. Here is an example of a simple configuration file with 13 lines:

```
remote feilner-it.dynalias.net
float
dev tun
tun-mtu 1500
ifconfig 10.79.10.1 10.79.10.2
secret my_secret_key.txt
port 5050
route 10.94.0.0 255.255.0.0 10.79.10.2
comp-lzo
keepalive 120 600
resolv-retry 86400
route-up "/sbin/firewall restart"
log-append /var/log/openvpn/ultrino.log
```

A command-line interface allows you to start temporary tunnels at your will, which is very useful when you're testing setups. The same parameters as in the configuration file are added to the command line, and the tunnels are started.

In the so-called server mode, OpenVPN can push various configuration data to the clients through the tunnel. Multiple tunnels can be run on one singular port, either UDP or TCP. OpenVPN can be tunneled through firewalls and proxies, if they allow HTTPS connections, and the server can tell the client to use the tunnel as default route to the Internet.

This offers a huge variety of possibilities; you can have your field workers open only one port to whatever network they are connected to. This is the port OpenVPN uses to connect to your company's VPN server. Once connected, all Internet traffic from this laptop is routed via the network of the company the VPN tunnel is connected to. In this way your company's firewall can also protect the road warriors. A road warrior is a member of a company (or a company's network) who is working outside of the company's walls and connects to the network frequently via different connections. A typical road warrior may be a salesman or saleswoman with his or her laptop, who needs to access the company's resources from his or her customer's network.

## Problems with OpenVPN

OpenVPN has a few weaknesses:

- It is not IPsec compatible, and IPsec is the standard VPN solution. Lots of devices like Cisco or Bintec routers use IPsec and can connect to applications of other manufacturers or software IPsec clients. At least they should be able to, because in practice many manufacturers tend to develop their own proprietary extensions to IPsec, which make their implementations practically incompatible with other IPsec devices.
- There are only a few people who know how to use OpenVPN, especially in difficult scenarios (though such are rare). So if you read on you can acquire a precious qualification.
- There is no working GUI for administration (but there are some promising projects).
- Today, you can only connect to other computers. But this is changing; there are some companies working on devices with integrated OpenVPN clients.

As you can see, the main weaknesses of OpenVPN are incompatibility to IPsec and lack of public knowledge about its features and hardware manufacturers. The first will probably never change, because the architectures differ too much, but the latter is already changing.

# OpenVPN Compared to IPsec VPN

Even though IPsec is the de facto standard, there are many arguments for using OpenVPN. If you want to convince your management about why your branches should be connected through OpenVPN instead of IPsec VPN, the following table can help your argument (points preceded by "+" are advantages and points preceded by "-" are disadvantages):

| IPsec VPN | OpenVPN |
|---|---|
| + The standard VPN technology | - Still rather unknown, not compatible with IPsec |
| + Hardware platforms (devices, appliances) | - Only on computers, but on all operating systems. Exception are devices, where embedded UNIXs are running like OpenWrt and similar |
| + Well-known technology | - New technology; still growing and rising |
| + Many GUIs for administration | - No professional GUI; however, there are some interesting and promising projects |
| - Complex modification of IP stack | + Simple technology |
| - Critical modification of kernel necessary | + Standardized network interfaces and packets |
| - Administrator privileges are necessary | + OpenVPN Software can run in user space, and can be chroot-ed |
| - Different IPsec implementations of different manufacturers can be incompatible | + Standardized encryption technologies |

| IPsec VPN | OpenVPN |
|---|---|
| - Complex configuration, complex technology | + Easy, well-structured, modular technology, easy configuration |
| - Steep learning curve for newbies | + Easy to learn, fast success for newbies |
| - Several ports and protocols in firewall necessary | + Only one port in firewall necessary |
| - Problems with dynamic addresses on both sides | + DynDNS works flawlessly, faster reconnects |
| - Security problems with IPsec technologies | +SSL/TLS as industry-standard cryptographic layer |
| | + Traffic shaping |
| | + Speed (up to 20 Mbps on a 1Ghz machine) |
| | + Compatibility with firewalls and proxies |
| | + No problems with NAT (both sides can be in NATed networks) |
| | + Possibilities for **road warriors** |

Probably the best argument is that you can use both VPN solutions in parallel, at least if you're using Linux or a Linux-based application. Due to the different approaches to networking, there are no conflicts between the two systems.

# Sources for Help and Documentation

If you want to learn more about OpenVPN (I bet you will), there are numerous resources in the Internet. Websites, mailing lists, forums, and private pages of OpenVPN fans can be found in abundance. Google finds more than three million hits for "open vpn". This list of course cannot be complete, but here you will find links to websites that were helpful to me when I started using OpenVPN and where I still look for help today.

# The Project Community

OpenVPN project has its own website, including downloads of new versions and updates, documentation, howtos, mailing lists, and links to various VPN-related pages. A project page can hardly be better than that of OpenVPN. You'll find it at `http://openvpn.net/`.

The most important source of help is the mailing lists: `http://openvpn.net/mail.html`.

Since we are using SSL/TLS for encryption purposes, you certainly want to understand this toolkit. The SSL/TLS Cryptographic libraries website provides detailed documentation and mailing lists, which can be found at `http://www.openssl.org/`.

The website of the TLS Charter by the TLS Working Group provides a list with many related RFCs and Internet drafts you might consider helpful: `http://www.ietf.org/html.charters/tls-charter.html`.

The Universal TUN/TAP driver can be downloaded from the following page: `http://vtun.sourceforge.net/tun/`. Nevertheless, this should not be necessary, since every modern distribution (and kernel) should have this feature *built-in*. But the FAQ of this project may be helpful for various questions.

## Documentation in the Software Packages

If you install OpenVPN from the binary packages for your distribution, you will have the standard documentation in the following directories:

| Distribution | Path to Documentation |
|---|---|
| Debian | `/usr/share/doc/openvpn` |
| SuSE | `/usr/share/doc/packages/openvpn` |
| Redhat | `/usr/share/doc/openvpn-2.0` |
| Windows | only online Documentation |

Other distributions may have different locations; check your package management system for details. RPM-based systems give a list of all files belonging to a specific package when you type "`rpm -ql openvpn`" as super user. Debian-based systems (like Ubuntu) should give the same information when root enters "`dpkg -L openvpn`". Simply replace `openvpn` with the name of the package you installed.

The source code package (tarball) contains several READMEs and documentation files. Just browse through the directories where you extracted OpenVPN to. And if you're interested, have a look in some of the source code files; the developer comments can be a great help to understand the depths of the software!

# Summary

OpenVPN offers great possibilities; especially the networking concept allows very transparent setups with firewalls or in road warrior configurations. James Yonan, the founder has made very good decisions when trusting the TUN/TAP network drivers and the SSL/TLS libraries. OpenVPN was first published in 2001; version 2 came out in 2005 and offers much more advanced features than the versions before. Multi-client support, the Windows version, and the push/pull options are only some of its features. OpenVPN is easy to configure and has only a few weaknesses, the most serious of which is its incompatibility to IPsec by design. But to name this a weakness is a tough verdict, if it is compared to IPsec as done in this chapter. IPsec still is the standard, but OpenVPN has much more features at a much better security level.

# 4
# Installing OpenVPN

Installing OpenVPN is easy and platform independent. In this chapter we will install it on Windows, Mac OS X, different Linux versions, and FreeBSD. Furthermore, we will compile the source code provided by the OpenVPN project and enable the required network support in your kernel for the TUN/TAP devices. We will start with the graphical installation under Windows, Mac OS X, and SuSE, and finish with building our own OpenVPN version from the source code, including hints for the configuration of an individual kernel.

## Prerequisites

Some prerequisites have to be fulfilled if you want to install OpenVPN on your system. Windows users must use Windows 2000 or XP; Mac OS X is required on Apple platforms. This is all that is required for these operating systems, but Linux/UNIX systems must meet the following demands:

- **Your system must provide support for the Universal TUN/TAP driver**:

  The kernels newer than version 2.4 of almost all modern Linux distributions provide support for TUN/TAP devices. Only if you are using an old distribution or if you have built your own kernel, will you have to add this support to your configuration. The section of this chapter *Enabling Linux Kernel Support for TUN/TAP Devices*, deals with this problem. This project's website can be found at: `http://vtun.sourceforge.net/tun/`.

- **OpenSSL Libraries have to be installed on your system**:

  I have not encountered modern Linux/UNIX systems that do not meet this requirement. However, if you want to compile OpenVPN from source code, the SSL development package may be necessary. The website is: `http://www.openssl.org/`.

- **The Lempel-Ziv-Oberhumer (LZO) Compression library has to be installed**:

  Again, most modern Linux/UNIX systems provide these packages, so there won't be any problem. LZO is a real-time compression library that is used by OpenVPN to compress data before sending. Packages can be found on `http://openvpn.net/download.html`, the website of this project is: `http://www.oberhumer.com/opensource/lzo/`.

Most Linux/UNIX systems' installation tools are able to solve these so-called dependencies on their own, but it might be helpful to know where to get the required software.

# Obtaining the Software

Basically, installation of OpenVPN can be done in one of the following ways:

- For Microsoft Windows operating systems, you have to download the binary `.exe` file from `http://openvpn.net/download.html` or the package containing a graphical user interface from `http://openvpn.se/`.
- On Macintosh systems running Mac OS X, there is a graphical installation wizard and management tool called **Tunnelblick**.
- Most commercial Linux systems, like SuSE, provide installation tools like **Yet Another Setup Tool** (**YaST**) and contain up-to-date versions of OpenVPN on their installation media (CD or DVD). Furthermore, systems based on RPM software can also install and manage OpenVPN Software at the command line.
- Linux systems like Debian use sophisticated package management tools that can install software provided by repositories on web servers. No local media is needed; the package management will resolve potential dependencies itself and install the newest or safest possible version of OpenVPN.
- FreeBSD (like other BSD-style systems).
- Like all open-source projects, OpenVPN source code is provided for download. These compressed `tar.gz` or `tar.bz2` archives can be downloaded from `http://openvpn.net/download.html` and unpacked to a local directory. This source code has to be configured and translated (compiled) for your operating system.
- You can also install unstable, developer, or older versions of OpenVPN from `http://openvpn.net/download.html`. This may be interesting if you want to test new features of forthcoming versions.
- Daily (unstable!) OpenVPN source code extracts can be obtained from `http://sourceforge.net/cvs/?group_id=48978`. Here you find the **Concurrent Versions System** (**CVS**) repository, where all OpenVPN developers post their changes to the project files.

> Please note that all OpenVPN versions not tagged as *stable* should never be used in the production environment. There may be security issues and bugs that cause the code to crash or open your complete network to intruders. The stable versions have been tested for stability and security flaws and will not be published as stable until they meet the developer team's requirements.

# Installing OpenVPN on Windows

If you want to install OpenVPN on Windows, you have to make a choice before downloading. You can install the original OpenVPN Software from `http://openvpn.net/download.html` or (this is my preferred suggestion) install the OpenVPN GUI from `http://openvpn.se/`. This package contains the OpenVPN Software plus a GUI to bring up or close down tunnels. Especially, if you set up an OpenVPN client—be it a laptop or desktop PC of a home worker, which is only connecting temporarily to your VPN—the Windows user will want to have an easy-to-use, clickable interface. However, if you do not want the users to interact with the VPN tunnels, the original OpenVPN Software will do.

OpenVPN can be run as a service on the Windows PC, which means it is started automatically on startup. It can be configured to enable the tunnel automatically or forced by a click of a mouse. The installation is pretty straightforward and should not pose any problem to the experienced Windows user. The following sections give you a guided installation process.

If you are prompted that the driver has not passed Windows Logo testing, click on **Continue anyway**.

## Downloading and Starting Installation

Download the newest version of the OpenVPN GUI from `http://openvpn.se/` to your local drive. Log in as administrator or privileged user and double-click on the downloaded file to start the setup wizard. If you are using a desktop firewall, you will be prompted to allow OpenVPN being installed and connecting to the Internet later.

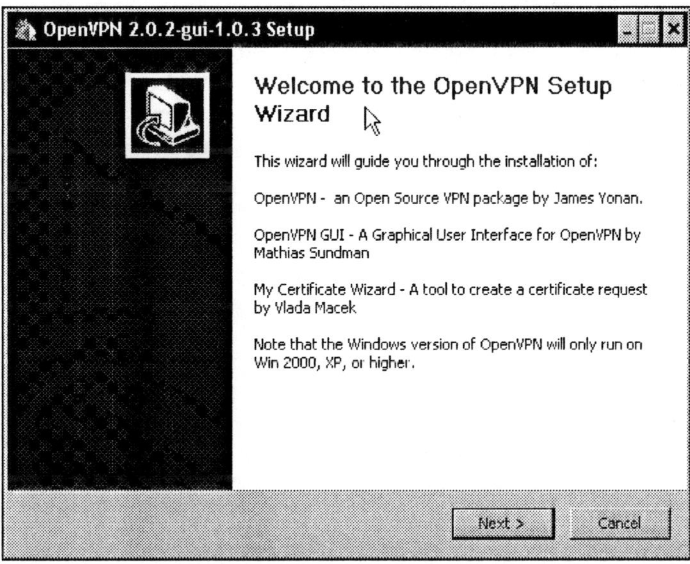


The OpenVPN GUI installation wizard, probably the most convenient way to install OpenVPN on Windows, is started. Click on **Next** to proceed.

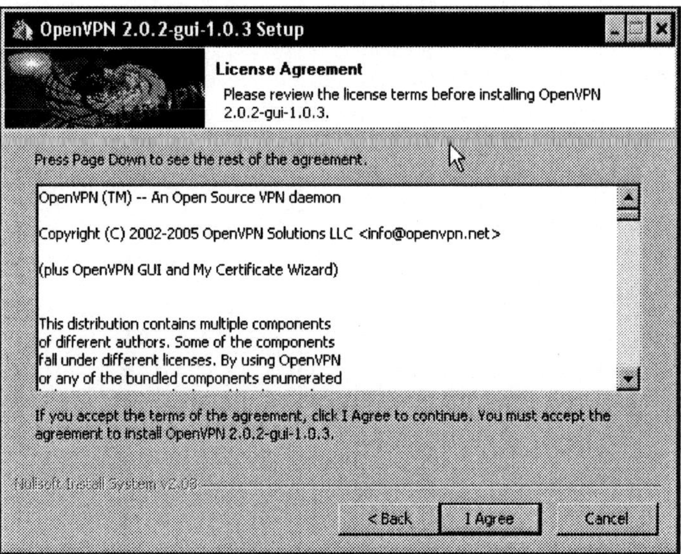


Even though OpenVPN and the OpenVPN GUI are completely available under the open source General Public License (GPL), you have to accept a license agreement. You should read the license to make sure that your planned use of OpenVPN conforms to it. Click on **I Agree** to proceed.

## Selecting Components and Location

The next dialog window offers a choice on the OpenVPN components you may want to install. Thus the standard selection of components makes sense in almost all cases.

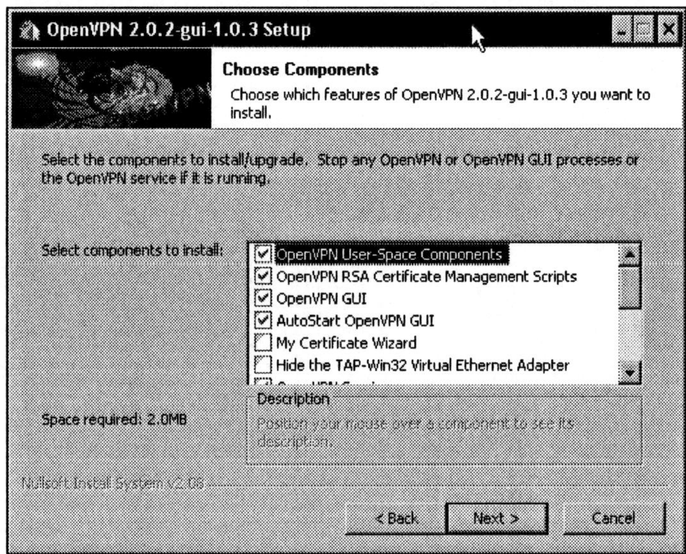

In this dialog, you have several options to choose from. Even if you normally don't need to make changes here, the following table gives an overview of the entries and when you should install which feature. The **Client Install** is a system that only connects to another OpenVPN system, whereas the **Server Install** is an OpenVPN system that allows incoming connections.

| Option | Feature | Client Install | Server Install |
|---|---|---|---|
| OpenVPN User-Space Components | The OpenVPN program | x | x |
| OpenVPN RSA Certificate Management Scripts | easy-rsa for Windows | | x |
| OpenVPN GUI | The graphical user interface | x | |
| AutoStart OpenVPN GUI | Link for auto start | x | |
| My Certificate Wizard | Certificate requests for a certificate authority | x | |
| Hide the TAP-Win32 VEA | Interface is not shown in network setup | | |
| OpenVPN Service | Configure OpenVPN as a service | | x |
| OpenVPN File Associations | Configuration files (`*.ovpn`) are associated with OpenVPN | x | x |
| OpenSSL DLLs | Dynamic link libraries | x | x |
| TAP-WIN32 VEA | Virtual network interface | x | x |
| Add OpenVPN to PATH | `openvpn.exe` is in the path of every user's command line | x | x |
| Add Shortcuts to Start Menu | Shortcut to start menu | x | x |

Newer versions also include the OpenSSL Utilities option.

As you can see, the only differences are the RSA Management and the option to run OpenVPN as a service. Both can be configured with different means, like the configuration file, the Windows system management, or software like **xca** that we will use to generate and administer certificates.

Press Next to continue installation.

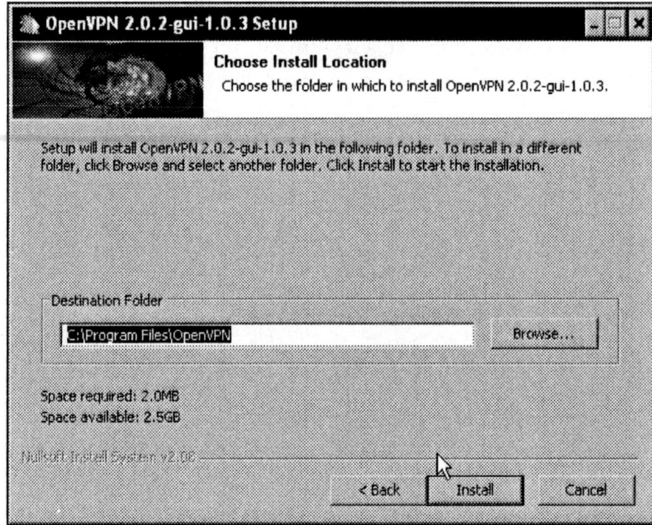


Now you have to select an installation directory for OpenVPN. The standard installation path of OpenVPN under Windows is `C:\Program Files\OpenVPN`, and this should work fine in almost any case. However, you can set this path as you please. After clicking on **Install**, the installation process is started.

## Finishing Installation

While OpenVPN is installing, you can read its output in the installation window and follow the creation of folders, files, and shortcuts and the installation of drivers (TAP) for networking.

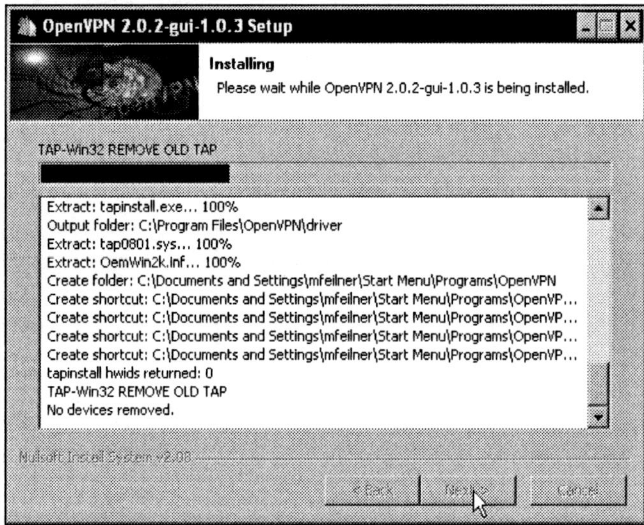

If you've made it so far, you have successfully installed OpenVPN on your Windows system. If you want to read the Readme file (as of September 2005 this is pretty poor and contains only a link to the website), activate the checkbox Show Readme before you click Finish.

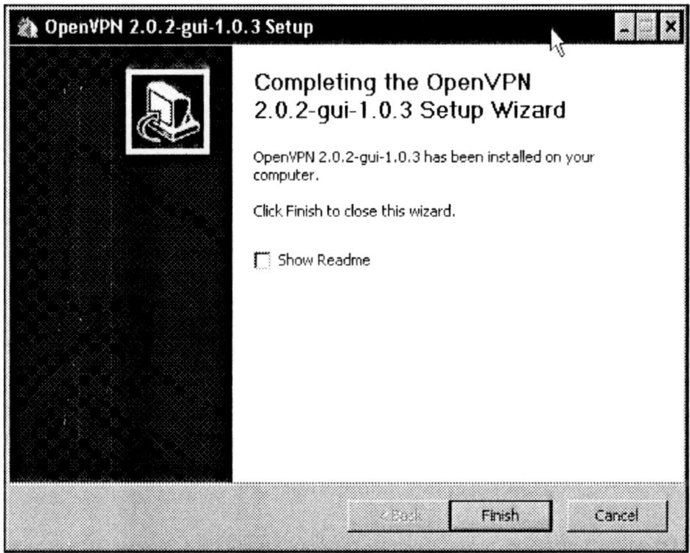


## Testing the Installation—A First Look at the Panel Applet

After the installation of OpenVPN GUI, OpenVPN is started and a panel applet is created. In the following screenshot, it is the icon close to the left:

This applet provides a convenient method for Windows users to control and configure (partly) OpenVPN. However, as there is no interface for configuration as yet, the configuration file can only be edited using an editor. And until a first configuration is created, the context menu may look rather poor. Right-click on the panel applet:

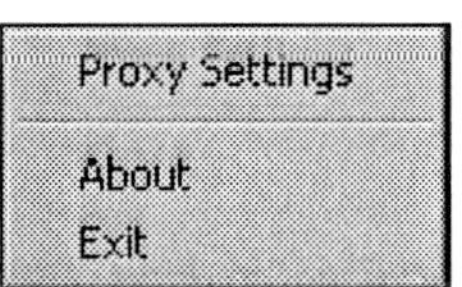

Once you have configured a first connection, this menu will be populated with new entries. With the entries Connect and Disconnect you can start and stop the configured tunnels.

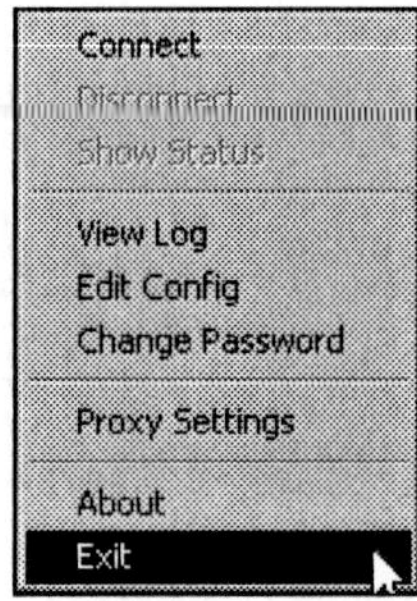


# Installing OpenVPN on Mac OS X (Tunnelblick)

Of course there is also OpenVPN software for Mac OS X. Its name is Tunnelblick, which is free open-source software, released under the BSD license, and it contains a graphical installation wizard. You can download it from `http://www.tunnelblick.net/`. Tunnelblick comes as a disk image file including the command-line application (by the OpenVPN project) and the Tunnelblick GUI for Macintosh computers.

If you need more detailed information on installing and uninstalling Tunnelblick, the online readme `http://www.tunnelblick.net/README.txt` file is the best place to look first. It contains a full list of files that are installed on your system. For version 3.0 these files are:

```
/System/Library/Extensions/tap.kext
/System/Library/Extensions/tun.kext
/System/Library/StartupItems/tap
/System/Library/StartupItems/tun
/usr/local/sbin/openvpn
/usr/local/sbin/openvpnstop
/usr/local/sbin/openvpnstart
/Applications/Tunnelblick.app
```

To uninstall Tunnelblick from your system, you just need to remove these files and reboot your machine.

But before that, let's install Tunnelblick. The installation is started simply by double-clicking on the file `Tunnelblick-Complete.mpkg` to start the installation wizard.

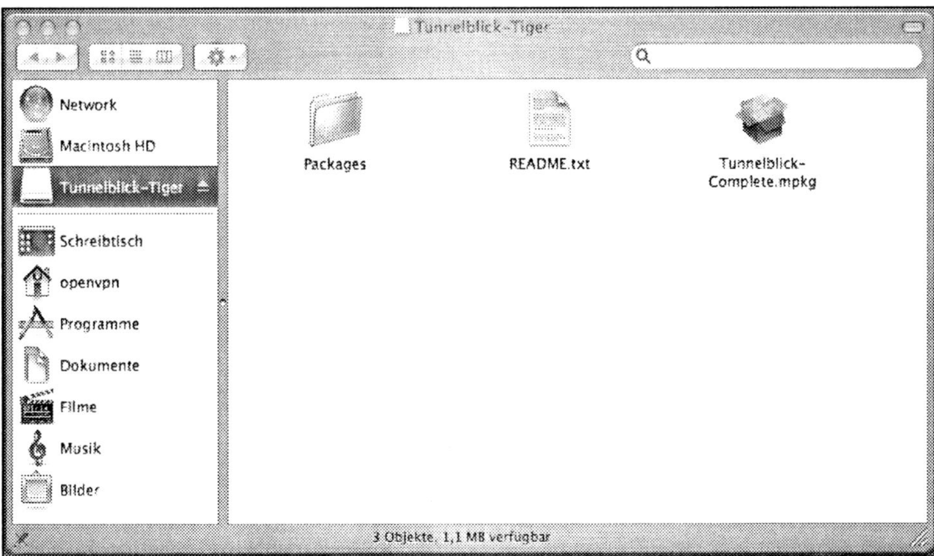


An installation wizard will guide you through five steps. Simply choosing the installation location and typing and the wizard will solve all questions for you. The file README.txt contains information on installing, uninstalling, and configuration of OpenVPN with special regards to Macintosh and OS X 10.3 or later.

## Testing the Installation—The Tunnelblick Panel Applet

After installation, you will find the Tunnelblick icon in the system tray of your panel:

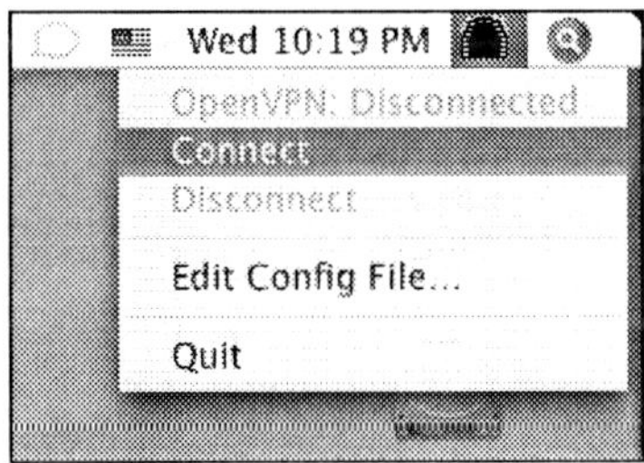

If you select the menu entry Edit Config File, you will be presented the standard configuration file in a text editor:

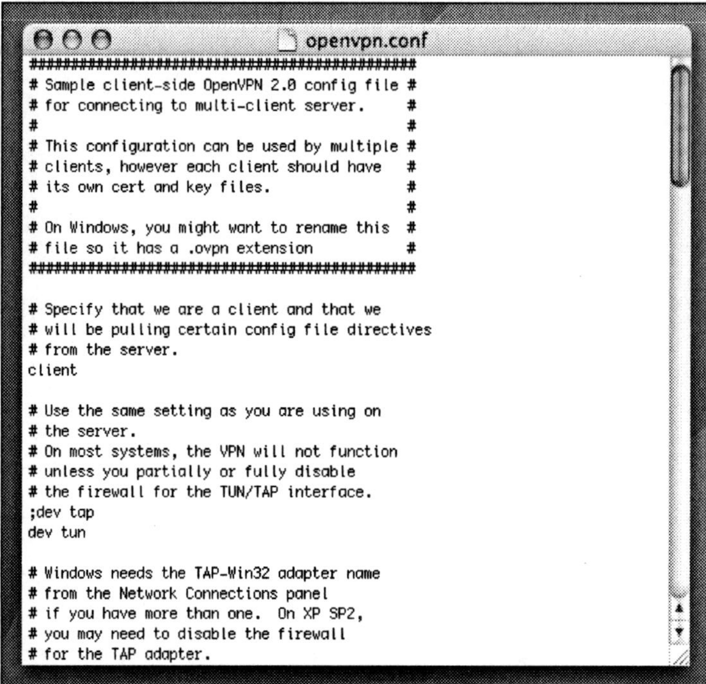


```
##############################################
# Sample client-side OpenVPN 2.0 config file #
# for connecting to multi-client server.     #
#                                            #
# This configuration can be used by multiple #
# clients, however each client should have   #
# its own cert and key files.                #
#                                            #
# On Windows, you might want to rename this  #
# file so it has a .ovpn extension           #
##############################################

# Specify that we are a client and that we
# will be pulling certain config file directives
# from the server.
client

# Use the same setting as you are using on
# the server.
# On most systems, the VPN will not function
# unless you partially or fully disable
# the firewall for the TUN/TAP interface.
;dev tap
dev tun

# Windows needs the TAP-Win32 adapter name
# from the Network Connections panel
# if you have more than one.  On XP SP2,
# you may need to disable the firewall
# for the TAP adapter.
```

If you need more information on OpenVPN on Macintosh, the following links are good places to visit:

- Detailed installation instructions for Mac OS 10.3:
  `http://www.helsinki.fi/atk/english/hy-ppp/hy-vpn/hy-vpn-mac.html`
- Homepage of the Tunnelblick OpenVPN GUI for Macintosh:
  `http://www.tunnelblick.net/`

# Installing OpenVPN on SuSE Linux

Installing OpenVPN on SuSE Linux is almost as easy as under Windows or on the Mac. Linux users may say that it is even easier. On SuSE Linux almost all administrative tasks can be done using the administration interface YaST. OpenVPN Software can be installed completely with YaST. The people distributing SuSE have always tried to include up-to-date software in their distribution and thus the installation media of SuSE 9.3 already contains version 2.0 of OpenVPN.

# Using YaST to Install Software

Start YaST. Under **K Desktop Environment** (**KDE**—the standard desktop under SuSE Linux), you will find YaST in the main menu under System | YaST. If you are logged in as a normal user, you will be prompted to enter your root password and confirm the same. The YaST control center is started.

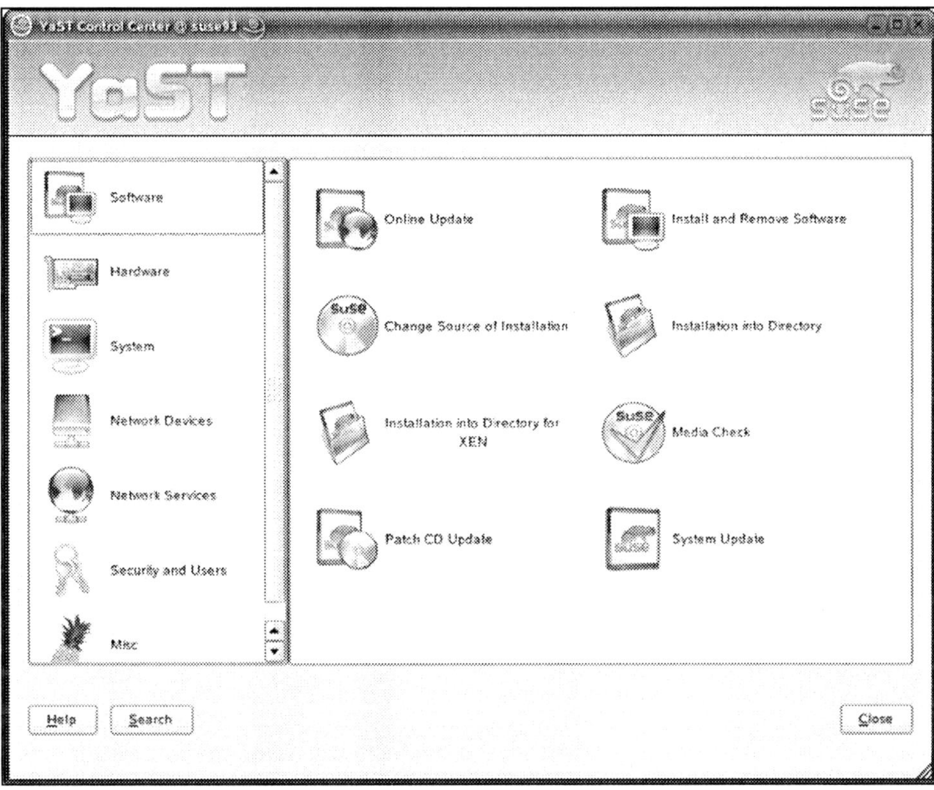


This administration interface consists of many different modules, which are represented by symbols in the right half of the window and grouped by the labels on the left. After starting YaST, click on the symbol labeled Install and Remove Software to start the software management interface of YaST.

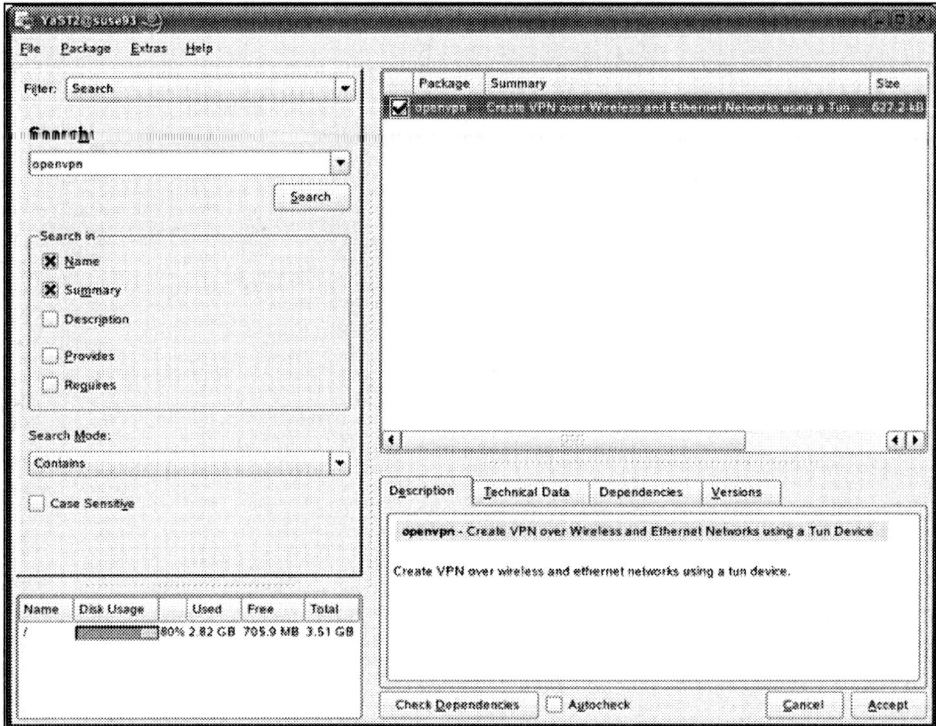

The software management tool in YaST is very powerful. Under SuSE, data about installed and installable software is kept in a database, which can be searched very comfortably. Select the entry **Search** in the drop-down list **Filter:** and enter **openvpn** in the **Search** field. YaST will find up to two entries that match your search value: **openvpn** and **openvpn-devel**. The first package is the one containing the OpenVPN Software. The second package provides software for developers who want to program with OpenVPN and may only be available if you have online installation sources in your setup. Select the entry **openvpn** by checking the box beside the entry in the first column. If you want to obtain information about the OpenVPN package, have a look at the lower half of the right side—here you will find the software **Description**, **Technical Data**, **Dependencies**, and more information about the package you selected.

Click on the button **Accept** to start the OpenVPN installation.

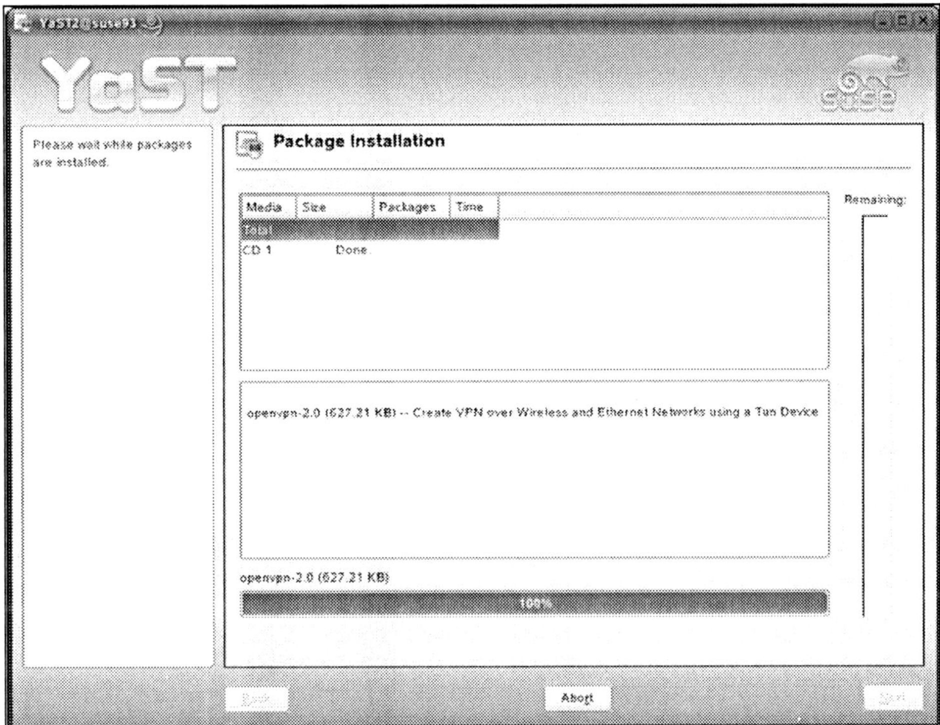


Put your CD or DVD in your local drive. YaST will retrieve the OpenVPN files from your installation media. If you have configured your system to use one of SuSE's web/FTP servers for installation, then this might take a while. The files are unpacked and installed into your system and YaST updates the configuration. This is managed by the script SuSEconfig and other scripts called by it.

SuSEconfig and YaST once were very infamous for deleting local configuration created by the local administrator or omitting relevant changes. This problem was only relevant on updating and re-installing software previously installed. The latest SuSE versions, however, have proven very reliable and the system configuration tools never delete configuration files you have added manually. Instead, the standard configuration files installed with the new software package may be renamed to `<file>.rpmnew` or similar and your configuration is loaded.

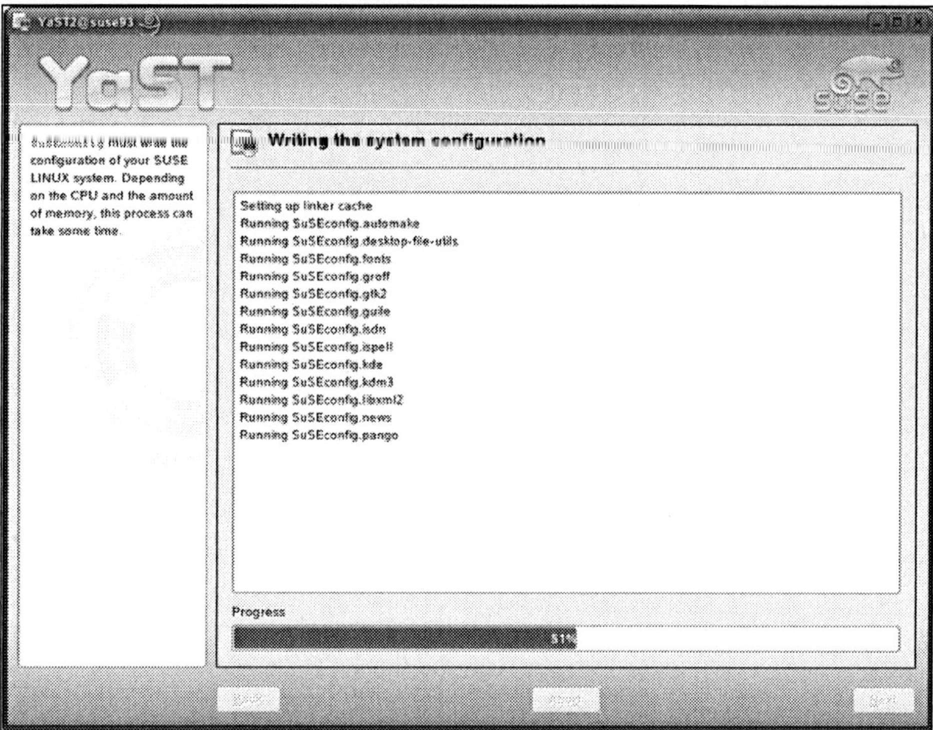


In the screenshot above, you see SuSEconfig calling several helper scripts and updating your configuration. After successful software installation, you are prompted if you want to install more packages or exit installation. Click the Finish button.

# Installing OpenVPN on Redhat Fedora Using yum

If you are using Redhat Fedora, the **Yellow dog Updater, Modified** (**yum**) is probably the easiest way to install software. It can be found on `http://linux.duke.edu/projects/yum/` and provides many interesting features like automatic updates, solving dependency problems, and managing installation of software packages.

Even though OpenVPN installation on Fedora can only be done on the command line, it still is a very easy task. The installation makes use of the commands `wget`, `rpm`, and `yum`.

- wget: A command-line download manager suitable for ftp or http downloads.
- rpm: The Redhat Package Manager is a software management system used by distributions like SuSE or Redhat. It keeps track of changes and can solve dependencies between programs.
- yum: This provides a simple installation program for RPM-based software.

To use yum, you have to adapt its configuration file as follows:

1. Log in as administrator (root).
2. Change to Fedora's configuration directory /etc.
3. Save the old, probably the original, configuration file yum.conf by renaming or moving it. You can use commands like mv yum.conf yum.conf_fedora_org to accomplish this.
4. The website http://www.fedorafaq.org/ provides a suitable configuration file for yum. Download the file http://www.fedorafaq.org/samples/yum.conf using wget. The command-line syntax is wget http://www.fedorafaq.org/samples/yum.conf.
5. At the same site a sophisticated yum configuration is available for download. Install this as well: rpm -Uvh http://www.fedorafaq.org/yum.

The following excerpt shows the output of these five steps on the system:

```
[root@fedora ~]# cd /etc
[root@fedora etc]# mv yum.conf yum.conf.org
[root@fedora etc]# wget http://www.fedorafaq.org/samples/yum.conf
--11:33:25--  http://www.fedorafaq.org/samples/yum.conf
           => `yum.conf'
Resolving www.fedorafaq.org... 70.84.209.18
Connecting to www.fedorafaq.org[70.84.209.18]:80... connected.
HTTP request sent, awaiting response... 200 OK
Length: 595 [text/plain]

100%[=============================================================================
=======================================>] 595          --.--K/s

11:33:25 (405.20 KB/s) - `yum.conf' saved [595/595]

[root@fedora etc]# rpm -Uvh http://www.fedorafaq.org/yum
Retrieving http://www.fedorafaq.org/yum
Preparing...                ########################################### [100%]
   1:yum-fedorafaq          ########################################### [100%]
[root@fedora etc]#
```

The rest of OpenVPN installation is very simple. Just enter yum install openvpn in your root shell. Now yum will start and give you a lot of output. We will have a short look at the things yum does:

```
[root@fedora ~]#yum install openvpn
Setting up Install Process
Setting up repositories
livna                     100% |=========================|  951 B    00:00
updates-released          100% |=========================|  951 B    00:00
base                      100% |=========================| 1.1 kB    00:00
extras                    100% |=========================| 1.1 kB    00:00
Reading repository metadata in from local files
primary.xml.gz            100% |=========================| 127 kB    00:00
```

```
livna      : ################################################## 380/380
Added 380 new packages, deleted 0 old in 1.36 seconds
primary.xml.gz            100% |=========================| 371 kB    00:00
updates-re: ################################################## 1053/1053
Added 0 new packages, deleted 13 old in 0.93 seconds
```

yum has set up the installation process and integrated online repositories for installation of software. This feature is the reason why Fedora does not need a URL source for installing OpenVPN. The repository metadata contains information about location, availability, and dependencies between packages. And resolving dependencies is yum's next step:

```
Parsing package install arguments
Resolving Dependencies
--> Populating transaction set with selected packages. Please wait.
---> Downloading header for openvpn to pack into transaction set.
openvpn-2.0.2-1.fc4.i386. 100% |=========================|  18 kB    00:00
---> Package openvpn.i386 0:2.0.2-1.fc4 set to be updated
--> Running transaction check
--> Processing Dependency: liblzo.so.1 for package: openvpn
--> Restarting Dependency Resolution with new changes.
--> Populating transaction set with selected packages. Please wait.
---> Downloading header for lzo to pack into transaction set.
lzo-1.08-4.i386.rpm       100% |=========================| 3.2 kB    00:00
---> Package lzo.i386 0:1.08-4 set to be updated
--> Running transaction check

Dependencies Resolved
```

OpenVPN needs the LZO library for installation, and yum is about to resolve this dependency. In a next step, yum tests whether this library has unresolved dependencies. This is not the case, and so we are presented with an overview over the packages to be installed:

```
=============================================================================
 Package                 Arch       Version           Repository        Size
=============================================================================
Installing:
 openvpn                 i386       2.0.2-1.fc4       extras           298 k
Installing for dependencies:
 lzo                     i386       1.08-4            extras            59 k

Transaction Summary
=============================================================================
Install      2 Package(s)
Update       0 Package(s)
Remove       0 Package(s)
Total download size: 357 k
Is this ok [y/N]:y
```

Confirm by entering y and press the *Enter* key. yum will start downloading the required packages.

```
Downloading Packages:
(1/2): lzo-1.08-4.i386.rp 100% |=========================|  59 kB    00:00
(2/2): openvpn-2.0.2-1.fc 100% |=========================| 298 kB    00:00
warning: rpmts_HdrFromFdno: Header V3 DSA signature: NOKEY, key ID 1ac70ce6
public key not available for lzo-1.08-4.i386.rpm
Retrieving GPG key from file:///etc/pki/rpm-gpg/RPM-GPG-KEY-fedora-extras
Importing GPG key 0x1AC70CE6 "Fedora Pre Extras Release <pre-
extras@fedoraproject.org>"
Is this ok [y/N]: y
```

The RPM process that yum is using to install the software packages has encountered a missing encryption key. This GPG key is used to control the authenticity of the packages selected for installation. Confirm the import of this key from http://www.fedoraproject.org by entering y and pressing the *Enter* key.

```
Key imported successfully
Running Transaction Test
Finished Transaction Test
Transaction Test Succeeded
Running Transaction
  Installing: lzo                                  ######################### [1/2]
  Installing: openvpn                              ######################### [2/2]

Installed: openvpn.i386 0:2.0.2-1.fc4
Dependency Installed: lzo.i386 0:1.08-4
Complete!
[root@fedora etc]#
```

That's all. yum has downloaded, checked, and has installed OpenVPN and the LZO libraries.

# Installing OpenVPN on RPM-Based Systems

On both SuSE and Fedora, there is another possible way to install OpenVPN. The command-line interface rpm is available on all systems using the Redhat package management system. rpm is a very powerful command that can install, remove, update, test, and query software packages. Installing software with rpm is done in three steps:

1. Downloading the software
2. Testing installation and resolving dependencies
3. Installing the RPM files with the appropriate rpm command

Whenever you run into problems with RPM, its manpage is the best reference for all of its abundant options.

The best place to look for the right version of OpenVPN under SuSE will be ftp://ftp.suse.com/. Fedora RPMs can be obtained from Dag Wieers' site http://dag.wieers.com/packages/openvpn/. The command-line extract in the following section shows the typical process of obtaining and installing OpenVPN on SuSE 9.3, but this procedure will work in exactly the same way on Fedora or any other RPM-based system.

## Using wget to Download OpenVPN RPMs

Enter wget 'ftp://ftp.suse.com/pub/suse/i386/9.3/suse/i586/openvpn-2.0-5.i586.rpm' on your SuSE system to download OpenVPN in version 2.0.5.

```
suse93:~/ # wget 'ftp://ftp.suse.com/pub/suse/i386/9.3/suse/i586/openvpn-2.0-
5.i586.rpm'
--09:17:50--  ftp://ftp.suse.com/pub/suse/i386/9.3/suse/i586/openvpn-2.0-
5.i586.rpm
           => `openvpn-2.0-5.i586.rpm.1'
Auflösen des Hostnamen »ftp.suse.com«.... 195.135.221.132
Connecting to ftp.suse.com|195.135.221.132|:21... verbunden.
Anmelden als anonymous ... Angemeldet!
```

```
==> SYST ... fertig.     ==> PWD ... fertig.
==> TYPE I ... fertig.   ==> CWD /pub/suse/i386/9.3/suse/i586 ... fertig.
==> PASV ... fertig.     ==> RETR openvpn-2.0-5.i586.rpm ... fertig.
Länge: 293,771 (287K) (unmaßgeblich)

100%[==========================================================================
=======================================>] 293,771        3.15K/s    ETA 00:00

09:19:38 (4.10 KB/s) - `openvpn-2.0-5.i586.rpm' saved [293771]

suse93:~/ #
```

After downloading the file, you can use rpm to test the installation.

## Testing Installation and Installing with rpm

One of the very interesting features of RPM is that you can test the installation of a specific RPM file in a "dry run". This is done with the command: `rpm -ivh --test openvpn-2.0.2-0.1.i586.rpm`. The options are simple:

- `-i` stands for install.
- `-v` means verbose output.
- `-h` prints a progress bar.
- `--test` lets RPM do a dry run to test installing the package.

In almost all cases you will receive the following output:

```
suse93:~ # rpm -ivh --test openvpn-2.0-5.i586.rpm
Preparing...                ########################################### [100%]
suse93:~ #
```

OK, rpm reports no errors, so we can install OpenVPN without the test switch:

```
suse93:~ # rpm -ivh --test openvpn-2.0-5.i586.rpm
```

## Installing OpenVPN and the LZO Library with wget and RPM

If your system is still missing the LZO library, our test-installation will fail. rpm reports an error, already pointing you to the solution: We have to download the RPM and install it. Again, wget is a good choice for this issue:

```
suse93:~ # wget 'ftp://ftp.suse.com/pub/suse/i386/9.3/suse/i586/lzo-1.08-
107.i586.rpm'
```

A good idea may be creating a local directory and downloading both RPM files to this directory.

```
suse93:~ # mkdir openvpn-rpms
suse93:~ # cd openvpn-rpms
suse93:~/openvpn-rpms # wget
'ftp://ftp.suse.com/pub/suse/i386/9.3/suse/i586/lzo-1.08-107.i586.rpm'
(...)
suse93:~/openvpn-rpms # wget
'ftp://ftp.suse.com/pub/suse/i386/9.3/suse/i586/openvpn-2.0-5.i586.rpm'
(...)
suse93:~/openvpn-rpms # rpm -ivh *rpm
```

```
Preparing...                ########################################### [100%]
   1:openvpn                ########################################### [ 50%]
   2:lzo                    ########################################### [100%]
suse93:~/openvpn-rpms #
```

As the last command shows, you can call RPM with wildcards and order it to install all RPM files it finds in this directory at once.

RPM can also have a remote location for the package to be installed, but this only works if there are no dependencies. Because this can only be checked after download, you may have to try several times. This is why `wget` is the better choice in most cases.

```
suse93:~ # rpm -Uvh 'ftp://ftp.suse.com/pub/suse/i386/9.3/suse/i586/openvpn-2.0-5.i586.rpm'
```

## Using rpm to Obtain Information on the Installed OpenVPN Version

You can use `rpm` to query the software database by adding options beginning with `-q` to the command:

```
[root@fedora openvpn]# rpm -qi openvpn
Name        : openvpn                      Relocations: (not relocatable)
Version     : 2.0.2                             Vendor: (none)
Release     : 1.fc4                         Build Date: Sat 27 Aug 2005
05:01:57 PM CEST
Install Date: Mon 29 Aug 2005 11:35:27 AM CEST      Build Host:
hammer1.fedora.redhat.com
Group       : Applications/Internet         Source RPM: openvpn-2.0.2-
1.fc4.src.rpm
Size        : 632024                           License: GPL
Signature   : DSA/SHA1, Sun 28 Aug 2005 10:19:53 PM CEST, Key ID
82ed95041ac70ce6
URL         : http://openvpn.net/
Summary     : A full-featured SSL VPN solution
Description :
OpenVPN is a robust and highly flexible tunneling application that uses all
of the encryption, authentication, and certification features of the
OpenSSL library to securely tunnel IP networks over a single UDP or TCP
port.  It can use the Marcus Franz Xaver Johannes Oberhumer's LZO library
for compression.
[root@fedora openvpn]#
```

Whereas `rpm -qi` provides information about the installed version, `rpm -qli` will print all files that have been installed by this software package including their full path:

```
[root@fedora ~]# rpm -ql openvpn
/etc/openvpn
/etc/rc.d/init.d/openvpn
/usr/lib/openvpn
/usr/lib/openvpn/plugin
/usr/lib/openvpn/plugin/lib
/usr/lib/openvpn/plugin/lib/openvpn-auth-pam.so
/usr/lib/openvpn/plugin/lib/openvpn-down-root.so
/usr/sbin/openvpn
/usr/share/doc/openvpn-2.0.2
/usr/share/doc/openvpn-2.0.2/AUTHORS
/usr/share/doc/openvpn-2.0.2/COPYING
/usr/share/doc/openvpn-2.0.2/COPYRIGHT.GPL
/usr/share/doc/openvpn-2.0.2/INSTALL
```

The following table shows the function of the most important directories and files of this list:

| Full Path and File Installed by OpenVPN | Function |
|---|---|
| /etc/openvpn | Directory containing configuration files |
| /etc/init.d/openvpn<br>/usr/sbin/rcopenvpn | Start/stop script for services |
| /usr/sbin/openvpn | The binary |
| /usr/share/doc/openvpn | Documentation files |
| /usr/share/man/man8/openvpn.8.gz | Manual page |
| /usr/share/doc/openvpn/examples/sample-config-files | Example configuration files |
| /usr/share/doc/openvpn/examples/sample-keys | Example keys and certificates |
| /usr/share/doc/openvpn/examples/easy-rsa | easy-rsa—a collection of scripts useful for creating tunnels |
| /usr/share/doc/openvpn/changelog.Debian.gz<br>/usr/share/doc/openvpn/changelog.gz | Version history |
| /usr/share/openvpn/verify-cn | verify-cn function (revoke command) |
| /usr/lib/openvpn/openvpn-auth-pam.so<br>/usr/lib/openvpn/openvpn-down-root.so | Libraries for PAM-Authentication and chroot mode |
| /usr/share/doc/packages/openvpn/suse<br>/usr/share/doc/packages/openvpn/suse/openvpn.init | SuSE-specific start/stop scripts |
| /var/run/openvpn | Process ID of the running OpenVPN process |

# Installing OpenVPN on Debian

Probably the easiest distribution on which to install OpenVPN is Debian. Just type `apt-get install openvpn`, answer two questions, and OpenVPN is installed and ready to be used.

The Debian package management system is capable of solving all issues that might occur during the installation. If your system is configured correctly, the automatic installation covers these steps:

1. The installation helper `apt-get` will find the software on the installation servers.
2. The helper will then download the chosen package and unpack it to your local system.
3. An interactive configuration script is executed, which configures your system and the newly installed software for later usage with the parameters you enter.

The following code extract is the standard output of `apt-get install openvpn` on a Debian system. This output may vary depending on your previous software selection, and in many cases the LZO compression library will have to be installed. On some systems `apt` will install OpenSSL libraries, but in most cases, `apt-get` is able to solve all problems for you.

```
debian01:~# apt-get install openvpn
Reading Package Lists... Done
Building Dependency Tree... Done
The following NEW packages will be installed:
  openvpn
0 upgraded, 1 newly installed, 0 to remove and 7 not upgraded.
Need to get 293kB of archives.
After unpacking 762kB of additional disk space will be used.
Get:1 http://ftp.uni-erlangen.de testing/main openvpn 2.0-4 [293kB]
Fetched 293kB in 1s (247kB/s)
Preconfiguring packages ...
Selecting previously deselected package openvpn.
(Reading database ... 9727 files and directories currently installed.)
Unpacking openvpn (from .../openvpn_2.0-4_i386.deb) ...
Setting up openvpn (2.0-4) ...
Restarting virtual private network daemon:.

debian01:~#
```

During this process, you will be prompted to answer the following two questions:

- You have to allow apt to create a TUN/TAP device for use by OpenVPN Software. If you select No, your tunnels will not be created and your tunnel software won't work.

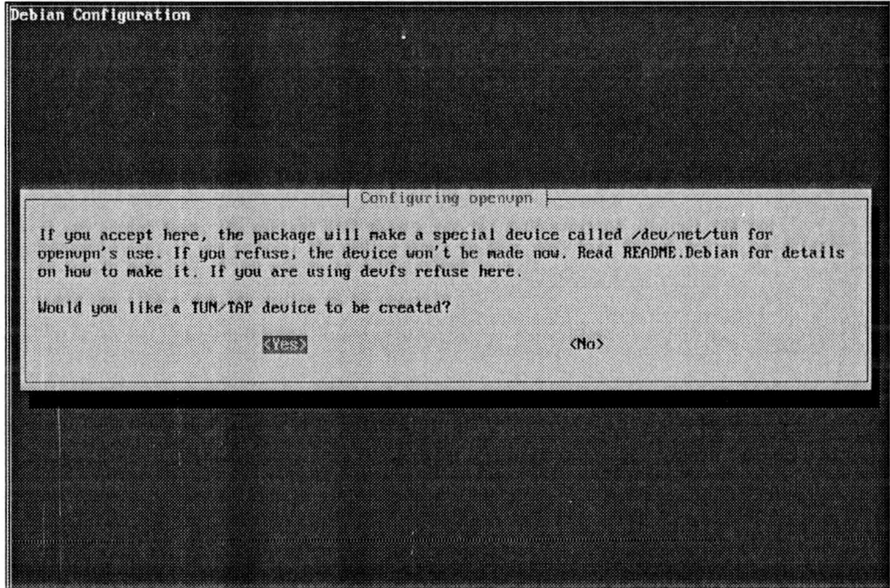

- The second question raises a security issue. OpenVPN Software should be stopped during an update, so you have to select YES and hit return.

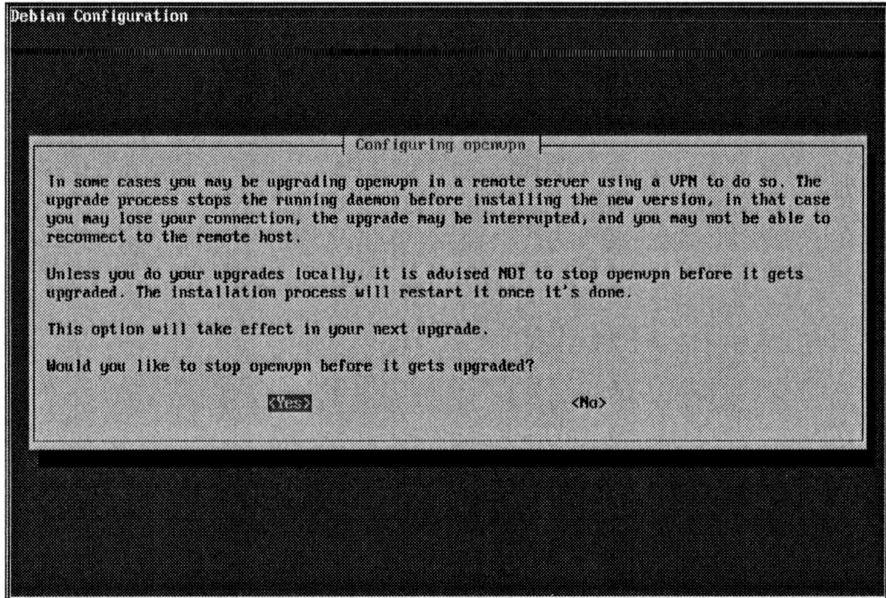


You have to stop the *old* tunnel software when an update is running. All tunneling will be stopped, and your users will not be able to connect to your system during this time. From now on, all tunnels are created by the new OpenVPN Software including patches and bugfixes. This is the safe way to go.

However, if you choose No, you risk that the old software and libraries are still running, even after installation of new OpenVPN Software. Bugfixes and patches of the new version may not apply to existing tunnels until they are started again. You may run into serious inconsistencies on your system, if you have several tunnels and they are running different versions of your software. Thus, it is safer to have a short time when users will not be able to connect.

## Installing Debian Packages

Software packages for Debian systems are provided in the so-called `.deb` file format. DEB files are usually stored in online repositories on FTP or web servers and every Debian system holds a list of repositories to be used for installation. You will find this list in `/etc/apt/sources.list`. The setup program `base-config` provides a menu-based configuration interface for `apt`.

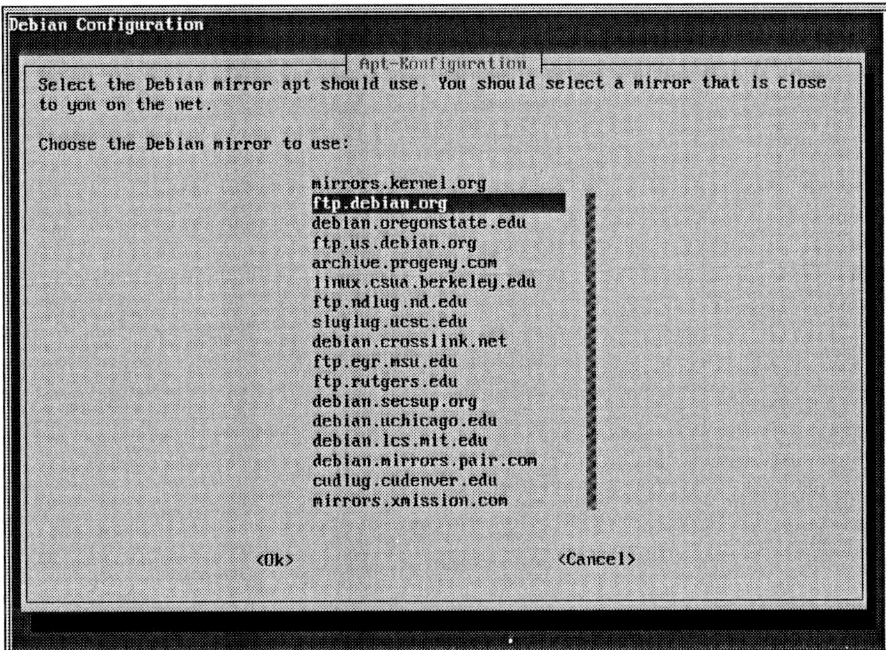


If you want to add source repositories to your Debian installation, type `base-config` and change to the menu `configure apt`. Select the country you live in and the repository of your choice. Select Ok. Now all software packages of this server can automatically be installed on your system, simply by typing `apt-get install` <package>.

A Debian package contains the software and information about it like name, version, description, contents, prerequisites, dependencies, and configuration scripts to be started after installation.

Debian systems offer some very powerful programs with which you can control software installation very specifically. Listing all programs and options would go far beyond the scope of this book, but here is a short overview of some handy package management commands:

| **Command** | **Function** |
|---|---|
| `apt-get install <package>` | Installs the selected package from repositories listed in `/etc/apt/sources.list` |
| `apt-get remove <package>` | Removes the selected package from your system |
| `apt-get update` | Updates the list of packages available on the repositories listed in `/etc/apt/sources.list` |
| `apt-get upgrade` | Installs the latest available versions of all your installed software |
| `apt-get dist-upgrade` | Installs the latest available software related to your configuration |
| `dpkg-reconfigure` | Restarts/Starts the configuration script inside the package, which will bring up the menu-based dialogs in the same way as after installation |

| Command | Function |
|---|---|
| apt-cache show <package> | Prints detailed information about the software package |
| dpkg -l <package> | Prints information on the installed software package |
| dpkg -L <package> | Lists all files installed by the software package |
| dpkg -i <file> | Installs a local (.deb) file to your system |
| dpkg -S <file> | Prints information about the software package owning <file> |
| apt-cache search <string> | Searches apt database for packages containing <string> in their name and description |

These programs should solve all possible questions, issues, and problems about the installation of software on Debian systems. Just try these commands with the freshly installed OpenVPN package on your system. Type `apt-cache show openvpn` to receive information about the installed package:

```
debian:~# apt-cache show openvpn
Package: openvpn
Priority: optional
Section: net
Installed-Size: 744
Maintainer: Alberto Gonzalez Iniesta <agi@inittab.org>
Architecture: i386
Version: 2.0-4
Depends: debconf, libc6 (>= 2.3.2.ds1-21), liblzo1, libssl0.9.7
Filename: pool/main/o/openvpn/openvpn_2.0-4_i386.deb
Size: 293492
MD5sum: dcc638e084f7b3143c614a33b26d5750
Description: Virtual Private Network daemon
 An application to securely tunnel IP networks over a single UDP or TCP port.
 It can be used to access remote sites, make secure point to point
connnections,
 enhance WiFi security, etc.
 .
 OpenVPN uses all of the encryption, authentication, and certification
features
 of the OpenSSL library (any cipher, key size, or HMAC digest).
 .
 OpenVPN may use static, pre-shared keys or TLS-based dynamic key exchange. It
 also supports VPNs with dynamic endpoints (DHCP or dial-up clients), tunnels
 over NAT or connection-oriented stateful firewalls (like Linux's iptables).
Tag: security::cryptography, interface::daemon

debian:~#
```

## Using Aptitude to Search and Install Packages

Although the Debian command-line tools are very powerful, there are more programs that help you retrieve and install software. Probably the most common software for this purpose is Aptitude. Type `aptitude` in a command line to start the menu-based installation interface.

> If Aptitude is not installed on your system, type `apt-get install aptitude`.

```
Actions  Undo  Package  Search  Options  Views  Help
f10: Menu  ?: Help  q: Quit  u: Update  g: Download/Install/Remove Pkgs
aptitude 0.2.15.9
--- New Packages
--- Installed Packages
--- Not Installed Packages
--- Virtual Packages
--- Tasks

These packages have been added to Debian since the last time you cleared the list of "new"
packages. (choose "Forget new packages" from the Actions menu to empty this list)
```

Aptitude consists of a menu at the top of the screen, a list of packages, and a window showing details on the software selected in the package list. If you have console mouse support, you can click on menu entries.

Click on the menu entry Search, or hit the *F10* key and navigate through the Search menu. Select the entry Find. You will be prompted with a search mask. Enter openvpn. While you are typing, aptitude is steadily updating the main window. Click OK and have a look at the output.

```
Actions  Undo  Package  Search  Options  Views  Help
f10: Menu  ?: Help  q: Quit  u: Update  g: Download/Install/Remove Pkgs
aptitude 0.2.15.9
i     pidentd                                               3.0.18-3    3.0.18-3
i     portmap                                               5-14        5-14
i     pppoe                                                 3.5-4       3.5-4
i     pppoeconf                                             1.7         1.7
i     shorewall                                             2.4.1-2     2.4.1-2
i     ssh                                                   1:3.8.1p1-  1:3.8.1p1-
i     telnet                                                0.17-29     0.17-29
i     traceroute                                            1.4a12-19   1.4a12-19
i     whois                                                 4.7.5       4.7.5
  --- oldlibs - Obsolete libraries
  --- otherosfs - Emulators and software to read foreign filesystems
  --- perl - Perl interpreter and libraries
  --- python - Python interpreter and libraries
  --- shells - Command shells and alternative console environments
  --- text - Text processing utilities
Virtual Private Network daemon
An application to securely tunnel IP networks over a single UDP or TCP port. It can be used
to access remote sites, make secure point to point connections, enhance WiFi security,
etc.

OpenVPN uses all of the encryption, authentication, and certification features of the
OpenSSL library (any cipher, key size, or HMAC digest).

OpenVPN may use static, pre-shared keys or TLS-based dynamic key exchange.  It also
supports VPNs with dynamic endpoints (DHCP or dial-up clients), tunnels over NAT or
connection-oriented stateful firewalls (like Linux's iptables).
```

Aptitude will find the OpenVPN version you have installed previously, and the entries in the menus Actions and Package help you select and install software. Depending on the selection of repositories that you have added to your `sources.list` during installation, Aptitude can also help you choose different versions of OpenVPN.

## OpenVPN—The Files Installed on Debian

The following table gives an overview of the files installed by the Debian package management system. Some of these files will be used in later chapters:

| Full Path and File Installed by OpenVPN | Function |
|---|---|
| `/etc/openvpn` | Directory containing configuration files |
| `/etc/network/if-up.d/openvpn`<br>`/etc/network/if-down.d`<br>`/etc/network/if-down.d/openvpn` | Start/stop openvpn when the network goes up/down |
| `/etc/init.d/openvpn` | Start/stop script for services |
| `/sbin/openvpn` | The binary |
| `/usr/share/doc/openvpn` | Documentation files |
| `/usr/share/man/man8/openvpn.8.gz` | Manual page |
| `/usr/share/doc/openvpn/examples/sample-config-files` | Example configuration files |
| `/usr/share/doc/openvpn/examples/sample-keys` | Example keys |
| `/usr/share/doc/openvpn/examples/easy-rsa` | `easy-rsa`—a collection of scripts useful for creating tunnels |
| `/usr/share/doc/openvpn/changelog.Debian.gz`<br>`/usr/share/doc/openvpn/changelog.gz` | Version history |
| `/usr/share/openvpn/verify-cn` | `verify-cn` function (revoke command) |
| `/usr/lib/openvpn/openvpn-auth-pam.so`<br>`/usr/lib/openvpn/openvpn-down-root.so` | Libraries for PAM-Authentication and chroot mode |

# Installing OpenVPN on FreeBSD

FreeBSD and BSD in general are UNIX systems of outstanding stability and security and are therefore very popular among network administrators. In practice, with FreeBSD you do not have to worry much about security issues of the software you install, but you may not always get up-to-date versions.

FreeBSD also has a modern software management system. Simply type `pkg_add -vr openvpn`, and OpenVPN Software is installed on your system. Calling `pkg_add` with the parameter `-r` installs software from remote servers, similar to `apt-get` or `rpm`. If you run into problems, increasing verbosity with the parameter `-v` can be helpful.

The following excerpt shows the ou

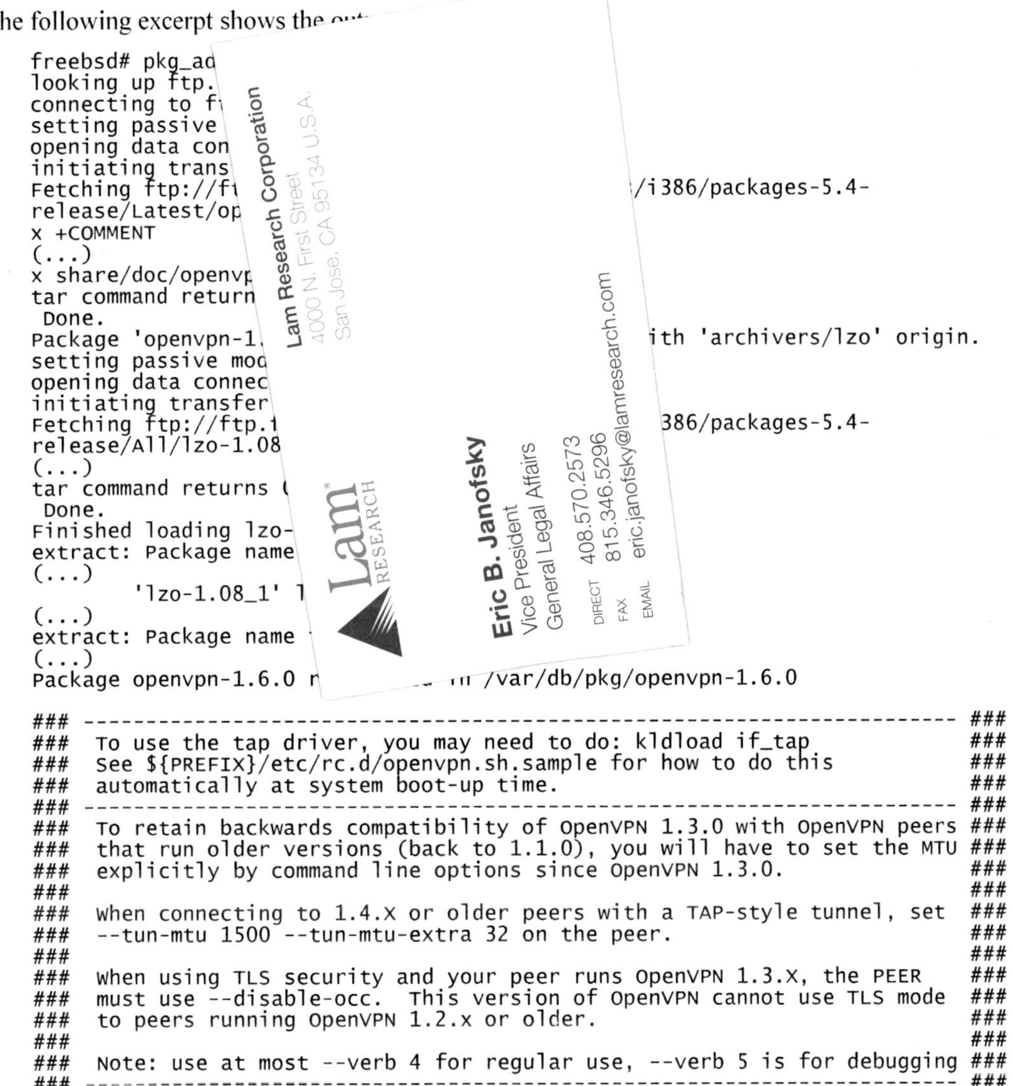

```
freebsd# pkg_ad
looking up ftp.
connecting to f
setting passive
opening data con
initiating trans
Fetching ftp://f                                          /i386/packages-5.4-
release/Latest/op
x +COMMENT
(...)
x share/doc/openvp
tar command return
 Done.
Package 'openvpn-1.                                       ith 'archivers/lzo' origin.
setting passive mod
opening data connec
initiating transfer
Fetching ftp://ftp.                                       386/packages-5.4-
release/All/lzo-1.08
(...)
tar command returns
 Done.
Finished loading lzo-
extract: Package name
(...)
        'lzo-1.08_1' 
(...)
extract: Package name
(...)
Package openvpn-1.6.0 r             /var/db/pkg/openvpn-1.6.0

### ------------------------------------------------------------------- ###
###  To use the tap driver, you may need to do: kldload if_tap          ###
###  See ${PREFIX}/etc/rc.d/openvpn.sh.sample for how to do this        ###
###  automatically at system boot-up time.                              ###
### ------------------------------------------------------------------- ###
###  To retain backwards compatibility of OpenVPN 1.3.0 with OpenVPN peers ###
###  that run older versions (back to 1.1.0), you will have to set the MTU ###
###  explicitly by command line options since OpenVPN 1.3.0.            ###
###                                                                     ###
###  When connecting to 1.4.x or older peers with a TAP-style tunnel, set ###
###  --tun-mtu 1500 --tun-mtu-extra 32 on the peer.                     ###
###                                                                     ###
###  When using TLS security and your peer runs OpenVPN 1.3.x, the PEER ###
###  must use --disable-occ.  This version of OpenVPN cannot use TLS mode ###
###  to peers running OpenVPN 1.2.x or older.                           ###
###                                                                     ###
###  Note: use at most --verb 4 for regular use, --verb 5 is for debugging ###
### ------------------------------------------------------------------- ###

freebsd#
```

`pkg_add` looks for an appropriate installation candidate, downloads it, and checks for dependencies. Because LZO is required but not installed, `pkg_add` starts over with downloading this package first. After successful installation of LZO, OpenVPN is installed. When called with the parameter `-v`, `pkg_add` also gives you a list of all files installed.

After this installation, there are four issues to be noticed:

- The OpenVPN binary is not in the standard path. Call OpenVPN with full path or add its path to your startup file.
- In our example, OpenVPN version 1.6.0 was installed. There are some features of version 2.0 that cannot be used. The section that follows shows how you can install a newer version on your system.
- The standard configuration file path is `/usr/local/etc/openvpn/`.
- The init script that is used to start OpenVPN and its tunnels at system boot must be edited before we can use it.

The OpenVPN installation on FreeBSD provides a sample startup script that needs a little editing after which it can be used at system boot. It is located in `/usr/local/etc/rc.d/openvpn.sh`. Copy this file to `/etc/rc.d/openvpn` and correct the path variables to your needs. To start OpenVPN at boot time, we have to change three entries in the file `/etc/rc.conf`, containing startup configuration for the services.

Simply add or edit the following lines in your `/etc/rc.conf` to these values:

```
openvpn_enable="YES"
openvpn_if=tun
openvpn-dir=/etc/openvpn
```

If you have set correct paths in your init script, OpenVPN will be started next time you boot your system.

## Installing a Newer Version of OpenVPN on FreeBSD—The Port System

If you want to install OpenVPN version 2.0 on FreeBSD, you can install a FreeBSD port of OpenVPN. But before that, we should uninstall the version of OpenVPN we have just installed. Just type `pkg_delete openvpn-1.6.0`.

```
freebsd# pkg_delete openvpn-1.6.0
```

Then browse to the FreeBSD website `http://www.freebsd.org`, which is the first place to look for documentation, help, and software for FreeBSD. Click on the Ports under the SHORTCUTS section, which will lead you to `http://www.freebsd.org/ports/index.html`. The *ports* are patches (`tar.gz` files) to the original source code of applications as well as download routines and information for the software installation management.

## Installing the Port System with sysinstall

To make use of these ports, the so-called port system has to be installed on your machine. This can easily be done with FreeBSD's setup tool called sysinstall. Start by typing `sysinstall`.

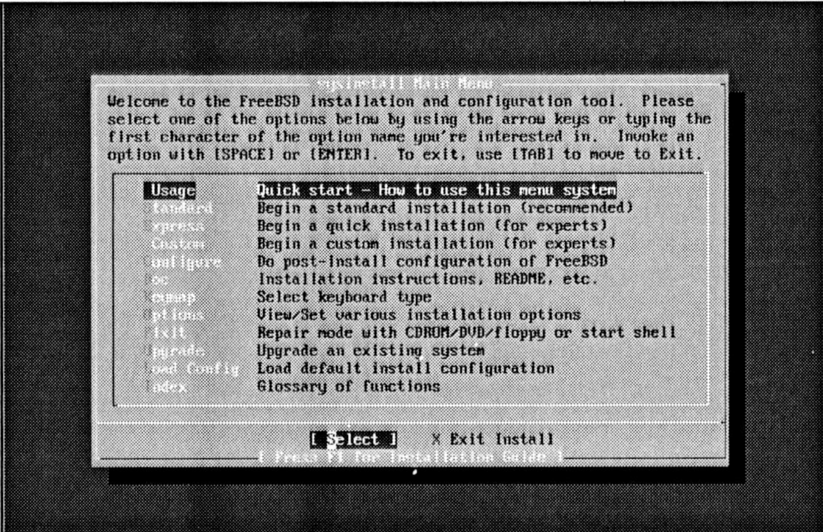


Use the up/down arrow keys to select the entry Configure and press *Enter*. In the following window called, "FreeBSD Configuration Menu", change to the module Distributions.

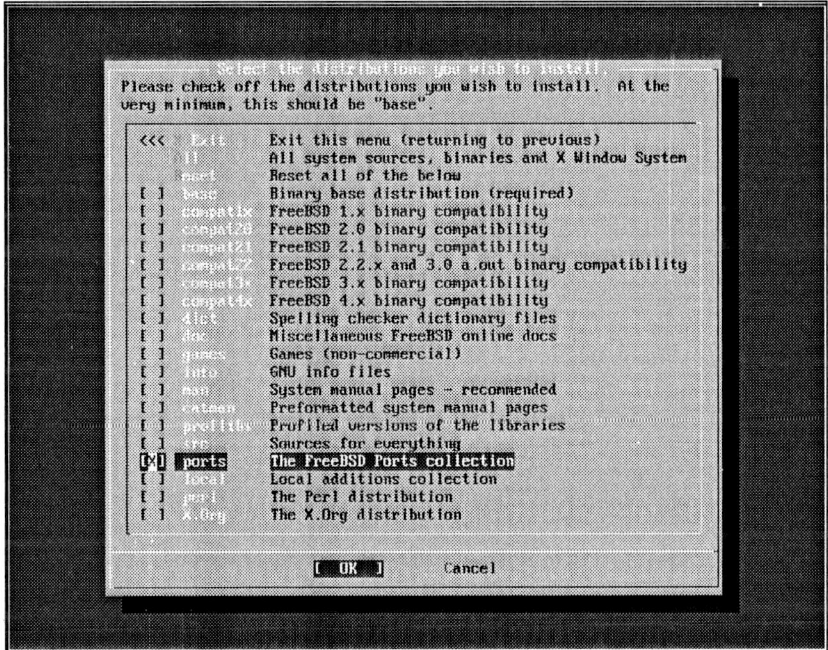

The distributions dialog contains many different distributions to install, but only The FreeBSD Ports collection is relevant for our purpose. Activate this entry with your *spacebar* and hit *Enter*. You will be asked to choose a source from which you want to install these ports; just confirm with *Enter* here (thrice). The port system is then downloaded and installed.

## Downloading and Installing a BSD Port

Now we must download the port package from the BSD website and extract it to a local folder. Point your browser to `http://www.freebsd.org/ports/index.html`, enter openvpn in the search field and click on the button Submit.

As result for your search you will be presented with OpenVPN in version 2.0.2 or newer in the security section. Click on the download link and save the **tarball** (`.tar` file) to a local directory.

Enter this directory and type `make`. The port system will fetch the appropriate sources for this port, patch them, and start the compilation process. When `make` is ready, type `make install` to install the binaries in your system.

```
freebsd# make install
===>  Installing for openvpn-2.0.2
===>   openvpn-2.0.2 depends on shared library: lzo.1 - found
===>   Generating temporary packing list
===>  Checking if security/openvpn already installed
test -z "/usr/local/sbin" || /root/openvpn/work/openvpn-2.0.2/install-sh -d
"/usr/local/sbin"
  install  -s -o root -g wheel -m 555 'openvpn' '/usr/local/sbin/openvpn'
(...)
      This port has installed the following files which may act as network
      servers and may therefore pose a remote security risk to the system.
/usr/local/sbin/openvpn

      This port has installed the following startup scripts which may cause
      these network services to be started at boot time.
/usr/local/etc/rc.d/openvpn.sh

      If there are vulnerabilities in these programs there may be a security
      risk to the system. FreeBSD makes no guarantee about the security of
      ports included in the Ports Collection. Please type 'make deinstall'
      to deinstall the port if this is a concern.

      For more information, and contact details about the security
      status of this software, see the following webpage:
http://openvpn.sourceforge.net/
freebsd#
```

That's it. A new version of OpenVPN has successfully been installed on your system. You can test it with `/usr/local/sbin/openvpn -version`.

If you need more details on installing and running OpenVPN, have a look at these websites: `http://blog.innerewut.de/articles/2005/07/04/openvpn-2-0-on-openbsd` and `http://blog.innerewut.de/articles/2005/07/08/improving-openvpn-s-security`.

# Troubleshooting—Advanced Installation Methods

Normally, the techniques discussed above should work fine for any platform. However, I want to provide advanced installation techniques that will enable you to install OpenVPN in situations where the other standard methods fail.

Our next installation example—installing from source code—will cover a procedure that is possible on every platform and enables the administrator to change the basic behavior of OpenVPN. Many developers and administrators consider that this *should be* standard installation procedure for all systems. There are some advantages regarding stability and performance that can only be optimized for your individual system by compiling as much relevant software as possible (the Gentoo approach...). In most cases, however, the installation tools provided with the systems are much easier to use. But if you are looking for detailed debugging information, the source code will be first choice.

When building OpenVPN from sources, there is also the possibility to produce RPM files for your SuSE or Redhat Systems, which is covered in the second section. The last troubleshooting hint may be useful for anybody running self-compiled kernels and who need to activate the TUN/TAP driver in the kernel, which should only seldom be necessary.

## Installing OpenVPN from Source Code

Provided that your system has installed several basic development tools like `make` and a C compiler, the following guideline is system independent. Based on a Debian system, we will download OpenVPN source code and install it using `make` and `configure`. As prerequisites, we have to install the compression library `liblzo1`, the corresponding development package `liblzo-devel`, and the headers of OpenSSL, `libssl-devel`. On Debian with kernel 2.6, simply type `apt-get install liblzo1 liblzo-dev libssl-dev`:

```
debian01:~# apt-get install liblzo1 liblzo-dev and libssl-dev
Reading Package Lists... Done
Building Dependency Tree... Done
The following NEW packages will be installed:
  and liblzo-dev liblzo1 libssl-dev
0 upgraded, 4 newly installed, 0 to remove and 7 not upgraded.
Need to get 23.5kB/2726kB of archives.
After unpacking 8040kB of additional disk space will be used.
Get:1 http://ftp.uni-erlangen.de testing/main and 1.2.1-2 [23.5kB]
Fetched 23.5kB in 0s (50.7kB/s)
Selecting previously deselected package and.
(Reading database ... 11232 files and directories currently installed.)
Unpacking and (from .../archives/and_1.2.1-2_i386.deb) ...
Selecting previously deselected package liblzo1.
Unpacking liblzo1 (from .../liblzo1_1.08-2_i386.deb) ...
Selecting previously deselected package liblzo-dev.
Unpacking liblzo-dev (from .../liblzo-dev_1.08-2_i386.deb) ...
Selecting previously deselected package libssl-dev.
Unpacking libssl-dev (from .../libssl-dev_0.9.7e-3_i386.deb) ...
Setting up and (1.2.1-2) ...
Starting auto nice daemon: and.

Setting up liblzo1 (1.08-2) ...

Setting up liblzo-dev (1.08-2) ...
Setting up libssl-dev (0.9.7e-3) ...
debian01:~#
```

As next step, we have to download the OpenVPN source code.

```
debian01:~# wget 'http://openvpn.net/release/openvpn-2.0.2.tar.gz'
```

We have to untar the `tar.gz` archive to a local directory:

```
debian01:~# ta
r -xzf openvpn-2.0.2.tar.gz
```

A directory called `openvpn-2.0.2` is created. The name of this directory depends on the version you downloaded. Change to this directory and type `./configure`.

```
debian01:~/openvpn-2.0.2# ./configure
checking for ifconfig... /sbin/ifconfig
checking for ip... ip
checking for route... /sbin/route
checking build system type... i686-pc-linux
checking host system type... i686-pc-linux
checking target system type... i686-pc-linux
checking for a BSD-compatible install... /usr/bin/install -c
checking whether build environment is sane... yes
checking for gawk... no
checking for mawk... mawk
checking whether make sets $(MAKE)... yes
checking for gcc... gcc
(...)
checking for SSL_CTX_new in -lssl... yes
configure: creating ./config.status
config.status: creating Makefile
config.status: creating openvpn.spec
config.status: creating config-win32.h
config.status: creating install-win32/openvpn.nsi
config.status: creating config.h
config.status: executing depfiles commands
debian01:~/openvpn-2.0.2#
```

You will receive some screens full of output. The configure script checks for software dependencies and compatibility of the source code with your system, and creates a so-called `makefile`, which is used as a sort of guideline for later compilation. The command `make` interprets the `makefile` and compiles the program and all needed libraries. Type `make` to start this process.

```
debian01:~/openvpn-2.0.2# make
make  all-am
make[1]: Entering directory `/root/openvpn-2.0.2'
if gcc -DHAVE_CONFIG_H -I. -I. -I.    -I.    -g -O2 -MT base64.o -MD -MP -MF
".deps/base64.Tpo" -c -o base64.o base64.c; \
then mv -f ".deps/base64.Tpo" ".deps/base64.Po"; else rm -f
".deps/base64.Tpo"; exit 1; fi
(...)
```

On slow systems, you can have a coffee now. OpenVPN and its components are compiled now. Make calls `gcc` with parameters according to the `makefile` that `configure` has created. `gcc` compiles the source code files to binary files that you (or your operating system) can execute. These binary files have to be installed to the proper places in your system. Type `make install` to accomplish that:

```
debian01:~/openvpn-2.0.2# make install
make[1]: Entering directory `/root/openvpn-2.0.2'
test -z "/usr/local/sbin" || mkdir -p -- . "/usr/local/sbin"
  /usr/bin/install -c 'openvpn' '/usr/local/sbin/openvpn'
```

```
test -z "/usr/local/man/man8" || mkdir -p -- . "/usr/local/man/man8"
 /usr/bin/install -c -m 644 './openvpn.8' '/usr/local/man/man8/openvpn.8'
make[1]: Leaving directory `/root/openvpn-2.0.2'
debian01:~/openvpn-2.0.2#
```

We see that only three files are installed: `/usr/local/sbin` and two manual pages. Now OpenVPN is ready to be used on your system. If you don't believe, just type `openvpn --version`

```
debian01:~/openvpn-2.0.2# openvpn --version
OpenVPN 2.0.2 i686-pc-linux [SSL] [LZO] [EPOLL] built on Sep  4 2005
Developed by James Yonan
Copyright (C) 2002-2005 OpenVPN Solutions LLC <info@openvpn.net>
debian01:~/openvpn-2.0.2#
```

The OpenVPN binary used was compiled (built) on September 4, 2005 and is available in your Path.

## Building Your Own RPM File from the OpenVPN Source Code

As you may have seen in the section on Redhat and SuSE, RPM files are quite handy: You can copy them to any other system of the same type and have them installed automatically. If you need to use a specific version of OpenVPN, you may want to create your own RPM files from a source code file, and distribute them to your servers. This may sound complicated, but it is done with one single command (and some prerequisites).

The program `rpmbuild` can create RPMs for your platform from an ordinary `tar.gz` source code archive. Download the newest stable version of OpenVPN and enter the command `rpmbuild -tb openvpn-2.0.2.tar.gz`. Replace the filename with the name of the file you want to install.

```
suse93:~ # wget 'http://openvpn.net/release/openvpn-2.0.2.tar.gz'
suse93:~ # rpmbuild -tb openvpn-2.0.2.tar.gz
error: Failed build dependencies:
        openssl-devel >= 0.9.6 is needed by openvpn-2.0.2-1
        pam-devel is needed by openvpn-2.0.2-1
suse93:~ #
```

`rpmbuild` has failed on this SuSE system because two libraries are missing. On SuSE systems, you simply install them with YaST, and on Redhat systems, you can use `yum`. After installing them, start `rpmbuild` again:

```
suse93:~ # rpmbuild -tb openvpn-2.0.2.tar.gz
Executing(%prep): /bin/sh -e /var/tmp/rpm-tmp.62341
+ umask 022
+ cd /usr/src/packages/BUILD
+ cd /usr/src/packages/BUILD
+ rm -rf openvpn-2.0.2
+ /usr/bin/gzip -dc /root/openvpn-2.0.2.tar.gz
+ tar -xf -
+ STATUS=0
+ '[' 0 -ne 0 ']'
+ cd openvpn-2.0.2
++ /usr/bin/id -u
+ '[' 0 = 0 ']'
+ /bin/chown -Rhf root .

(...)
Requires(preun): /bin/sh
```

```
Requires: openssl >= 0.9.6 lzo >= 1.07 pam
Checking for unpackaged file(s): /usr/lib/rpm/check-files /var/tmp/openvpn-
root
Wrote: /usr/src/packages/RPMS/i586/openvpn-2.0.2-1.i586.rpm
Executing(%clean): /bin/sh -e /var/tmp/rpm-tmp.68581
+ umask 022
+ cd /usr/src/packages/BUILD
+ cd openvpn-2.0.2
+ '[' /var/tmp/openvpn-root '!=' / ']'
+ rm -rf /var/tmp/openvpn-root
+ exit 0
```

While you receive several screens of output, the OpenVPN source code is configured and compiled. At the end the RPM file is placed in `/usr/src/packages/RPMS/i586/` and can be installed with RPM from this location:

```
suse93:~ # rpm -ivh /usr/src/packages/RPMS/i586/openvpn-2.0.2-1.i586.rpm
Preparing...                ########################################### [100%]
   1:openvpn                ########################################### [100%]
openvpn                   0:off  1:off  2:off  3:on   4:off  5:on   6:off
Shutting down openvpn:                                                  done
Starting openvpn:                                                       done
suse93:~ #
```

## Building and Distributing Your Own DEB Packages

One great feature of the Debian package management is automatic installation and update of software packages. You can install your own (individually improved and tested) OpenVPN version on all your tunnel servers automatically, simply by placing a file in your own repository. Five prerequisites have to be fulfilled for this purpose:

- Configure one of your HTTP or FTP servers to act as a Debian repository. A detailed howto can be found here: `http://www.debian.org/doc/manuals/repository-howto/repository-howto.en.html`.
- Add your repository to the `sources.list` of all the Debian systems you want to automatically install your software.
- Add a cronjob to your Debian systems that runs `apt-get` upgrade on a regular basis.
- Create your own OpenVPN Debian file from the source code. The Debian New Maintainers' Guide (`http://www.debian.org/doc/manuals/maint-guide/index.en.html`) describes how you build Debian binaries.
- Place the binaries on your repository server.

The next time your Debian server runs the software update, it will automatically download the new OpenVPN Software.

## Enabling Linux Kernel Support for TUN/TAP Devices

If your kernel does not support TUN/TAP devices, you have to enable it in the kernel configuration. All modern Linux/UNIX distributions support TUN/TAP devices, so it is very unlikely for you to run into this problem. Probably, this will only happen if you have built your own kernel. In this case, you will already guess how to enable TUN/TAP support.

If you are not running your own kernel, but your system does not support TUN/TAP devices, you have to build a kernel of your own. Even though this process is not that complicated, the documentation would go beyond the scope of this book.

> The process of kernel compilation is documented at `www.linuxhaven.de/dlhp/HOWTO/DE-Kernel-HOWTO.html` and the Linux kernel source code can be obtained from `http://www.kernel.org/`.

In short, you have to:

- Install the sources of the kernel of your choice.
- Change to the directory where you installed the sources. In most cases they can be found in `/usr/src/linux`.
- Configure the kernel with one of the appropriate configuration tools like **menuconfig** or **Xconfig**.
- Compile the kernel and the modules using `make` and `make modules`.
- Install the kernel and configure your boot manager's settings.

If you want TUN/TAP device support, you have to select the driver during the process of kernel configuration. This can be done with various tools like `xconfig` or `menuconfig`. `xconfig` is probably best when you have a workstation with a running X-Server, whereas `menuconfig` is best on a simple command line.

## Using Menuconfig to Enable TUN/TAP Support

The following three steps show you how to enable module support for your Linux kernel before building it. Type `make menuconfig` to configure the sources of your kernel. You can navigate through `menuconfig` using the up/down and *Tab* keys. Select an entry by highlighting it with your cursor and pressing *Enter*.

1. Select the entry Device Drivers and press *Enter* to receive the list of available devices that the kernel source code supports.

```
Linux Kernel v2.6.11.4-21.8 Configuration

Arrow keys navigate the menu. <Enter> selects submenus --->. Highlighted letters are
hotkeys. Pressing <Y> includes, <N> excludes, <M> modularizes features. Press <Esc><Esc>
to exit, <?> for Help, </> for Search. Legend: [*] built-in [ ] excluded <M> module < >
module capable

    [*] rovide RTC interrupt
        ode maturity level options --->
        eneral setup --->
        oadable module support --->
        rocessor type and features --->
        ower management options --->
        us options (PCI etc.) --->
        xecutable file formats / Emulations --->
        Device Drivers --->
        irmware Drivers --->
        ile systems --->
        rofiling support --->
        ernel hacking --->
        ecurity options --->
        ryptographic options --->
        ibrary routines --->
    ---
        oad an Alternate Configuration File
        ave Configuration to an Alternate File

        <Select>    < Exit >    < Help >
```

2. Select Networking Support and press *Enter*.

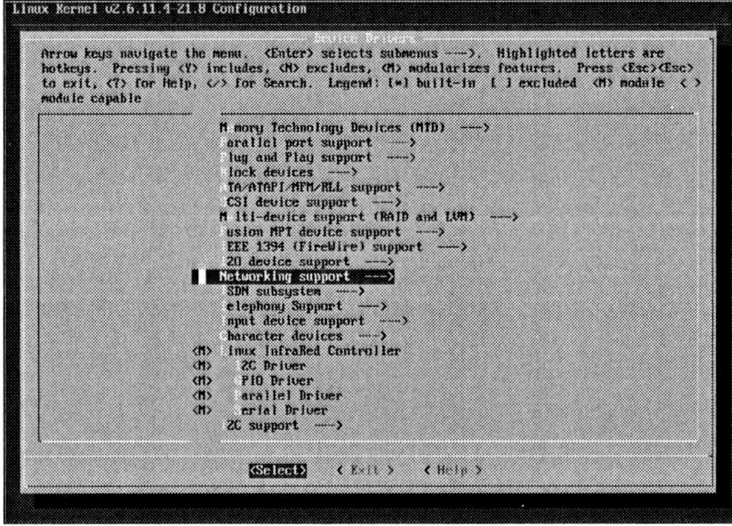


3. In the list of available network drivers you will see the entry Universal TUN/TAP driver. By pressing the *spacebar* you can select if the driver is loaded permanently, as a module, or not at all. In the first column, a letter will show your selection. (M is for "module", * for "permanent", empty for "not to be installed").

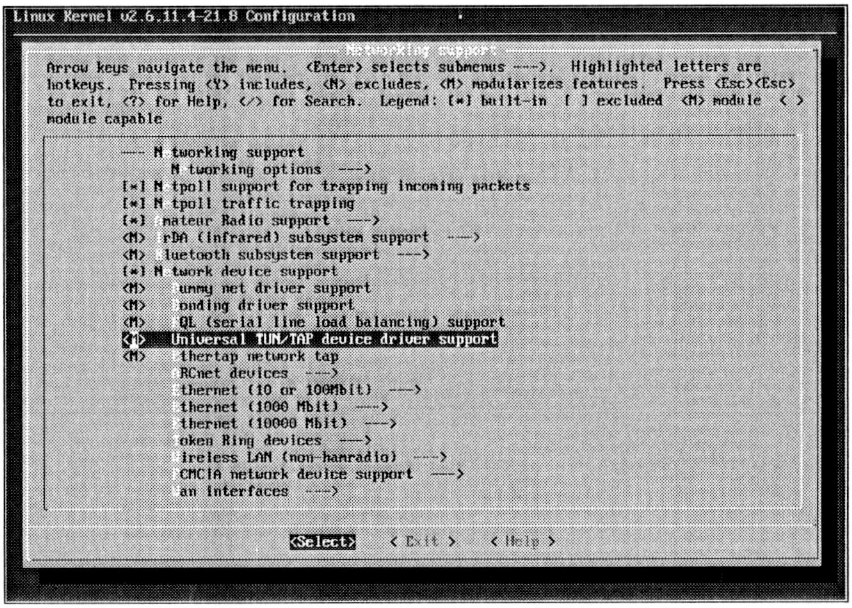

In the screenshot above, this driver is selected as a module, which means the driver is only loaded when needed. This is probably the best selection, because the tunnel driver is unloaded when it is not needed and system's resources are set free.

Now you can continue your kernel configuration. After compilation, installation, and reboot, your system should be able to provide TUN/TAP devices.

# Internet Links, Installation Guidelines, and Help

This section of links can give you help for the installation of OpenVPN on various platforms:

- OpenVPN and Debian:
  `http://www.debian-administration.org/articles/35`
- OpenVPN and Redhat:
  `http://mia.ece.uic.edu/~papers/volans/openvpn.html`
- Installing OpenVPN devices run by OpenWrt:

  OpenWrt is a Linux variant designed to run on devices like Linksys or Asus, WLAN or DSL routers. These appliances have about 4 MB Flash chips, which can be used for Linux hotspots, VPN servers, Internet Gateways, and Firewalls: `http://martybugs.net/wireless/openwrt/openvpn.cgi`

# Summary

In this chapter we have seen in numerous installations on different systems, that installation of OpenVPN is very easy. Apart from Linux systems like SuSE, Redhat, Debian, or FreeBSD, which provide sophisticated installation and package management systems, OpenVPN can also easily be installed on other systems like Windows. And there are several possibilities for installing OpenVPN from source and generating installation packages for your own systems.

# 5

# Configuring an OpenVPN Server—The First Tunnel

In this chapter we will create an encryption key for OpenVPN and use it to set up our first OpenVPN tunnel between two Windows systems in the same network. By doing so, we have a test-bed environment where no problems with firewalls or routers will interfere with our OpenVPN setup, and we can concentrate on learning how to create tunnels.

A little work on the configuration file needs to be done and the key has to be exchanged between these systems. After this, the tunnel will be started and tested with the `ping` command. We will then copy the key on a Linux system and connect this system with a tunnel to the first Windows machine. As a last step, we will ensure that OpenVPN is run automatically on both systems and have a look at the Service Manager on Windows and the `init` system on Linux.

## OpenVPN on Microsoft Windows

During the process of installation OpenVPN has created the following entries in Windows' main menu:

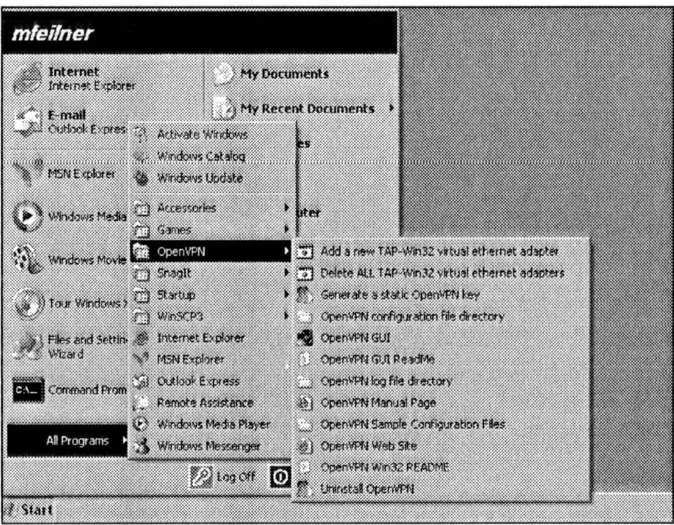

Depending on your Windows version and installed programs, the exact location in the menu can vary.

At this point, only the following five entries in this menu are relevant (beginning from the top):

| Title | Function |
|---|---|
| Generate a static OpenVPN key | Creates a static encryption key that can be used for creating tunnels |
| OpenVPN configuration file directory | Opens an Explorer window in the directory `C:\Program Files\OpenVPN\config`, where the configuration data for OpenVPN is stored |
| OpenVPN GUI | Starts the OpenVPN GUI that plugs in the system tray of the taskbar |
| OpenVPN log file directory | Opens an Explorer window in the directory `C:\Program Files\OpenVPN\log`, where the log files for OpenVPN are kept |
| OpenVPN Sample Configuration Files | Opens an Explorer window in the directory `C:\Program Files\OpenVPN\sample-config`, where example configuration files for OpenVPN can be found |

Apart from these entries, you will find information on OpenVPN in the online manual page, a readme file, a link to the website, and some entries helping you manage the network interfaces that OpenVPN creates.

## Generating a Static OpenVPN Key

Before we can connect two systems with an OpenVPN tunnel, we have to create a static key that will be used for encryption of the traffic. This key must be provided on both systems because in this case of symmetric encryption both sides will use the same key.

Select the entry Generate a static OpenVPN key in Windows' OpenVPN menu.

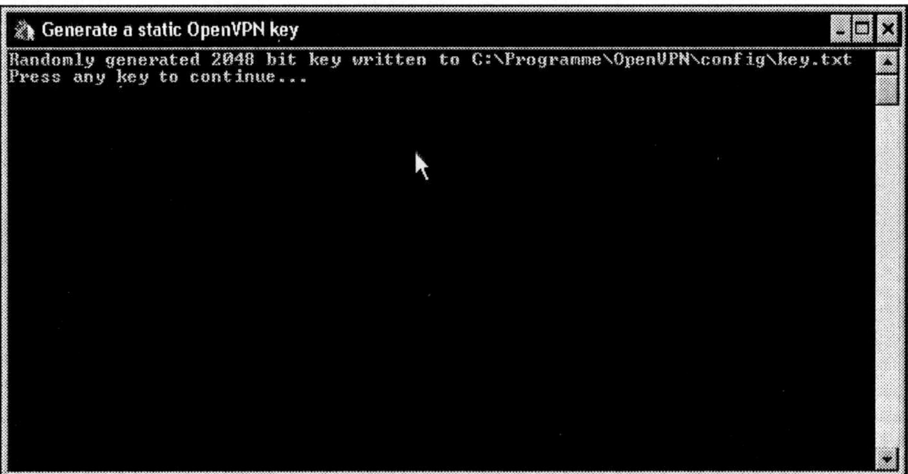

OpenVPN will open a command-line window and generate a 2048 bit long encryption key. This key is saved in the standard configuration directory with the name `key.txt`. This key should only be used for testing and learning purposes, but for our little test setup it is necessary.

> Do not use this key for anything but testing OpenVPN connections.

This process is also done by the `openvpn.exe` program. In the next chapter we will explain the use of the OpenVPN command-line interface.

The menu entry **OpenVPN GUI** starts the OpenVPN panel applet. After the installation this applet is already running, so clicking this menu entry will only bring up the window stating, **OpenVPN GUI is already running**. If you stopped the GUI, this entry will restart the panel applet.

The other three menu entries open Explorer windows in three different directories:

- The directory `C:\Program Files\OpenVPN\config\` is the default place where OpenVPN will look for configuration and key files. Have a look at the screenshot of the key generation progress opposite and you will see that the key we generated is written to `C:\Program Files\OpenVPN\config\key.txt`.
- In the directory `C:\Program Files\OpenVPN\sample-config\`, we find configuration files for standard setup. These files have to be changed slightly and can be used to test VPN functionality.
- The output of the tunnel software is written to text files in the directory `C:\Program Files\OpenVPN\log\`.

The following screenshot shows an arrangement of Explorer windows of the three directories:

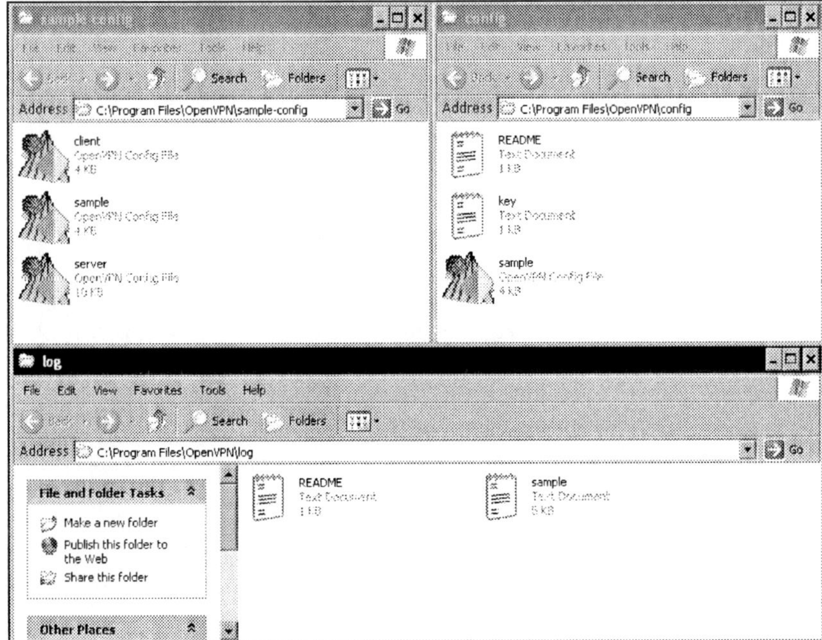

## Creating a Sample Connection

We will now create a sample VPN connection to see how the OpenVPN GUI works. Open all three directories by clicking on the entries in the main menu. Copy the sample configuration file `sample` from the sample configuration directory into the configuration directory. You can use drag-and-drop to accomplish that. That's all. Your new OpenVPN configuration could be started via the panel applet—if your network suits the needs of the sample configuration.

Right-click on the panel applet. You will see the context menu has some more entries now. Select the entry Connect to start the sample configuration now.

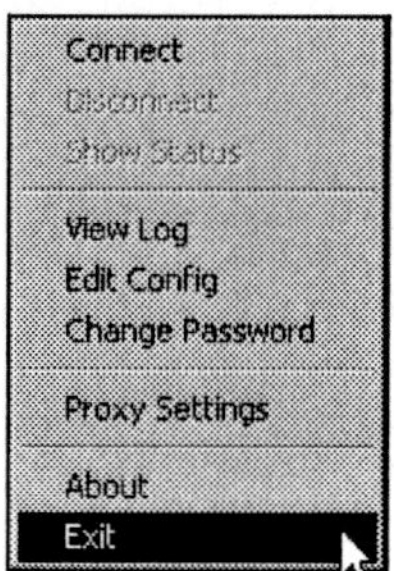


The window OpenVPN Connection (sample) is opened. In this window the protocol output of the sample connection, which is also written to a log file in the log directory, is shown. You can see that there is still some configuration work to be done: in the sample configuration, OpenVPN is advised to connect to a remote server called myremote. If you don't happen to have an OpenVPN server with this name in your local network, you should see a window exactly like the one that follows. This means that your Windows OpenVPN software is up and running, but that it cannot create a tunnel.

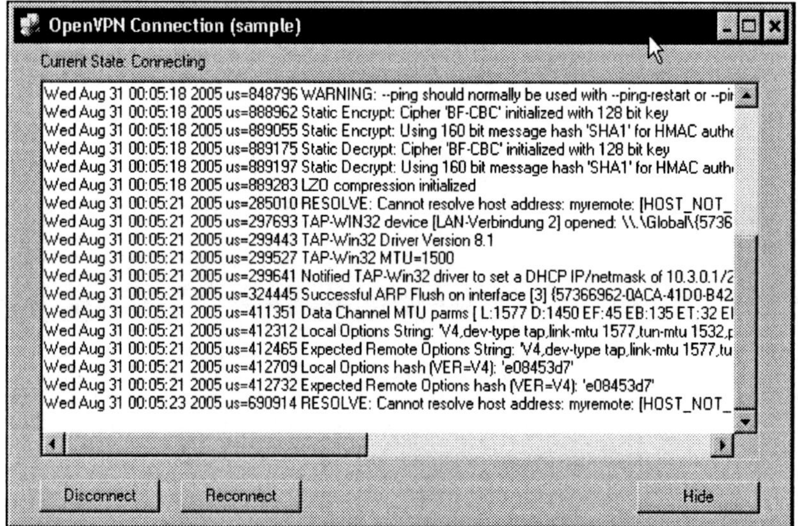

## Adapting the Sample Configuration File Provided by OpenVPN

Obviously, we have to change our configuration a little. Select the entry OpenVPN configuration file directory from the Windows main menu and double-click on the sample configuration file we copied here. Notepad starts up and shows us the sample configuration file.

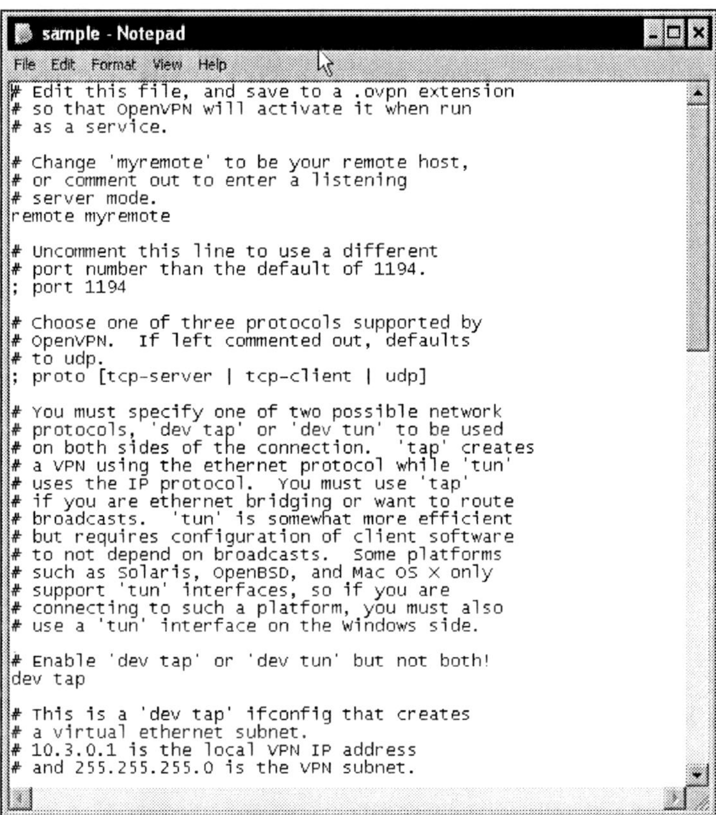



```
# Edit this file, and save to a .ovpn extension
# so that OpenVPN will activate it when run
# as a service.

# Change 'myremote' to be your remote host,
# or comment out to enter a listening
# server mode.
remote myremote

# Uncomment this line to use a different
# port number than the default of 1194.
; port 1194

# Choose one of three protocols supported by
# OpenVPN.  If left commented out, defaults
# to udp.
; proto [tcp-server | tcp-client | udp]

# You must specify one of two possible network
# protocols, 'dev tap' or 'dev tun' to be used
# on both sides of the connection.  'tap' creates
# a VPN using the ethernet protocol while 'tun'
# uses the IP protocol.  You must use 'tap'
# if you are ethernet bridging or want to route
# broadcasts.  'tun' is somewhat more efficient
# but requires configuration of client software
# to not depend on broadcasts.  Some platforms
# such as Solaris, OpenBSD, and Mac OS X only
# support 'tun' interfaces, so if you are
# connecting to such a platform, you must also
# use a 'tun' interface on the Windows side.

# Enable 'dev tap' or 'dev tun' but not both!
dev tap

# This is a 'dev tap' ifconfig that creates
# a virtual ethernet subnet.
# 10.3.0.1 is the local VPN IP address
# and 255.255.255.0 is the VPN subnet.
```

In this file, we have to change or enter the following three settings:

- The name or IP address of the other VPN host
- The name of the key file
- The IP addresses for the VPN and the host

Obviously, OpenVPN needs the IP address of the other tunnel endpoint in order to know where to connect to. To make sure both sides are using the same encryption key, we must specify the file in which the key is kept. And last but not least, the tunnel net itself must be equipped with IPs. These IPs are the ones assigned to the virtual network adapter. Every tunnel has one virtual network adapter on either side, and both sides can only communicate with each other if they are in the same network segment. Thus we have to choose an IP address for each host; in my example I use the IPs provided by the sample file set, 10.3.0.1 and 10.3.0.2.

Once you have chosen appropriate parameters for these settings, you can easily connect two systems. Just keep in mind that you need to have the settings for the IPs mirrored.

The following table shows my OpenVPN configuration file entries for two hosts connected via OpenVPN that are in the same subnet:

| **Host A (10.10.10.103)** | **Host B (10.10.10.104)** |
|---|---|
| remote 10.10.10.104 | remote 10.10.10.103 |
| ifconfig 10.3.0.1 255.255.255.0 | ifconfig 10.3.0.2 255.255.255.0 |
| secret `key.txt` | secret `key.txt` |

Only these three configuration parameters in OpenVPN configuration files are important to set up our example tunnel.

- `remote` defines the other end of the tunnel. Here you can use IPs or DNS entries.
- `ifconfig` sets the local IP and netmask for the tunnel interface secret tells OpenVPN which key file to use, relative to the configuration directory.

The following graphic should help to clarify this a little:

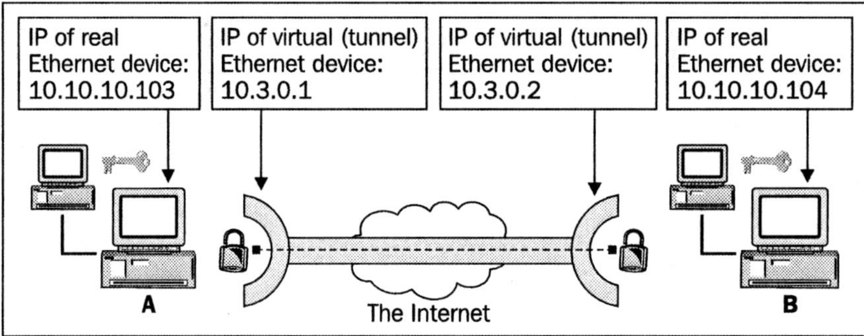


For an OpenVPN tunnel there are four network devices involved. Two of them are real Ethernet cards and the other two are merely virtual tunnel devices (TUN or TAP). The real network devices have IPs assigned to them under which the system is reachable in its local net. The virtual network devices have IPs assigned to them that are used to set up the tunnel.

In our little example, Host A with the LAN IP 10.10.10.103 tries to connect to Host B with the LAN IP 10.10.10.104. The IP of the virtual network interface (in the tunnel network) for Host A is 10.3.0.1; Host B has 10.3.0.2. The name of the key file is `key.txt` on both systems.

> OpenVPN can have IPs and DNS names as options to the configuration parameter `remote`. If you use DNS names, you have to make sure that domain name resolution on your system is configured properly; in any case, you must make sure the other host is reachable—check DNS, routing, and firewall configuration.

You may have noticed that the two hosts in our example are in the same subnet. This is a simple setup, where no routing, DNS, or firewall issues will interfere with our tunnels. All we need are two PCs running OpenVPN. The option `remote` is the only option that needs to be changed later, when we set up a tunnel between two Internet sites.

Now copy the key file `key.txt` to the second system, and edit this system's configuration file. An easy way to do this is creating a shared folder on one system and mapping it as a network drive on the other system.

## Starting and Testing the Tunnel

After both systems are prepared, start the OpenVPN GUI (or make sure it is running) and select the entry Connect from its context menu on both systems.

If everything has worked out fine, the icons of OpenVPN on both systems will change to green like the ones here:

If you see a red light here, no OpenVPN tunnel is connected. Yellow is shown while a connection is being set up, and once this process is successful, the icon switches to green.

However, if you are using a local firewall on either system, be sure that it is not blocking these packets. The Windows XP firewall, like most firewall systems, is per default not blocking outgoing packets, which means that an OpenVPN connection should always be established. If you run into connection problems, check the section *Troubleshooting Firewall Issues* at the end of this chapter.

Select the entry Show Status from the OpenVPN GUI context menu to receive more detailed information about the process of connecting:

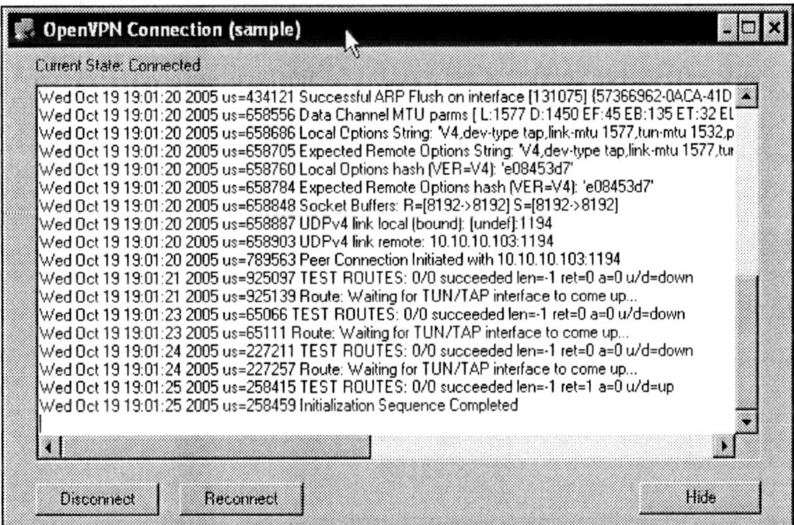

For now, only the last line of this output is important: Initialization Sequence Completed is OpenVPN's message of success. Your tunnel is up and running and both systems should show this message in the status log.

Let's now test the tunnel with the `ping` command. Start a DOS shell by selecting the Windows main menu Run and entering cmd.exe. You will be presented with a command-line interface as in the following screenshot. Type `ping 10.3.0.2` on Host A to check if the ping packets are correctly transferred to Host B. On Host B, you will have to enter `ping 10.3.0.1` if you used the same network addresses as in the aforementioned example.

If you receive output like in the following screenshot, the `ping` command is successful and the OpenVPN tunnel is working.

```
Command Prompt
Microsoft Windows XP [Version 5.1.2600]
(C) Copyright 1985-2001 Microsoft Corp.

C:\Documents and Settings\mfeilner>ping 10.3.0.1

Pinging 10.3.0.1 with 32 bytes of data:

Reply from 10.3.0.1: bytes=32 time=9ms TTL=128
Reply from 10.3.0.1: bytes=32 time<1ms TTL=128
Reply from 10.3.0.1: bytes=32 time<1ms TTL=128

Ping statistics for 10.3.0.1:
    Packets: Sent = 3, Received = 3, Lost = 0 (0% loss),
Approximate round trip times in milli-seconds:
    Minimum = 0ms, Maximum = 9ms, Average = 3ms
Control-C
^C
C:\Documents and Settings\mfeilner>
```

## A Brief Look at Windows OpenVPN Network Interfaces

On your Windows system, open the Control Panel and change to the Network Connections. As you can see, for every OpenVPN tunnel you configure, a virtual network interface is added. The following screenshot shows the active interface—the default when the tunnel is up. This appears like a real network interface and can be used like any other interface. If you do not believe this, have a look at the properties dialog in the context menu of the interface's icon. Apart from the fact that this interface is presented as a TAP-Win32 Adapter V8, every setting possible on real network adapters can be chosen here too.

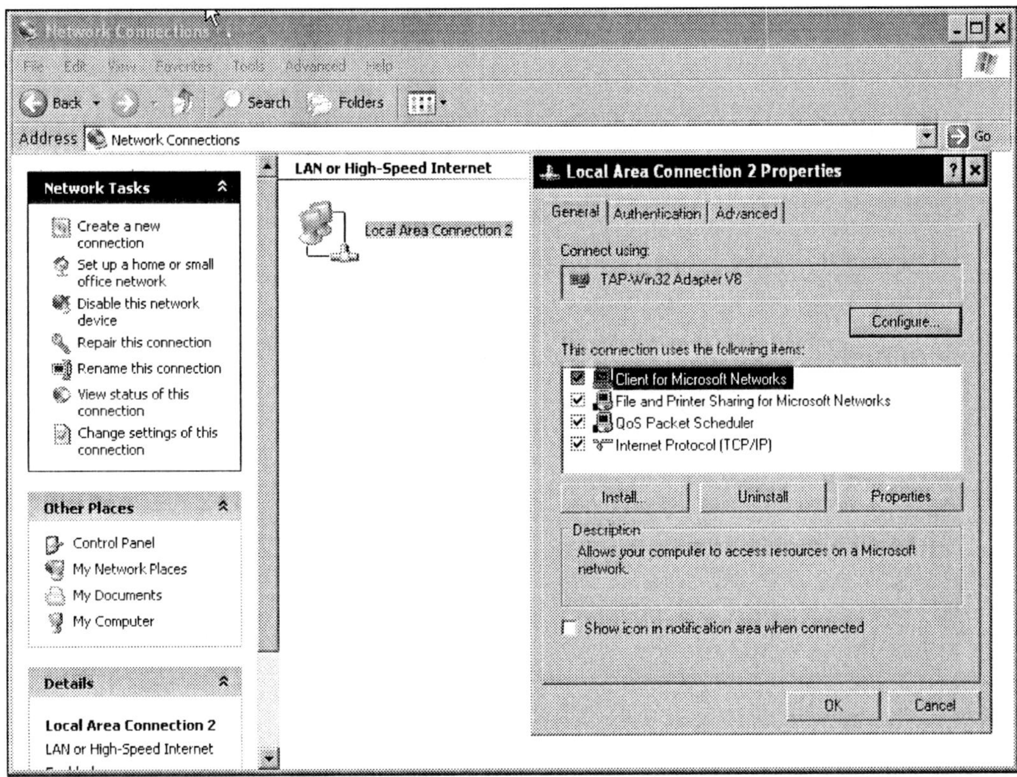


You can disable this interface by simply double-clicking on its icon here, but keep in mind that the tunnel won't be connected automatically after you enable the interface again; you must reconnect manually by selecting the entry in OpenVPN's context menu.

If you need detailed information on network interfaces, the command `ipconfig /all` is very helpful. Open a DOS Shell under Windows and enter `ipconfig /all`. Windows will list all available network interfaces, the IPs, and routing data.

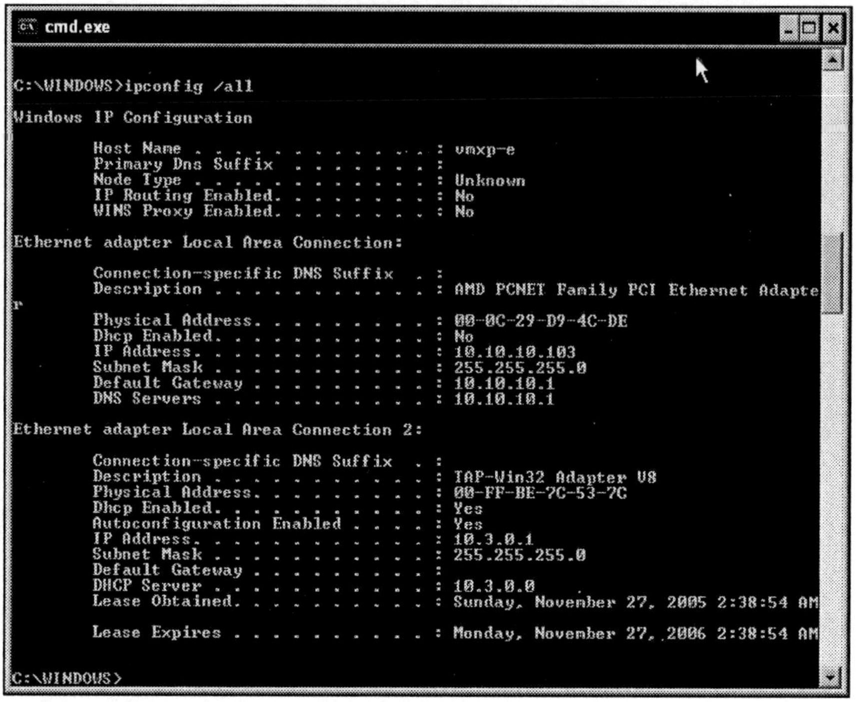

```
cmd.exe

C:\WINDOWS>ipconfig /all

Windows IP Configuration

        Host Name . . . . . . . . . . . . : vmxp-e
        Primary Dns Suffix  . . . . . . . :
        Node Type . . . . . . . . . . . . : Unknown
        IP Routing Enabled. . . . . . . . : No
        WINS Proxy Enabled. . . . . . . . : No

Ethernet adapter Local Area Connection:

        Connection-specific DNS Suffix  . :
        Description . . . . . . . . . . . : AMD PCNET Family PCI Ethernet Adapte
r
        Physical Address. . . . . . . . . : 00-0C-29-D9-4C-DE
        Dhcp Enabled. . . . . . . . . . . : No
        IP Address. . . . . . . . . . . . : 10.10.10.103
        Subnet Mask . . . . . . . . . . . : 255.255.255.0
        Default Gateway . . . . . . . . . : 10.10.10.1
        DNS Servers . . . . . . . . . . . : 10.10.10.1

Ethernet adapter Local Area Connection 2:

        Connection-specific DNS Suffix  . :
        Description . . . . . . . . . . . : TAP-Win32 Adapter V8
        Physical Address. . . . . . . . . : 00-FF-BE-7C-53-7C
        Dhcp Enabled. . . . . . . . . . . : Yes
        Autoconfiguration Enabled . . . . : Yes
        IP Address. . . . . . . . . . . . : 10.3.0.1
        Subnet Mask . . . . . . . . . . . : 255.255.255.0
        Default Gateway . . . . . . . . . :
        DHCP Server . . . . . . . . . . . : 10.3.0.0
        Lease Obtained. . . . . . . . . . : Sunday, November 27, 2005 2:38:54 AM

        Lease Expires . . . . . . . . . . : Monday, November 27, 2006 2:38:54 AM

C:\WINDOWS>
```

# Connecting Windows and Linux

Connections between these two operating systems are almost as simple as those described in the previous section. The steps that need to be taken are exactly the same. However, there are two pitfalls that you must avoid, and both of the pitfalls are connected to transferring files from Windows to Linux (or back).

## File Exchange between Windows and Linux

On Linux, remote command execution and data exchange through the SSH is the standard. SSH also uses OpenSSL for encryption, like OpenVPN. Windows, however, has no built-in support for encrypted data exchange.

Windows systems use the **Server Message Block** (**SMB**) protocol to communicate and exchange data. Linux has no native support for this, but there is a powerful server suite called **Samba,** which can be used to make Linux machines appear like Windows PCs (and even integrate them into Active Directory domains).

So how do we copy the `key` file from a Windows machine to a Linux server? There are two possibilities. Either we set up Samba on Linux to act as a Windows client or server or (this is by far the better choice) we install SSH software on Windows. A very simple tool for this purpose is **WinSCP**, which can be downloaded freely from `http://winscp.net/`. WinSCP is an Explorer-style application that provides drag-and-drop copying over secure connections.

## Installing WinSCP

Download WinSCP and double-click on the EXE file. Start the installation by clicking **Next** twice. (You are asked to accept its license—the free GPL.)

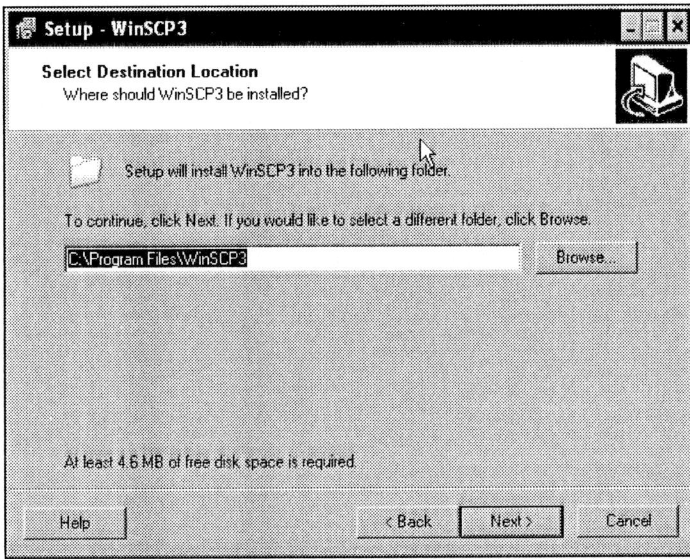


If you want a different location for this program, enter its path in the third dialog.

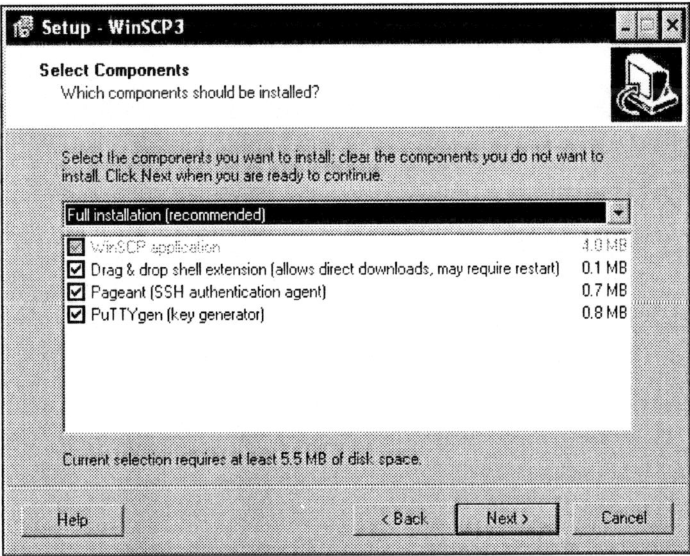


You are now asked to decide on the components you want to install. A full installation like that selected by default is best in most cases, but the compact installation may also be enough if you only want file copying. The full installation provides enhanced key-usage features for encrypted connections like creation of your own encryption keys or usage of existing keys.

Click **Next** twice to accept your choice and the default menu entry for the Windows main menu.

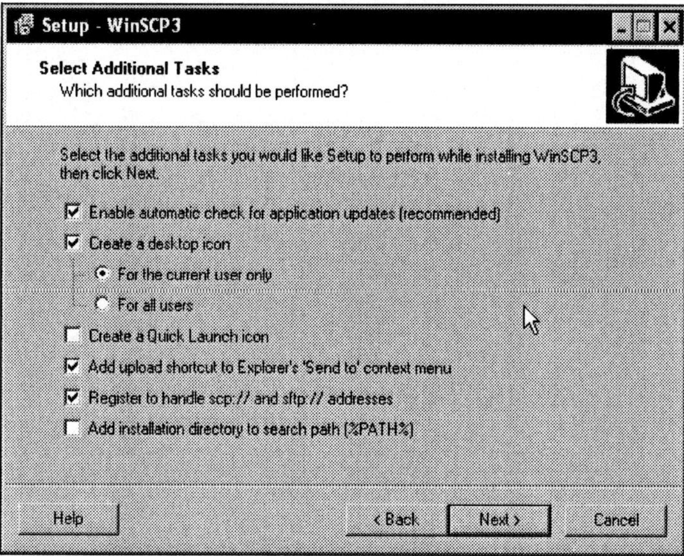


WinSCP can do additional tasks for you. Besides the usual desktop icons and regular automatic updates, you can have context menu entries and support for URLs like `scp://` and `sftp://` for Windows Explorer, which become very convenient features once you get used to them. Click **Next** again to confirm the default selection.

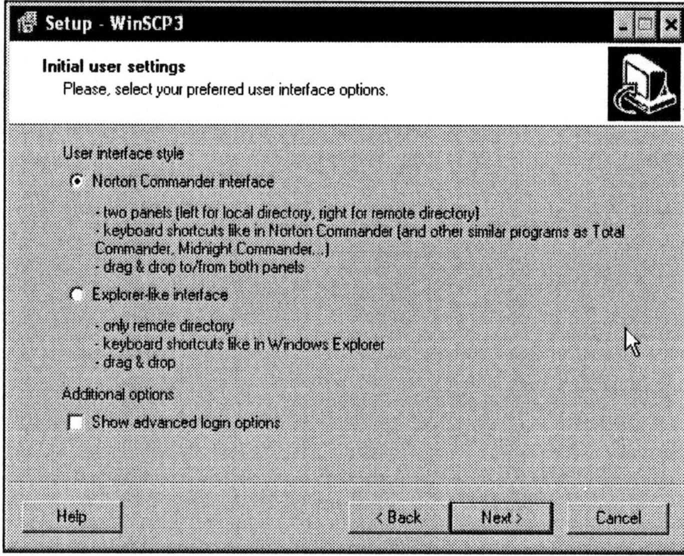

This dialog lets you choose the default look of WinSCP. If you choose the Norton Commander interface, you will be presented with a file manager window split into two parts, a local and a remote directory. This is the default selection and might be the most useful one. However, if you prefer the Windows Explorer style, then select the button Explorer-like interface, which presents the remote directory in one single window.

Finish installation by clicking on Next, and then on Install in the following dialog. The setup program then extracts and sets up WinSCP. After clicking Finish, WinSCP will start automatically.

## Transferring the Key File from Windows to Linux with WinSCP

After WinSCP is started, you have to tell it where to connect to. Enter the IP address or DNS name of your Linux system in the field Host name, the name of the Linux user (the administrator "root") in the field User name, and the password in the field Password. All other options are not necessary at this point. Click on Login to start the connection. If you are connecting for the first time, WinSCP will ask you if you are sure of the authenticity of the host you want to connect to. If you click OK here, WinSCP will remember this host's signature next time.

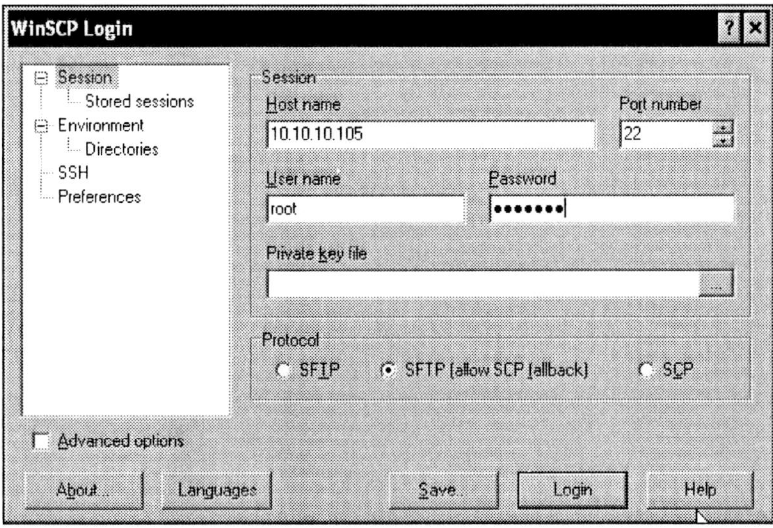


WinSCP presents a window similar to the following screenshot. On the left side of the window there should be a local directory listing, while the right side shows a directory on the remote server. The small drop-down menus above the listings allow fast selection and change of working directories.

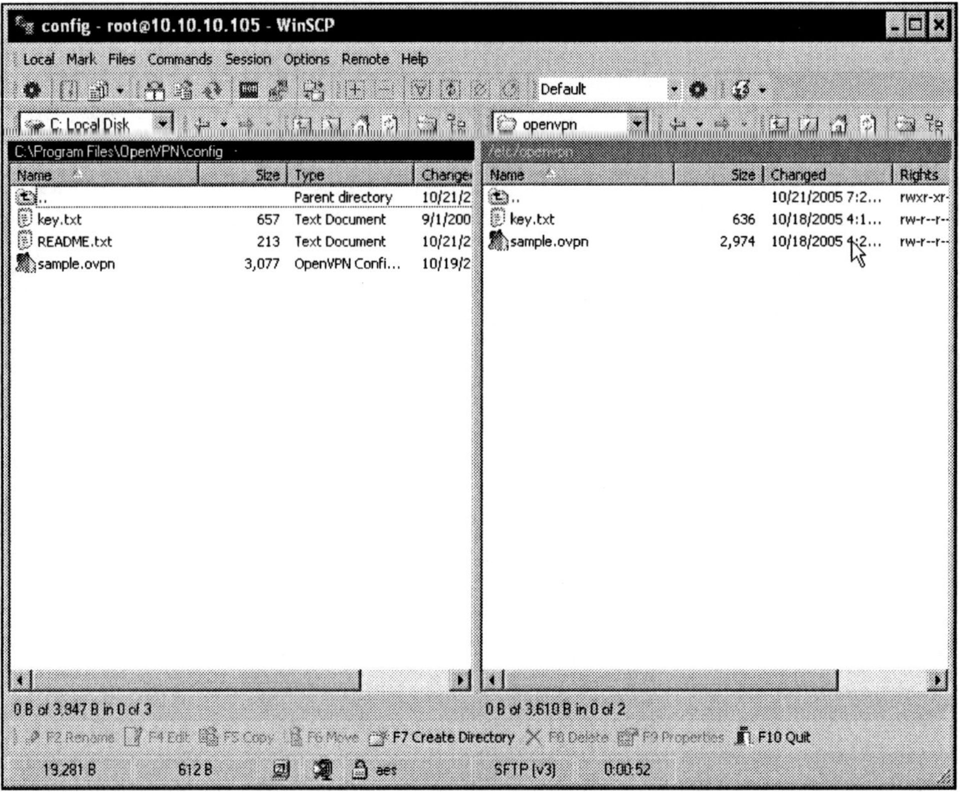


Now let's copy the key file and the configuration file from Windows to the Linux system. On the Windows machine change to the directory `C:\Program Files\OpenVPN\config`; on Linux change to `/etc/openvpn`. Drag and drop the `key.txt` file and the configuration file `sample.ovpn` to the Linux system.

> `.ovpn` is the standard extension for OpenVPN's Windows configuration files; `.conf` is the OpenVPN standard extension on Linux.

## The Second Pitfall—Carriage Return/End of Line

Exchanging text files between Linux and Windows always produces another problem. On UNIX systems, the *new line* character signifies the end of a line; on DOS/Windows, the characters *return* and *new line* are always used together to signify this.

Thus text files copied from a DOS system to a UNIX system always have superfluous characters at the end of the lines and files copied the other way always miss line feeds. Because this problem is very common, the Linux community has developed the **dos2unix** and **unix2dos** utilities. `dos2unix` converts text files from DOS/Windows format into correct UNIX format, and `unix2dos` does the other way.

In our example, we have to convert both the key file and the configuration file into UNIX format. If your `sample.ovpn` looks like this (like my `vi` shows it):

```
(...)
# Change 'myremote' to be your remote host,^M
# or comment out to enter a listening^M
# server mode.^M
remote 10.10.10.104^M
^M
# Uncomment this line to use a different^M
# port number than the default of 1194.^M
; port 1194^M
^M
# Choose one of three protocols supported by^M
# OpenVPN.  If left commented out, defaults^M
# to udp.^M
(...)
```

then you have copied the file from Windows to UNIX. To convert it to UNIX format simply type:

```
debian01:~# dos2unix sample.ovpn
```

and have a look in this file again. Everything should be alright now. Repeat this step for the key file (`key.txt`). If you forget this step, OpenVPN will find different keys on both systems and therefore deny setting up the tunnel.

> `dos2unix` is contained in the `sysutils` package of Debian systems. Run `apt-get install sysutils` to install these tools.

## Configuring the Linux System

In our next step we have to adapt the Linux configuration, just as we did on the Windows systems before. We will use exactly the same configuration as in our first example; only three lines have to be changed. The following figure gives an overview on how the interfaces will be set up.

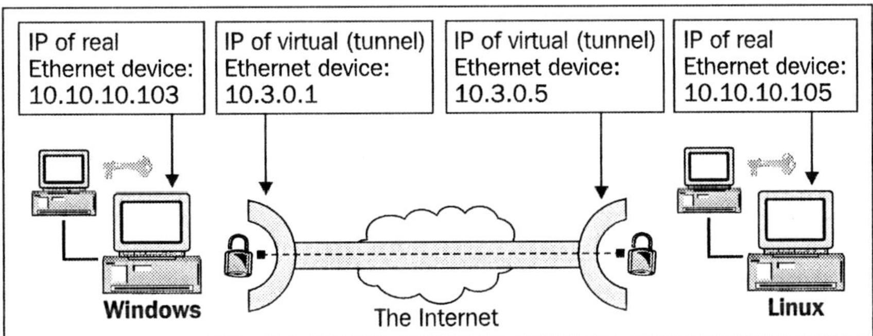

The Linux OpenVPN configuration is as simple as its Windows counterpart. Just modify the following lines in your `sample.ovpn`:

- `remote 10.10.10.103`
- `ifconfig 10.3.0.5 255.255.255.0`
- `secret key.txt`

and adapt them to your needs. The IP specified in the line `remote 10.10.10.103` must be replaced with that of your Windows server; the IP specified in the line `ifconfig 10.3.0.5 255.255.255.0` defines the IP of the virtual tunnel network interface. You may have noticed that this IP can be chosen freely in this network segment.

After you have done so, fire up the tunnel by typing the following command:

```
openvpn --config sample.ovpn
```

in the configuration directory. This command is the main part of OpenVPN, no matter what operating system you are using. For Linux there is no graphical interface, which may be due to the fact that on most Linux systems no graphical environment is running. However, the `openvpn` command is an adequate way to start tunnels for testing purposes and is also called by the scripts that provide OpenVPN services.

You will receive output similar to this:

```
Wed Oct 19 00:23:01 2005 us=318267 TUN/TAP device tap0 opened
Wed Oct 19 00:23:01 2005 us=318335 TUN/TAP TX queue length set to 100
Wed Oct 19 00:23:01 2005 us=318372 /sbin/ifconfig tap0 10.3.0.5 netmask
255.255.255.0 mtu 1500 broadcast 10.3.0.255
Wed Oct 19 00:23:01 2005 us=334639 Data Channel MTU parms [ L:1577 D:1450
EF:45 EB:135 ET:32 EL:0 AF:3/1 ]
Wed Oct 19 00:23:01 2005 us=334726 Local Options String: 'V4,dev-type
tap,link-mtu 1577,tun-mtu 1532,proto UDPv4,ifconfig 10.3.0.0
255.255.255.0,comp-lzo,cipher BF-CBC,auth SHA1,keysize 128,secret'
Wed Oct 19 00:23:01 2005 us=334740 Expected Remote Options String: 'V4,dev-
type tap,link-mtu 1577,tun-mtu 1532,proto UDPv4,ifconfig 10.3.0.0
255.255.255.0,comp-lzo,cipher BF-CBC,auth SHA1,keysize 128,secret'
Wed Oct 19 00:23:01 2005 us=334806 Local Options hash (VER=V4): 'e08453d7'
Wed Oct 19 00:23:01 2005 us=334831 Expected Remote Options hash (VER=V4):
'e08453d7'
Wed Oct 19 00:23:01 2005 us=334886 Socket Buffers: R=[109568->131072]
S=[109568->131072]
Wed Oct 19 00:23:01 2005 us=334961 UDPv4 link local (bound): [undef]:1194
Wed Oct 19 00:23:01 2005 us=334975 UDPv4 link remote: 10.10.10.103:1194
Wed Oct 19 00:23:03 2005 us=513994 Peer Connection Initiated with
10.10.10.103:1194
Wed Oct 19 00:23:03 2005 us=514046 Initialization Sequence Completed
```

This program is also part of the Windows installation. Start a command line and change to the directory containing the configuration file. Type the command `openvpn --config sample.ovpn` and press *Enter*. You will receive a lot of output as in the following screenshot. As you see, OpenVPN's behavior is almost identical to its Linux version.

Unfortunately, if you start a tunnel manually like this, the OpenVPN GUI does not notice.

```
[sample.ovpn] OpenVPN 2.0.2 F4:EXIT F1:USR1 F2:USR2 F3:HUP
C:\Program Files\OpenVPN\config>openvpn --config sample.ovpn
Sat Oct 29 19:30:56 2005 us=739680 Current Parameter Settings:
Sat Oct 29 19:30:56 2005 us=740085   config = 'sample.ovpn'
Sat Oct 29 19:30:56 2005 us=741119   mode = 0
Sat Oct 29 19:30:56 2005 us=741264   show_ciphers = DISABLED
Sat Oct 29 19:30:56 2005 us=741415   show_digests = DISABLED
Sat Oct 29 19:30:56 2005 us=741788   show_engines = DISABLED
Sat Oct 29 19:30:56 2005 us=741950   genkey = DISABLED
Sat Oct 29 19:30:56 2005 us=742091   key_pass_file = '[UNDEF]'
Sat Oct 29 19:30:56 2005 us=742233   show_tls_ciphers = DISABLED
Sat Oct 29 19:30:56 2005 us=742375   proto = 0
Sat Oct 29 19:30:56 2005 us=742565 NOTE: --mute triggered...
Sat Oct 29 19:30:56 2005 us=742755 178 variation(s) on previous 10 message(s) su
ppressed by --mute
Sat Oct 29 19:30:56 2005 us=742969 OpenVPN 2.0.2 Win32-MinGW [SSL] [LZO] built o
n Aug 25 2005
Sat Oct 29 19:30:56 2005 us=788778 IMPORTANT: OpenVPN's default port number is n
ow 1194, based on an official port number assignment by IANA.  OpenVPN 2.0-beta1
6 and earlier used 5000 as the default port.
Sat Oct 29 19:30:56 2005 us=789155 WARNING: --ping should normally be used with
--ping-restart or --ping-exit
Sat Oct 29 19:30:56 2005 us=790014 Static Encrypt: Cipher 'BF-CBC' initialized w
ith 128 bit key
Sat Oct 29 19:30:56 2005 us=790387 Static Encrypt: Using 160 bit message hash 'S
HA1' for HMAC authentication
Sat Oct 29 19:30:56 2005 us=790663 Static Decrypt: Cipher 'BF-CBC' initialized w
ith 128 bit key
```

## Testing the Tunnel

And now it's time to test the tunnel. Simply use `ping` again to test the reachability of the other tunnel endpoint. On our Linux system:

```
debian01:~# ping 10.3.0.1
PING 10.3.0.1 (10.3.0.1) 56(84) bytes of data.
64 bytes from 10.3.0.1: icmp_seq=1 ttl=128 time=2.77 ms
64 bytes from 10.3.0.1: icmp_seq=2 ttl=128 time=0.982 ms
64 bytes from 10.3.0.1: icmp_seq=3 ttl=128 time=0.872 ms
64 bytes from 10.3.0.1: icmp_seq=4 ttl=128 time=0.836 ms

--- 10.3.0.1 ping statistics ---
4 packets transmitted, 4 received, 0% packet loss, time 3020ms
rtt min/avg/max/mdev = 0.836/1.366/2.774/0.814 ms
```

Both tunnel endpoints are reachable. Our Windows-Linux tunnel is working.

## A Look at the Linux Network Interfaces

As we did on Windows, we will have a short look at the Linux network interfaces right now. Type `ifconfig` to have Linux show you all available interfaces:

```
debian01:~# ifconfig
eth0      Link encap:Ethernet  HWaddr 00:0C:29:4B:46:B3
          inet addr:10.10.10.105  Bcast:10.10.10.255  Mask:255.255.255.0
          UP BROADCAST RUNNING MULTICAST  MTU:1500  Metric:1
          RX packets:11346 errors:0 dropped:0 overruns:0 frame:0
          TX packets:8687 errors:0 dropped:0 overruns:0 carrier:0
          collisions:0 txqueuelen:1000
          RX bytes:1593787 (1.5 MiB)  TX bytes:1458734 (1.3 MiB)
          Interrupt:18 Base address:0x1080

lo        Link encap:Local Loopback
          inet addr:127.0.0.1  Mask:255.0.0.0
          UP LOOPBACK RUNNING  MTU:16436  Metric:1
          RX packets:644 errors:0 dropped:0 overruns:0 frame:0
```

```
          TX packets:644 errors:0 dropped:0 overruns:0 carrier:0
          collisions:0 txqueuelen:0
          RX bytes:73352 (71.6 KiB)  TX bytes:73352 (71.6 KiB)
tap0      Link encap:Ethernet  HWaddr 00:FF:0E:87:FA:DD
          inet addr:10.3.0.5  Bcast:10.3.0.255  Mask:255.255.255.0
          UP BROADCAST RUNNING MULTICAST  MTU:1500  Metric:1
          RX packets:10 errors:0 dropped:0 overruns:0 frame:0
          TX packets:9 errors:0 dropped:0 overruns:0 carrier:0
          collisions:0 txqueuelen:100
          RX bytes:921 (921.0 b)  TX bytes:666 (666.0 b)
debian01:~#
```

On this system, there is an Ethernet card `eth0` configured as `10.10.10.105` and a loopback interface `lo`. The device `tap0` is the TAP device used by OpenVPN and has the IP `10.3.0.5` assigned. This TAP device is a virtual Ethernet device that runs OpenVPN's bridging mode. On UNIX systems, you can choose between bridging mode with TAP devices and routing mode with TUN devices, but for Windows systems there is only a TAP driver available.

## Running OpenVPN Automatically

If your want your OpenVPN machine to provide remote access and therefore act like a VPN server, you will simply need to start the OpenVPN process (task) and have it run permanently. Once a client like those we configured before connects, the tunnel is up. On Windows this task is done with the Services module of the Control Panel.

## OpenVPN as Server on Windows

From the main menu, select the entry Control Panel | Administrative Tools | Services to start the service manager.

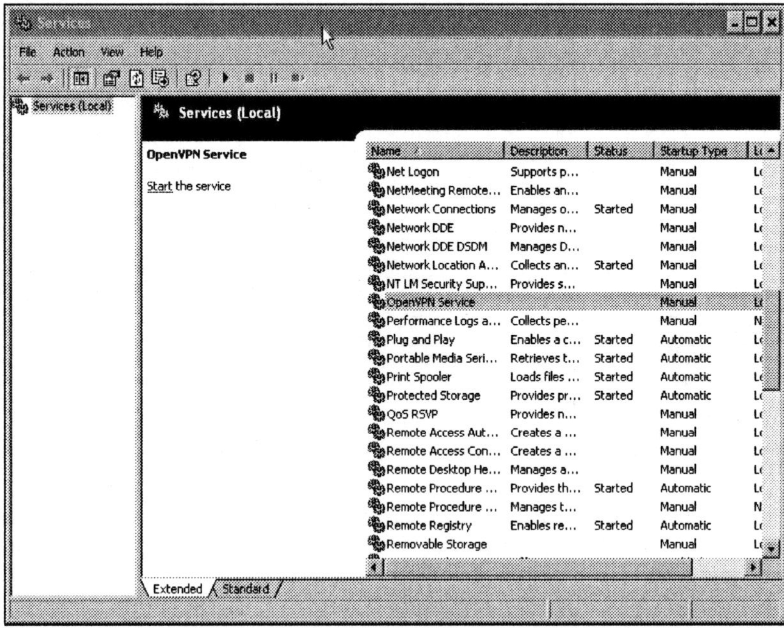

Scroll down this list until you find the entry OpenVPN Service. The fourth column shows the Startup Type for OpenVPN and is set to Manual by default. Double-click this entry and you will see the following properties window:

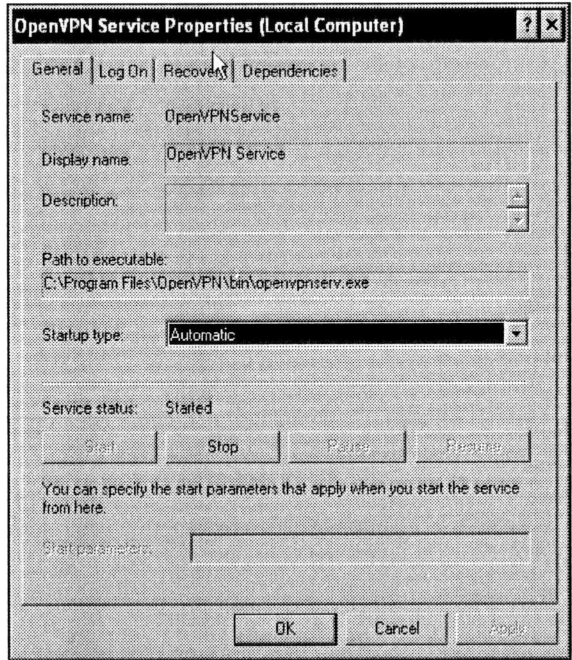


Select the entry Automatic from the Startup type drop-down menu to provide tunnel access from boot time. Confirm by clicking on OK and closing the services dialog. You have successfully turned your system into a simple VPN server.

To test this, simply reboot your system and have a look at the remote system's log file. You will find some entries saying Connection refused or No route to host, but after the restart, the tunnel will be started automatically, the log file will show Connection initiated, and pings will be successful.

> OpenVPN will try to start a tunnel for every `.ovpn` file it finds in the `config` directory, if it is called via the service manager (e.g. on reboot).

## OpenVPN as Server on Linux

During the Linux installation on Debian-based systems, you would have been asked whether you wanted OpenVPN to be started automatically. This is the standard if you entered *Enter* all the time. On Windows you have the services dialog and on Linux there is the directory `/etc/init.d` containing start scripts for an abundance of server processes. A typical script in this directory can be called with the options `start` and `stop` (among others) and therefore starts or stops the server process described in its code. After you have installed OpenVPN, there is a script `/etc/init.d/openvpn` on your system that you can use to stop and start your server.

Some examples of calling the OpenVPN script on Linux:

| Script Syntax | Function |
|---|---|
| `/etc/init.d/openvpn start` | Starts the OpenVPN server |
| `/etc/init.d/openvpn stop` | Stops the OpenVPN server |
| `/etc/init.d/openvpn restart` | Stops and then re-starts the OpenVPN server |
| `/etc/init.d/openvpn reload` | Forces the OpenVPN server to reload its configuration, applying changes |

## Runlevels and init Scripts on Linux

Every Linux system can be run at different runlevels. Like the gears of a car that offer different combinations of speed and power, every runlevel on a Linux system provides different server processes and possibilities. Runlevel 1 for example, is normally used for maintenance mode and provides only single-user access, no networking, and no GUI. Runlevel 5 mostly is used for a full-featured desktop system with network access and most servers run in runlevel 3, where no graphical interface is started, but both networking and multi-user support are available.

Of course you can configure exactly which service is to be run in which runlevel. The following description explains how:

A tree of directories with start/stop scripts is used to configure starting and stopping of services during boot time or runlevel change. On Debian systems you find this tree under `/etc` in the directories `rc0.d` to `rc6.d`; on SuSE and Redhat these directories can be found under `/etc/init.d`. Each of these directories contains links to the `/etc/init.d/` service files. The links have names starting with `K` or `S` indicating that this service is to be stopped (`K`—killed) or started (`S`) for this runlevel, while the number after the `K` or `S` is used to order the services. Thus, all necessary processes for a server can be started in the correct order before the server process starts itself. OpenVPN for example, needs `network` and `syslog` support to work correctly. Therefore, the link has a number higher than the link files of the `network` and `syslog` daemons. On a SuSE Linux system for example, network services are started via `S05network`, then `S06syslog` starts the logging facilities, and OpenVPN is started with `S12openvpn`.

For each runlevel, a directory exists containing a collection of links following the scheme explained above. The links in the directory `/etc/rc3.d`, for example, on a Debian system start and stop the services for runlevel 3. An OpenVPN start script called via the link `S20openvpn` in the directory `/etc/rc3.d` will be started on entering runlevel 3 after all scripts with names from `S1` to `S19` are started.

Three command-line programs are relevant for management of system services on Linux: `init`, `runlevel`, and `update-rc.d`. The following table gives an overview:

| The Program | Used For |
|---|---|
| init <runlevel> | Change to runlevel number <runlevel> |
| runlevel | Lists the active (and the last) runlevel |
| update-rc.d <options> | Helps you arrange the processes automatically |

## Using runlevel and init to Change and Check Runlevels

Both `runlevel` and `init` are very easy-to-use programs. `init 1` switches your system to runlevel 1—mostly configured as single user mode for maintenance. `init 5` switches to runlevel 5, which is the desktop user mode.

In the following example, we will first find out at which runlevel our system is and as a next step, switch to runlevel 5. Again, we check if the runlevel was changed successfully and then change back to runlevel 3, where we were before.

```
debian01:~# runlevel
N 2
debian01:~#init 5
INIT: Switching to runlevel: 5
(...)
debian01:~# runlevel
2 5
debian01:~#init 3
INIT: Switching to runlevel: 3
(...)
debian01:~# runlevel
5 3
debian01:~#
```

## The System Control for Runlevels

The configuration file `/etc/inittab` contains the information the program `init` uses to determine:

- The standard runlevel (the runlevel in which the system will be after boot)
- Which directories are to be used for which runlevel
- Many other useful options (e.g. what happens when you press *Ctrl+Alt+Delete*)

Here is an extract from the `inittab` file on Debian systems:

```
# /etc/inittab: init(8) configuration.
# $Id: inittab,v 1.91 2002/01/25 13:35:21 miquels Exp $

# The default runlevel.
id:2:initdefault:

(...)
```

The last line defines the standard runlevel after reboot—on this system it is runlevel 2 and the following comments indicate where `init` shows how the runlevels on this Debian system are supposed to work:

```
(...)
# /etc/init.d executes the S and K scripts upon change
# of runlevel.
#
# Runlevel 0 is halt.
```

```
# Runlevel 1 is single-user.
# Runlevels 2-5 are multi-user.
# Runlevel 6 is reboot.
(...)
```

## Managing init Scripts

The third important tool for managing server processes on Debian Linux is `update-rc.d`. This Perl script can check, create, and delete `init` scripts suitable for your system configuration.

| Options for update-rc.d | Explanation |
|---|---|
| `update-rc.d <service> <options> <action>` | Configures the links in your `init` directories for your needs (according to the options passed) |
| `update-rc.d -n <options>` | Dry-run mode; only shows what it would do |
| `update-rc.d <options> remove` | Removes the start/stop scripts listed in `options` |
| `update-rc.d -f <options>` | Ignore warnings |

Let's do some examples: the command `update-rc.d -n openvpn remove` removes all links to OpenVPN, but not really, only in a dry run to test if there would be problems. After this command, OpenVPN would not be started anymore in any runlevel. In our example, we encounter a little problem, which can easily be fixed by the "force" switch `-f`, `update-rc.d -n -f openvpn remove` gives us a list of files that would be deleted.

```
debian01:/etc/rc3.d# update-rc.d -n openvpn remove
update-rc.d: /etc/init.d/openvpn exists during rc.d purge (use -f to force)
debian01:/etc/rc3.d# update-rc.d -n -f openvpn remove
update-rc.d: /etc/init.d/openvpn exists during rc.d purge (continuing)
 Removing any system startup links for /etc/init.d/openvpn ...
   /etc/rc0.d/K20openvpn
   /etc/rc1.d/K20openvpn
   /etc/rc2.d/S16openvpn
   /etc/rc3.d/S16openvpn
   /etc/rc4.d/S16openvpn
   /etc/rc5.d/S16openvpn
   /etc/rc6.d/K20openvpn
debian01:/etc/rc3.d# ls -l /etc/rc2.d/S16openvpn

lrwxrwxrwx  1 root root 17 2005-09-04 16:23 /etc/rc2.d/S16openvpn ->
../init.d/openvpn

debian01:/etc/rc3.d#
```

As you can see in the last line, the files are still there. Repeat these steps without the option `-n`, and the links will be deleted permanently.

`update-rc.d` can also create the links for you. Its syntax is easy:

`update-rc.d <options> <service name><start/stop><service number><runlevel>`

Thus the following command is supposed to `start` `openvpn` with service number `16` in runlevel `3`:

```
debian01:/etc/rc3.d# update-rc.d -f openvpn start 16 3 .
 Adding system startup for /etc/init.d/openvpn ...
   /etc/rc3.d/S16openvpn -> ../init.d/openvpn
debian01:/etc/rc3.d# ls -l /etc/rc3.d/S16openvpn
lrwxrwxrwx  1 root root 17 2005-10-21 12:37 /etc/rc3.d/S16openvpn ->
../init.d/openvpn
debian01:/etc/rc3.d#
```

Now try to create the links that you have deleted above.

> If you want to revert to the default configuration of OpenVPN—like that after installation—simply enter `dpkg-reconfigure openvpn`. This program starts the post-install configuration dialog and process again, and installs the default links to your runlevel directories.

## Using Webmin to Manage init Scripts

Webmin is a great tool to administer your Linux machines remotely using only a browser. All you need is an HTTPS-enabled browser and then almost all system settings can be set from this interface. Even though the installation of Webmin will be covered in Chapter 9, here is a brief example of the advantages of this tool.

The module Bootup and Shutdown in the category System can be used to start and stop services and has proven very useful to control Linux servers. The following screenshot shows a long list of all services available (the first column to the left). Services that are supposed to be started at boot time are indicated with a black Yes in the second column, whereas available services that are not started have a red No. A description of the service rounds up this table, and the text link Return to bootup and shutdown actions on the bottom of the page brings us back to the list of services.

Furthermore, this module lets you reboot or shutdown the remote Linux system. With buttons at the lower end of the displayed page, services can be started, stopped interactively or at boot time, and you can change the runlevel of the system.

To make changes on a running service, simply activate the checkbox before the service entry in the list and press the appropriate button at the end of the page.

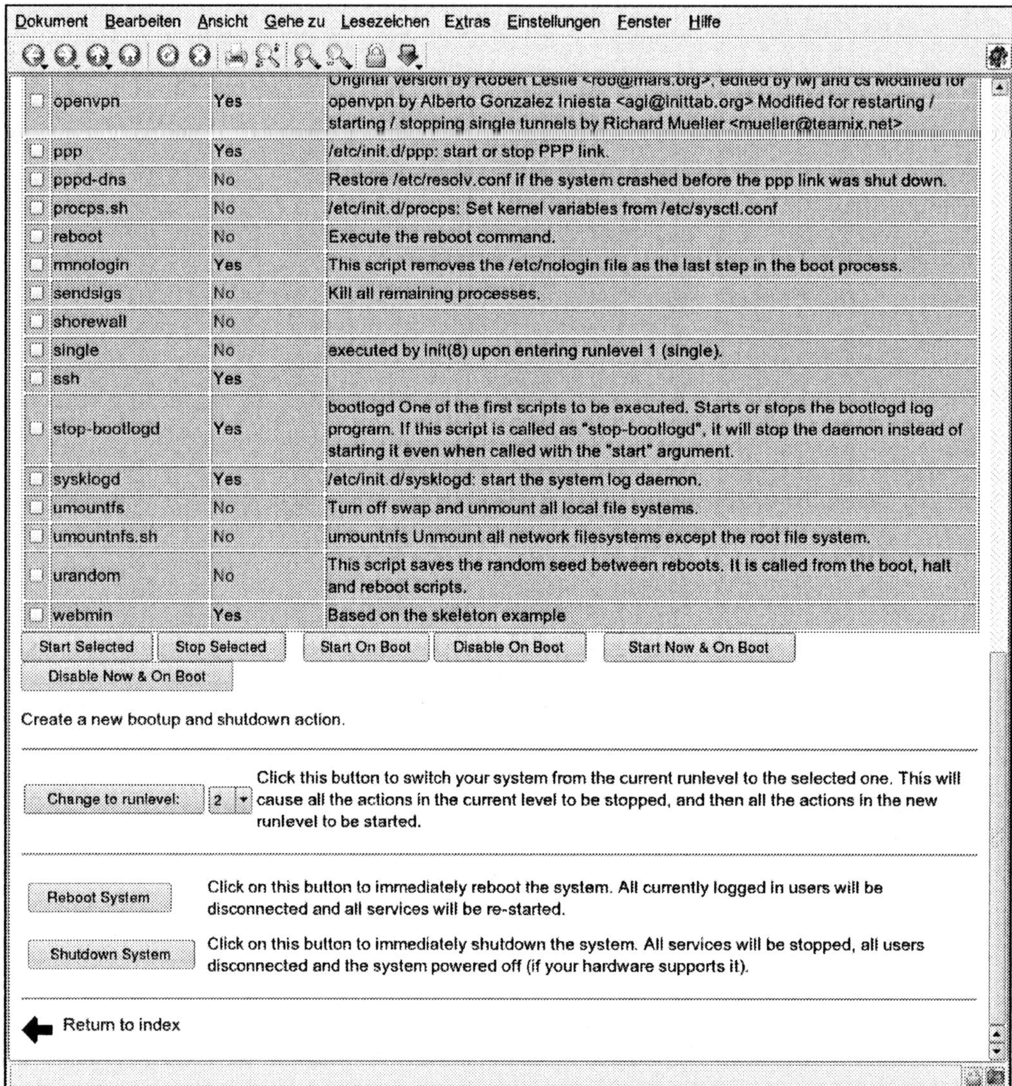


The names of the services are represented with hyperlinks, and if you click on these links, a detailed service menu will open. The dialog Edit Action offers an editor with the possibility to edit and rename the `init` script in `/etc/init.d`, and in the lower part of the screen we find a nice GUI to set our startup preferences for the service. In this dialog, we can define exactly the runlevel and the point of time when OpenVPN is started and stopped during boot or runlevel change. The buttons Start Now, Restart, and Stop Now let you activate or stop the tunnel remotely.

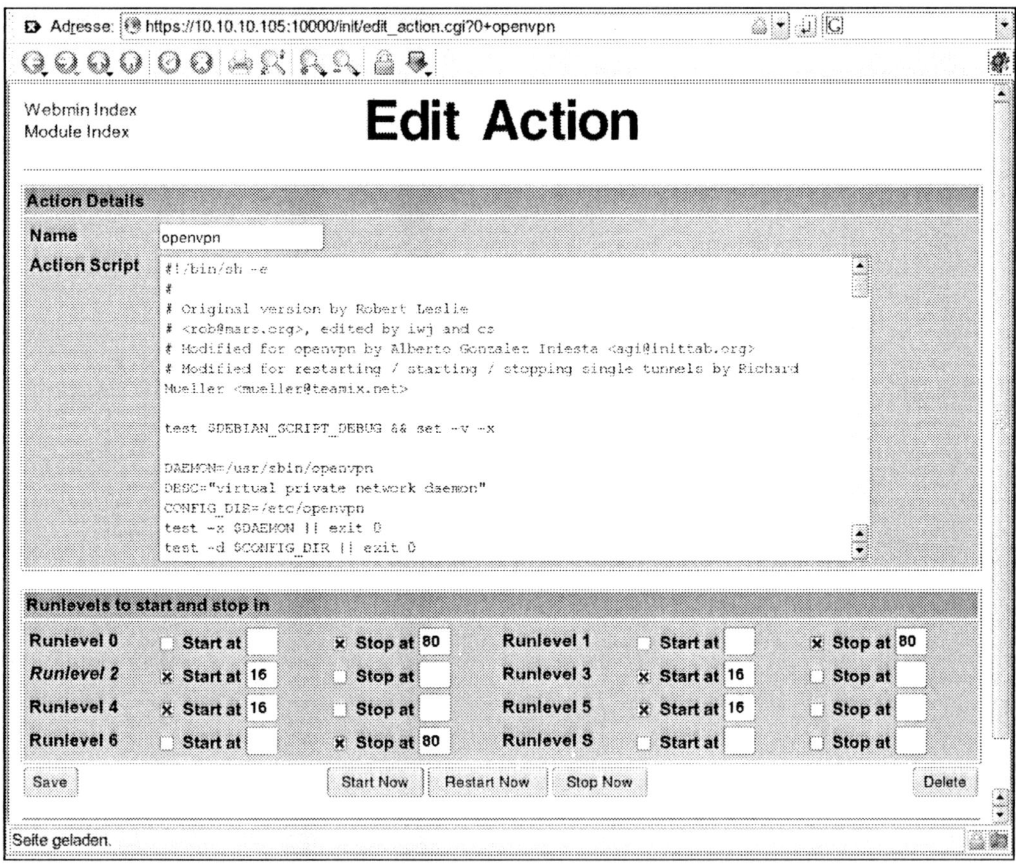


## Using SuSE's YaST Module System Services (Runlevel)

SuSE systems have a sophisticated tool for maintenance of your server processes. The System Services editor can be found in the YaST module System:

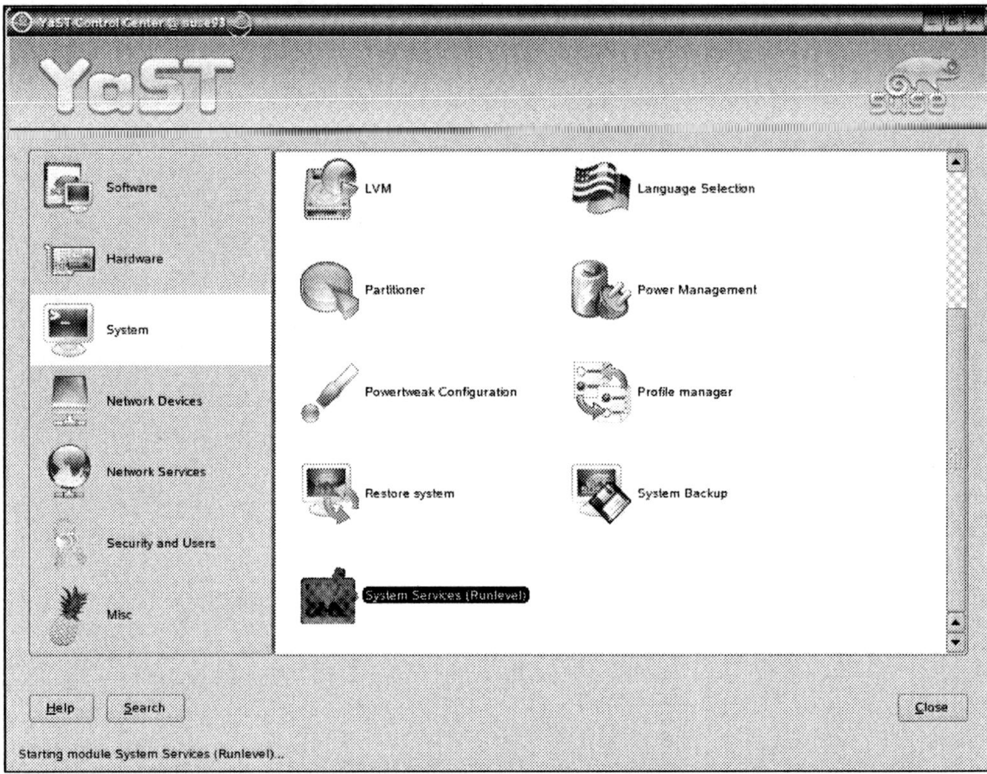


This runlevel editor can be run in two modes: Simple Mode and Expert Mode. In Simple Mode, you can simply switch services on or off and YaST takes care of all considerations necessary for you. You are presented a list with all available services and two buttons, Enable and Disable.

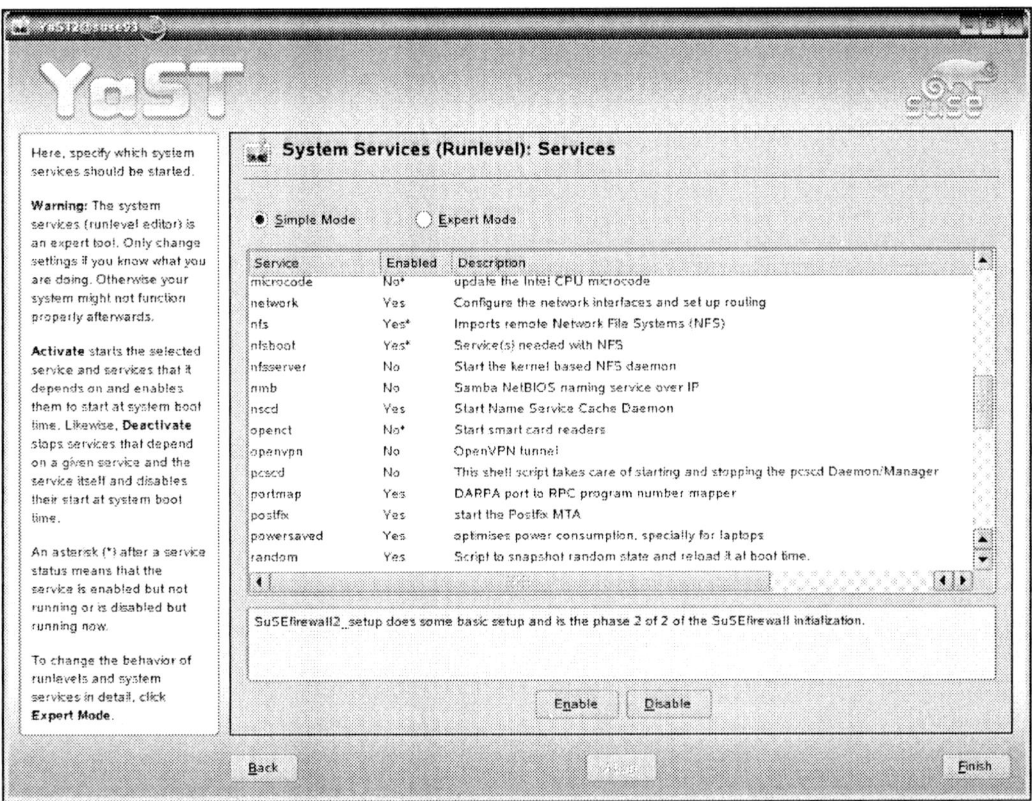

If you want to enable openvpn, simply highlight it in the list and press Enable. The entry in the second column of the line openvpn in the list will change to Yes and a status window reports OpenVPN started. Try to activate or deactivate the service openvpn several times.

Even though the Simple Mode is a convenient and fast method to retrieve an overview of the running services, there may be some disadvantages caused by the standard settings. In Expert Mode, however, you can explicitly define the runlevels in which the different services will be started:

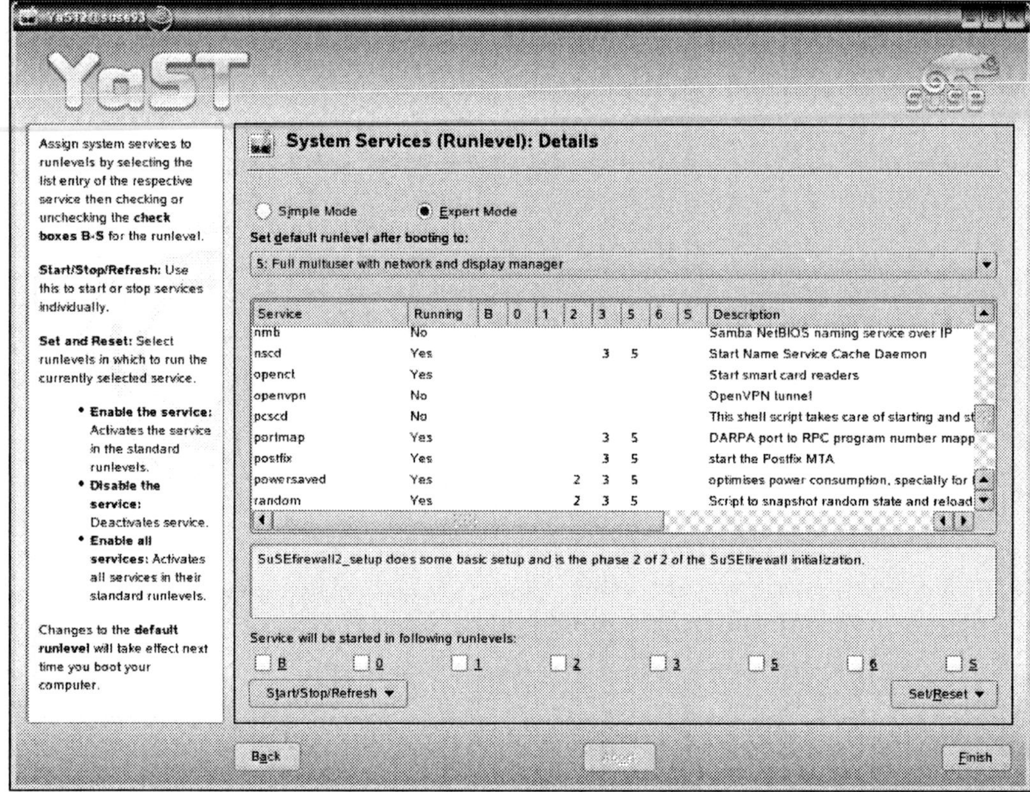


You see a separate column for each runlevel and a list of checkboxes with which you can easily activate the service in a single runlevel. Select openvpn in the list and activate it in runlevel 3 by activating the checkbox. You can accomplish this with the mouse or by simply entering *Alt+3*.

In either mode, click on Finish to activate your changes.

# Troubleshooting Firewall Issues

Windows XP and SuSE Linux have firewall systems installed that are activated automatically after installation. Like most (personal or desktop) firewalls these are configured to allow traffic originating from the local system and destined to the Internet or the local network. This configuration is sufficient for OpenVPN in almost every case. However, if your tunnels won't start and you receive messages announcing connection problems, perhaps it's the fault of a mis-configured desktop firewall. As only SuSE Linux and Windows XP come with pre-installed firewalls, we will learn how to deactivate these firewalls quickly.

# Deactivating Windows XP Service Pack 2 Firewall

On Windows XP with service pack 2, you will find the firewall configuration as an entry in the Control Panel. If you have service pack 2 installed, you will find an icon Windows Firewall in the list of available control panel modules.

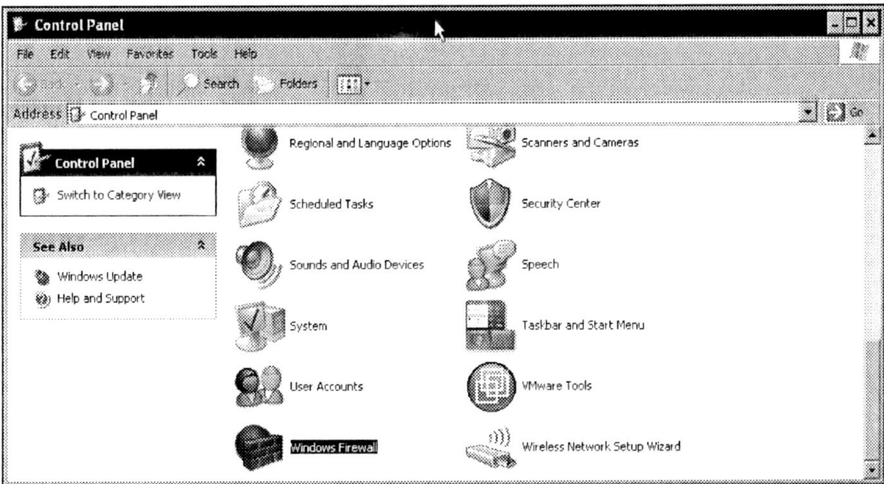


Double-click the icon Windows Firewall to start the configuration dialog of the firewall. A window like the following will appear:

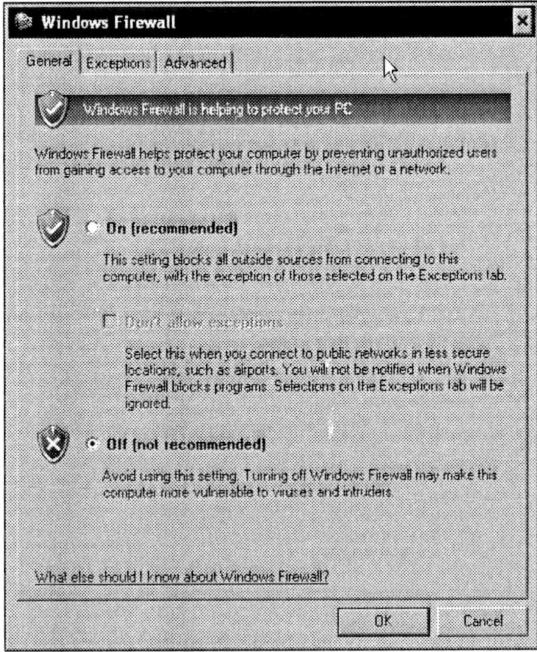

Activate the button Off (not recommended) to deactivate the Windows Firewall. Click on OK to finish the setup. Your Windows system is unprotected now.

> It must be considered unwise to have a running Windows system without a firewall, but for our OpenVPN test-bed, this is acceptable. Please do not use this in production environments. In Chapter 8, we will deal with the proper firewall setup for an OpenVPN host.

If you do not want to deactivate your Windows firewall, you can explicitly allow OpenVPN access to the Internet. If you start an OpenVPN connection, you may be asked by your firewall software:

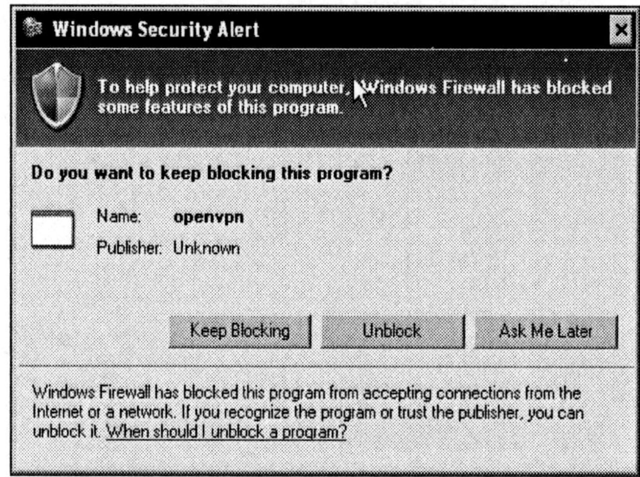


This Windows Security Alert dialog informs you that a local program called openvpn (strange, isn't it?) wants to accept connections from the Internet. Click Unblock here, and OpenVPN should work fine with the Windows firewall.

## Stopping the SuSE Firewall

On SuSE Linux you can use YaST to deactivate your desktop firewall. Start YaST from the main menu and enter your root password. Change to the Security and Users module and left-click on the icon Firewall. The following dialog is opened:

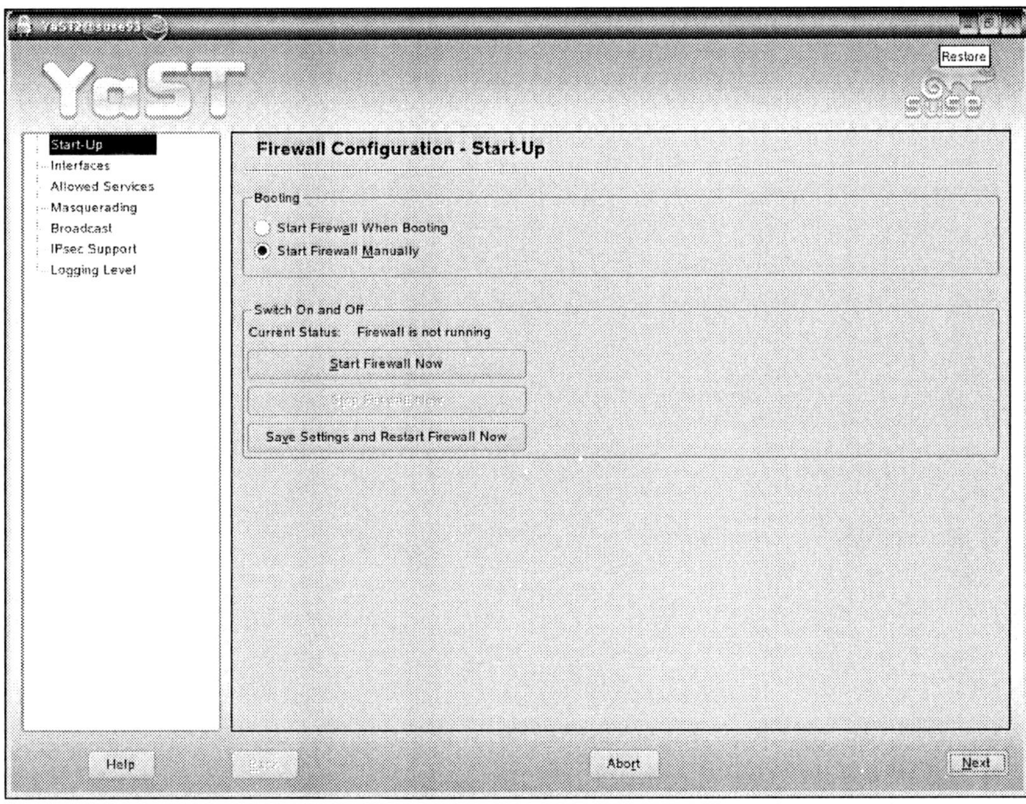


This window will show the actual state of your firewall, depending on your settings (and your selections during installation); it may be active or inactive, and can be started manually or automatically. Set your firewall configuration as in the screenshot above, which means that it is not started automatically, and it is not running:

- Click on the Stop Firewall Now button to stop the firewall on your SuSE system.
- Activate the Start Firewall Manually button to prevent the firewall from being started at boot time.

> Even though there are no viruses and fewer security issues related to Linux systems, you should always protect your systems with a firewall. Consider the deactivation of the firewall only reasonable for testing purposes.

If you have a different firewall system running on your OpenVPN host, you will have to check the documentation of this software. The following hint may be helpful:

Standard OpenVPN configuration initializes connections on UDP port 1194. If you want your system to answer OpenVPN connection requests, you have to allow this port.

# Summary

In this chapter we have successfully configured our first tunnels. We have connected Windows and Linux systems and safely transferred the encryption keys necessary using WinSCP. We had to use the tool `dos2unix` to correct the plaintext files exchanged. After that we have tested the tunnels and activated them at boot time on both systems, including a short introduction to the Linux `init` system and runlevels. The last topic we discussed was about Windows and SuSE Linux firewall issues, including stopping and deactivating these firewalls.

# 6

# Setting Up OpenVPN with X509 Certificates

In this chapter we will create X509 server and client certificates for use with OpenVPN. We will create a certificate authority, and sign and distribute new certificates. We will use `easy-rsa`, which comes with OpenVPN and exists both for Windows and Linux. This tool allows creation and administration of certificates that have to be transferred to the machines that are supposed to take part in the VPN.

## Creating Certificates

In the last chapter we successfully set up our first tunnels using pre-shared keys with static encryption, but in the initial chapters we learned why X509 certificates provide a much better level of security than pre-shared keys do. There is, however, slightly more work to be done to set up and connect two systems with certificate-based authentication. The following five steps have to be accomplished:

1. Create a CA certificate for your CA with which we will sign and revoke client certificates.
2. Create a key and a certificate request for the clients.
3. Sign the request using the CA certificate and thereby making it valid.
4. Provide keys and certificates to the VPN partners.
5. Change the OpenVPN configuration so that OpenVPN will use the certificates and keys, and restart OpenVPN.

There are a number of ways to accomplish these steps. `easy-rsa` is a command-line tool that comes with OpenVPN, and exists both on Linux and Windows. On Windows systems you could create certificates by clicking on the batch files in the Windows Explorer, but starting the batch files at the command-line prompt should be the better solution. On Linux you type the full path of the scripts, which share the same name as on Windows, simply without the extension `.bat`.

# Certificate Generation on Windows XP with easy-rsa

Open the Windows Explorer and change to the directory `C:\\Program Files\ OpenVPN\easy-rsa\`. The Windows version of `easy-rsa` consists of thirteen files. On Linux systems you will have to check your package management tools to find the right path to the `easy-rsa` scripts. On Debian Linux you will find them in `/usr/share/doc/openvpn/examples/easy-rsa/`.

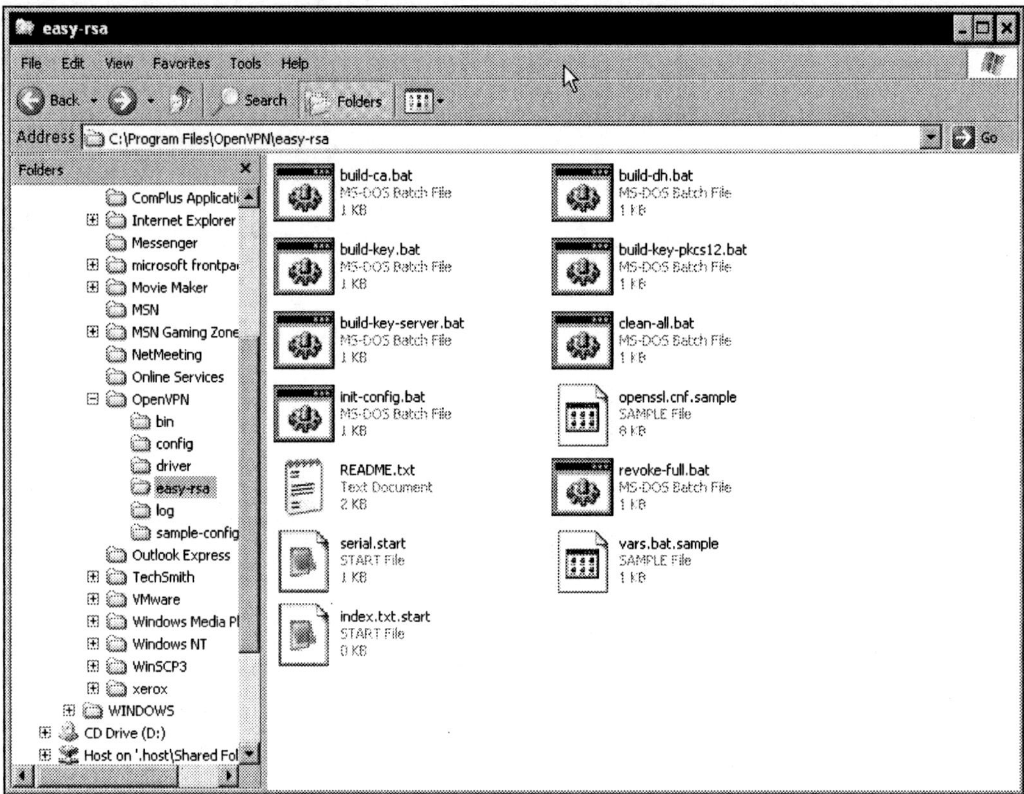


You find there are eight batch files, four configuration files, and a README (which is actually not really helpful). However, we must now create a directory called `keys`, copy the files `serial.start` and `index.txt.start` into it, and rename them to `serial` and `index.txt` respectively. The keys and certificates created by `easy-rsa` will be stored in this directory. These files are used as a database for certificate generation.

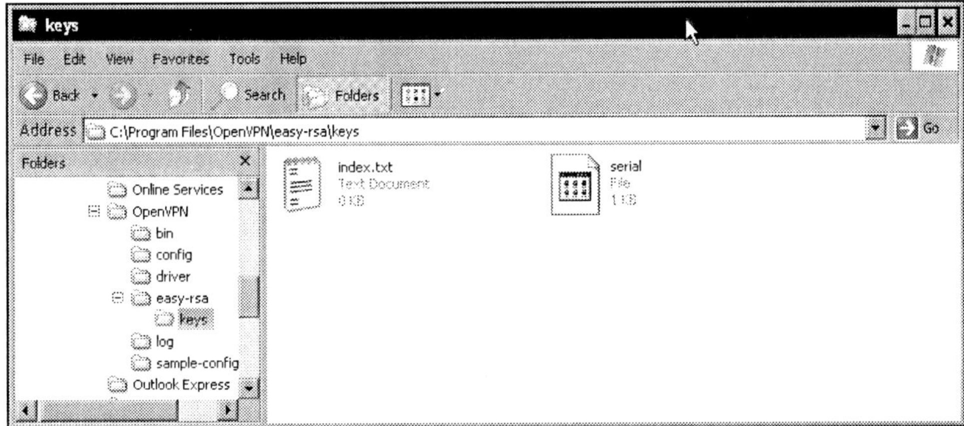


Now we let `easy-rsa` prepare the standard configuration for our certificates. Double-click on the file `C:\\Program Files\ OpenVPN\easy-rsa\init-config.bat` or start this batch file at a command-line prompt. It simply copies the template files `vars.bat.sample` to `vars.bat` and `openssl.cnf.sample` to `openvpn.ssl`. While the file `openssl` is a standard OpenSSL configuration, the file `vars.bat` contains variables used by OpenVPN's scripts to create our certificates, and needs some editing in the next step.

## Setting Variables—Editing vars.bat

Right-click on the `vars.bat` file's icon and select Edit from the menu.

vars.bat - Notepad

File Edit Format View Help

```
@echo off
rem Edit this variable to point to
rem the openssl.cnf file included
rem with easy-rsa.

set HOME=%ProgramFiles%\OpenVPN\easy-rsa
set KEY_CONFIG=openssl.cnf

rem Edit this variable to point to
rem your soon-to-be-created key
rem directory.
rem
rem WARNING: clean-all will do
rem a rm -rf on this directory
rem so make sure you define
rem it correctly!
set KEY_DIR=keys

rem Increase this to 2048 if you
rem are paranoid.  This will slow
rem down TLS negotiation performance
rem as well as the one-time DH parms
rem generation process.
set KEY_SIZE=1024

rem These are the default values for fields
rem which will be placed in the certificate.
rem Change these to reflect your site.
rem Don't leave any of these parms blank.

set KEY_COUNTRY=US
set KEY_PROVINCE=CA
set KEY_CITY=SanFrancisco
set KEY_ORG=FortFunston
set KEY_EMAIL=mail@host.domain
```

In this file, several parameters are set that are used by the certificate generation scripts later. The following table gives a quick overview of the entries in the file:

| Entry in vars.bat | Function |
|---|---|
| set HOME=%ProgramFiles%\OpenVPN\easy-rsa | The path to the directory where easy-rsa resides. |
| set KEY_CONFIG=openssl.cnf | The name of the OpenSSL configuration file. |
| set KEY_DIR=keys | The path to the directory where the newly generated keys are stored—relative to $HOME as set above. |
| set KEY_SIZE=1024 | The length of the SSL key. This parameter should be increased to 2048. |
| set KEY_COUNTRY=US<br>set KEY_PROVINCE=CA<br>set KEY_CITY=SanFrancisco<br>set KEY_ORG=FortFunston<br>set KEY_EMAIL=mail@host.domain | These five values are used as suggestions whenever you start a script and generate certificates with the easy-rsa software. |

Only the entry KEY_SIZE must be changed (unless you don't care much about security), but setting the last five entries to your needs might be very helpful later. Every time we generate a certificate, easy-rsa will ask (among others) for these five parameters, and give a suggestion that could be accepted simply by pressing *Enter*. The better the default values set here in vars.bat fit our needs, the less typing work we will have later. I leave it up to you to change these settings here.

The next step is easy. Run vars.bat to set the variables. Even though you could simply double-click on its explorer icon, I recommend that you run it in a shell window. Select the entry Run from Windows' main menu, type cmd.exe, and change to the easy-rsa directory by typing **cd "C:\\Program Files\ OpenVPN\easy-rsa\"** and pressing *Enter*. By doing so, we will proceed in exactly the same way as we would do on a Linux system (except for the .bat extensions).

## Creating the Diffie-Hellman Key

Now it is time to create the keys that will be used for encryption, authentication, and key exchange. For the latter, a Diffie-Hellman key is used by OpenVPN. The Diffie-Hellman key agreement protocol enables two communication partners to exchange a secret key safely. No prior secrets or safe lines are needed; a special mathematical algorithm guarantees that only the two partners know the used shared key. If you would like to know exactly what this algebra is about, have a look at this website: http://www.rsasecurity.com/rsalabs/node.asp?id=2248.

easy-rsa provides a script (batch) file that generates the key for you: C:\\Program Files\ OpenVPN\easy-rsa\build-dh.bat. Start it by typing build-dh.bat. A Diffie-Hellman key is being generated. The batch file tells you, This is going to take a long time, which is only true if your system is really old or if you are not patient enough. However, on modern systems some minutes may be a time span horribly long!

```
C:\WINDOWS\System32\cmd.exe - build-dh.bat
Microsoft Windows XP [Version 5.1.2600]
(C) Copyright 1985-2001 Microsoft Corp.

C:\Documents and Settings\mfeilner>cd "\Program Files\OpenVPN\easy-rsa"

C:\Program Files\OpenVPN\easy-rsa>vars.bat

C:\Program Files\OpenVPN\easy-rsa>build-dh.bat
Loading 'screen' into random state - done
Generating DH parameters, 2048 bit long safe prime, generator 2
This is going to take a long time
....................................................................................
....................................................................................
............+.......................................................................
.................................................+..................................
....................................................................................
............................................................
```

## Building the Certificate Authority

OK, now it's time to generate our first CA.

Enter `build-ca.bat`. This script generates a self-signed certificate for a CA. Such a certificate can be used to create and sign client certificates and thereby authenticate other machines.

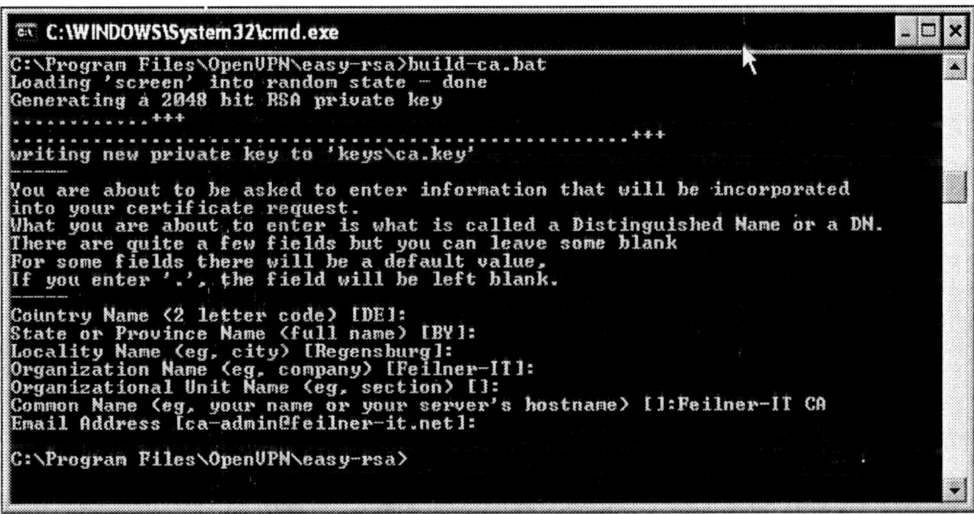

```
C:\WINDOWS\System32\cmd.exe
C:\Program Files\OpenVPN\easy-rsa>build-ca.bat
Loading 'screen' into random state - done
Generating a 2048 bit RSA private key
............+++
........................................................+++
writing new private key to 'keys\ca.key'
-----
You are about to be asked to enter information that will be incorporated
into your certificate request.
What you are about to enter is what is called a Distinguished Name or a DN.
There are quite a few fields but you can leave some blank
For some fields there will be a default value,
If you enter '.', the field will be left blank.
-----
Country Name (2 letter code) [DE]:
State or Province Name (full name) [BY]:
Locality Name (eg, city) [Regensburg]:
Organization Name (eg, company) [Feilner-IT]:
Organizational Unit Name (eg, section) []:
Common Name (eg, your name or your server's hostname) []:Feilner-IT CA
Email Address [ca-admin@feilner-it.net]:

C:\Program Files\OpenVPN\easy-rsa>
```

Depending on the data you entered in your `vars.bat` file, `build-ca.bat` will suggest different default parameters during the process of generating this certificate. Five of the last seven lines are taken from the variables set in `vars.bat`. If you edited these parameters, a simple return will do here and the certificate for the CA is generated in the `keys` directory.

Let's now have a look in this directory. Point your Windows Explorer to it, and you will see that the following files have been created:

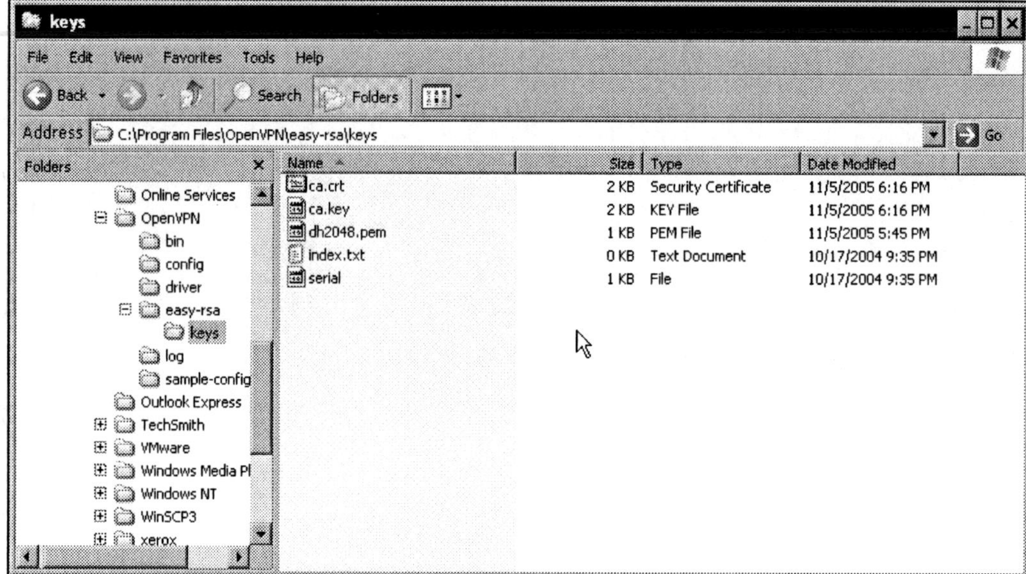


`easy-rsa`'s `build-ca.bat` script has created a certificate file `ca.crt` and a CA key file `ca.key`. The `build-dh.bat` script has built a `dh2048.pem` Diffie-Hellman key file, where the length of this key is part of the filename—if you use 1024-bit keys, this file will be named `dh1024.pem`. Really paranoid (but patient) readers may find a `dh4096.pem` file.

The file `ca.crt` is needed by all machines that are supposed to connect to your server, whereas the `dh2048.pem` file must only be available on the server.

> Please note that whoever owns the file `ca.key` (and `ca.crt`) is able to sign requests for your CA. Therefore, this file must be kept absolutely secret and should never leave the CA server. This file is essential and is the central key to your VPN. It should be kept protected on one computer strictly. Many experts advise you to use a dedicated machine without network connection (local login only) and strict access rules for this purpose.

## Generating Server and Client Keys

Our next step is to provide a VPN server certificate and a key, and have it signed from the CA. Or, to be more precise, we will create a certificate request that will be signed by the CA. An unsigned request cannot be used. Like a passport not stamped or unsigned by your local authority, no one will trust an unsigned certificate (request). Again, batch files are provided to fulfill this task. Start **`build-key-server.bat VPN-Server`** at your command-line prompt. The parameter you give to this script is the template name used for the files. In this example, we will use `VPN-Server` as an example.

A 2048-bit private RSA key is generated. Again, the values derived from the parameters in your `vars.bat` are provided as default and can be accepted by simply pressing *Enter*. Only in the field `Common Name`, you should be very specific and enter a distinguished name for your VPN server. Every time you generate a certificate/key pair, you should enter the name for the machine you want to use this certificate/key pair on. I suggest that you use the same name you chose as command-line argument. As we will see later in this book, OpenVPN can have different configurations based on and distinguished by the value that you enter here, and choosing names skillfully here can save a lot of work later.

```
C:\WINDOWS\System32\cmd.exe
C:\Program Files\OpenVPN\easy-rsa>build-key-server.bat VPN-Server
Loading 'screen' into random state - done
Generating a 2048 bit RSA private key
....................+++
...+++
writing new private key to 'keys\VPN-Server.key'
-----
You are about to be asked to enter information that will be incorporated
into your certificate request.
What you are about to enter is what is called a Distinguished Name or a DN.
There are quite a few fields but you can leave some blank
For some fields there will be a default value,
If you enter '.', the field will be left blank.
-----
Country Name (2 letter code) [DE]:
State or Province Name (full name) [BY]:
Locality Name (eg, city) [Regensburg]:
Organization Name (eg, company) [Feilner-IT]:
Organizational Unit Name (eg, section) []:
Common Name (eg, your name or your server's hostname) []:VPN-Server
Email Address [ca-admin@feilner-it.net]:

Please enter the following 'extra' attributes
to be sent with your certificate request
A challenge password []:
An optional company name []:
Using configuration from openssl.cnf
Loading 'screen' into random state - done
Check that the request matches the signature
Signature ok
The Subject's Distinguished Name is as follows
countryName           :PRINTABLE:'DE'
stateOrProvinceName   :PRINTABLE:'BY'
localityName          :PRINTABLE:'Regensburg'
organizationName      :PRINTABLE:'Feilner-IT'
commonName            :PRINTABLE:'VPN-Server'
emailAddress          :IA5STRING:'ca-admin@feilner-it.net'
Certificate is to be certified until Nov  4 02:52:21 2015 GMT (3650 days)
Sign the certificate? [y/n]:y


1 out of 1 certificate requests certified, commit? [y/n]y
Write out database with 1 new entries
Data Base Updated

C:\Program Files\OpenVPN\easy-rsa>
```

If you want, you can also enter some extra attributes, like a password that needs to be entered every time the certificate is used or an optional company name. However, if you enter a password here, no one (including no service) can set up a connection without this password. I leave it up to you to decide if this makes sense; if you are a little inclined to paranoia it will.

After the certificate request is generated, the batch script asks you if you want to have it signed by the CA. Simply enter *Y* twice, and the request is signed.

Let's again have a look at the `keys` directory. Three files whose name starts with `VPN-Server` have been generated: `VPN-Server.key`, `VPN-Server.crt`, and `VPN-Server.csr`. The file with the extension `.key` is the server key, the file with the extension `.crt` contains the server certificate, and the file `VPN-Server.csr` holds the certificate signing request signed in the step before.

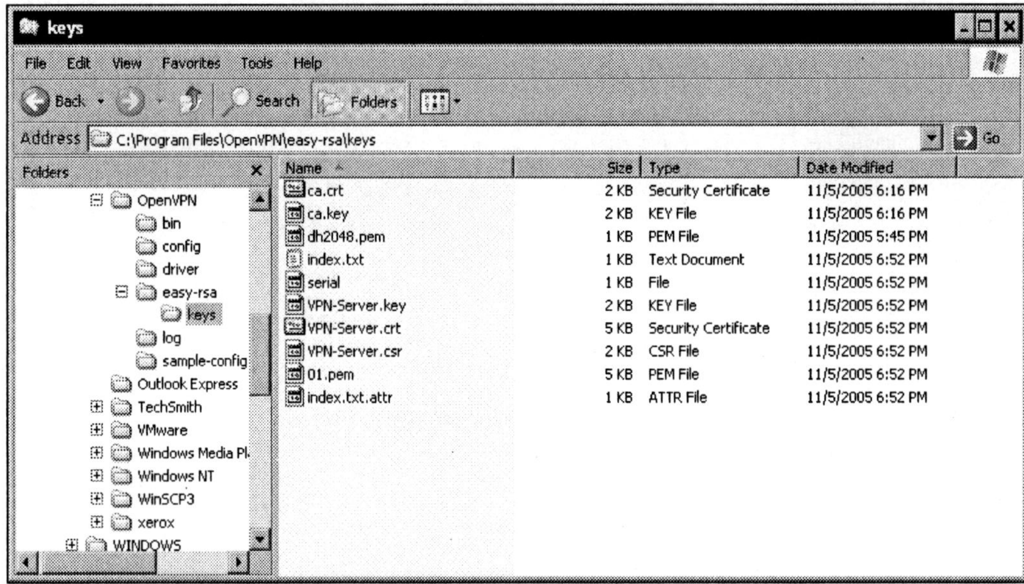


What does that mean now? Right, we have a certificate/key pair for our VPN server that tells everybody that the machine owning and using this pair is (or was) trusted by the CA we created before. What a pity, that nobody else knows this authority up to now. Let's hurry to change this and create a certificate for a client:

Not very surprisingly, another batch file will help us here. It's called `build-key.bat` and you should give the name of the VPN client as a command-line parameter. I chose `VPN-client` just to have a simple, recognizable name.

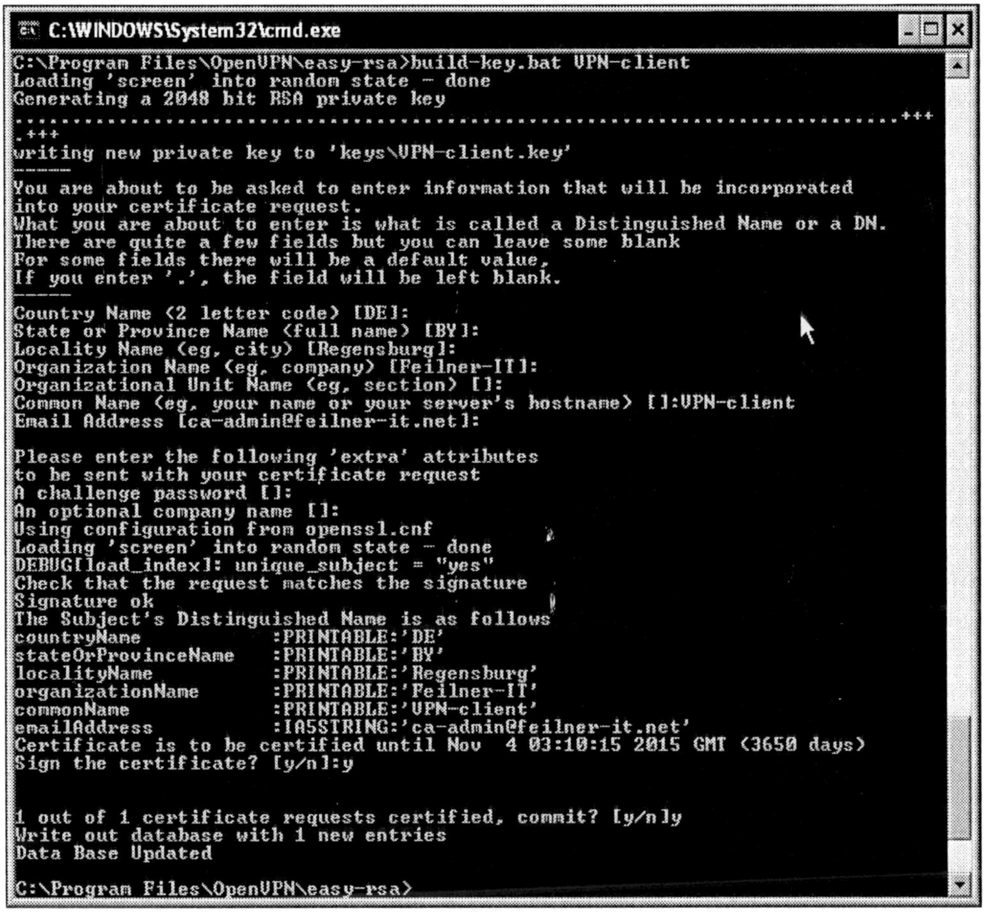

```
C:\WINDOWS\System32\cmd.exe
C:\Program Files\OpenVPN\easy-rsa>build-key.bat VPN-client
Loading 'screen' into random state - done
Generating a 2048 bit RSA private key
...........................................................................+++
.+++
writing new private key to 'keys\VPN-client.key'
-----
You are about to be asked to enter information that will be incorporated
into your certificate request.
What you are about to enter is what is called a Distinguished Name or a DN.
There are quite a few fields but you can leave some blank
For some fields there will be a default value,
If you enter '.', the field will be left blank.
-----
Country Name (2 letter code) [DE]:
State or Province Name (full name) [BY]:
Locality Name (eg, city) [Regensburg]:
Organization Name (eg, company) [Feilner-IT]:
Organizational Unit Name (eg, section) []:
Common Name (eg, your name or your server's hostname) []:VPN-client
Email Address [ca-admin@feilner-it.net]:

Please enter the following 'extra' attributes
to be sent with your certificate request
A challenge password []:
An optional company name []:
Using configuration from openssl.cnf
Loading 'screen' into random state - done
DEBUG[load_index]: unique_subject = "yes"
Check that the request matches the signature
Signature ok
The Subject's Distinguished Name is as follows
countryName           :PRINTABLE:'DE'
stateOrProvinceName   :PRINTABLE:'BY'
localityName          :PRINTABLE:'Regensburg'
organizationName      :PRINTABLE:'Feilner-IT'
commonName            :PRINTABLE:'VPN-client'
emailAddress          :IA5STRING:'ca-admin@feilner-it.net'
Certificate is to be certified until Nov  4 03:10:15 2015 GMT (3650 days)
Sign the certificate? [y/n]:y


1 out of 1 certificate requests certified, commit? [y/n]y
Write out database with 1 new entries
Data Base Updated

C:\Program Files\OpenVPN\easy-rsa>
```

Create another (or many) signed certificate(s) for the other tunnel partner(s) with the batch script `build-key-server.bat`.

# Distributing the Files to the VPN Partners

Again, in your `keys` directory you will find three new files `VPN-client.csr`, `VPN-client.key`, and `VPN-client.crt`, two of which need to be transferred to the VPN partner. Do you know which ones, already? The following table gives an overview of the files we have created up to now and the ones that have to be transferred to our client.

| File | Location and purpose |
|---|---|
| `VPN-Server.crt` | Signed certificate of the `VPN-Server`, must be on `VPN-Server` |
| `VPN-Server.key` | Private RSA key of the `VPN-Server`, must be on `VPN-Server` |
| `VPN-Server.csr` | Certificate signing request of `VPN-Server`, can be deleted |
| `VPN-client.crt` | Signed certificate of the `VPN-client`, must be on `VPN-client` |
| `VPN-client.key` | Private RSA key of the `VPN-client`, must be on `VPN-client` |
| `VPN-client.csr` | Certificate Signing request of `VPN-Client`, can be deleted |
| `ca.crt` | CA certificate, must be available on both machines |
| `ca.key` | The key to the CA, must be kept only on CA; must be kept very secret |
| `dh2048.pem` | The Diffie-Hellman key, must only be available on `VPN-Server` |

OK, we must transfer three files, `VPN-client.crt`, `VPN-client.key`, and `ca.crt` to our VPN client. Remember that we have to use a secure transfer method to do so. If the client is a Linux machine, we will use WinSCP to accomplish that. Start WinSCP and change to the remote directory `/etc/openvpn` on the Linux machine. Create a directory `/etc/openvpn/keys`. Although this is not really necessary, a reasonable directory structure is very helpful and makes administration much easier.

Copy the three files by drag-and-drop to the remote directory.

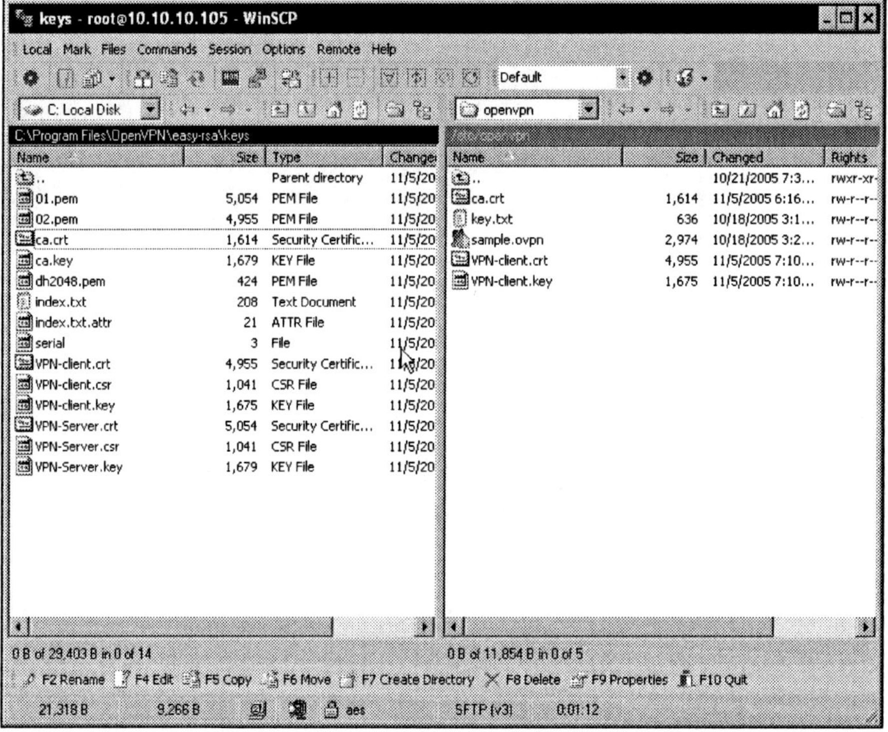

Then create a directory called keys under C:\\Program Files\OpenVPN\ and copy the three files VPN-Server.crt, VPN-Server.key, and ca.crt into this directory. These are the files needed on the VPN server.

As a last step, we must adapt our configuration files so that OpenVPN uses X509 certificates and knows where to find them.

# Configuring OpenVPN to Use Certificates

Open the configuration file in your favorite editor; of course you may also use Notepad:

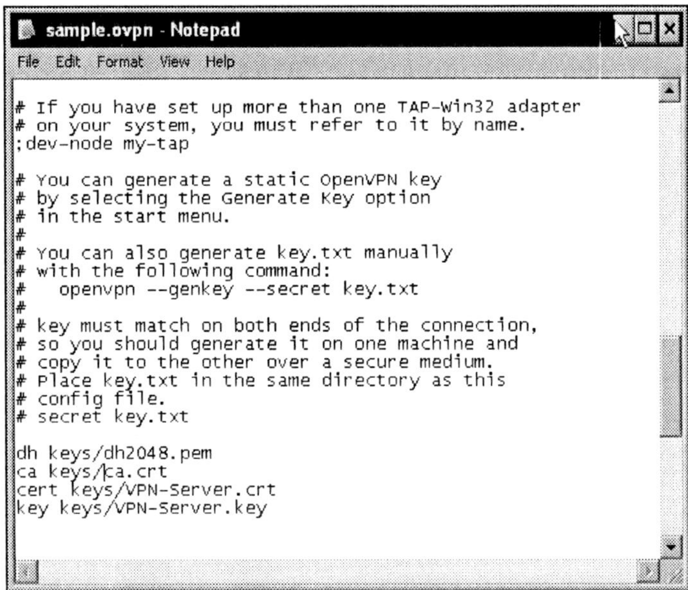


All you have to do here is put # in front of the entry **secret key.txt**, which we adapted in our last chapter, and add the following five entries:

| Entry in config file | Function |
|---|---|
| tls-server | OpenVPN will run in TLS-server mode (on a client you will have to add TLS-client) |
| dh keys/dh2048.pem | Use the Diffie-Hellman key stored in keys/dh2048.pem |
| ca keys/ca.crt | Use the CA certificate in keys/ca.crt |
| cert keys/VPN-Server.crt | Use my certificate in keys/VPN-Server.crt |
| key keys/VPN-Server.key | Use my key in keys/VPN-Server.key |

In my test-bed network, where the local net is 10.10.10.0/24, and the tunnel network is 10.3.0.0/24, the simplest possible configuration file (`C:\\Program Files\OpenVPN\config\sample.ovpn` on Windows) for an X509-enabled OpenVPN server is:

```
dev tap
ifconfig 10.3.0.1 255.255.255.0
tls-server
dh keys/dh2048.pem
ca keys/ca.crt
cert keys/VPN-Server.crt
key keys/VPN-Server.key
```

And the simplest possible configuration file for a client is:

```
remote 10.10.10.103
dev tap
tls-client
ifconfig 10.3.0.2 255.255.255.0
dh keys/dh2048.pem
ca keys/ca.crt
cert keys/VPN-Client.crt
key keys/VPN-Client.key
```

Change the OpenVPN configuration on the two systems to the values above.

It's as simple as that. And the best thing is that this configuration is the same on all platforms. Simply edit your `openvpn` configuration file on the Linux machine as in the previous example, restart your `openvpn` services, and the tunnels will come up, but this time safe and secure with X509 certificates.

```
debian01:/etc/openvpn/keys# openvpn --config /etc/openvpn/sample.ovpn
Sun Nov  6 06:34:02 2005 OpenVPN 2.0.2 i486-pc-linux-gnu [SSL] [LZO] [EPOLL]
built on Oct  9 2005
Sun Nov  6 06:34:02 2005 IMPORTANT: OpenVPN's default port number is now 1194,
based on an official port number assignment by IANA.  OpenVPN 2.0-beta16 and
earlier used 5000 as the default port.
Sun Nov  6 06:34:02 2005 WARNING: No server certificate verification method
has been enabled.  See http://openvpn.net/howto.html#mitm for more info.
Sun Nov  6 06:34:02 2005 WARNING: file '/etc/openvpn/keys/VPN-Client.key' is
group or others accessible
Sun Nov  6 06:34:02 2005 TUN/TAP device tap0 opened
Sun Nov  6 06:34:02 2005 /sbin/ifconfig tap0 10.3.0.2 netmask 255.255.255.0
mtu 1500 broadcast 10.3.0.255
Sun Nov  6 06:34:02 2005 UDPv4 link local (bound): [undef]:1194
Sun Nov  6 06:34:02 2005 UDPv4 link remote: 10.10.10.103:1194
Sun Nov  6 06:34:03 2005 [VPN-Server] Peer Connection Initiated with
10.10.10.103:1194
Sun Nov  6 06:34:04 2005 Initialization Sequence Completed
```

If you do not believe, check it by `ping` on either side of the tunnel:

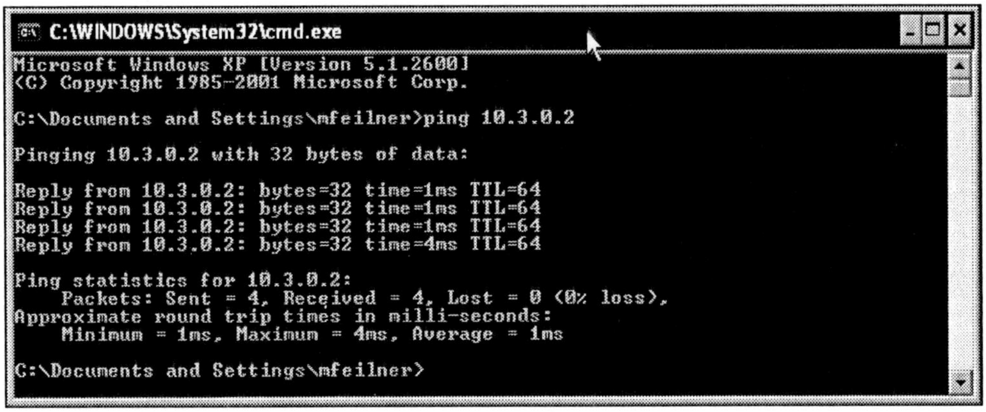

```
C:\WINDOWS\System32\cmd.exe
Microsoft Windows XP [Version 5.1.2600]
(C) Copyright 1985-2001 Microsoft Corp.

C:\Documents and Settings\mfeilner>ping 10.3.0.2

Pinging 10.3.0.2 with 32 bytes of data:

Reply from 10.3.0.2: bytes=32 time=1ms TTL=64
Reply from 10.3.0.2: bytes=32 time=1ms TTL=64
Reply from 10.3.0.2: bytes=32 time=1ms TTL=64
Reply from 10.3.0.2: bytes=32 time=4ms TTL=64

Ping statistics for 10.3.0.2:
    Packets: Sent = 4, Received = 4, Lost = 0 (0% loss),
Approximate round trip times in milli-seconds:
    Minimum = 1ms, Maximum = 4ms, Average = 1ms

C:\Documents and Settings\mfeilner>
```

Use `ping` to test the tunnel once OpenVPN reports "Peer Connection Initiated".

# Using easy-rsa on Linux

We have learned earlier that `easy-rsa` is a part of OpenVPN and available on all platforms. Because we have worked through the generation of certificates on Windows, we will now have a look at the same process on a Linux system. On Debian Linux, `easy-rsa` can be found in the directory `/usr/share/doc/openvpn/examples/easy-rsa`. Start a root shell and change to this directory:

```
debian01:/# cd /usr/share/doc/openvpn/examples/easy-rsa
debian01:/usr/share/doc/openvpn/examples/easy-rsa# ls -l
total 80
drwxr-xr-x  2 root root 4096 2005-11-19 09:31 2.0
-rwxr-xr-x  1 root root  242 2005-11-01 12:06 build-ca
-rwxr-xr-x  1 root root  228 2005-11-01 12:06 build-dh
-rwxr-xr-x  1 root root  529 2005-11-01 12:06 build-inter
-rwxr-xr-x  1 root root  516 2005-11-01 12:06 build-key
-rwxr-xr-x  1 root root  424 2005-11-01 12:06 build-key-pass
-rwxr-xr-x  1 root root  695 2005-11-01 12:06 build-key-pkcs12
-rwxr-xr-x  1 root root  662 2005-11-01 12:06 build-key-server
-rwxr-xr-x  1 root root  466 2005-11-01 12:06 build-req
-rwxr-xr-x  1 root root  402 2005-11-01 12:06 build-req-pass
-rwxr-xr-x  1 root root  280 2005-11-01 12:06 clean-all
-rw-r--r--  1 root root  264 2005-11-01 12:06 list-crl
-rw-r--r--  1 root root  268 2005-11-01 12:06 make-crl
-rw-r--r--  1 root root 7487 2005-11-01 12:06 openssl.cnf
-rw-r--r--  1 root root 2619 2005-11-01 12:06 README.gz
-rw-r--r--  1 root root  268 2005-11-01 12:06 revoke-crt
-rwxr-xr-x  1 root root  593 2005-11-01 12:06 revoke-full
-rwxr-xr-x  1 root root  411 2005-11-01 12:06 sign-req
-rw-r--r--  1 root root 1266 2005-11-01 12:06 vars
debian01:/usr/share/doc/openvpn/examples/easy-rsa#
```

As you can see, this directory contains all the scripts we have used on Windows, and some more too. On Linux, there is a file called `vars`, which is a shell script that contains all the information and variables like its Windows counterpart, `vars.bat`.

On Linux, easy-rsa is located in /usr/share/doc/openvpn/examples/easy-rsa. Start a root shell and change to this directory.

## Preparing Variables in vars

Open vars with your favorite editor and change the certificate values to fit your needs. Don't forget to point the entry export KEY_DIR to an existing directory or create the directory /usr/share/doc/openvpn/examples/easy-rsa/keys. Create the two files index.txt and serial in this directory before proceeding.

On Windows, vars.bat is a batch file that simply is executed; on Linux it is **sourced**, which means that the shell reads this file and sets the environment variables you defined in it—a very common way to read configuration files on Linux. The command for this purpose is called source, and its abbreviation is simply a dot.

Now type source vars or simply . vars to have your shell read the configuration variables you edited:

```
debian01:/usr/share/doc/openvpn/examples/easy-rsa# . vars
NOTE: when you run ./clean-all, I will be doing a rm -rf on
/usr/share/doc/openvpn/examples/easy-rsa/keys
debian01:/usr/share/doc/openvpn/examples/easy-rsa#
```

The note you receive is important. In this directory, there is a script called clean-all, which removes all old configurations and keys you created previously from the keys directory you enter in vars. If you want to execute clean-all, be sure to back up all files you might need later on. Normally there should be no need to run clean-all.

## Creating the Diffie-Hellman Key and the Certificate Authority

As our next step we will create a Diffie-Hellman key with the script build-dh. On most Linux systems, the working directory is not in the path of the user root, so you have to invoke it with ./build-dh:

```
debian01:/usr/share/doc/openvpn/examples/easy-rsa# ./build-dh
Generating DH parameters, 1024 bit long safe prime, generator 2
This is going to take a long time
....+........+.+......+.....................+..............................
.............+.
(...)
```

Now your system might be occupied for some time, busily calculating a 1024-bit prime number. If you want to set the key size to 2048, have a look in /usr/share/doc/openvpn/examples/easy-rsa/vars -like we did on Windows. And once we're ready again, create the certificate for the CA:

```
debian01:/usr/share/doc/openvpn/examples/easy-rsa# ./build-ca
Generating a 2048 bit RSA private key
.........................................++++++
.............++++++
writing new private key to 'ca.key'
-----
You are about to be asked to enter information that will be incorporated
into your certificate request.
What you are about to enter is what is called a Distinguished Name or a DN.
```

```
There are quite a few fields but you can leave some blank
For some fields there will be a default value,
If you enter '.', the field will be left blank.
-----
Country Name (2 letter code) [DE]:
State or Province Name (full name) [BY]:
Locality Name (eg, city) [Regensburg]:
Organization Name (eg, company) [Feilner-IT]:
Organizational Unit Name (eg, section) []:
Common Name (eg, your name or your server's hostname) []:CA-Server
Email Address [security@feilner-it.net]:
debian01:/usr/share/doc/openvpn/examples/easy-rsa#  ls -l keys
total 12
-rw-r--r--  1 root root 1245 2005-11-20 00:17 ca.crt
-rw-------  1 root root  887 2005-11-20 00:17 ca.key
-rw-r--r--  1 root root  245 2005-11-20 00:14 dh1024.pem
debian01:/usr/share/doc/openvpn/examples/easy-rsa#
```

Certificate and key have been created in the directory /usr/share/doc/openvpn/examples/easy-rsa/keys.

## Creating the First Server Certificate/Key Pair

Now we can create the first certificate/key pair for our first VPN server. Remember, that the Common Name can be used to recognize a client authenticating with this certificate, so choose a distinguishing name here. After generation of the certificate, we are prompted if we want to sign the certificate using the CA's certificate.

Start creation of a certificate/key pair called VPN-Server with the command ./build-key-server VPN-Server:

```
debian01:/usr/share/doc/openvpn/examples/easy-rsa# ./build-key-server VPN-
Server
Generating a 1024 bit RSA private key
......++++++
...++++++
writing new private key to 'VPN-Server.key'
-----
You are about to be asked to enter information that will be incorporated
into your certificate request.
What you are about to enter is what is called a Distinguished Name or a DN.
There are quite a few fields but you can leave some blank
For some fields there will be a default value,
If you enter '.', the field will be left blank.
-----
Country Name (2 letter code) [DE]:
State or Province Name (full name) [BY]:
Locality Name (eg, city) [Regensburg]:
Organization Name (eg, company) [Feilner-IT]:
Organizational Unit Name (eg, section) []:
Common Name (eg, your name or your server's hostname) []:VPN-Server
Email Address [security@feilner-it.net]:

Please enter the following 'extra' attributes
to be sent with your certificate request
A challenge password []:
An optional company name []:
Using configuration from /usr/share/doc/openvpn/examples/easy-rsa/openssl.cnf
Check that the request matches the signature
Signature ok
The Subject's Distinguished Name is as follows
countryName           :PRINTABLE:'DE'
```

```
stateOrProvinceName    :PRINTABLE:'BY'
localityName           :PRINTABLE:'Regensburg'
organizationName       :PRINTABLE:'Feilner-IT'
commonName             :PRINTABLE:'VPN-Server'
emailAddress           :IA5STRING:'security@feilner-it.net'
Certificate is to be certified until Nov 17 23:40:04 2015 GMT (3650 days)
Sign the certificate? [y/n]:y

1 out of 1 certificate requests certified, commit? [y/n]y
Write out database with 1 new entries
Data Base Updated
debian01:/usr/share/doc/openvpn/examples/easy-rsa#
```

Enter a distinguishing `Common Name` and enter *Y* twice to have the certificate signed. The certificate and key file are created in `/usr/share/doc/openvpn/examples/easy-rsa/keys`:

```
debian01:/usr/share/doc/openvpn/examples/easy-rsa# ls -l keys/
total 44
-rw-r--r--  1 root root 3653 2005-11-20 00:40 01.pem
-rw-r--r--  1 root root 1233 2005-11-20 00:39 ca.crt
-rw-------  1 root root  887 2005-11-20 00:39 ca.key
-rw-r--r--  1 root root  245 2005-11-20 00:37 dh1024.pem
-rw-r--r--  1 root root  104 2005-11-20 00:40 index.txt
-rw-r--r--  1 root root   21 2005-11-20 00:40 index.txt.attr
-rw-r--r--  1 root root    0 2005-11-20 00:31 index.txt.old
-rw-r--r--  1 root root    3 2005-11-20 00:40 serial
-rw-r--r--  1 root root    3 2005-11-20 00:31 serial.old
-rw-r--r--  1 root root 3653 2005-11-20 00:40 VPN-Server.crt
-rw-r--r--  1 root root  688 2005-11-20 00:40 VPN-Server.csr
-rw-------  1 root root  887 2005-11-20 00:40 VPN-Server.key
debian01:/usr/share/doc/openvpn/examples/easy-rsa#
```

Now we have the certificate for the CA and a certificate and key for the first OpenVPN machine.

## Creating Further Certificates and Keys

Let's repeat the last step for a second machine, which is called `VPN-client`:

```
debian01:/usr/share/doc/openvpn/examples/easy-rsa# ./build-key-server VPN-
Client
Generating a 1024 bit RSA private key
........................++++++
(...)
```

That's it. Repeat the last command for every machine you want to equip with a certificate. You will find the certificate, key, and CA certificate in `/usr/share/doc/openvpn/examples/easy-rsa/keys` (or the path you specified in the file `vars`). Transfer these files to the machines involved in your VPN using a secure method. WinSCP works perfectly here, if you have Windows clients, the command-line tool `scp` (from the **sshd** package) is the best choice for data exchange between systems with SSH servers (most Linux/UNIX systems).

# Troubleshooting

If you run into problems, check the following:

- Ensure basic network connectivity between the two systems. Can they `ping` each other without problems? Are there firewalls involved between them?

- Disable all firewalls on both systems during testing the tunnels. We will later set them up properly. Remember that both Windows XP and SuSE activate their firewall solutions by default.
- OpenVPN and X509 certificates need synchronized time on both systems. For testing purposes you can set the time by hand. On Linux, the commands `date` and `hwclock` will help you, for the production environment a time server client should be set up. On Linux, Xntp is probably the most common one; its homepage offers documentation: `http://www.eecis.udel.edu/~ntp/`.
- If you copy the files from a Windows machine to a Linux machine, remember to have `dos2unix` run and convert the end-of-line characters. The same applies to configuration files, certificates, and keys created on Linux and transferred to Windows—apply `unix2dos` before transfer. Depending on your Linux system and OpenVPN version, it may be necessary to change the file access permissions in the `keys` directory as follows:

```
debian01:~# cd /etc/openvpn/keys
debian01:/etc/openvpn/keys# ls -l
total 16
-rw-------  1 root root 1606 2005-11-05 09:54 ca.crt
-rw-------  1 root root 4948 2005-11-05 09:55 VPN-Client.crt
-rw-------  1 root root 1679 2005-11-05 09:55 VPN-Client.key
debian01:/etc/openvpn/keys#
```

- If file permissions are set less restrictively, some OpenVPN versions may refuse to start.
- Check the data you enter during the process of creating the certificates. Ensure that you have not misspelled anything and that there are no typos. Any character different in the certificates can cause the process of connecting the systems to fail.

If you have checked this, repeat the process of certificate generation with `easy-rsa` and enter your data carefully. Analyze the log file entries in the Windows main menu and context menu of the OpenVPN GUI or have a look at the output of `openvpn` at the command line when invoked manually.

# Summary

In this chapter we have used the scripts in the `easy-rsa` directory, provided with OpenVPN, to create a CA, a Diffie-Hellman key, and both keys, certificate requests, and keys for the two VPN partners. The client and server certificates were automatically signed during creation. After having them transferred to the VPN partner (Windows or Linux), we started the new, secure tunnel.

# 7

# The Command openvpn and its Configuration File

In this chapter we will have a look at the syntax of the command-line tool openvpn, which enables us to build tunnels quickly. By analyzing the standard configuration file we used to set up a tunnel with a pre-shared key, we will now dive into the depths of the configuration options of openvpn. This way, we will learn about basic tunnel network setup and control, compression, and debug output.

As a next step, the configuration file containing the certificate-based tunnel created in Chapter 6 will be in our focus. From then on we will go through several groups of parameters that can be given to openvpn (be it in a configuration file or at the command-line prompt). We will deal with examples for many of these parameters and look at scenarios where they might prove helpful. Parameters available in server and client mode, encryption, and Windows-specific options are explained.

Many of the following options are explained in detail on the manual page of OpenVPN (Version 2.1 can be found at `http://openvpn.net/man-beta.html`). The explanations (especially in the tables) are close to the explanations in the manpage; some details and examples have been added, some removed. If you feel unsure about some options, have a closer look at the manpage, which is updated regularly on the website.

## Syntax of openvpn

In the previous chapters we have invoked openvpn at the command line several times. On Windows, this is an easy way to get more detailed output during troubleshooting; on Linux it is the normal way to set up a tunnel quickly. And on both systems this is what lies beneath the services layer of the services or the GUI Tools.

OpenVPN on both Windows and Linux is called by start scripts that add special parameters to the command openvpn. Normally, there is (among others) the parameter `--config` (followed by a filename) which lets openvpn read a configuration file; on Linux a file in `/etc/openvpn/`. On Windows configuration files have the extension `.ovpn`, on Linux `.conf`. The start scripts will read all configuration files in the configuration file directory and start the tunnels described in them. If you have three `.conf` files in your Linux configuration directory, openvpn will try to start three tunnels. The same applies for `.ovpn` files on Windows and if you double-click such a file on Windows, a tunnel should be started.

# OpenVPN Command-Line Parameters

Our first tunnel from the Linux system was configured in a configuration file transferred from the Windows VPN partner. OpenVPN had to be told where this configuration file is to be found, so we started it with openvpn --config sample.ovpn. We now know that the extension .ovpn is typical for the Windows version of OpenVPN. Basically, you could use any extension you like, but only tunnels described in .ovpn and .conf files will be started automatically. The Linux system would not start a tunnel described in this file automatically until you rename the file to a .conf extension (and restart the service).

However, this was the first time we called openvpn, but it already shows its syntax:

```
openvpn <option1> <parameter(s)> ... <optionn> <parameter(s)>
```

Parameters and options for OpenVPN are either stored in a configuration file or called at the command-line prompt. Normally there is no difference between the name of the command-line option and the configuration file parameter, of course with the exception of the following parameters:

- --config <file>: Directs to the location of the configuration file
- --help: Gives you a brief introduction to the syntax of openvpn
- --version: Prints the installed version and copyright information

| Parameter | Options | Function | Usage |
|---|---|---|---|
| config | <file> | Directs openvpn to the location of the configuration file | Command line only |
| help | - | Prints help and a list of options | Command line only |
| version | - | Prints the version of OpenVPN | Command line only |

The following code extract shows the first lines of the output of openvpn --help:

```
debian01:~# openvpn --help
OpenVPN 2.0.5 i486-pc-linux-gnu [SSL] [LZO] [EPOLL] built on Nov  7 2005

General Options:
--config file   : Read configuration options from file.
--help          : Show options.
--version       : Show copyright and version information.

Tunnel Options:
--local host    : Local host name or ip address.
--remote host [port] : Remote host name or ip address.
--remote-random : If multiple --remote options specified, choose one randomly.
--mode m        : Major mode, m = 'p2p' (default, point-to-point) or 'server'.
--proto p       : Use protocol p for communicating with peer.
                  p = udp (default), tcp-server, or tcp-client
--connect-retry n : For --proto tcp-client, number of seconds to wait
                  between connection retries (default=5).
(...)
```

# Using OpenVPN at the Command Line

In the course of this book we have already invoked openvpn several times from a command line. As a first example, we built a tunnel with a pre-shared key and a rather simple configuration file. Even though there are some other parameters set in the standard configuration file we used, the easiest command to start a tunnel with a static key is:

```
debian01:/etc/openvpn# openvpn --remote <IP of System B> --dev tun1 --ifconfig
10.3.0.1 10.3.0.2 --secret /etc/openvpn/key.txt
```

You see, it's very easy to connect two systems with an openvpn tunnel, when we know their IPs. All we need is a pre-shared key, a tunnel IP, and a decision on which device type to use.

If the second tunnel endpoint is a Linux system already provided with the pre-shared key /etc/openvpn/key.txt, then all we need to do to start our tunnel is enter the aforementioned command on system A, and enter the following command on system B:

```
/etc/openvpn# openvpn --remote <IP of System A> --dev tun1 --ifconfig 10.3.0.2
10.3.0.1 --secret /etc/openvpn/key.txt
```

That's all. Your tunnel is up and running. However, this tunnel is rather temporary and will be closed when you exit the shell around it. Nevertheless, you may consider it a convenient method to start and stop quick tunnels, especially for testing purposes.

The following table gives an overview on the parameters used here:

| Parameter | Options | Function | Usage | Example |
|---|---|---|---|---|
| remote | <hostname><br><IP> | Points to the other tunnel endpoint | Command line and config file | --remote vpn.dyndns.org |
| dev | <device> | Tells openvpn which network device (type) to use | Command line and config file | --dev tun<br>--dev tap |
| ifconfig | For TUN devices:<br><local IP><br><remote IP><br>For TAP devices:<br><local IP><br><subnet mask> | Sets tunnel endpoints' virtual IPs and netmasks in the tunnel | Command line and config file | --ifconfig 10.3.0.2 10.3.0.1<br>--ifconfig 10.3.0.2 255.255.255.0 |
| secret | File containing the pre-shared key | Tells openvpn the location of the pre-shared key | Command line and config file | --secret key.txt |

> The parameter remote specifies the machine on which the OpenVPN Software is running and takes IPs or DNS entries as parameters.

In combination with DynDNS entries, we can build VPNs between dial-up network lines based on cheap DSL Lines, on both sides of the tunnel!

Depending on the device type we select, `ifconfig` must set the IP/netmask combination differently. TUN devices are virtual point-to-point devices, and therefore `ifconfig` must be provided with the virtual IP of the other point-to-point partner. TAP devices, however, are virtual network devices and thus `ifconfig` needs a netmask for this virtual network segment.

In our example above, openvpn is called in `tun` mode and the parameter `ifconfig` is used with the options `10.3.0.2 10.3.0.1`. This means that a virtual point-to-point network is created between the two OpenVPN servers, with `10.3.0.1` and `10.3.0.2` as virtual endpoints.

The example below shows the correct `ifconfig` syntax for a `tap` device: `--ifconfig 10.3.0.2 255.255.255.0`. Since TAP devices provide virtual Ethernet segments, a netmask is needed.

> TUN devices provide routing mode and start a virtual point-to-point connection; TAP devices provide bridging mode and start a virtual network segment. The parameter `ifconfig` needs the two tunnel IPs when we are using `tun` devices, and the local IP along with netmask, when we are using `tap` devices.

## Parameters Used in the Standard Configuration File for a Static Key Client

When we want to connect a Linux system to a Windows XP system with the standard configuration file that we used (and adapted slightly) in Chapter 5, we have to change this command a little bit:

```
debian01:/etc/openvpn# openvpn --remote 10.10.10.103 --dev tap --ifconfig
10.3.0.2 255.255.255.0 --secret key.txt --comp-lzo
Fri Nov 18 22:35:15 2005 OpenVPN 2.0.2 i486-pc-linux-gnu [SSL] [LZO] [EPOLL]
built on Oct  9 2005
Fri Nov 18 22:35:15 2005 IMPORTANT: OpenVPN's default port number is now 1194,
based on an official port number assignment by IANA.  OpenVPN 2.0-beta16 and
earlier used 5000 as the default port.
Fri Nov 18 22:35:15 2005 LZO compression initialized
Fri Nov 18 22:35:15 2005 TUN/TAP device tap0 opened
Fri Nov 18 22:35:15 2005 /sbin/ifconfig tap0 10.3.0.3 netmask 255.255.255.0
mtu 1500 broadcast 10.3.0.255
Fri Nov 18 22:35:15 2005 UDPv4 link local (bound): [undef]:1194
Fri Nov 18 22:35:15 2005 UDPv4 link remote: 10.10.10.103:1194
```

## Compressing the Data

Until OpenVPN 1.5, Windows needed TAP devices, thus the option `--dev` has the parameter `tap` instead of `tun`, and in the standard configuration file the `lzo` compression is activated; that's why I typed `-comp-lzo` at the end of my command line.

| **Parameter** | **Options** | **Function** | **Usage** | **Example** |
|---|---|---|---|---|
| `comp-lzo` | `<yes>`<br>`<no>`<br>`<adaptive>`<br>(default) | openvpn uses `lzo` library to compress tunnel traffic | Command line and config file | `--comp-lzo` |

Normally, we do not need any option to this parameter, unless you want to control compression of tunnel data more specifically (such as switching compression on/off on-the-fly in server mode); the manual page will provide detailed information also here.

> The parameter `comp-lzo` activates compression of tunnel data.

Without further options, `comp-lzo` will use its adaptive algorithm. OpenVPN checks compression efficiency regularly and adapts it to the results. By doing so, compressed data will very likely not be compressed again, but other data have a high probability of being compressed.

Now let's have a look at the other parameters used in the OpenVPN standard configuration files. In Chapter 5, we adapted the configuration file for a client that uses static keys.

On Windows, open the file `C:\Program Files\OpenVPN\sample-config\sample.ovpn` in Notepad. On Linux, open the configuration file copied from the Windows system.

In this file, there are some more parameters that we did not talk about. Some of them are commented, either by a semi-colon or by a hash mark at the beginning of a line. The following table gives an overview of ports, protocols, and network devices:

| Parameter | Options | Function | Usage | Example |
|---|---|---|---|---|
| `port` | `<port number>` | Specifies the port (both local and remote) which OpenVPN will use. | Command line and config file | `--port 5001` |
| `proto` | `<udp>` `<tcp-client>` `<tcp-server>` | Sets the protocol OpenVPN uses. A TCP client will try to start connections, while a TCP server only waits for clients. | Command line and config file | `--proto udp` `--proto tcp-client` `--proto tcp-server` |
| `tun-mtu` | `<mtu size>` | Sets the maximum transmission units. | Command line and config file | `--tun-mtu 1200` |
| `dev-node` | `<interface name>` | Specifies the name of the interface to be used. | Command line and config file | `--dev-node openvpn1` |

You may have noticed that I left out two parameters: `fragment` and `mssfix`. These two are relevant if you run into problems with Maximum Transmission Units (MTUs) and datagram sizes when you are using UDP. I never ran into such problems, but if you need more information, the online manpage is very detailed.

With the parameter `dev-node`, you can tell `openvpn` to use a specific network device. In the aforementioned example, I have entered `openvpn1` as name of the device. This is the name I gave the network adapter in the Network Connections module of the Windows Control Panel. On Linux you can also simply set the name of the device as an option to the parameter `dev`.

```
debian01:/etc/openvpn# openvpn --remote 10.10.10.103 --dev tap --ifconfig
10.3.0.2 255.255.255.0 --secret key.txt --verb 1 --comp-lzo --dev tap1
```

This command will have the tunnel created over the network device tap1. On Windows you would need to add the parameter --dev-node followed by the name of the network device you want to use.

# Controlling and Restarting the Tunnel

The following parameters from our standard file can be used by OpenVPN to determine whether a tunnel is still up or already down.

| Parameter | Options | Function | Usage | Example |
|---|---|---|---|---|
| ping | <seconds> | Sends a ping to the other tunnel partner through the tunnel after <seconds> without traffic | Command line and config file | --ping 10 |
| ping-restart | <seconds> | After <seconds> without receiving any packet from remote, the tunnel will be restarted | Command line and config file | --ping-restart 60 |
| ping-timer-rem | - | ping-restart runs only when a remote address is given | Command line and config file | --ping-timer-rem |
| persist-tun | - | Keeps tun/tap devices up when openvpn is restarted | Command line and config file | --persist-tun |
| persist-key | - | openvpn will not re-read the keys on a restart | Command line and config file | --persist-key |
| resolv-retry | <seconds> | This sets the time for which openvpn will try to resolve a hostname before giving up | Command line and config file | --resolv-retry 86400 |

OpenVPN brings some sophisticated tools to check tunnels and restart them, if they are not working anymore.

- ping: This parameter is used to send ping packages through the tunnel to the tunnel partner on a regular schedule.
- ping-restart: If the sender does not receive any traffic for the time span defined by the parameter, openvpn assumes that this tunnel is dead and will try to establish it again by restarting it.
- ping-timer-rem: If you add the parameter ping-timer-rem, openvpn will only start a tunnel if a remote address for the tunnel is given—thus a server only listening for clients will not try to reconnect. If the option persist-tun is set, openvpn will keep up the network devices used.

- `persist-key`: This parameter will prevent openvpn from re-reading the key files on a restart. This should only be necessary when openvpn runs as a non-privileged user without access to the key files.

## Debugging Output—Troubleshooting

And last but not least, the parameters that define the verbosity and debugging output of OpenVPN:

| Parameter | Options | Function | Usage | Example |
|---|---|---|---|---|
| verb | <verbosity level> | Sets level of verbosity, 0 is lowest, 11 is maximum detail level | Command line and config file | --verb 4 |
| mute | <number of messages> | openvpn will print only 10 consecutive messages from the same category | Command line and config file | --mute 10 |

The parameter verb offers a range from 0 to 11 for the verbosity of the output openvpn provides. Default for this parameter is 1, which should provide enough output in most cases. Selecting 0 here will make openvpn provide messages only when fatal errors occur. While levels 1-4 provide an increasing level of verbosity, which is useful for administration, the levels 5 and above are ideal only for debugging. Following is an example for the output of openvpn concerning the successful initialization of our sample connection:

```
debian01:/etc/openvpn# openvpn --remote 10.10.10.103 --dev tap --ifconfig
10.3.0.2 255.255.255.0 --secret key.txt --verb 1 --comp-lzo --dev tap1 --verb
11

(...)

t Nov 19 01:07:21 2005 us=949416 UDPv4 read returned 60
Sat Nov 19 01:07:21 2005 us=949642 UDPv4 READ [60] from 10.10.10.103:1194:
DATA 01edfefe f6ed7f34 019f0f09 9c560481 084241cc 63d35cfd 71f001d8
d640fbe[more...]
Sat Nov 19 01:07:21 2005 us=949815 DECRYPT IV: 63d35cfd 71f001d8
Sat Nov 19 01:07:21 2005 us=950033 DECRYPT TO: 00000220 43844441 fa2a187b
f3641eb4 cb07ed2d 0a981fc7 48
Sat Nov 19 01:07:21 2005 us=950197 PID TEST 0:0 1132741697:544
Sat Nov 19 01:07:21 2005 us=950378 Peer Connection Initiated with
10.10.10.103:1194
Sat Nov 19 01:07:21 2005 us=950687 RECEIVED PING PACKET
Sat Nov 19 01:07:21 2005 us=950709 Initialization Sequence Completed
Sat Nov 19 01:07:21 2005 us=950724 TIMER: coarse timer wakeup 1 seconds
Sat Nov 19 01:07:21 2005 us=950741 PO_CTL rwflags=0x0001 ev=3 arg=0x08090424
Sat Nov 19 01:07:21 2005 us=950768 PO_CTL rwflags=0x0001 ev=4 arg=0x08090420
Sat Nov 19 01:07:21 2005 us=950788 I/O WAIT TR|Tw|SR|Sw [1/185372]
Sat Nov 19 01:07:23 2005 us=150719  event_wait returned 0
Sat Nov 19 01:07:23 2005 us=150773 I/O WAIT status=0x0020
Sat Nov 19 01:07:23 2005 us=150791 TIMER: coarse timer wakeup 5 seconds
Sat Nov 19 01:07:23 2005 us=150813 PO_CTL rwflags=0x0001 ev=3 arg=0x08090424
Sat Nov 19 01:07:23 2005 us=150851 PO_CTL rwflags=0x0001 ev=4 arg=0x08090420
Sat Nov 19 01:07:23 2005 us=150870 I/O WAIT TR|Tw|SR|Sw [5/185372]
```

A very helpful level of verbosity can be set by using `--verb 5`:

```
debian01:/etc/openvpn# openvpn --remote 10.10.10.103 --dev tap --ifconfig
10.3.0.2 255.255.255.0 --secret key.txt --verb 1 --comp-lzo --dev tap1 --verb
5

(...)

Sat Nov 19 01:38:53 2005 us=827058 UDPv4 link local (bound): [undef]:1194
Sat Nov 19 01:38:53 2005 us=827200 UDPv4 link remote: 10.10.10.103:1194
RSat Nov 19 01:39:01 2005 us=970557 Peer Connection Initiated with
10.10.10.103:1194
Sat Nov 19 01:39:01 2005 us=970938 Initialization Sequence Completed
WRRwrWRwrWRwrWRwrWrWRwRw
```

As you can see in the last line, OpenVPN prints w's and r's for each packet traveling through the tunnel. A capital letter stands for a packet read or written to the TUN/TAP adapter, a small letter stands for a packet written or read in the tunnel. This is really very useful, because you can easily track packets (like pings) and find out how far they come. Set up your tunnel with `verb 5` on both sides, ping the other host from either side, and watch the debug output—there are four letters for each ping: RwrW.

# Configuring OpenVPN with Certificates—Simple TLS Mode

In Chapter 6, we worked with a configuration file like the following:

```
remote 10.10.10.103
dev tap
tls-client
ifconfig 10.3.0.2 255.255.255.0
dh keys/dh2048.pem
ca keys/ca.crt
cert keys/VPN-Client.crt
key keys/VPN-Client.key
```

In line 3 of our little configuration file, we find the parameter `tls-client`; on our Windows system we entered `tls-server` here. These entries cause `openvpn` to start TLS to protect the data transferred. All machines involved in the VPN need the same CA certificate and a local certificate and key pair issued by this CA. On connection, the two partners exchange their local certificates and validate the partner's certificate by checking if it was signed by the common CA. OpenVPN must know which files contain the CA and local certificate and key.

The following table shows the main parameters that we need to adapt for the use with certificates:

| Parameter | Options | Function | Usage | Example |
|---|---|---|---|---|
| `dh` | `<file>` | Defines the Diffie-Hellmann key | Command line and config file | `--dh keys/dh2048.pem` |
| `ca` | `<file>` | Defines the certificate file of the CA | Command line and config file | `--ca keys/ca.crt` |
| `cert` | `<file>` | Defines the local machine's certificate file | Command line and config file | `--cert keys/VPN-Client.crt` |

| Parameter | Options | Function | Usage | Example |
|---|---|---|---|---|
| key | <file> | Defines the local machine's key file | Command line and config file | --key keys/VPN-Client.key |
| tls-server | - | Local machine acts as TLS server | Command line and config file | --tls-server |
| tls-client | - | Local machine acts as TLS client | Command line and config file | --tls-client |

The options `tls-server` and `tls-client` affect only the way in which the TLS handshake is dealt with and have no further consequences for OpenVPN.

# Overview of OpenVPN Parameters

The table in the following section is a detailed list of all parameters OpenVPN offers concerning basic tunnel options. They can be used both at the command line and in configuration files.

## General Tunnel Options

Most of these options are used to determine the way in which openvpn connects to the tunnel partner and how it deals with connections not responding or changing.

| Parameter | Options | Function | Usage |
|---|---|---|---|
| local | <host> | Binds local service to the address of <host>. Useful if you want openvpn to run only on one interface of a host, with multiple home sites. | --local 192.168.0.50 |
| remote | <host> | Connects to the host. IP or DNS are equivalent, DynDNS is possible. | --remote feilner-it.net |
| remote-random | | Simple load balancing, Specify multiple --remote addresses and openvpn will randomly connect to one of them. | --remote-random |
| float | | Allows the remote VPN partner to change the remote IP address (e.g. with DynDNS). | --float |
| ipchange | <cmd> | Calls the program <cmd> if the IP address has changed. | --ipchange /script-ip.sh |
| connect-retry | <seconds> | Retries to connect for <seconds> if connection fails. | --connect-retry 60 |
| connect-retry-max | <n> | n is the maximum number of retries that can be done if the connection can't be established. | --connect-retry-max |
| resolv-retry | <seconds> | If openvpn can't resolve the hostname of the tunnel partner, it will try to reconnect after n seconds. | --resolv-retry 86400 |
| proto | <tcp/udp> | Protocol to use. | --proto udp |

| Parameter | Options | Function | Usage |
|---|---|---|---|
| port | <port> | Uses this port for connections (both local and remote). | --port 5493 |
| lport | <port> | Uses this local port to bind OpenVPN. | --lport 1194 |
| rport | <port> | Uses this remote port to bind OpenVPN. | --rport 5000 |
| nobind | | Uses dynamic port to connect (only client). | --nobind |
| shaper | <Bytes> | Throttles the outgoing data bandwidth of your tunnel (only client; only outgoing bandwidth). | --shaper 10000 |
| ip-win32 | <method> | Sets the Windows network adapter's IP and netmask using <method>. | --ip-win32 ipapi |

Unfortunately, it's impossible to deal with all options in detail within the scope of this book. Nevertheless, we will have a close look at various parameters that have proven useful.

- If your system has several NICs or several IPs, you may want OpenVPN to run only on one of them. This can easily be done with the parameter `--local` followed by the IP you want to bind OpenVPN to. This option might be very interesting for routers or firewalls providing VPN services, too.
- We have learned about the option `remote`, and that it supports DNS entries (and therefore DynDNS) but we need to set the `float` parameter to allow the other tunnel endpoint change its IP without needing to restart the tunnel. The parameter `ipchange` specifies a command that can be executed on such an event.

> With the option `float`, OpenVPN does not need to restart tunnels when the IP of a partner changes.

- If you specify multiple `--remote` addresses, the parameter `remote-random` enables automatic load balancing between the hosts by choosing randomly which to connect to.
- The options `connect-retry`, `connect-retry-max`, and `resolv-retry` define how (often and long) OpenVPN will try to establish a connection when errors occur. (86400 seconds are one day).
- The parameter `proto` switches `udp` and `tcp` mode within OpenVPN. UDP should always be preferred, as there are some problems with TCP
- Furthermore, the options `port`, `lport`, `rport`, and `nobind` give us the possibility to define exactly from which local port to which remote port our tunnel shall be connected. And if we like, `--nobind` will use dynamically assigned ports—almost randomly.
- Probably the handiest parameter in this section is `--shaper`. Using `--shaper 10000` will limit outgoing bandwidth of the `openvpn` tunnel to `10000` byte/sec. Only outgoing traffic can be shaped (do you know why?), so if you want your tunnel to use 10k of bandwidth as a maximum, you have to set this on both sides!

- And the last parameter is one I have not needed to use up to today: `--ip-win32` lets you decide the method with which the Windows network adapter receives its IP and netmask. This method may be one of adaptive, IPAPI, Netsh, Dynamic or Manual. More information on this can be found in the manual page.

The following example shows an excerpt from a configuration file. Can you explain what `openvpn` is supposed to do according to this file?

```
(...)
local 192.168.0.150
remote feilner-it.net
remote ultrino.de
remote openvpn.dyndns.org
remote-random
float
resolv-retry 86400
proto tcp-client
lport 22222
rport 22223
connect-retry 86400
shaper 10000
(...)
```

These lines make `openvpn` set up a tunnel:

- Listening only on the local IP `192.168.0.150`
- Trying to connect randomly to `feilner-it.net`, `ultrino.de`, and `openvpn.dyndns.org`
- Ignoring changing IP of the other tunnel partner, as long as encryption is OK
- Running as `tcp-client` on local port `22222`
- Trying to connect to remote port `22223`
- If the connection fails, `openvpn` will retry for a day
- Outgoing traffic is limited to `10000` bytes/sec

# Routing

The parameters in this section deal with routing of the traffic inside, to, and from the tunnel. We have already learned about the parameter `ifconfig` and that it needs different parameters for TAP or TUN devices. A second important point in this section is the parameter `route`. Many people seem to have difficulties with connecting networks over OpenVPN, but it's really easy.

| Parameter | Options | Function | Usage |
|---|---|---|---|
| `ifconfig` | `<local remote>` | Sets the IP address and netmask for the tunnel on TAP devices<br>Sets the local and remote IP address for the tunnel on TUN devices | `--ifconfig 10.1.0.1 10.1.0.2`<br>`--ifconfig 10.1.0.1 255.255.255.0` |
| `route` | `<network>` | Sets a specific route on the VPN host when openvpn has successfully started the tunnel | `--route 10.0.10.0 255.255.255.252` |

| Parameter | Options | Function | Usage |
|---|---|---|---|
| route-gateway | <IP> | Sets the gateway on the VPN host | --route-gateway 192.168.0.22 |
| route-delay | <seconds> | Waits n seconds before setting the routes | --route-delay 5 |
| route-up | <cmd> | Calls a program if the routes are up | --route-up /script.sh |
| redirect-gateway | | Sets default route through the tunnel | --redirect-gateway |

- `--ifconfig`: Sets the IPs of the tunnel. Here you need to give the two IPs of a point-to-point VPN, based on TUN devices, or the IP and netmask of a TAP-based VPN-bridge.
- `--route`, `--route-gateway`, and `--redirect-gateway`: Affects the routing of packets on the VPN host. After our tunnel is set up correctly, we have to make sure that both VPN servers are forwarding traffic (perhaps we need a firewall?), and that the connected networks are routed correctly on the other side. A later example will deal with this setup. `--redirect-gateway` is an excellent feature, for example, for notebooks of road warriors.
- `--route-up`: Enables us to run scripts when the routes are set up.
- `--route-delay`: Tells openvpn to wait a little before setting the routes when the tunnel is set up.

There are many possibilities to use `ifconfig`, `route`, and `route-up` commands for an openvpn tunnel:

```
(...)
ifconfig 10.3.0.1 10.3.0.2
route 192.168.0.0 255.255.255.0 10.3.0.2
route-up "/sbin/FW_openvpn_1 start"
route-up "route add -net 192.168.1.0 netmask 255.255.255.0 gw 192.168.0.1"
route-delay 2
(...)
```

This example provides a tunnel, where a firewall script is started after routing is set up. A `route` is defined into a subnet `192.168.0.0` behind the other tunnel endpoint. Another `route` is defined into a third subnet on the other side of the tunnel using the `route-up` parameter and the Linux system tool `route`. And last but not least, openvpn waits 2 seconds between setting up the tunnel and configuring routing.

## Controlling the Tunnel

| Parameter | Options | Function | Usage |
|---|---|---|---|
| inactive | <seconds> | The TUN/TAP device is closed after <seconds> of inactivity | --inactive 120 |
| ping-exit | <seconds> | After <seconds> with no packet received, shutdown OpenVPN | --ping-exit 120 |
| keepalive | <seconds> | Simply ping and ping-restart | --keep-alive 10 60 |

| Parameter | Options | Function | Usage |
|---|---|---|---|
| persist-local-ip | <IP> | Keeps local IP over restarts | |
| persist-remote-ip | <IP> | You can't restart the tunnel if the IP was changed | --persist-remote-ip 62.184.232.1 |

In this context the parameters `--ping`, `--ping-restart`, `--ping-timer-rem`, `--persist-tun`, and `--persist-key` should also be mentioned. We met them as part of the standard configuration.

All these parameters influence `openvpn`'s behavior concerning testing and restarting a tunnel. If there is no traffic in the tunnel for the amount of seconds specified by the `ping` parameter, `openvpn` will send a ping packet through the tunnel. If no packet is received for the amount of seconds defined with `--ping-restart`, the tunnel is started over.

The parameter `--keepalive` is a shortcut for a combination of `ping` and `ping-restart`; you can express:

```
ping 100
ping-restart 200
```

by the simple directive:

```
keepalive 100 200
```

Since OpenVPN ping packets are only sent in one direction, both sides of the tunnel must be configured to send pings on a regular basis. In the standard configuration file these are included, but remember to check every configuration you create for this purpose. (Don't worry, you will notice when you have forgotten this, your tunnel won't work long.)

The parameters `--ping`, `--ping-restart`, `--ping-exit`, and `--inactive` can be combined in many ways, depending on your setup and goals. Can you imagine what the following example does?

```
(...)
ping 20
ping-restart 120
inactive 3600
(...)
```

These directives cause `openvpn` to send pings after `20` seconds of inactivity. After two minutes of inactivity, `openvpn` will restart the tunnel. After an hour without tunnel data being exchanged, `openvpn` will exit.

# Scripting

OpenVPN has several points of time when scripts can be executed. We have already learned about one of them, `--route-up <command>`. Here is a list of more parameters that allow scripts to be run:

| Parameter | Options | Function | Usage |
|---|---|---|---|
| up | <command> | Calls program when the TUN/TAP device is up | --up script-up.sh |
| up-delay | <seconds> | Waits n seconds after connect for the up-script | --up-delay 5 |
| down | <command> | Calls program when the TUN/TAP device is down | --down script-down.sh |
| down-pre | <command> | Calls script before TUN/TAP shuts down | --down-pre |
| up-restart | <command> | Calls script after every reconnect | --up-restart |
| route-up | <command> | Calls a program when the routes are up | --route-up script.sh |
| ipchange | <command> | Calls script when the IP changes | -- ipchange script.sh |

> With openvpn we can have our own scripts executed before and after the interface is brought up or down, when we are reconnected, when the routes are set up, and when our IP changes.

# Logging

Besides the debugging parameters --verb and --mute that we learned about when dealing with our standard configuration file, there are several parameters useful for directing openvpn's output:

| Parameter | Options | Function | Usage |
|---|---|---|---|
| log | <file> | Defines the log file where the output of messages for this tunnel is supposed to be written to | --log /var/log/vpn.log |
| log-append | <file> | Appends messages to the log file—does not overwrite it | --log-append /var/log/openvpn/messages.log |
| status | <file> | Writes a status file of the connections to <file> | --status /var/log/openvpn/status.log |

You should add the following two lines to every tunnel you configure:

```
log-append /var/log/openvpn/packt.log
status /var/log/openvpn/packt.status
```

The first entry in a configuration file will cause openvpn to write debug information and messages in the specified file. The latter will print status information like the following in a status log file:

```
debian01:/etc/openvpn # cat /var/log/openvpn/packt.status
OpenVPN STATISTICS
Updated,Thu Nov 24 09:11:02 2005
TUN/TAP read bytes,3189334
TUN/TAP write bytes,3783482
TCP/UDP read bytes,4847840
```

```
TCP/UDP write bytes,4248748
Auth read bytes,3801636
pre-compress bytes,579459
post-compress bytes,546430
pre-decompress bytes,489729
post-decompress bytes,678607
END
debian01:/etc/openvpn #
```

These data are updated automatically and can be very helpful for statistic programs like Nagios, Munin, or Cacti.

## Specifying a User and Group

On Linux, we can specify a certain user and group under whose privileges openvpn shall run—a good idea to reduce the number of processes running with root privileges and increase security:

| Parameter | Options | Function | Usage |
|---|---|---|---|
| user | UNIX-Account | For more security | --user nobody |
| group | UNIX-Account | For more security | --group nogroup |

Please note that openvpn will be started with root privileges, but once a tunnel configured with --user nobody is started, it switches to the environment of this user. This may lead into problems, when key or certificate files are not readable to the user you defined in your configuration, as root openvpn can read the key files and start the tunnel. Later, this tunnel is restarted due to some parameter passed (like --ping-restart), and now, openvpn will try to re-read the key files. If the unprivileged user (nobody) has no right to read these files, this will fail and the tunnel won't be set up. You can avoid this by using the parameter --persist-key. The same applies to the network devices—you can avoid this problem with the parameter --persist-tun.

## The Management Interface

OpenVPN provides a management interface available via Telnet. This interface is designed for use by management tools like **OpenVPN-Admin** that allow GUI management of tunnels.

| Parameter | Options | Function | Usage |
|---|---|---|---|
| management | <IP> <port> <pw-file> | Management interface of OpenVPN | --management 127.0.0.1 5702 |
| --management-hold | - | The tunnel will not be set up until the command hold release is entered in the management console | --management-hold |
| --management-log-cache | <number> | Caches the number of lines for use with the management interface | --management-log-cache 10 |

If you want to activate the management interface, you simply need to add a line like the following to your configuration file:

```
management 10.10.10.105 5702
```

To connect to the management interface is easy—just type `telnet <IP> <Port>` and replace `IP` and `Port` with the values you placed in the configuration file. After you have connected, type `help` to get a list of available commands:

```
mfeilner@shuttle:~> telnet 10.10.10.105 5702
Trying 10.10.10.105...
Connected to 10.10.10.105.
Escape character is '^]'.
>INFO:OpenVPN Management Interface Version 1 -- type 'help' for more info
>HOLD:Waiting for hold release
help
Management Interface for OpenVPN 2.0.5 i486-pc-linux-gnu [SSL] [LZO] [EPOLL]
built on Nov  7 2005
Commands:
auth-retry t           : Auth failure retry mode (none,interact,nointeract).
echo [on|off] [N|all]  : Like log, but only show messages in echo buffer.
exit|quit              : Close management session.
help                   : Print this message.
hold [on|off|release]  : Set/show hold flag to on/off state, or
                         release current hold and start tunnel.
kill cn                : Kill the client instance(s) having common name cn.
kill IP:port           : Kill the client instance connecting from IP:port.
log [on|off] [N|all]   : Turn on/off realtime log display
                         + show last N lines or 'all' for entire history.
mute [n]               : Set log mute level to n, or show level if n is
absent.
net                    : (Windows only) Show network info and routing table.
password type p        : Enter password p for a queried OpenVPN password.
signal s               : Send signal s to daemon,
                         s = SIGHUP|SIGTERM|SIGUSR1|SIGUSR2.
state [on|off] [N|all] : Like log, but show state history.
status [n]             : Show current daemon status info using format #n.
test n                 : Produce n lines of output for testing/debugging.
username type u        : Enter username u for a queried OpenVPN username.
verb [n]               : Set log verbosity level to n, or show if n is absent.
version                : Show current version number.
END
```

If you have set the verbosity level to any level higher than 2, you will receive entries in your log file like the following every time a client connects.

```
Sat Nov 19 09:10:58 2005 us=877891 MANAGEMENT: Client connected from
10.10.10.105:5702
Sat Nov 19 09:11:02 2005 us=432643 Peer Connection Initiated with
10.10.10.103:1194
Sat Nov 19 09:11:02 2005 us=432692 Initialization Sequence Completed
Sat Nov 19 09:12:05 2005 us=10509 MANAGEMENT: Client disconnected
```

- The management console can be password-protected; simply put your password in a file and add the path to this file in your configuration file.
- Tunnels can be started in suspended mode, which means that they are only started after a command sent from the management console. Just add `--management-hold` to the configuration. The tunnel will not be started until you log in to this tunnel's management interface and type `hold release`.

# Proxies

Since OpenVPN uses SSL/TLS for encryption, and UDP or TCP as transport protocol, it can be easily tunneled through an HTTP-proxy. Similarly, we can have our tunnels proxied over a **SOCKetS (SOCKS)** proxy server. The following parameters are available for proxy support:

| Parameter | Options | Function | Usage |
|---|---|---|---|
| `http-proxy` | `<server port [auth]>` | OpenVPN can tunnel through proxies. Specify the proxy and the port here. Optionally, authentication is supported. | `--http-proxy 192.168.0.12 8080` |
| `http-proxy-retry` | - | Retries indefinitely if connection fails. | `--http-proxy-retry` |
| `http-proxy-timeout` | `<seconds>` | Considers connection to proxy as failed after `<seconds>` inactivity. | `--http-proxy-timeout 5` |
| `socks-proxy` | `<server port>` | Tunneling through a socks5 gateway. | `--socks-proxy 192.168.0.12 8080` |
| `socks-proxy-retry` | - | Retries indefinitely if connection fails. | `--socks-proxy-retry` |
| `auto-proxy` | | Tries to determine the proxy automatically; needs OpenVPN 2.1 or higher. | `--auto-proxy` |

> OpenVPN tunnels can be tunneled through both HTTP and SOCKS proxies.

# Encryption Parameters

Chapter 8 in this book deals with security options for OpenVPN, but we will have a short (introductory) look at the parameters OpenVPN's cryptographic layer provides. The most important ones are here in the following table, and we already know many of them:

| Parameter | Options | Function | Usage |
|---|---|---|---|
| `secret` | `<file>` | Points to the file with the static key | `--secret /kex.txt` |
| `cipher` | `<alg>` | Specifies the algorithm to use for encryption of packets | `--cipher AES-256-CBC` |
| `keysize` | `<n>` | Specifies the size of the cipher key in bits | `--keysize 128` |
| `auth` | `<alg>` | Defines the message digest algorithm `<alg>` used by the HMAC authentication algorithm | `--auth SHA1` |
| `tls-server` | | Uses SSL certificates and acts as TLS server during TLS handshake | `--tls-server` |
| `tls-client` | | Uses SSL certificates and act as TLS client during TLS handshake | `--tls-client` |
| `ca` | `<file>` | Your generated CA file | `--ca /CA.crt` |
| `dh` | `<file>` | Your generated Diffie-Hellman key | `--dh /DH.pem` |

| Parameter | Options | Function | Usage |
|---|---|---|---|
| cert | <file> | Your server's local certificate file | --cert /SERVER.crt |
| key | <file> | Your server's local key file | --key /SERVER/key.pem |
| pkcs12 | <file> | PKCS12 file (containing certificate, key, and CA in one file) | --pkcs12 /file |
| crl-verify | <file> | Certificate revocation list | --tls-verify /revoke.crl |
| no-replay | | Disables OpenVPN's protection against replay attacks | --no-replay |
| no-iv | | Disables OpenVPN's use of Cipher Initialization Vector (IV) | --no-iv |

The following parameters may be new to you. In most cases you do not need to make any changes here:

- cipher: Here you can specify a different algorithm for transport encryption. Have a look at the option --show-ciphers below to receive a list of available algorithms.
- keysize: You can specify a different key size for the cipher algorithm that you chose with the --cipher parameter. The option --show-ciphers (below) shows the default key sizes.
- auth: OpenVPN uses SHA1 with HMAC to authenticate packets. No changes should be necessary here, but with the option auth none you could disable authentication.
- pkcs12: This is a file format in which CA certificate, server certificate, and local key are packed together. Using such a file would replace the directives --ca, --cert, and --key.
- no-replay and no-iv: These disable basic security mechanisms that OpenVPN provides. Do not deactivate these unless you know what you are doing. These parameters switch off basic security functions and will leave your system insecure.
- crl-verify: This defines the file in which a certificate revocation list is stored. Such a list contains certificates that are no longer valid for use with our OpenVPN tunnels.

> The parameter crl-revoke <file> specifies the file containing the certificate revocation list.

## Testing the Crypto System with --test-crypto

With the command-line parameter --test-crypto we will now test the cryptographic system of our VPN server with a static key.

| Parameter | Options | Function | Usage |
|---|---|---|---|
| test-crypto | | Command line only. Do a self-test of OpenVPN's crypto options by encrypting and decrypting test packets using the data channel encryption options specified above. | --test-crypto |

```
debian01:/etc/openvpn# openvpn --test-crypto --secret /etc/openvpn/key.txt
Sat Nov 19 10:20:38 2005 OpenVPN 2.0.5 i486-pc-linux-gnu [SSL] [LZO] [EPOLL]
built on Nov  7 2005
Sat Nov 19 10:20:38 2005 OpenVPN 2.0.5 i486-pc-linux-gnu [SSL] [LZO] [EPOLL]
built on Nov  7 2005
Sat Nov 19 10:20:38 2005 WARNING: file '/etc/openvpn/key.txt' is group or
others accessible
Sat Nov 19 10:20:38 2005 Entering OpenVPN crypto self-test mode.
Sat Nov 19 10:20:38 2005 TESTING ENCRYPT/DECRYPT of packet length=1
Sat Nov 19 10:20:38 2005 TESTING ENCRYPT/DECRYPT of packet length=2
Sat Nov 19 10:20:38 2005 TESTING ENCRYPT/DECRYPT of packet length=3
Sat Nov 19 10:20:38 2005 TESTING ENCRYPT/DECRYPT of packet length=4
Sat Nov 19 10:20:38 2005 TESTING ENCRYPT/DECRYPT of packet length=5
Sat Nov 19 10:20:38 2005 TESTING ENCRYPT/DECRYPT of packet length=6

(..)
Sat Nov 19 10:19:56 2005 TESTING ENCRYPT/DECRYPT of packet length=1495
Sat Nov 19 10:19:56 2005 TESTING ENCRYPT/DECRYPT of packet length=1496
Sat Nov 19 10:19:56 2005 TESTING ENCRYPT/DECRYPT of packet length=1497
Sat Nov 19 10:19:56 2005 TESTING ENCRYPT/DECRYPT of packet length=1498
Sat Nov 19 10:19:56 2005 TESTING ENCRYPT/DECRYPT of packet length=1499
Sat Nov 19 10:19:56 2005 TESTING ENCRYPT/DECRYPT of packet length=1500
Sat Nov 19 10:19:56 2005 OpenVPN crypto self-test mode SUCCEEDED.
debian01:/etc/openvpn#
```

Everything looks fine; the crypto system is working well. It has successfully encrypted and decrypted `1500` packets with our pre-shared key without any errors.

## SSL Information—Command Line

| Parameter | Function |
|---|---|
| `openvpn --show-ciphers` | Shows all available cipher algorithms for use with the `--cipher` option |
| `openvpn --show-digests` | Shows all available message digest algorithms to use with the `--auth` option |
| `openvpn --show-tls` | Shows the available TLS ciphers in a list sorted from highest preference and security to lowest |
| `openvpn --engine` | Uses a specific SSL-based hardware encryption engine |
| `openvpn --show-engines` | Shows available hardware-based crypto engines |

The following examples give an overview of the standard output of OpenVPN's cryptographic engines. First, we will ask for a list of the cipher algorithms that can be used for transport encryption, which can be set using the `--cipher` parameter:

```
debian01:/etc/openvpn# openvpn --show-ciphers
The following ciphers and cipher modes are available
for use with OpenVPN.  Each cipher shown below may be
used as a parameter to the --cipher option.  The default
key size is shown as well as whether or not it can be
changed with the --keysize directive.  Using a CBC mode
is recommended.

DES-CBC 64 bit default key (fixed)
RC2-CBC 128 bit default key (variable)
DES-EDE-CBC 128 bit default key (fixed)
DES-EDE3-CBC 192 bit default key (fixed)
DESX-CBC 192 bit default key (fixed)
```

```
BF-CBC 128 bit default key (variable)
RC2-40-CBC 40 bit default key (variable)
CAST5-CBC 128 bit default key (variable)
RC2-64-CBC 64 bit default key (variable)
AES-128-CBC 128 bit default key (fixed)
AES-192-CBC 192 bit default key (fixed)
AES-256-CBC 256 bit default key (fixed)

debian01:/etc/openvpn#
```

The last entry, `AES-256-CBC 256`, is the safest one; `BF-CBC 128` is the default. Remember that using safer algorithms causes more traffic overhead—maybe a price to pay.

The parameter `--show-digests` lists all available digest methods for use with the `--auth` parameter in the configuration file:

```
debian01:/etc/openvpn# openvpn --show-digests
The following message digests are available for use with
OpenVPN.  A message digest is used in conjunction with
the HMAC function, to authenticate received packets.
You can specify a message digest as parameter to
the --auth option.

MD2 128 bit digest size
MD5 128 bit digest size
RSA-MD2 128 bit digest size
RSA-MD5 128 bit digest size
SHA 160 bit digest size
RSA-SHA 160 bit digest size
SHA1 160 bit digest size
RSA-SHA1 160 bit digest size
DSA-SHA 160 bit digest size
DSA-SHA1-old 160 bit digest size
DSA-SHA1 160 bit digest size
RSA-SHA1-2 160 bit digest size
DSA 160 bit digest size
RIPEMD160 160 bit digest size
RSA-RIPEMD160 160 bit digest size
MD4 128 bit digest size
RSA-MD4 128 bit digest size
ecdsa-with-SHA1 160 bit digest size
RSA-SHA256 256 bit digest size
RSA-SHA384 384 bit digest size
RSA-SHA512 512 bit digest size
RSA-SHA224 224 bit digest size
SHA256 256 bit digest size
SHA384 384 bit digest size
SHA512 512 bit digest size
SHA224 224 bit digest size

debian01:/etc/openvpn#
```

The standard is `SHA 160`; the entries in this list rank from insecure (but fast) to safe and slow.

This does not applies for the list of TLS methods available; this list is in `order of preference`, which means the first method is the safest (and slowest) one.

```
debian01:/etc/openvpn# openvpn --show-tls
Available TLS Ciphers,
listed in order of preference:

DHE-RSA-AES256-SHA
DHE-DSS-AES256-SHA
AES256-SHA
```

```
EDH-RSA-DES-CBC3-SHA
EDH-DSS-DES-CBC3-SHA
DES-CBC3-SHA
DHE-RSA-AES128-SHA
DHE-DSS-AES128-SHA
AES128-SHA
DHE-DSS-RC4-SHA
RC4-SHA
RC4-MD5
EXP1024-DHE-DSS-DES-CBC-SHA
EXP1024-DES-CBC-SHA
EXP1024-RC2-CBC-MD5
EDH-RSA-DES-CBC-SHA
EDH-DSS-DES-CBC-SHA
DES-CBC-SHA
EXP1024-DHE-DSS-RC4-SHA
EXP1024-RC4-SHA
EXP1024-RC4-MD5
EXP-EDH-RSA-DES-CBC-SHA
EXP-EDH-DSS-DES-CBC-SHA
EXP-DES-CBC-SHA
EXP-RC2-CBC-MD5
EXP-RC4-MD5

debian01:/etc/openvpn#
```

And last, but not least, OpenVPN (and SSL/TLS in particular) can support hardware encryption devices. The parameter `--show-engines` lists available engines for such devices.

```
debian01:/etc/openvpn# openvpn --show-engines
OpenSSL Crypto Engines

Dynamic engine loading support [dynamic]
debian01:/etc/openvpn#
```

In our configuration file or at the command line, such an engine can be specified for usage with the `--engine` parameter.

> OpenVPN provides several tools that list available cryptographic algorithms: `--show-tls`, `--show-ciphers`, and `--show-digests`. OpenVPN can be instructed to use a specific mechanism in the configuration file or at the command line.

## Server Mode

A very powerful parameter has been available since OpenVPN version 2: `--server`. This parameter can replace the `ifconfig` directive that is used to set up networking over TUN/TAP devices, and provide IPs and network config dynamically for clients.

| Parameter | Options | Function | Usage |
|---|---|---|---|
| `server` | `<network>` `<mask>` | Sets the network addresses that are assigned to clients | `--server 10.3.0.0 255.255.255.0` |

We must notice that `--server` implies TLS mode automatically, thus a directive like `--server 10.3.0.0 255.255.255.0` implies the following:

- The VPN Software on this machine acts as a server for the tunnel described in this configuration (or in this command)
- This tunnel will be run in TLS-server mode— certificates are required
- Clients logging into this tunnel will be provided with an IP address from the network mask specified as option.

In our example above, TLS-certified clients will receive IPs between `10.3.0.1` and `10.3.0.254`. With TUN devices (running a virtual point-to-point connection), a /30 subnet is necessary for every connection, thus 128 clients can connect to this server. If we need a bridged network, the directive `server-bridge` is very helpful:

| Parameter | Options | Function | Usage |
|---|---|---|---|
| `server-bridge` | `gateway mask pool` | Server mode for bridging devices (TAP) | `--server bridge 10.3.0.1 255.255.255.0 10.3.0.128 10.3.0.254` |

The example would provide addresses from `10.3.0.128` to `10.3.0.254` and tell the (TLS-authenticated only) clients to use `10.3.0.1` as gateway in a bridged tunnel setup.

To be honest, `--server` is only a sort of *shortcut* for the directives setting server mode, TLS server, and network addresses. We will deal with these parameters in the next section, just note that there is a parameter called `--mode` that can be called with an option `server`.

| Parameter | Options | Function | Usage |
|---|---|---|---|
| `<mode>` | `<server>` | Switches on openvpn server mode (since version 2) | `--mode server` |
| | `<p2p>` (default) | mode p2p is not necessary | `--mode p2p` |

> `--mode server` switches on server mode in an OpenVPN tunnel. The directives `--server` and `--server-bridge` are handier, since they allow setting relevant easily data and switch on TLS automatically.

## Server Mode Parameters

You may have noticed that there are several functions included in the parameter `--server` that we have not dealt with, like defining an IP range for clients logging into the VPN. The following table gives an overview of parameters useful for such issues:

| Parameter | Options | Function | Usage |
|---|---|---|---|
| `push` | `<options>` | Allows *pushing* of configuration data to the client. (See later section for further options.) | `--push route 192.168.0.0 255.255.255.0` |

| Parameter | Options | Function | Usage |
|---|---|---|---|
| ifconfig-pool | <start-IP> <end-IP> <mask> | Defines a range of IP addresses to be used for the tunnel subnet. | --ifconfig-pool 10.1.0.1 10.1.0.10 255.255.255.0 |
| ifconfig-pool-persist | <file> <seconds> | Ensures IP associations for clients—so that clients will always (hopefully) be assigned the same IP. IP-to-client associations will be written to <file> every <seconds>. | --ifconfig-pool-persist /etc/openvpn/IPs 100 |
| client-to-client | - | All clients are allowed to connect to each other. | --client-to-client |
| tmp-dir | <directory> | Specifies a directory for temporary files. | --tmp-dir /etc/openvpn/tmp |
| max-clients | <number> | Maximum number of clients allowed to connect. | --max-clients 5 |
| max-routes-per-client | <number> | Maximum number of routes possible for a single client. | --max-routes-per-client 5 |
| connect-freq | <number> <seconds> | A client is allowed to connect this <number> of connections per specified <seconds> as maximum. | --connect-freq 5 120 |
| learn-address | <cmd> | Shell script command <script> to validate client virtual addresses or routes. | --learn-address /etc/openvpn/script.sh |
| auth-user-pass-verify | <script> <method> | OpenVPN will execute script as a shell command to validate the username/password provided by the client. | --auth-user-pass |
| client-cert-not-required | | Doesn't require client certificate; client will authenticate using username/password only. | - -client-cert-not-required |
| duplicate -cn | - | Uses one client certificate for several (or all) clients. | --duplicate.cn |

The following parameters are my favorites in server mode:

- `--push`: A complete new scope of VPN functionality is opened up here. The table in the section *Push Options* shows how you can *push* configuration options to clients connecting to the VPN on initialization of the connection.
- `--ifconfig-pool` and `--ifconfig-pool-persist`: Define in detail how and which IP addresses the server is supposed to provide to clients connecting.
- `--client-to-client`: If your VPN clients need connections between them, this option will help. Simply adding

  ```
  (...)
  client-to-client
  (...)
  ```

  to the configuration file will enable clients to connect to each other through the tunnels.

- `--max-clients` and `--max-routes-per-client`: Restrict the number of clients that are allowed to connect to the VPN server and the number of routes that are allowed to be set to one client.
- `--client-cert-not-required` and `--duplicate-cn`: You may *loosen* certificate restrictions a little, but this may be dangerous!
- `--auth-user-pass-verify <script><method>`: This is really handy. A script is called for authentication; the method specified is used to pass authentication data received from the client to this script.

The method `via-env` for example, calls a script with the parameters `username` and `password`, expecting a return code of 0 for success, 1 for failure. Can you imagine what a simple Perl script can do here? Authentication against Active Directory, **Lightweight Directory Access Protocol (LDAP)**, and many more are possible. Sample scripts can be found in the source-code package of OpenVPN, in the file `sample-scripts/auth-pam.pl`.

The file `/usr/share/doc/openvpn/README.auth-pam` holds information on the usage of the Linux Authentication Standard **Pluggable Authentication Modules (PAM)** for authentication of VPN clients. PAM itself is built on a modular basis, so that none of your wishes should be unfulfilled.

> OpenVPN in server mode can assign IPs dynamically to clients, but you can specify exceptions. Client-to-client connections are possible, and certificates can be used for multiple clients. The parameter `--auth-user-pass-verify` can be used to verify passwords and usernames against PAM or arbitrary scripts.

## --client-config Options

We have learned by now that TLS clients can be assigned individual configurations based on the common name of their certificates. For this purpose, we only need to create a client configuration directory, tell openvpn where this directory is to be found, and put our client configurations in this directory. The name of the client configuration file must be identical with the common name of the certificate the client uses. This is very important: Only with this field in the certificate can openvpn distinguish the clients. A client with the common name `server1` in its certificate must be configured with `server1.conf` in the client configuration directory. The name of this file can not be chosen.

The parameter `-client-config-dir` is used to tell openvpn where to look for the clients' configurations:

| Parameter | Options | Function | Usage |
|---|---|---|---|
| `client-config-dir` | `<directory>` | The path to our client configuration directory | `--client-config-dir /etc/openvpn/clients` |
| `ccd-exclusive` | | Requires, as a condition of authentication that a connecting client has a `--client-config-dir` file | `--ccd-exclusive` |

The parameter ccd-exclusive allows connections only for clients that have a client configuration file in the client configuration directory.

In a client configuration file almost all parameters and options used in a normal configuration file can be used along with the following parameters, which are only valid in a client configuration file:

| Parameter | Options | Function | Usage |
|---|---|---|---|
| client-connect | <script> | Runs script when a client connects successfully | --client-connect /file.sh |
| client-disconnect | <script> | Runs script when a client disconnects successfully | --client-disconnect |
| ifconfig-push | <IP> <IP> | Pushes IP endpoints for client tunnels, overriding the settings from ifconfig-pool—useful in client-specific configurations (on the server) | |
| iroute | <network> <netmask> | Generates an internal route to a specific network via a VPN client | --iroute 10.94.0.0 255.255.255.0 |

- --client-connect and -client-disconnect: Allow execution of scripts on connection or disconnection of a client of our VPN—another handy possibility for solving many interesting issues.
- --ifconfig-push: Sets the IP of the tunnel endpoints for this connection to different values than specified with ifconfig-pool; a convenient method of specifying a fixed IP for a client.
- --iroute: Allows setting an internal route to a network *behind* a VPN client, enabling partners on the server side to access the network behind the tunnel (on the client's side).This parameter is very interesting in a scenario like the following: Mr. Smith connects to the VPN server of his company from the LAN at his home with the network address 10.94.0.0/24. He is working on the terminal server in the central branch of his company. Now he wants to print a document, but on a network printer 10.94.0.200 in his home LAN. To fulfill this, the terminal server must have configured this network printer, and therefore it needs to know how to route to 10.94.0.200. Besides setting the route on the company's default gateway pointing to the VPN server, the VPN server itself must also know that this network address is behind the VPN client. All machines that act as routers in this scenario must be configured to do forwarding, including correct firewall setup and access rights to the printer. In our scenario, both VPN partners (also the VPN client machine) must have forwarding enabled!

## Client Mode Parameters

The following table shows parameters that are relevant if your VPN machine acts as a TLS client to a VPN server. --client stands here, similarly to --server, as a shortcut for two parameters: --tls-client and -pull. We have talked about --tls-client, but not about -pull, which simply tells openvpn to try to get routes and network configuration from the VPN server.

| Parameter | Options | Function | Usage |
|---|---|---|---|
| client | | Simply pull TLS server option. | --client |
| pull | | Gets pushed routes and more from the server. | --pull |
| auth-user-pass | <file> | Authenticates to the server using the username/password pair specified on two lines in <file>. | --auth-user-pass /etc/openvpn/passes |
| auth-retry | <interact><br><noninteract><br><none> | Determines the client's behavior on authentication failure.<br><interact>: The client will prompt the user.<br><non-interact>: The client will keep on trying.<br><none>: The client will exit with an error message. | --auth-retry noninteract |

- auth-user-pass and auth-retry: They are the client's settings for authentication with a password, where auth-user-pass simply wants a file with a username/password pair in it. If called as -auth-user-pass up, openvpn will prompt for the username/password pair. All of this will only work if the server has -auth-user-pass-verify configured properly.
- auth-retry: With this parameter, we can specify how OpenVPN clients deal with authorization errors or failures. Unattended systems should be set to --non-interactive because otherwise they would stop connecting if a connection error occurs. A road warrior's laptop can be configured to prompt the user because there might be other problems that prevent the tunnel (firewalls?). And none is the best solution for the paranoid—If authentication fails just once, no further attempt to set up a tunnel will be made; the openvpn process exits.

## Push Options

Pushing configuration parameters to clients is one of the really great features of openvpn.

| Parameter | Options | Function | Usage |
|---|---|---|---|
| push | <configuration options> | Push the <configuration options> to the client. | push "route 192.168.20.0 255.255.255.0" |

An OpenVPN server (running in server mode) can push the following settings to a client (that has the *pull* parameter enabled). You should know most of them by now; can you imagine how they work without looking in the right column? (Only the last two are new.)

| Push Parameter Option | Function |
|---|---|
| `--route` | The client will set a route. |
| `--route-gateway` | The client will set its gateway. |
| `--route-delay` | The client will wait a little before setting its routes. |
| `--redirect-gateway` | The client will redirect its gateway through the VPN. |
| `--inactive` | The client will exit after a specified time. |
| `--ping`, `--ping-exit`, `--ping-restart` | The client will change its ping behavior. |
| `--persist-key`, `--persist-tun` | The client will change its behavior on restart. |
| `--comp-lzo` | The client will use compression. |
| `--dhcp-option` | The client will use specific DHCP options (Windows only, see below). |
| `--ip-win32` | The client will use the method specified to set IPs and network addresses (Windows only, see below). |

It's very important to set the quotation marks correctly. Anything between them will be sent to the client as a configuration directive.

> A VPN server can push routing, network, and DHCP options to a client. Ping behavior and other features can be controlled by the server and set on connection initialization.

# Important Windows-Specific Options

A fast-growing number of options can only be used on Windows clients, because other systems can't deal with the methods used. The following table gives an overview of these:

| Parameter | Options | Function | Usage |
|---|---|---|---|
| `dhcp-option` | `WINS <IP>`<br>`DNS <IP>`<br>`DOMAIN <name>`<br>`NBDD <IP>`<br>`NTP <IP>`<br>`NBT <type>`<br>`NBS <scope-id>`<br>`DISABLE-NBT` | Sets specific DHCP data over the VPN for Windows clients:<br>Sets a specific DNS or WINS server via DHCP, set domain name, NetBIOS server address, network time server, and more. | `--push "dhcp-option DNS 10.94.46.11"` |
| `route-method` | `ipapi`<br>`exe` | Sets the method Windows uses to set routes, either by executing the route command (`exe`) or by using the IPAPI interface. | `--route-method ipapi` |
| `ip-win32` | `<method>` | Sets the Windows Network adapter's IP and netmask using `<method>` | `--ip-win32 ipapi` |

Are you ready for an example? Read the following command line and write down what it does:

```
openvpn --port 5001 --proto udp --dev tun --ca ca1.crt --cert opteron.crt --
key opteron.pem   /
--crl-verify revoke.crl --dh dh2048.pem --server 10.79.2.0 255.255.255.0  /
--push "route 10.19.46.0 255.255.255.0" --push "route 10.18.46.0
255.255.255.0"  /
--push "dhcp-option DNS 10.10.16.15"  --push "dhcp-option WINS 10.10.16.12"  /
--client-to-client --keepalive 10 60 --comp-lzo  /
--status /var/log/openvpn/openvpn-road-status2.log  /
--log-append  /var/log/openvpn/openvpn-road2.log  --verb 4
```

Here is the solution:

This openvpn command starts a TLS server listening on port UDP 5001 with the specified certificates, key, and revoke list files. The virtual network has the address 10.79.2.0/24, clients are *pushed* several routes and DHCP options, (which means they are probably Windows clients), clients are allowed to connect to each other, the traffic is compressed, and log and status messages are written to files in /varlog/openvpn at a verbosity of 4.

# Summary

In this chapter we started with explaining the syntax of openvpn and its configuration file. Parameters that are in our standard configuration file were followed by the ones used during setup of a certificate-based tunnel. From then on we traveled through the basic tunnel parameters, encryption, server and client mode, and we finished this chapter with parameters that are only available on Windows systems.

# 8

# Securing OpenVPN Tunnels and Servers

In this chapter we will learn how to make the example tunnels we created safer and persistent by choosing a safe combination of configuration file parameters. We will then discuss how to install and use a firewall with a convenient web-based configuration interface on a standard Linux system, namely Shorewall on a Debian system. After that we will have a look at the **SuSEfirewall 2** that comes with OpenSuSE. A short look will deal with how to configure the Windows XP firewall for use with OpenVPN. Last but not least, we will discuss the possibilities that the Linux command line offers (especially with the examples that come with OpenVPN).

## Securing and Stabilizing OpenVPN

Up to now, we have built several tunnels and all of them were built with simple mechanisms and focused on simplicity. In this chapter, we will set up an OpenVPN server and tunnels that can be used in a production environment. For this purpose we will use strong encryption layers, which OpenVPN offers, and set some parameters in our config file to make sure that OpenVPN keeps running. This will be our first task.

Here is a configuration file for our VPN server for enabling access only for one client. Perhaps it's a good idea that you have a look at the following options and parameters before you read on. This is far from perfect, especially because there is a constant development concerning security going on and hence I do not try to give an example with the highest possible security. Nevertheless, there are some features enabled in this configuration that have proven very helpful:

```
float
dev tunVPN0
tun-mtu 1500
ifconfig 10.179.10.1 10.179.10.2
port 5000
route 10.194.0.0 255.255.0.0 10.179.10.2
comp-lzo
auth SHA512
cipher AES-256-CBC
tls-cipher DHE-RSA-AES256-SHA
tls-auth keys/tls-key.txt
tls-server
tls-remote "/C=DE/ST=BY/O=Feilner-IT/CN=VPN-
```

```
Client/emailAddress=security@feilner-it.net"
ca certs/ca.crt
cert certs/server.crt
key certs/server.key
dh dh2048.pem
keepalive 10 60
shaper 20000
route-up "/sbin/firewall restart"
log-append /var/log/openvpn/feilner-it.log
status /var/log/openvpn/feilner-it.status 5
```

An explanation of the options and parameters of the config file is as follows:

- `float`: The VPN server accepts connections from clients even if their IPs change.
- `dev tunVPN0`: We will use the network device `tunVPN0` for connections. Because the name of the device can be chosen freely, it may be a good idea to use a significant name.
- `ifconfig`: These are the virtual IPs of our tunnel network.
- `port`: We will use port `5000` for the VPN communication.
- `route`: This server is told that the subnet `10.194.0.0` is behind the other end of the tunnel.
- `comp-lzo`: All traffic will be compressed before transport
- We tell OpenVPN to use stronger encryption methods than the standard methods:

  ```
  auth SHA512
  cipher AES-256-CBC
  tls-cipher DHE-RSA-AES256-SHA
  ```

  Use the commands `openvpn --show-ciphers`, `openvpn --show-digests`, and `openvpn --show-tls` to find out the encryption mechanisms available on both systems. There will be differences depending on the operating systems and software versions used. You must use methods that both systems are capable of.

  The values in the file listed are merely examples that will differ from your real setup.
- `tls-auth`: This provides a simple **Denial of Service** (**DOS**) protection. DOS is a kind of attack where somebody tries to *flood* your machine and thereby slow down (or stop) regular connections. An OpenVPN machine with `tls-auth` activated will only accept packets encrypted with the correct HMAC signature generated from the key specified in the file (e.g. `tls-key.txt`). The OpenVPN manpage speaks of an "HMAC Firewall". This option should always be applied when your system is accepting connections from varying IPs.
- `tls-server`: Specifies the role that the OpenVPN machine will take for setting up the tunnel and exchanging certificates.
- `tls-remote "/C=DE/ST=BY/O=Feilner-IT/CN=server2/emailAddress=security@feilner-it.net"`: Specifies the exact subject line of the VPN partner's certificate. This line makes sure that only the VPN partner presenting this certificate is allowed to connect to our VPN. You can extract this line from your certificate file. At a verbosity level of `5` or higher, you will also find this "subject" line explicitly in the log file of your VPN machines.

- The following lines specify the location of TLS certificates and keys and the Diffie-Hellman key:
  ```
  ca certs/ca.crt
  cert certs/server.crt
  key certs/server.key
  dh dh2048.pem
  ```
- `keepalive 10 60`: We add these parameters ensuring that the tunnel will be restarted automatically
- `shaper`: This option must be used on both sides, and limits the traffic through this tunnel to about 20K
- The last three lines define a firewall script that is run when the tunnel is set up and the location of log and status files.

Our VPN client should receive basically the same configuration, with changes only to the location and names of files and certificates. We will need to type the subject line of the certificate of the server here and we will need a `remote` directive telling our client where to connect to and that our system will be trying to resolve the other hostname for one day before giving up:

```
remote xxx.dyndns.org
(...)
tls-remote "/C=DE/ST=BY/O=Feilner-IT/CN=VPN-
Server/emailAddress=security@feilner-it.net"
(...)
resolv-retry 86400
```

So how can we sum this up in a nutshell?

> With the configuration above:
>
> Our OpenVPN server will only start the connection setup process from an OpenVPN client that authenticates with the correct HMAC signature generated by a static, pre-shared key. The connection process will only be successful, if both partners know and can handle the correct ciphers and encryption methods specified. Only the machine offering the X509 certificate specified in the line starting with `tls-remote` will be accepted.

Some lines of this configuration help re-establishing the tunnel after connection errors and make sure that the systems will try to resolve DNS for one day before giving up.

I guess this configuration is not yet paranoid, but already quite secure, as long as we are careful with our keys and certificates.

# Linux and Firewalls

Now that OpenVPN is configured safely, how about the system that it runs on? On Linux there are several excellent firewall solutions that can be used with OpenVPN. On the following pages we will deal with two firewalls, which offer graphical interfaces for configuration—Shorewall (with Webmin) and the SuSEfirewall as delivered with OpenSuSE 10.

## Debian Linux and Webmin with Shorewall

Webmin is an excellent GUI for Linux system management, if your preference is for web-based administration. Webmin can be found on www.webmin.com and offers almost full control over your Linux systems. It brings a small web server of its own and supports SSL encryption, user management, and more. However, I do not want to conceal the fact that there are Perl scripts that set system variables in files at /etc, which is not considered best practice. However, as always, security and usability are enemies and the compromises may vary. If we use Webmin, we must secure access to it. A good idea is a separate OpenVPN tunnel for it.

### Installing Webmin and Shorewall

Besides Webmin, we will enable SSH access to our Debian system. If you haven't installed an SSH server, simply type apt-get install ssh on your system. Don't forget to update your package database and software before you install new software. Enter apt-get update && apt-get upgrade and make sure that this works. Next, let's install Webmin. One of the beautiful features of Debian Linux is the fact that the package management system resolves all problems for us. Thus we simply type apt-get install webmin-shorewall and all of Webmin, Shorewall, and related modules will be installed automatically for us:

```
debian03:~# apt-get install webmin-shorewall
Reading Package Lists... Done
Building Dependency Tree... Done
The following extra packages will be installed:
  gawk iproute libatm1 libauthen-pam-perl libmd5-perl libnet-ssleay-perl
man2html openssl perl
  perl-modules shorewall webmin webmin-core webmin-mailboxes
Suggested packages:
  manpages-dev swish++ lynx www-browser ca-certificates libterm-readline-gnu-
perl
  libterm-readline-perl-perl shorewall-doc kernel-image-2.4 kernel-image-2.6
linux-image-2.6 make
  webmin-lvm mdctl mdadm
Recommended packages:
  apache httpd-cgi perl-doc logcheck
The following NEW packages will be installed:
  gawk iproute libatm1 libauthen-pam-perl libmd5-perl libnet-ssleay-perl
man2html openssl perl
  perl-modules shorewall webmin webmin-core webmin-mailboxes webmin-shorewall
0 upgraded, 15 newly installed, 0 to remove and 24 not upgraded.
Need to get 11.7MB of archives.
After unpacking 51.6MB of additional disk space will be used.
Do you want to continue? [Y/n]
```

Enter *Y* to start download and installation. The software will be downloaded and the configuration script is started. You are told that Webmin uses a separate password file in /etc/webmin/miniserv.users. Confirm this dialog with the Ok button.

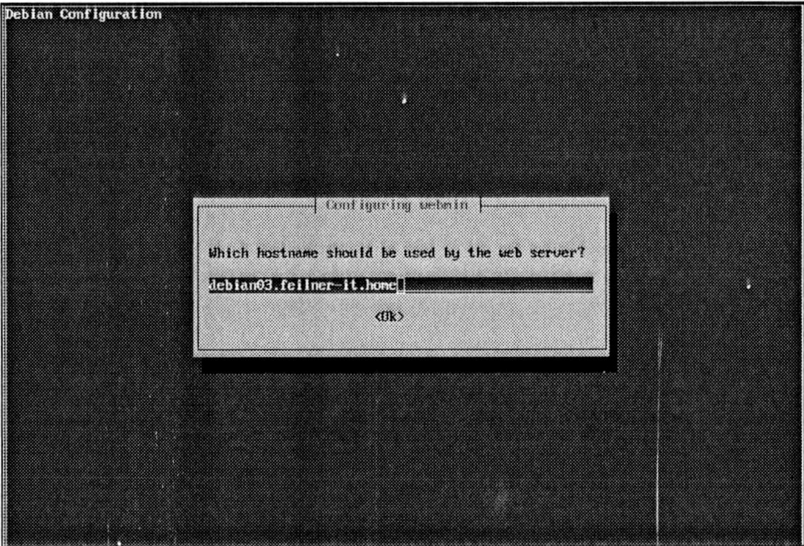


The second dialog needs some input from you. Enter your fully qualified hostname here and confirm with Ok. That's all—Webmin and Shorewall are downloaded and installed. The following lines of output are the feedback you get when everything works fine:

```
(...)
Setting up shorewall (3.0.1-1) ...
#### WARNING ####
the firewall won't be started/stopped unless it is configured

please configure it and then edit /etc/default/shorewall
and set the "startup" variable to 1 in order to allow
shorewall to start
#################

Setting up webmin (1.230-1) ...
md5sum: miniserv.pem: No such file or directory
Starting webmin: webmin.

Setting up webmin-core (1.230-1) ...

Setting up webmin-mailboxes (1.200-1) ...

Setting up webmin-shorewall (1.220-1) ...

debian03:~#
```

However, there are some small adjustments that you need to make:

- Webmin must be secured and configured.
- Shorewall must be configured and started. (You can see from the earlier output that this is not done automatically.)

## Preparing Webmin and Shorewall for the First Start

After installation, you find Webmin installed in `/usr/share/webmin` and the Webmin configuration in `/etc/webmin`. The file `miniserv.conf` contains the basic configuration for access and authentication:

```
debian03:/etc# cat /etc/webmin/miniserv.conf
root=/usr/share/webmin
mimetypes=/etc/mime.types
port=10000
host=debian03.feilner-it.home
addtype_cgi=internal/cgi
realm=Webmin Server
logfile=/var/log/webmin/miniserv.log
pidfile=/var/run/webmin.pid
logtime=168
ssl=1
env_WEBMIN_CONFIG=/etc/webmin
env_WEBMIN_VAR=/var/log/webmin
logout=/etc/webmin/logout-flag
listen=10000
userfile=/etc/webmin/miniserv.users
keyfile=/etc/webmin/miniserv.pem
libwrap=1
alwaysresolve=1
allow=127.0.0.1
blockhost_time=300
no_pam=0
logouttime=5
passdelay=1
session=1
blockhost_failures=3
syslog=1
log=1
logclear=
loghost=1
preroot=debiantheme
ppath=
atboot=1
denyfile=\.pl$
extraroot_0=/usr/local/share/webmin
debian03:/etc#
```

The Webmin documentation on the website is the best place to look for the meaning of these options; at this point you will only need to change one line:

Change the line `allow=127.0.0.1` to the address of the client that you want to use for accessing Webmin and type `/etc/init.d/webmin restart`.

Webmin can now be reached from the system you specified with a standard browser (supporting cookies and JavaScript is recommended, but not necessary) on the URL `https://ip-of-our-webmin-server:10000`.

There are only two small changes to configuration files in the Shorewall setup that need editing:

1. Set the parameter `startup=0` to `startup=1` in `/etc/default/shorewall`:

```
# prevent startup with default configuration
# set the below variable to 1 in order to allow shorewall to start
startup=1

# if your shorewall's configuration need to detect the ip address of a ppp
# interface you must list such interface in "wait_interface" to get
```

```
# shorewall to wait until the interface is configured otherwise the script
# will fail because it won't be able to detect the address.
#
# Example:
#    wait_interface="ppp0"
# or
#    wait_interface="ppp0 ppp1"
# or, if you have defined  in /etc/shorewall/params
#    wait_interface=

# EOF
```

2. Enable forwarding in `/etc/shorewall/shorewall.conf` by changing the line `IP_FORWARDING=Keep` to `IP_FORWARDING=On`.

```
#
# ENABLE IP FORWARDING
#
# If you say "On" or "on" here, IPV4 Packet Forwarding is enabled. If you
# say "Off" or "off", packet forwarding will be disabled. You would only
# want to disable packet forwarding if you are installing Shorewall on a
# standalone system or if you want all traffic through the Shorewall
# system to be handled by proxies.
#
# If you set this variable to "Keep" or "keep", Shorewall will neither
# enable nor disable packet forwarding.
#
IP_FORWARDING=On
```

## Starting Webmin

Start your favorite browser and enter the IP address of your Webmin server in the URL field followed by the port number `10000`. In my example, I log in to Webmin through a VPN tunnel. The screenshot is taken from Firefox on an OpenSuSE system, which has the (tunnel) IP `10.179.10.1`. Therefore, I enter `https://10.179.10.1:10000` in the URL field of my browser.

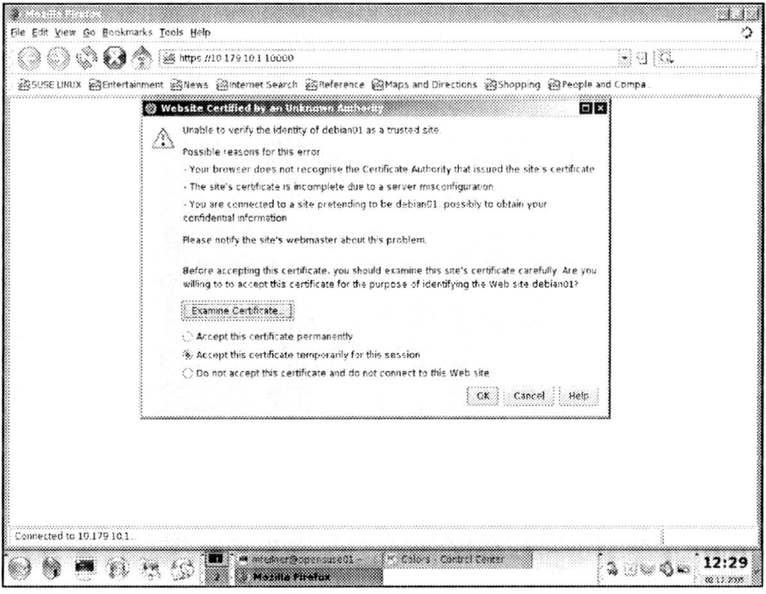

As you can see, the Webmin connection is secured by SSL again. I leave it up to you to decide which machines are allowed to access Webmin under what circumstances, but a HTTPS-secured connection over a OpenVPN tunnel should be safe enough (especially, if you have configured your tunnel as described earlier).

At this moment, Webmin will still use the standard certificate that is delivered with the software. Click on the button OK to accept this certificate temporarily, and log into Webmin in the next dialog:

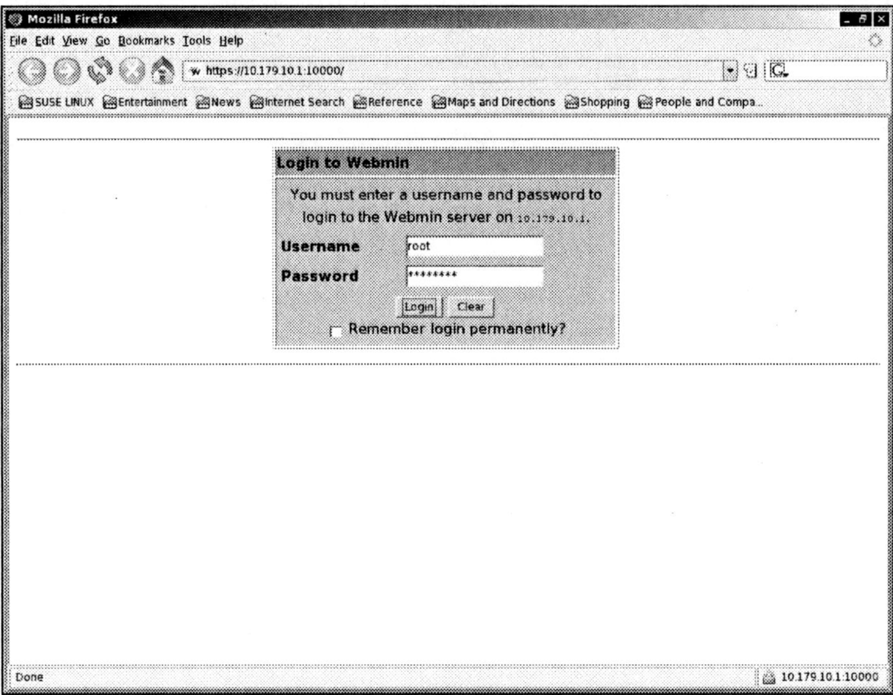


In this dialog, you must enter the root password for your Webmin machine. It is a good idea to add a non-privileged Webmin user who is allowed only to access specific Webmin services.

The following screenshot shows the standard Webmin interface. There are categories and modules. Categories are aligned horizontally, and each category holds a list of available modules represented by icons. We are now in the category Webmin, where we can adjust the configuration of Webmin itself:

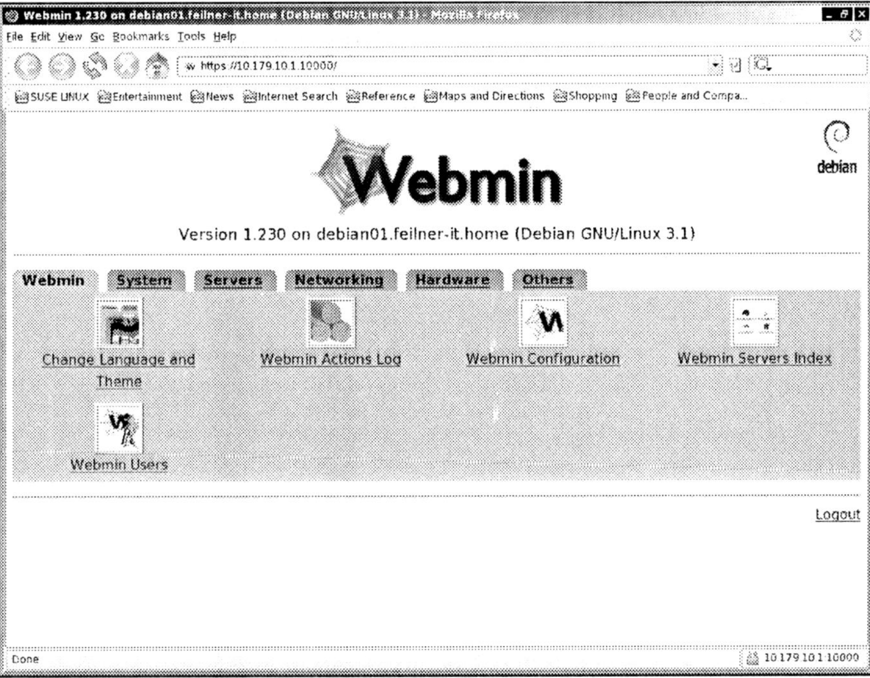


Click on the Webmin Configuration option and then on SSL Encryption.

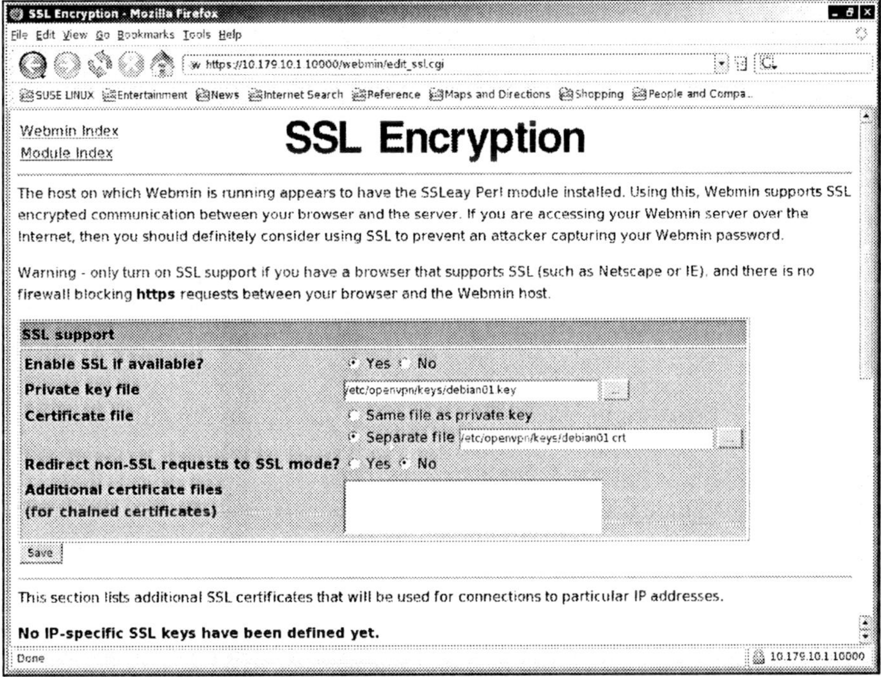

There are two settings in this module that are relevant for us: Private key file and Certificate file.

Of course we can use the certificates generated by OpenVPN's `easy-rsa` for Webmin too, and the best way to do this is generating certificates for Webmin. Perhaps you type something like `webmin-server01` or similar in the Common Name field of the certificate and key. If you have certificates, you only have to put them on the server running Webmin and enter the path in the fields in this dialog. By doing so, you have certificates nobody else is using, which is definitely not true of the original Webmin certificates. In the example above, the keys are placed in `/etc/openvpn/keys`, but you can choose the location freely.

Click on Save to make your changes valid.

Now let's add a user for us to use with Webmin only for firewall configuration. Go to Webmin | Webmin Users and click on the Create a new Webmin user hyperlink.

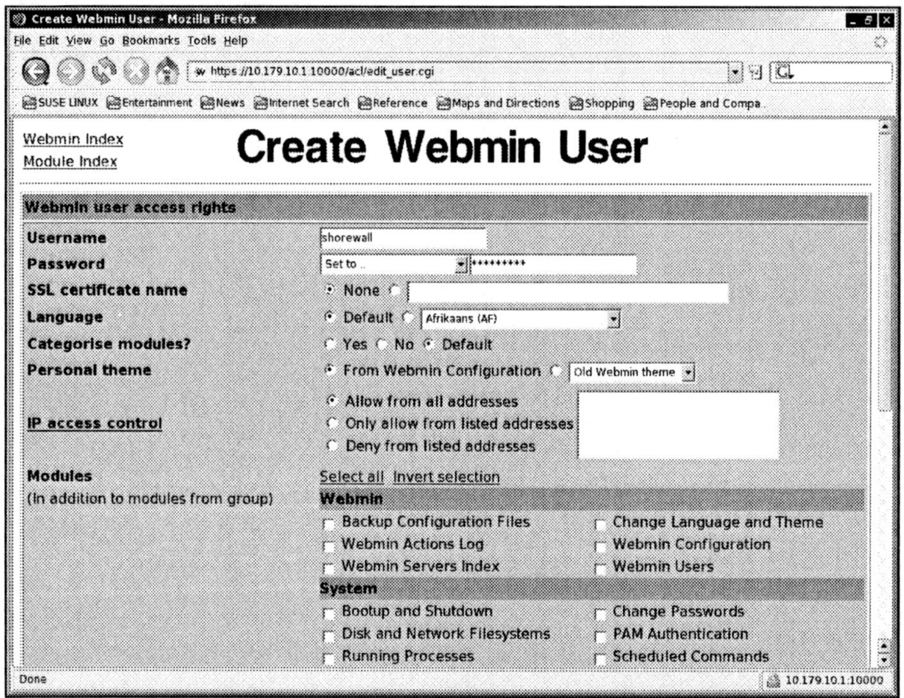


Enter a username and a password for this user. If you want, you can specify different IP addresses from which this user is allowed to connect, but the most important selection is to activate the module Shorewall Firewall in the Modules | Networking section of this dialog. You will have to scroll down a little to accomplish this. Click on the button Save to return to the Webmin Users dialog.

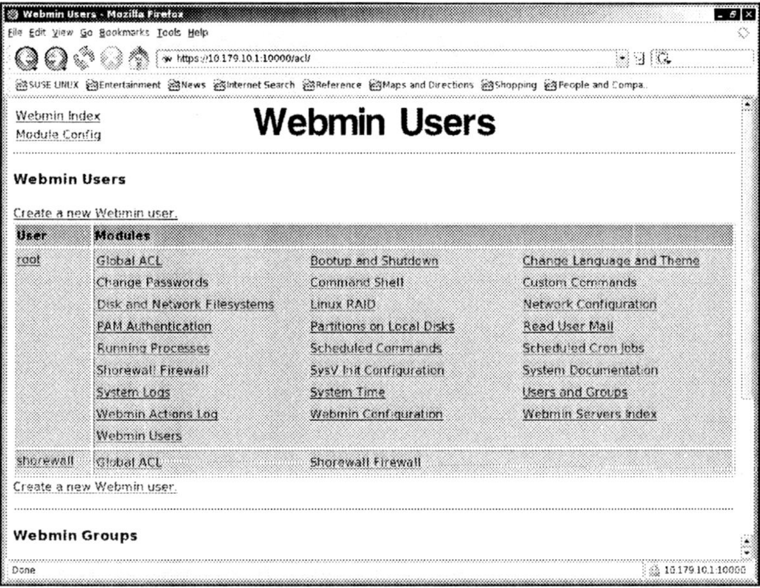


We can see the user added to Webmin and that this user has only access to two modules, one of which is the Shorewall Firewall. Now let's return to the Webmin Index (the hyperlink on the top left of the page) and log out of Webmin with the hyperlink Logout on the bottom right of the Webmin dialog.

## Configuring the Shorewall with Webmin

Now log into Webmin with your newly created user account. After login you will only see the Shorewall Firewall module. Click on its icon to start this module.

Before we proceed, we need to collect some information:

- What port and protocol is OpenVPN running (by default it's UDP port is 1149)?
- What are the names of the network interfaces?
- What is the IP address or DNS name of the VPN partner?

We will now enter this data in our firewall configuration and close all other access except SSH traffic. Thus our firewall will have only two ports open from outside: SSH and OpenVPN. What you want or need to open from your internal network will depend on the other services that you run on this server. I recommend and assume that no other services are running, thus the firewall will be closed also to the internal network as well, which gives the following firewall rules. Of course, if your Firewall/VPN server is gateway to the Internet for the local net, there may be some rules to be added.

The Firewall on our OpenVPN server will:

- Allow SSH access from everywhere (remote and local)
- Allow OpenVPN traffic (UDP port 1194, or whatever you opt for)
- Forward traffic between the local network and the remote network (connected by the VPN)

The typical proceeding to set up such rules is as follows:

- **Add network zones**: Here we define "what is outside", "what is inside", etc.
- **Define network interfaces and link them to network zones**: We bind the zones "outside", "inside", etc. to network cards—real or virtual ones.
- **Define default policies**: This declares the standard procedure for traffic that is not defined by rules (see next point).
- **Define firewall rules**: We define exact rules for the traffic based on its IP, port, or protocol.

You can see in the previous screenshot that the four icons in the first line are all that we need, but the Shorewall can do much more. The online help on its homepage is a very concise description of its capabilities.

## Creating Zones

Now click on Network Zones and then on the hyperlink Add a new network zone.

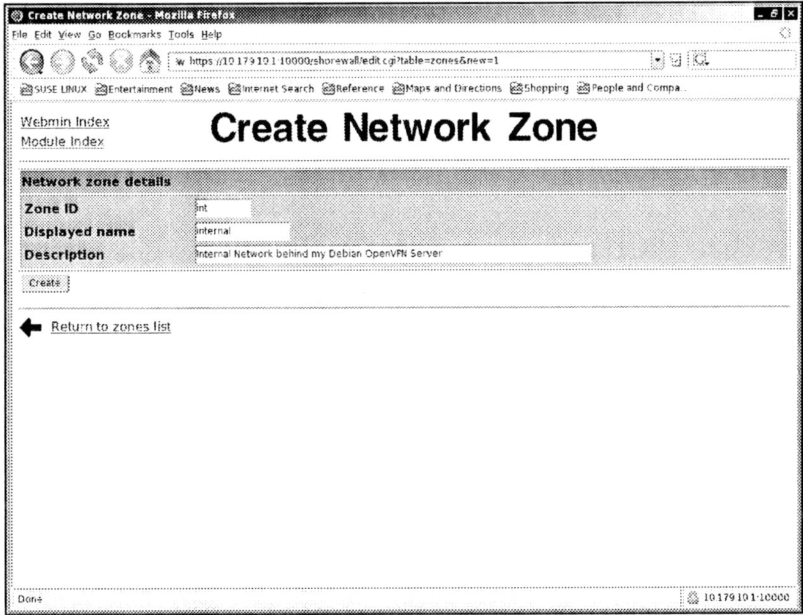


Enter a short ID, a display name, and a longer description for your internal network, and click on Create. Repeat this step for every zone you will need—in my setup, twice.

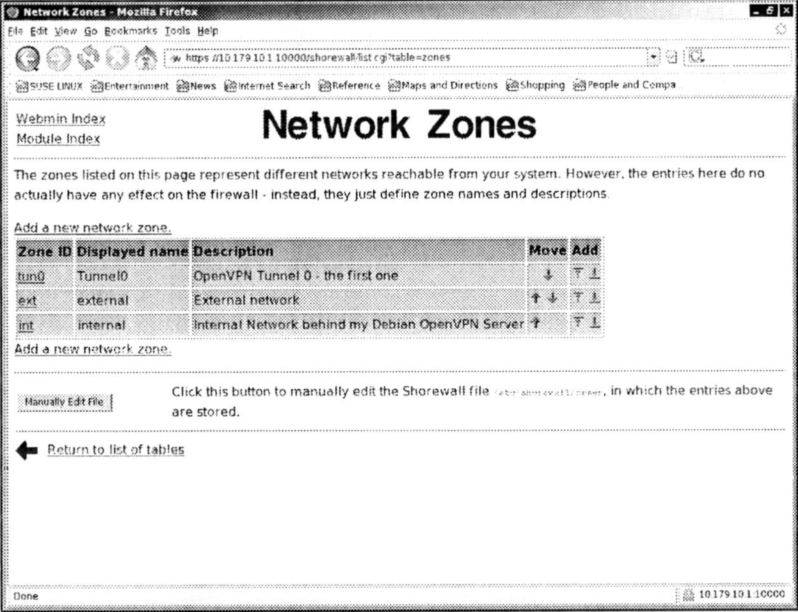

I added one zone for my tunnel device and one for the external network, which is connected to the Internet. There is always one more zone, which is not listed here: the zone describing the firewall machine itself, which is called firewall or FW.

Click on the hyperlink Return to list of tables and select the Network Interfaces, which should present an empty list. Click on the hyperlink Add a new network interface.

## Editing Interfaces

In this dialog we can enter the network interfaces and select the corresponding network zones.

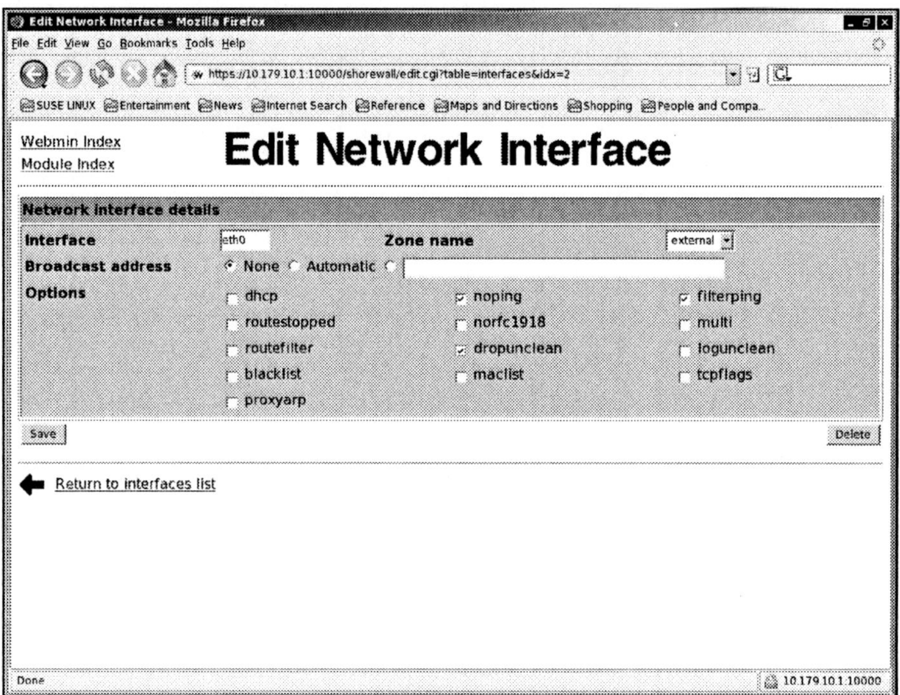


Type the name of your network interface in the field Interface and select its network zone from the drop-down menu on the right. Repeat this step for all your network devices, no matter if they are real or virtual (OpenVPN TUN/TAP) devices. If you run into problems with the name of the OpenVPN device, try a standard name—like tun0 or tap0. It may be a good idea to activate some security options for the external interface here, like `noping`, `filterping`, and `dropunclean`. With these options, the firewalls will not answer pings and unclean packages from outside. If you want to know more about these features, the Shorewall website is the place to look.

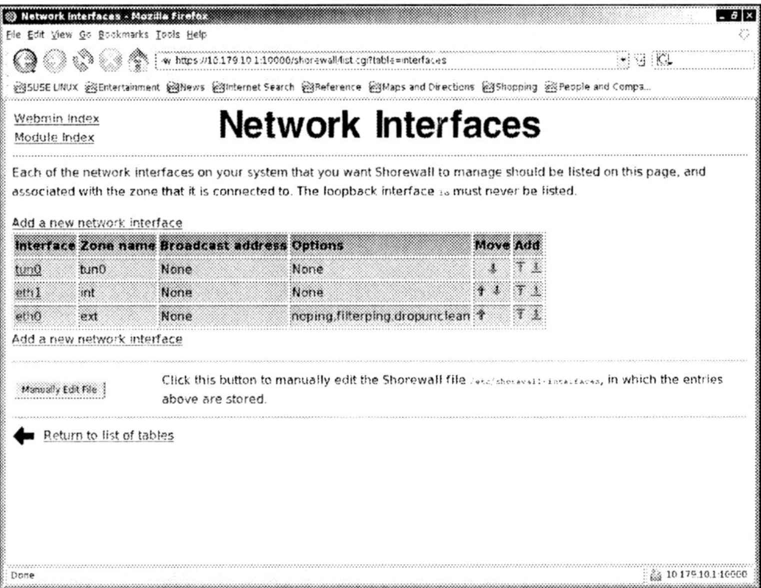


In this screenshot you can see my zone/interface setup for the three zones. Our next step is to define default policies for our networks. Click on Return to list of tables and select the icon Default Policies.

## Default Policies

This list should still be empty. Click on the Add a new default policy hyperlink, and we will see the policy editor:

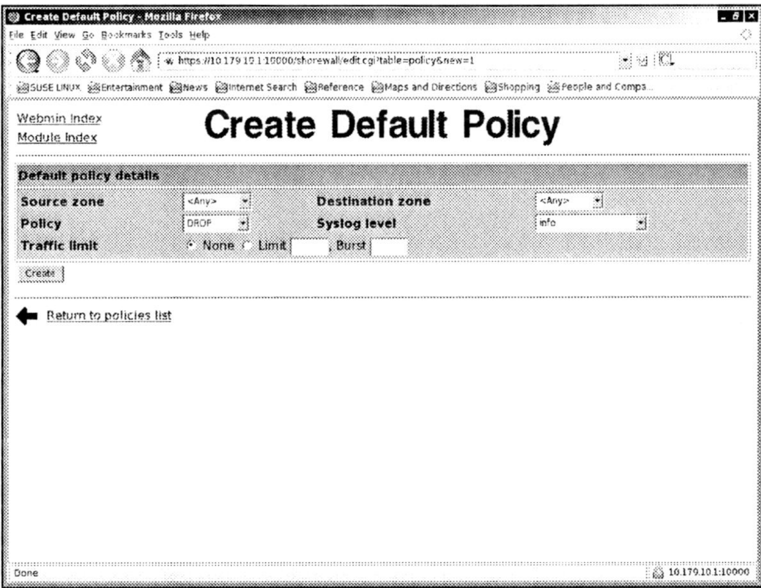

The most important rule in our firewall is described with the simple sentence: "Drop anything that I have not specified otherwise...". This can be extended to the Shorewall rule "Any to Any DROP", which simply means that traffic from any zone to any other zone will be dropped unless it's defined otherwise in specific rules. Of course, any traffic that is dropped by our firewall should be logged for later evaluation by the administrator. Thus in this dialog we select:

- Source zone: <Any>
- Destination zone: <Any>
- Policy: DROP
- Syslog level: info

The drop-down menu Policy offers basic functionalities of a firewall: the firewall can accept, reject, and drop packets. I guess accept may be clear, but what's the difference between reject and drop?

Rejected packets cause an answer—the sender is informed that a firewall has rejected the connection. Dropped packets seem to vanish into oblivion—at least the sender will perceive it like this. Dropping will always be the better solution, because it causes less traffic and does not offer information to an attacker.

But now that we have dropped all traffic, we will need more default rules to allow our tunnel traffic and permit the firewall to access the Internet and the local net:

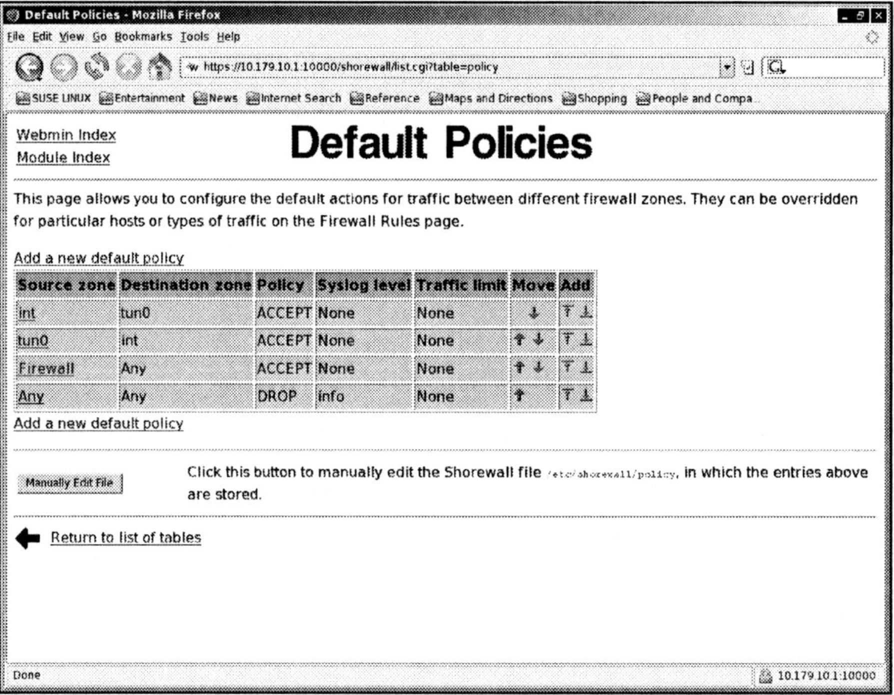

Add the following policies:

- The firewall is allowed to access both Internet (external) and local net (internal) (Firewall to Any ACCEPT)
- Traffic from internal network is permitted into the tunnel (int to tun0 ACCEPT)
- Traffic from the tunnel to the local net is permitted (tun0 to int ACCEPT)
- Anything else is prohibited (Any to Any DROP)

## Adding Firewall Rules

Now let's add some firewall rules. Select the icon Firewall Rules in the Shorewall module and click on the Add a new firewall rule hyperlink.

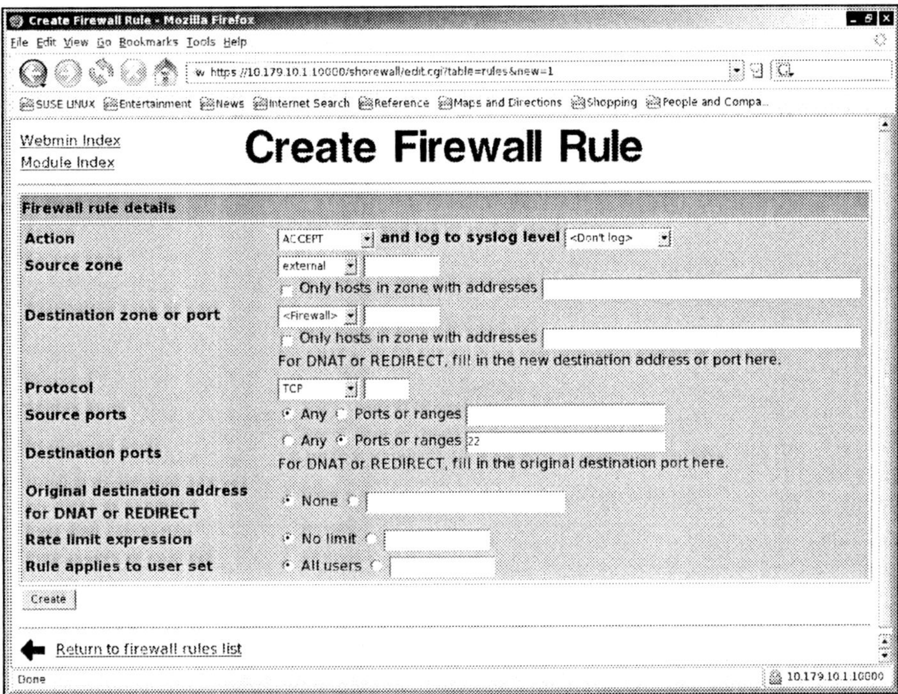


As first rule, we will activate the SSH access on the external interface:

| Fields in the "Create Firewall Rule" Dialog | Parameters to Enter/Select |
|---|---|
| Action | ACCEPT |
| Source zone | external |
| Destination zone | <Firewall> |
| Protocol | TCP |
| Destination ports | 22 |

We tell the Shorewall to ACCEPT any traffic from outside that is traffic bound for the firewall itself and is of protocol TCP and headed for destination port 22. Click on the Create hyperlink to save this rule, and in the list of rules, click on Add a new firewall rule again.

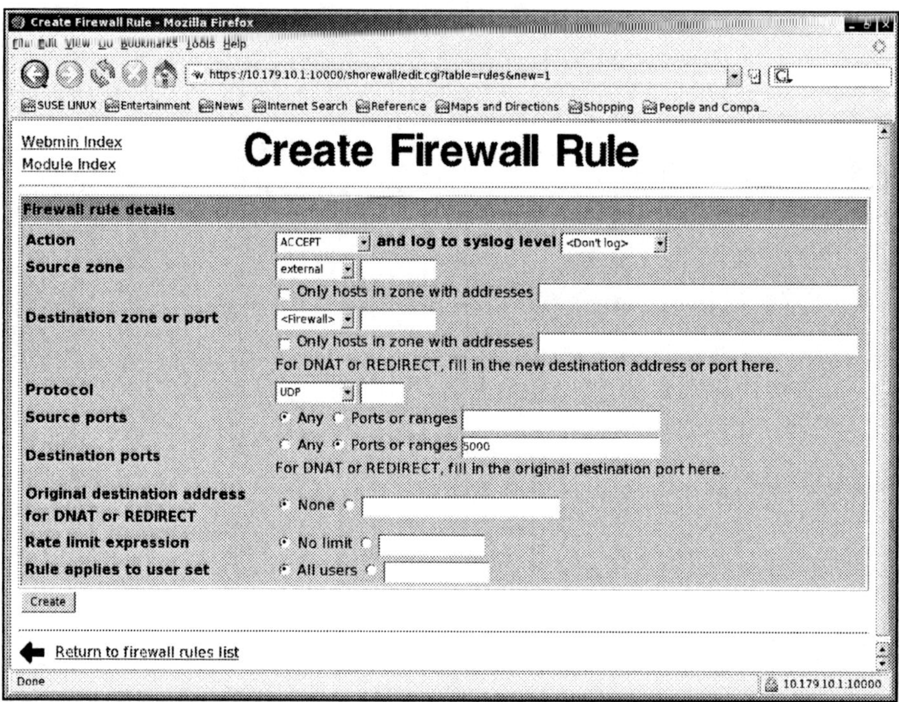


Our second rule activates UDP packets on port 5000, (which we have configured in the OpenVPN configuration at the beginning of this chapter) on the external interface:

| Fields in the Dialog "Create Firewall Rule" | Parameters to Enter/Select |
|---|---|
| Action | ACCEPT |
| Source zone | external |
| Destination zone | Firewall |
| Protocol | UDP |
| Destination ports | 5000 |

We tell the Shorewall to ACCEPT any traffic from outside that is traffic bound for the firewall itself and is of protocol UDP and headed for destination port 5000. Click on the Create hyperlink to save this rule.

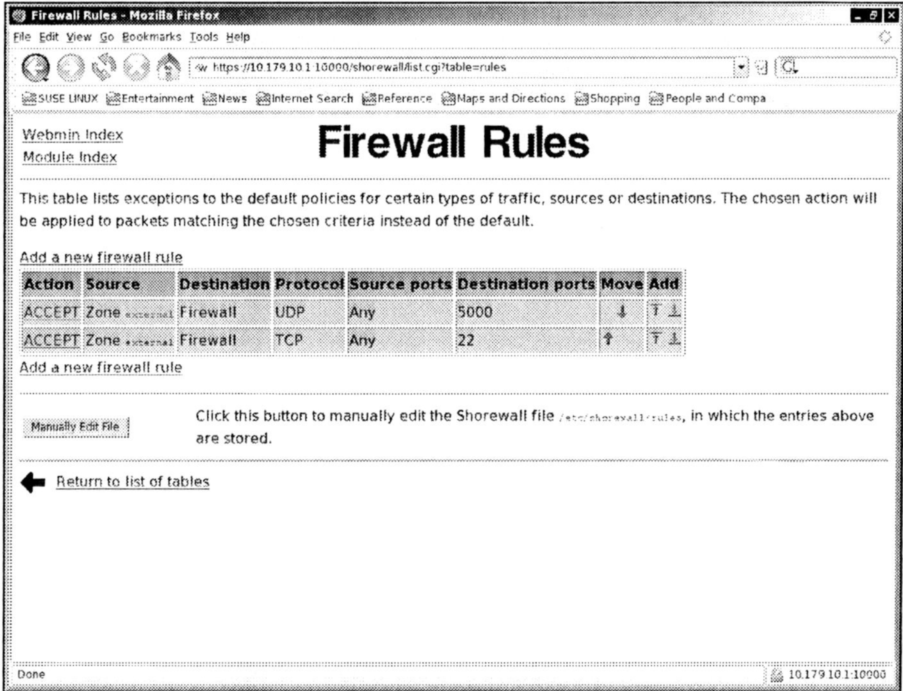


That's all. Click on the Return to list of tables hyperlink to return to the list of Shorewall icons.

> There is a known problem with Shorewall 3.0.1-1 and Webmin 1.240-1 (which were installed by default on my Debian system in December 2005). The Webmin module does not write a correct configuration file for the Shorewall zones configuration file. With all other Shorewall, Webmin, and **webmin-shorewall** software versions this works fine and the earlier proceedings are correct. If you run into problems here, have look in the troubleshooting section that follows.

The Shorewall can now be started. Click on the button Check Firewall. You should receive a long list of feedback, with a very positive ... your configuration looks OK at the end. If everything works fine, you can click on Start Firewall to enable Shorewall. Every time you make changes to your firewall setup, you should run a check and then click on Apply Changes.

## Troubleshooting Shorewall—Editing the Configuration Files

The Shorewall is configured by configuration files that are placed in `/etc/shorewall`. The GUI tool may be the best for the lazy (Windows) administrator, but editing the configuration files is the fastest way to adjust Shorewall behavior. The following table shows the files and the corresponding Webmin modules and functionality of the Shorewall:

| Configuration File | Webmin Module | Function |
|---|---|---|
| `zones` | Network Zones | Defines the zones (like external, internal, tunnel) for the firewall |
| `interfaces` | Network Interfaces | Links zones and network devices |
| `policy` | Default Policies | How traffic not specified by any firewall rule is treated |
| `rules` | Firewall Rules | Exact definition of firewall treatment of traffic |

If we want to make changes here, we proceed in the same way as we do with Webmin:

1. Edit the zones.
2. Bind interfaces to zones.
3. Define policies for zones.
4. Define rules that are different than the policies.

The syntax of these files is simple. The `rules` file created with Webmin looks like this:

```
debian01:/etc/shorewall# cat rules
ACCEPT   ext      $FW      udp      5000
ACCEPT   ext      $FW      tcp      22
debian01:/etc/shorewall#
```

The target action is specified in the first column, followed by source zone, destination zone, protocol, and port number. Almost the same system can be used to read the `policy` file:

```
debian01:/etc/shorewall# cat policy
$FW      all      ACCEPT
all      all      DROP     info
tun0     int      ACCEPT
int      tun0     ACCEPT
tun0     $FW      ACCEPT
$FW      tun0     ACCEPT
debian01:/etc/shorewall#
```

`$FW` stands for firewall and `all` is a shortcut for all interfaces (like the parameter for Any in Webmin). The first column is the source zone, the second shows the destination zone, and the third column, a target action. Optional logging is defined in the fourth column. The policy file shows two new entries at the end, which I have added to allow traffic from the tunnel to access the OpenVPN firewall.

The `interfaces` file shows our network interfaces as we have defined them in Webmin:

```
debian01:/etc/shorewall# cat interfaces
int      eth1
ext      eth0    -        noping,filterping,dropunclean
tun0     tunVPN0 -
debian01:/etc/shorewall#
```

The first column shows the short name, the second column the real name of the network interface in the system, and optional further columns can define other options.

The last file (which was the first we set up with Webmin) is the one that can cause problems with some versions of the Shorewall software—the zones file:

```
debian01:/etc/shorewall# cat zones
tun0     Tunnel0 OpenVPN Tunnel 0 - the first one
ext      external        External network
int      internal        Internal Network behind my Debian OpenVPN Server
debian01:/etc/shorewall#
```

This is the content of the file after the editing in Webmin. This configuration works fine with all versions of Shorewall before 3.0.1; however, newer versions will need the file in the following format:

```
debian01:/etc/shorewall# cat zones
fw       firewall
tun0     ipv4
ext      ipv4
int      ipv4
debian01:/etc/shorewall#
```

Since version 3.0.1 of Shorewall, a new field has been introduced to the definitions in this file, the "interface type", which usually should be set to ipv4. The Webmin module does not yet know this change and therefore writes the "displayed name" in this column, which prevents Shorewall from starting. The good news is: once set up at the command line, Webmin will work fine with this file, and there should not be a need to change the network zones for a firewall very often. (A bugfix from Shorewall is on its way.)

There is also a command shorewall, which can be used to start, stop, restart, and check the Shorewall:

| Shorewall Command | Function |
|---|---|
| shorewall check | Checks the Shorewall configuration files |
| shorewall start | Starts the Shorewall firewall |
| shorewall stop | Stops the Shorewall firewall |
| shorewall restart | Stops and then starts the Shorewall firewall |
| shorewall show | Shows a detailed list of firewall rules, including statistics |

# OpenVPN and SuSEfirewall

On SuSE Linux, there is a very sophisticated firewall solution with an administration GUI embedded in YaST. This firewall can also be set up very easily to work with OpenVPN. We will configure the SuSEfirewall for use with the OpenVPN configuration from the beginning of this chapter.

Start YaST on your SuSE Linux system and change to the Firewall module, which can be found in Security and Users:

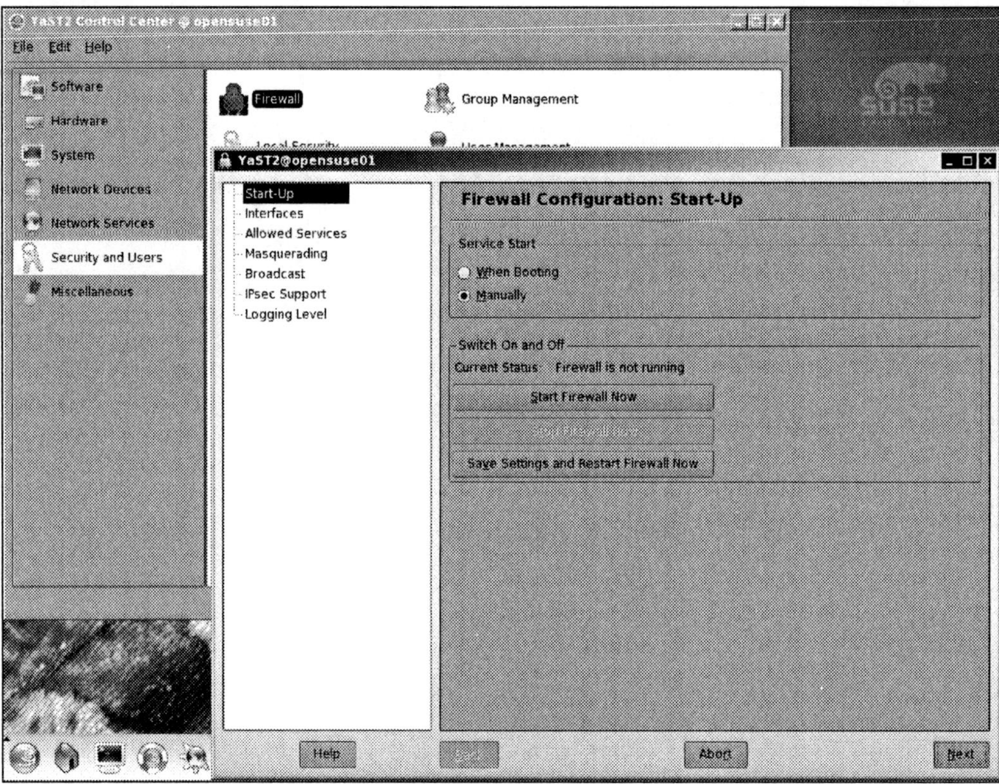


The YaST firewall setup is very straightforward; in the left part of the window we can select the dialogs to be set up for the interfaces, services, and some special features like logging, etc., and in the right part of the window the parameters and options for these features are entered. The following list will give a step-by-step configuration:

1. Let the SuSEfirewall start at boot time. Activate When Booting in Service Start.
2. Change to the entry Interfaces in the left part of the window. Look up the MAC addresses of your network cards; double-click them in the interface list, and select the proper entry from the drop-down menu Interface Zone. Here you must define your internal and external device.
3. Click on the entry Allowed Services in the list on the left. Select External Zone in the drop-down menu Allowed Services for Selected Zone and SSH from the Service to Allow drop-down menu. Click on the Add button to confirm your changes. Now SSH access on the external interface is permitted.

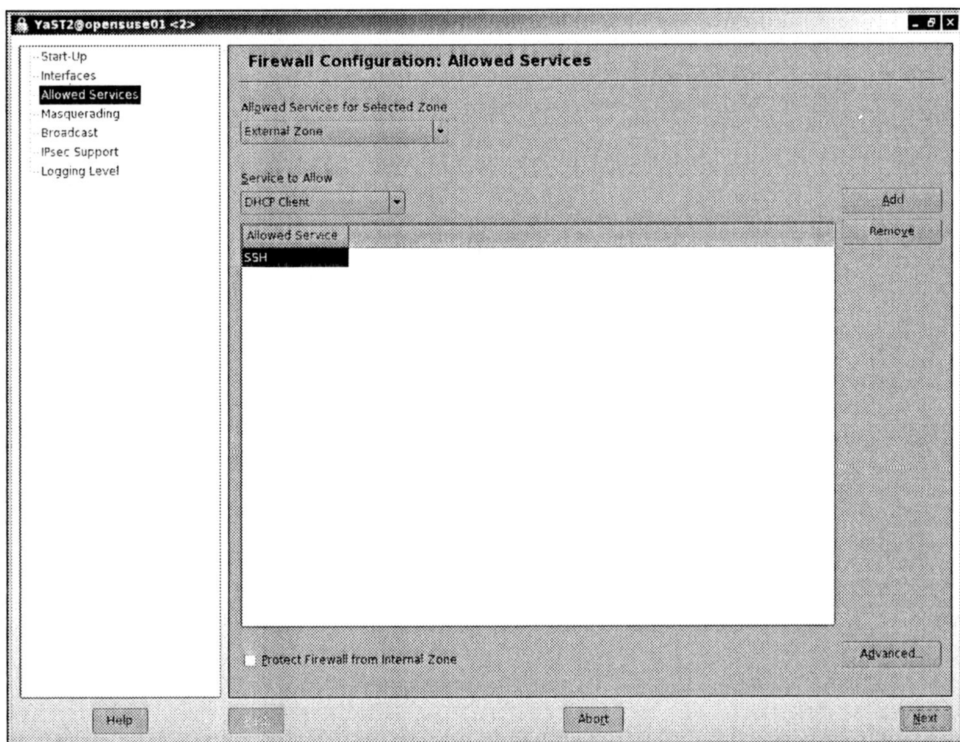


4. Next, click on the button **Advanced** to add our OpenVPN service. The UDP Port 5000 is not yet part of the standard SuSEfirewall drop-down menu, so we will have to add it using the advanced dialog. Enter 5000 in the field **UDP Ports**:

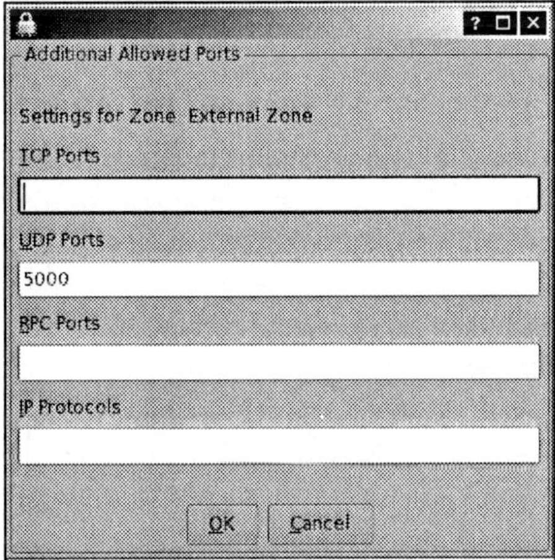


5. Click on **OK** and on the **Next** button to finish SuSEfirewall setup. Check the settings displayed and click on **Accept**.

Now we have the SuSEfirewall configured to deny any access via the external interface except OpenVPN and SSH. What is missing? You may know it by now: forwarding and network traffic from inside the tunnel. These options need to be set up with the **sysconfig Editor** tool of YaST, in the **System** category.

6. Start the YaST module **System | /etc/sysconfig Editor**.

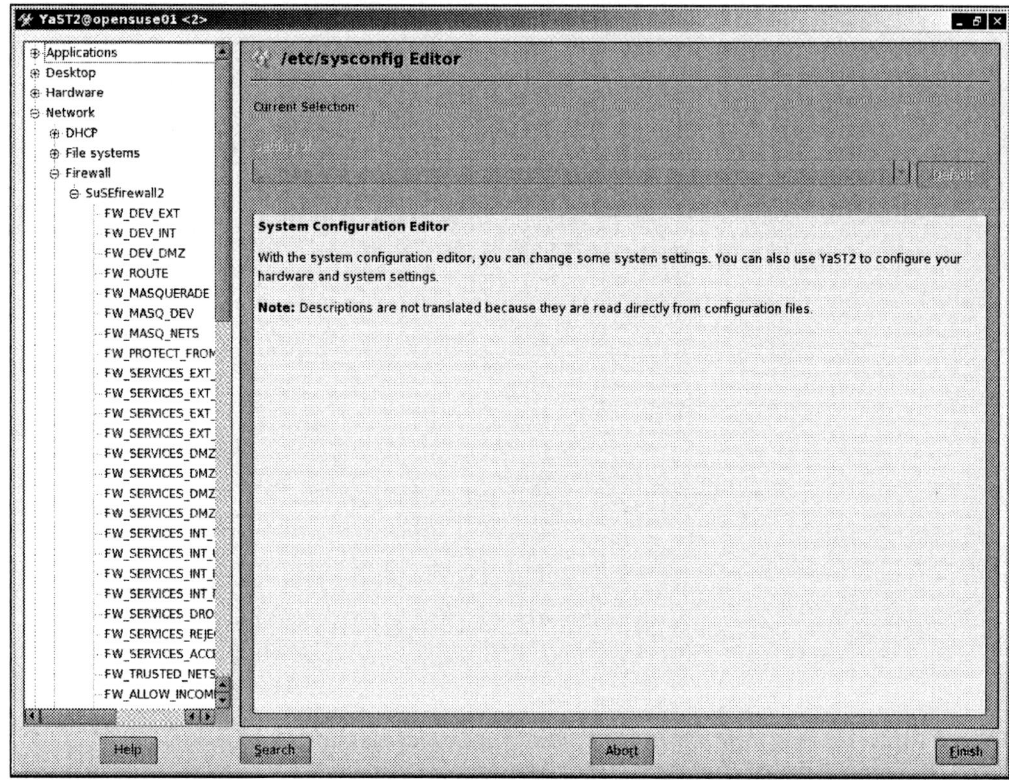


The **sysconfig Editor** is a useful tool on SuSE Linux that enables setting of various configuration options that otherwise can only be set on the command line. It consists of a list of variables on the left and fields where our parameters can be entered in the right half of the window.

We need to enter the following three options:

1. The OpenVPN interface is an interface that should be treated like the internal network interface.
2. SuSEfirewall must start routing functionality.
3. The firewall must route packets between the two networks connected with OpenVPN.

7. Select the entry Network | Firewall | SuSEfirewall2 in the long list of variables on the left. We will only need to change the values of the following three variables:

| Variable | Value |
|---|---|
| FW_DEV_INT | eth-id-00:0c:29:88:9c:b0 tunVPN0 |
| FW_ROUTE | yes |
| FW_FORWARD | 172.16.76.0/24,192.168.250.0/24<br>192.168.250.0/24,172.16.76.0/24 |

In my example network the two networks connected are 172.16.76.0/24 and 192.168.250.0/24. The tunnel interface is `tunVPN0`, and the MAC address of my internal network card is eth-id-00:0c:29:88:9c:b0.

8. Probably the most interesting value in this list is the last line: here we tell the SuSEfirewall that all traffic from 172.16.76.0/24 to 192.168.250.0/24, and from 192.168.250.0/24 to 172.16.76.0/24 shall be allowed.
9. Click on the Finish button. You will be asked to confirm a list of the changes you have made. Click on OK to commit your changes. Now we must start the YaST firewall module again and restart the SuSEfirewall. Simply start YaST and go to Security and Users | Firewall and click on the button Save settings and restart firewall.
10. Your SuSEfirewall is up and running.

# Troubleshooting OpenVPN Routing and Firewalls

We have now successfully connected the two networks. Please note that you always need two systems that do routing to connect two networks. If you do not need a firewall on these systems, or if you have problems and do not find the reason for your problems, it may be helpful to enable forwarding without firewall functionality.

## Configuring a Router without a Firewall

The following command activates forwarding of TCP/IP traffic from one network interface to another.

```
opensuse01:~ # echo "1" > /proc/sys/net/ipv4/ip_forward
opensuse01:~ #
```

If your routing setup is correct, then this is absolutely sufficient to make a Linux box a temporary router. Temporary router—because this setting will be gone after a reboot. If you add this command to one of your startup files (or call it from one of the OpenVPN scripts), then your Linux box can act as a router automatically.

## iptables—The Standard Linux Firewall Tool

Almost every Linux firewall uses `iptables` as the standard tool. It may be very helpful to know basic features of this tool, not only for debugging, but also to understand what is happening behind firewall GUIs like Shorewall or YaST.

`iptables` is a simple command-line tool that controls the kernel's IP tables. In these tables rules that define how network packets are treated on this system can be stored. As always, the simple commands offer the best solutions when they are combined with an abundance of options. There is a vast number of options and extensions for `iptables`, so this short description is far from perfect and far from complete. However, I hope that it may help in some cases.

The `iptables` syntax is very simple:

`iptables <rule command> <chain> <matching extensions><target>`

A typical rule command is `-A`, which means to "Add the following rule". Since `iptables` use different chains (by default, `INPUT`, `FORWARD`, and `OUTPUT`), we must declare the chain that this rule is to be added to. The following table shows three examples:

| iptables Command | Function |
|---|---|
| `iptables -A INPUT <rule>` | Adds a rule to the `INPUT` chain, which affects all incoming packets heading for the firewall itself. |
| `iptables -A OUTPUT <rule>` | Adds a rule to the `FORWARD` chain, which affects all packets that are supposed to be forwarded by the firewall. |
| `iptables -A FORWARD <rule>` | Adds a rule to the `OUTPUT` chain, which affects all outgoing packets originating from the firewall. |

Another typical command is `-P`, which sets the default policy for a chain. This should always be set to `DROP`, because then all packets "arriving" in this chain are dropped if not specified explicitly by another rule. This is the only way to make sure that only the traffic allowed by us is handled and any unspecified traffic is dropped.

A typical example for this is:

```
opensuse01:~ # iptables -P FORWARD DROP
opensuse01:~ #
```

Then there are `iptables`' targets. A target can be `DROP`, `REJECT`, or `ACCEPT` (among others), and is invoked by the switch `-j`. Furthermore, so-called "matching extensions" are like a filter specifying exactly which packet is meant.

Thus a rule like `iptables -A INPUT <matching extension> -j DROP` means: "Drop every packet that is headed for my firewall and that matches the `<matching extension>`."

| Matching Extension | Meaning |
|---|---|
| `-i <interface>` | The incoming interface of the datagram |
| `-o <interface>` | The outgoing interface of the datagram |
| `-p <protocol>` | The IP protocol of the datagram |
| `--dport <destination port>` | The destination port of the datagram |
| `--sport <source port>` | The source port of the datagram |
| `-s <source IP>` | The source IP of the sender |
| `-d <destination IP>` | The destination IP of the recipient |

There are many other matching extensions, but these here should be sufficient to understand the basics of `iptables`. Have a look at these lines:

```
#!/bin/bash
echo "1" > /proc/sys/net/ipv4/ip_forward

iptables -P INPUT DROP
iptables -P OUTPUT DROP
iptables -P FORWARD DROP

iptables -A INPUT -i eth0 -p tcp --dport 22 -j ACCEPT
iptables -A INPUT -i eth0 -p udp --dport 5000 -j ACCEPT
iptables -A INPUT -i eth0 -j DROP

iptables -A OUTPUT -o eth0 -p tcp --sport 22 -j ACCEPT
iptables -A OUTPUT -o eth0 -p udp --dport 5000 -j ACCEPT
iptables -A OUTPUT -o eth0 -j DROP

iptables -A INPUT -i tun0 -j ACCEPT
iptables -A OUTPUT -o tun0 -j ACCEPT
iptables -A FORWARD -i tun0 -j ACCEPT

iptables -A INPUT -i eth1 -j ACCEPT
iptables -A OUTPUT -o eth1 -j ACCEPT
iptables -A FORWARD -i eth1 -j ACCEPT
```

Do you already understand them? If you do, congratulations; if not, don't worry, it's easy. These lines represent a simple shell script that can be used to start a very simple firewall example. `iptables` is a command-line tool and therefore is simply called from a script with parameters such as the following:

| **Command** | **Meaning** |
|---|---|
| `iptables -P INPUT DROP` | Drop all incoming packets that are not specified by any other rule |
| `iptables -P OUTPUT DROP` | Drop all outgoing packets that are not specified by any other rule |
| `iptables -P FORWARD DROP` | Do not forward any packets that are not specified by any other rule |
| `iptables -A INPUT -i eth0 -p tcp --dport 22 -j ACCEPT` | Accept TCP connections for port 22 coming in on network interface `eth0` |
| `iptables -A INPUT -i eth0 -p udp --dport 5000 -j ACCEPT` | Accept UDP connections for port 5000 coming in on network interface `eth0` |
| `iptables -A INPUT -i eth0 -j DROP` | Drop everything (else) incoming on interface `eth0` |
| `iptables -A OUTPUT -o eth0 -p tcp --sport 22 -j ACCEPT` | Accept outgoing TCP connections for port 22 going out on network interface `eth0` |
| `iptables -A OUTPUT -o eth0 -p udp --dport 5000 -j ACCEPT` | Accept outgoing UDP connections for port 5000 going out on network interface `eth0` |
| `iptables -A OUTPUT -o eth0 -j DROP` | Drop everything (else) going out on interface `eth0` |
| `iptables -A INPUT -i tun0 -j ACCEPT` | Accept traffic coming from the tunnel headed for the firewall |

| Command | Meaning |
|---|---|
| `iptables -A OUTPUT -o tun0 -j ACCEPT` | Accept traffic headed for the tunnel |
| `iptables -A FORWARD -i tun0 -j ACCEPT` | Accept traffic to be forwarded coming from the tunnel |
| `iptables -A INPUT -i eth1 -j ACCEPT` | Allow incoming traffic from the local network interface `eth1` |
| `iptables -A OUTPUT -o eth1 -j ACCEPT` | Allow outgoing traffic to the local network interface `eth1` |
| `iptables -A FORWARD -i eth1 -j ACCEPT` | Accept traffic to be forwarded coming from the local network `eth1` |

In a nutshell:

- `eth0` is the external interface, where all traffic except SSH and OpenVPN will be dropped.
- `tun1` is the tunnel interface; forwarding to `eth1` is allowed.
- `eth1` is the local network; forwarding into the tunnel is allowed.

If you need more information, the manual page of `iptables` is the best place to look for help.

The OpenVPN software package contains a sample script that could be adapted for firewall purposes. The script can be found in `/usr/share/doc/openvpn/examples/sample-config-files/firewall.sh` and can be adapted to your needs. However, this script makes use of some special features of `iptables` that would go beyond the scope of this book.

> Every Linux system (since kernel 2.4) uses `iptables` to set up the rules for its firewall.

# Configuring the Windows Firewall for OpenVPN

Microsoft Windows XP with installed service pack 2 offers firewall software too. In the control panel there is an icon called Windows Firewall. Double-click on this icon.

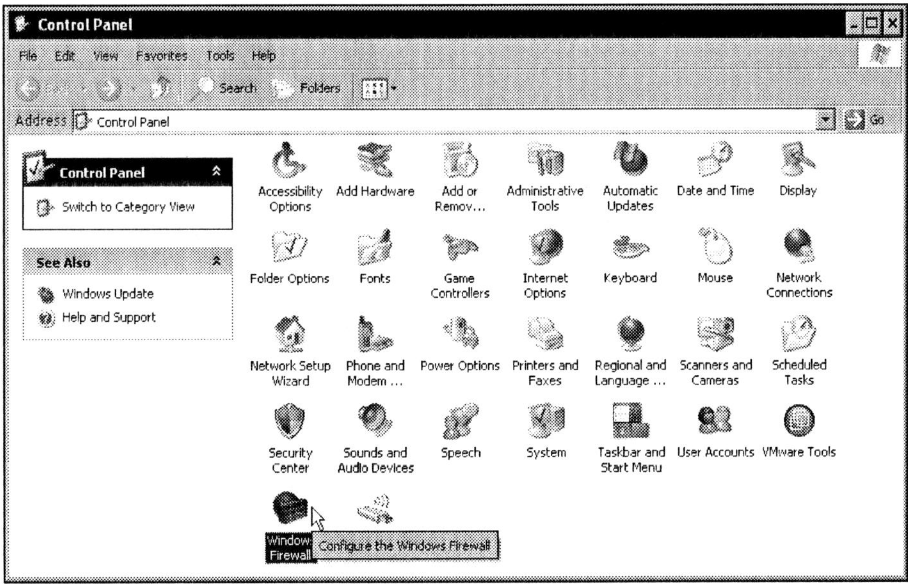


The Windows Firewall is activated as default, blocking all connections from outside to the local host. The Windows machine can connect to any host; even OpenVPN as a client can be run without any changes. If you want to connect to this Windows machine with OpenVPN, then some changes have to be made. The Windows Firewall offers the possibility to switch off the firewall service completely (which should only be done for testing purposes) and as an alternative to add exceptions to the firewall behavior. This is what we will have a look at later.

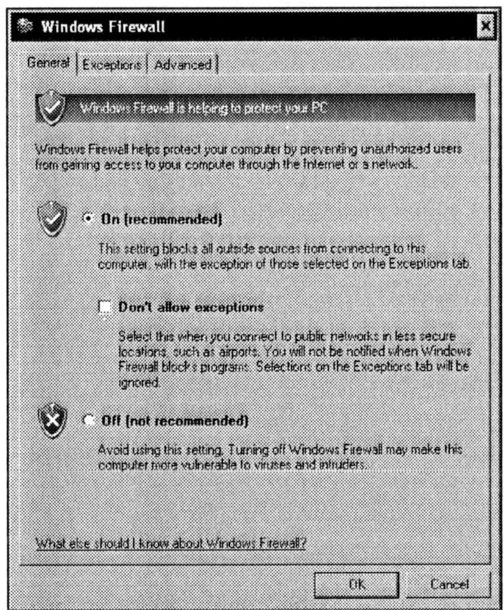

However, if we want to start an OpenVPN server process that binds to a local port and expects other machines' connection, then the Windows Firewall causes a security alert with a dialog box like the one that follows. This is probably the easiest way to activate OpenVPN in the Windows Firewall:

Click the Unblock button.

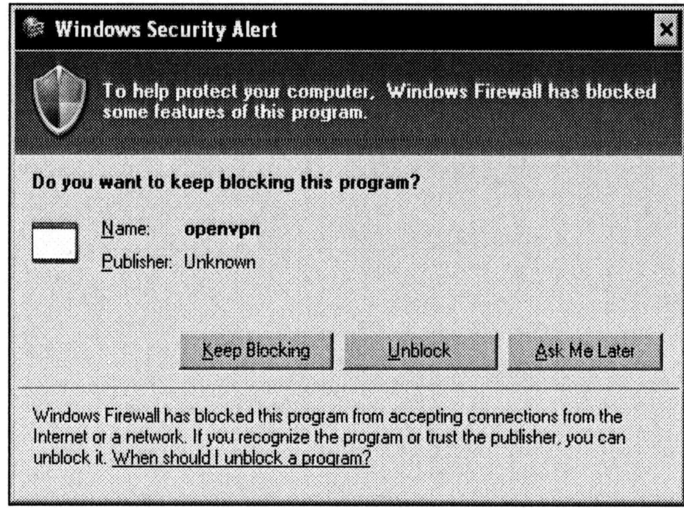


As soon as the OpenVPN process is started, another (small) pop-up window will appear and indicate that the OpenVPN process is ready to accept connections.

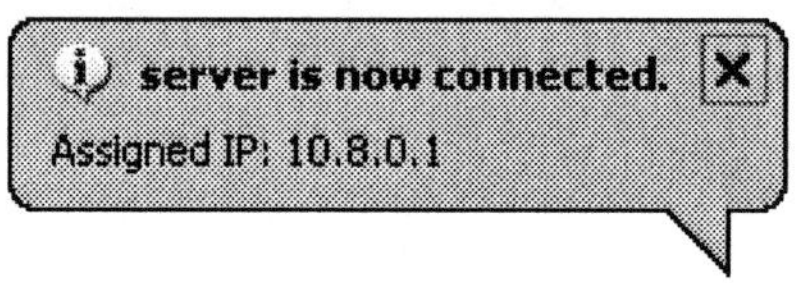


What happened when we clicked Unblock? The Windows Firewall has automatically created a rule (or so-called exception) that allows incoming connections to the OpenVPN process. Let's click on the Exceptions tab in the Windows Firewall dialog:

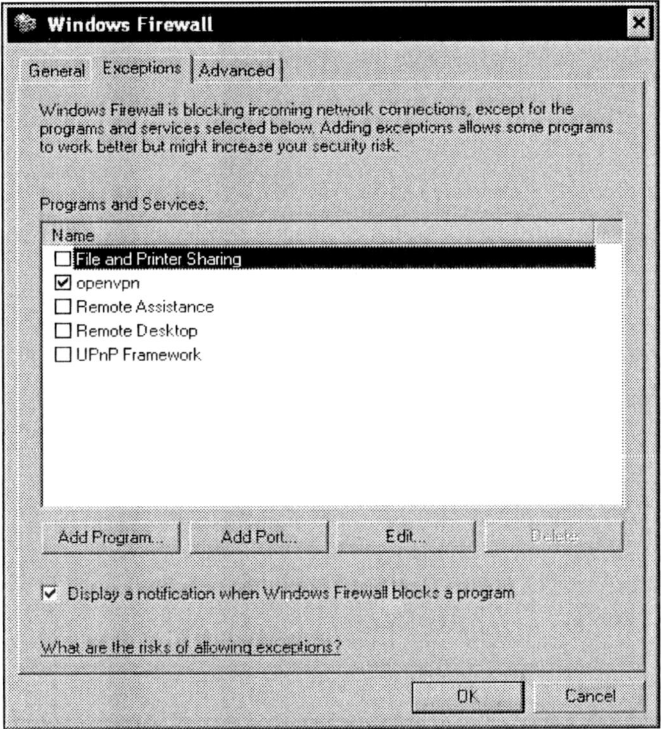


Here is a new rule that was generated when OpenVPN tried to open the port. Click on the Edit button, if you want to have a closer look at this rule. With the Add Port button we can add any firewall rule to the Windows Firewall setup.

Click on Add Port. The following dialog below shows that we have three options to set up a rule:

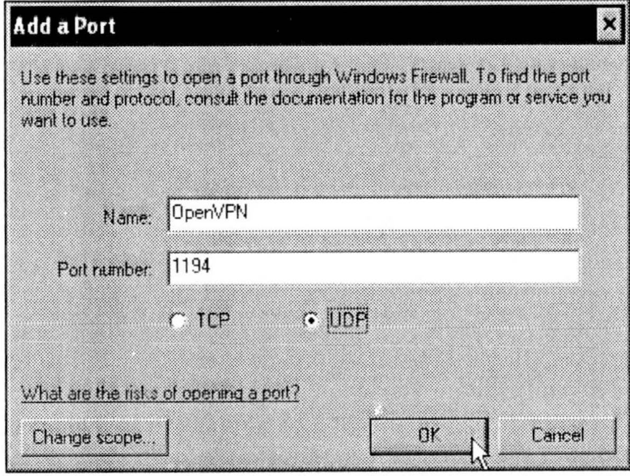

We can enter:

- Name for the rule—Unblock usually takes the name of the program
- Port number
- Protocol (UDP or TCP) for the connection

In this example the standard port of OpenVPN is entered—port 1194 and protocol UDP.

More options can be declared if we click on the Change Scope button. Another window pops up, where we can define the source of the connection that is to be allowed.

Three possibilities are offered:

- No restrictions—Any computer (including those on the Internet)
- The local subnet—My network (subnet) only
- A Custom list of IPs that are allowed to connect to this process

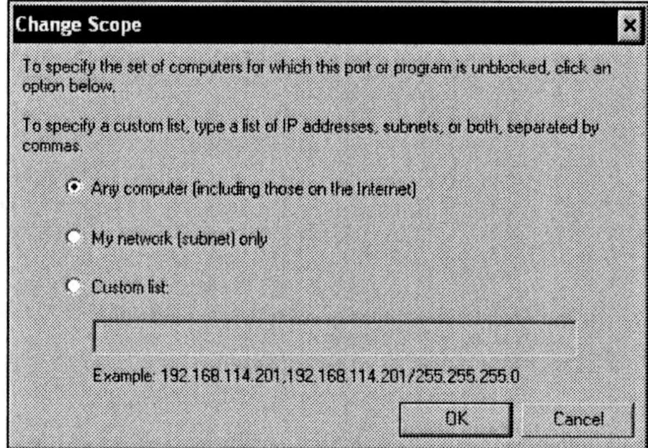


> On Microsoft Windows XP with service pack 2 the firewall can easily be configured with the control panel module Windows Firewall. In the Exceptions tab, we can enter ports, protocols, and sources for connections.

# Summary

In this chapter we have set up a secure OpenVPN connection between two partners based on certificates and using strong encryption plus some non-standard security features. In the next step we configured a Debian system with a firewall, which was the Shorewall that offers a nice GUI together with Webmin. A short look at the configuration files of the Shorewall Firewall and possible troubleshooting hints followed before we proceeded with the SuSEfirewall of OpenSuSE. After that we configured two different firewall systems that could connect to each other through the secure OpenVPN tunnel. We looked at `iptables`, and finally learned how to configure the Windows Firewall on Microsoft Windows XP.

# 9

# Advanced Certificate Management

In this chapter we will learn how to install and use xca, an advanced tool for Windows with which we can easily manage our X509 certificates. We will also learn how to use its Linux alternative, TinyCA2, which can even manage multiple certificate authorities. Both tools can be used to generate certificate revocation lists that are used to block unwanted connections by formerly authorized clients, like stolen notebooks.

## Certificate Management and Security

I think it's quite obvious that a computer that is used to sign certificates and keys granting or restricting access to a company's network will deserve special focus for everybody interested in accessing this network. My recommendation for a **certificate server** is to disconnect it from the network. Transfer keys and certificates with USB sticks or other non-network-media.

This advice has been published before very often because it is simply reasonable and true.

However, anybody who really does separate a certificate server computer from the local net and does not control the network of a secret service like a bank or similar infrastructure may send me an email. Most people simply wouldn't. In reality, certificate servers are merely programs running as a background job or as an application run by a non-privileged user. They say there are even Windows machines out there that do certificate management!

Nevertheless, there are some really cool and very reliable tools for certificate management that can be run on Windows and on Linux desktops; my favorites being xca (especially for Windows) and TinyCA2 (for Linux).

## Installing xca

Installing xca is easy. Just download the `.exe` file by searching for it on `http://www.sourceforge.net`. You will find a version newer than version 0.4.6—an `.exe` file of about 2MB. Download it to your Windows and double-click it to start installation.

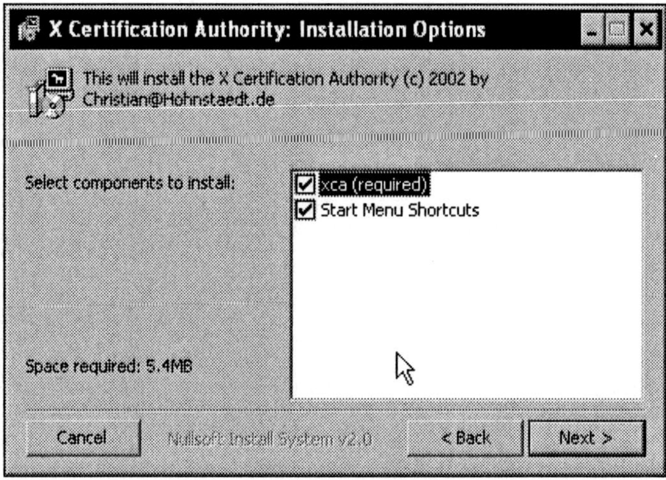


In the first step you are asked to accept the BSD-style license. If you are unsure, read it carefully and then click on the agreement, if it suits your needs. You will then be asked to select the components to be installed. (Well, in fact you can only choose not to install the Start Menu Shortcuts.) Click Next again, and xca will ask you which path to install in.

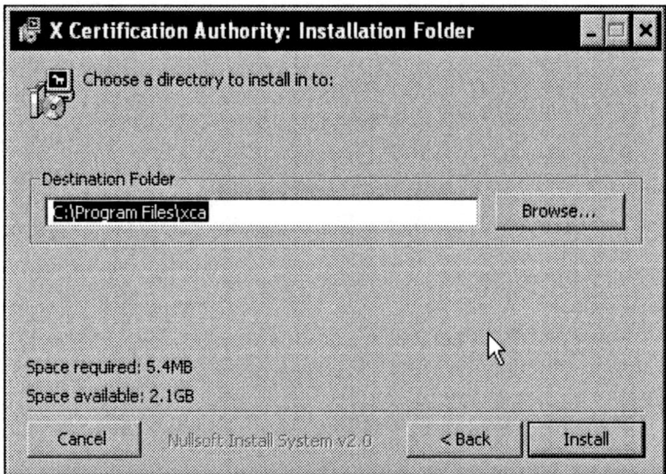

Once you've clicked on Install in this dialog, xca is installed in a few seconds. Now select the entry start | Programs | xca | xca to start it.

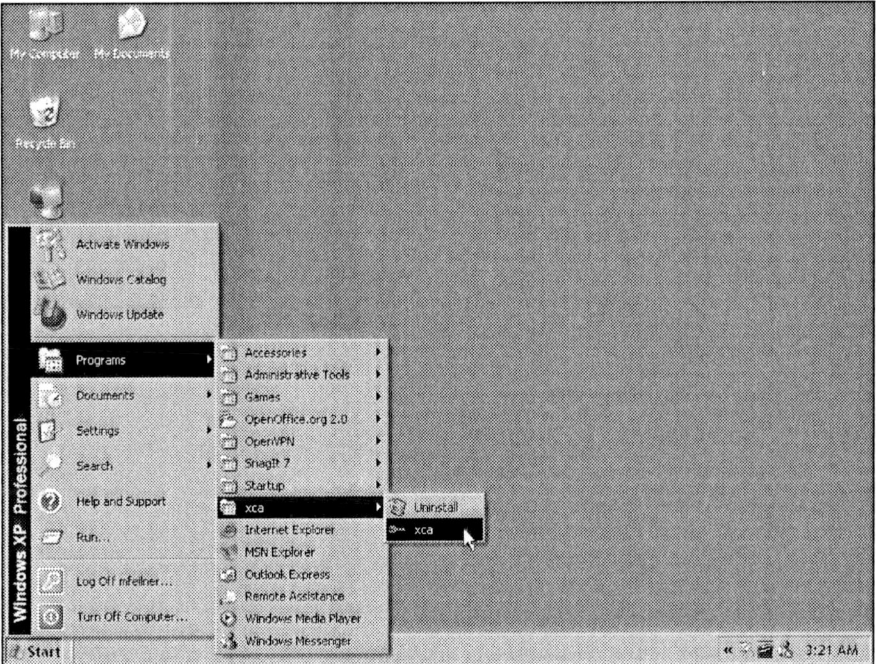


# Using xca

Upon first start, xca may inform you that its data directory (`C:\Documents and Settings\USERNAME\Application Data\xca`) is created; click on OK to close this window. xca is started. As a first step when running xca, we need to create a database where xca stores metadata on the certificates.

## Creating a Database

Select Open DataBase from the File menu of xca:

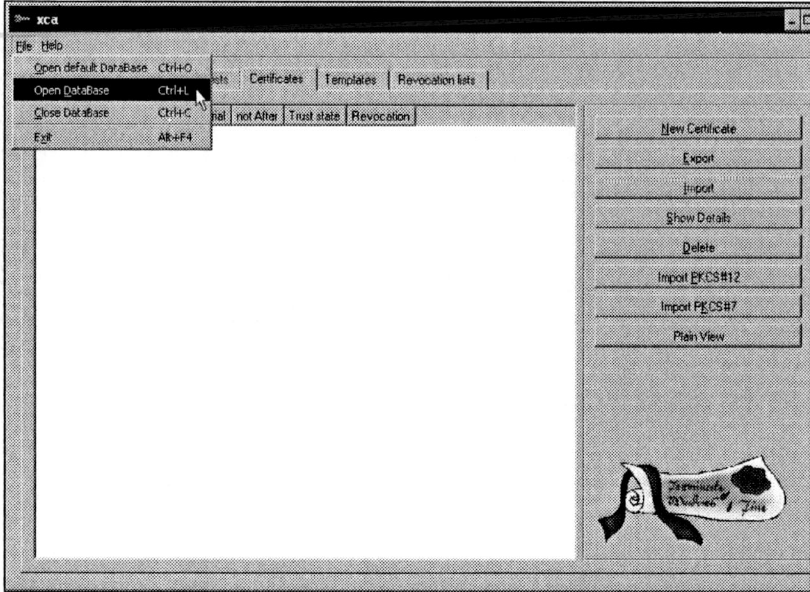

In the Open XCA Database dialog, we can select an existing database. However, since we have started xca for the first time, there will not be a database, and we will have to create one. For this purpose, we can simply enter a new file name in the field File name using the file name extension .db. This is very important, because xca may not recognize the database correctly later if the extension is missing. Click on the Save button to commit the creation of the database.

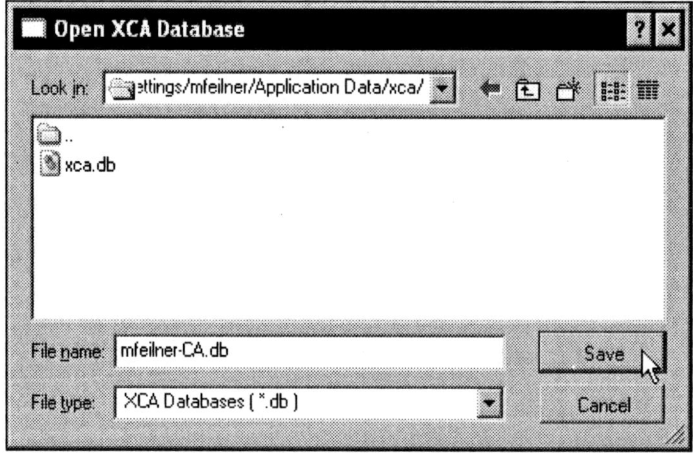

Now we must define a password for this database. This password will be needed to encrypt the keys in the database file. If you transfer this database to a different machine and want to reopen it, you will have to enter it again.

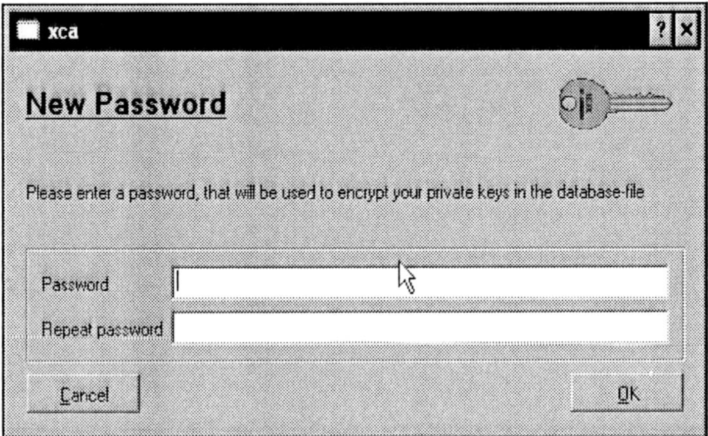


## Importing a CA Certificate

xca's main window offers the following five tabs:

- RSA Keys
- Certificate signing requests
- Certificates
- Templates
- Revocation lists

Except for the Templates tab, we will explain and use all the other tabs.

Let's first import the CA certificate that we created with `easy-rsa` before. Change to the tab Certificates and right-click to open the context menu. Select the entry Import to have xca import a certificate authority.

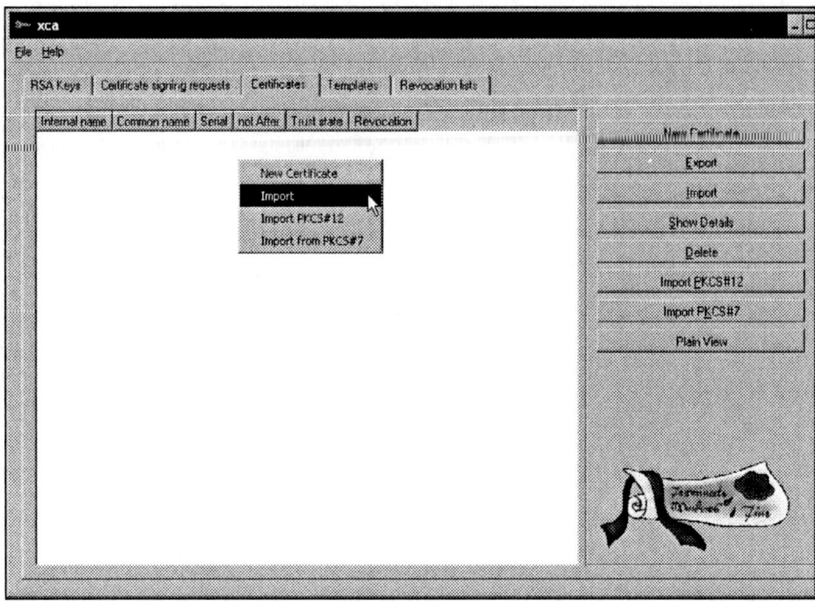


The Import X.509 Certificate window is displayed. Change to the directory containing your xca keys. According to our examples, this is `C:/Program Files/OpenVPN/easy-rsa/keys`. Select the `ca.crt` file and commit by clicking on the Open button.

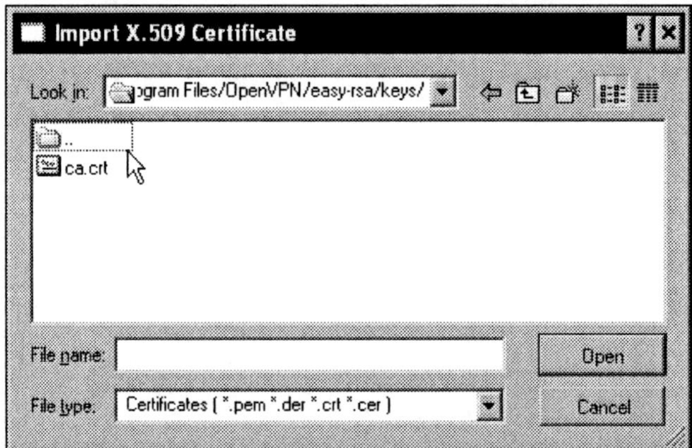


We see a new certificate in our list that is marked with a red question mark. This signifies the fact that the certificate is still unknown and untrustworthy. Right-click on the certificate and select the entry Trust to make this certificate a trusted one.

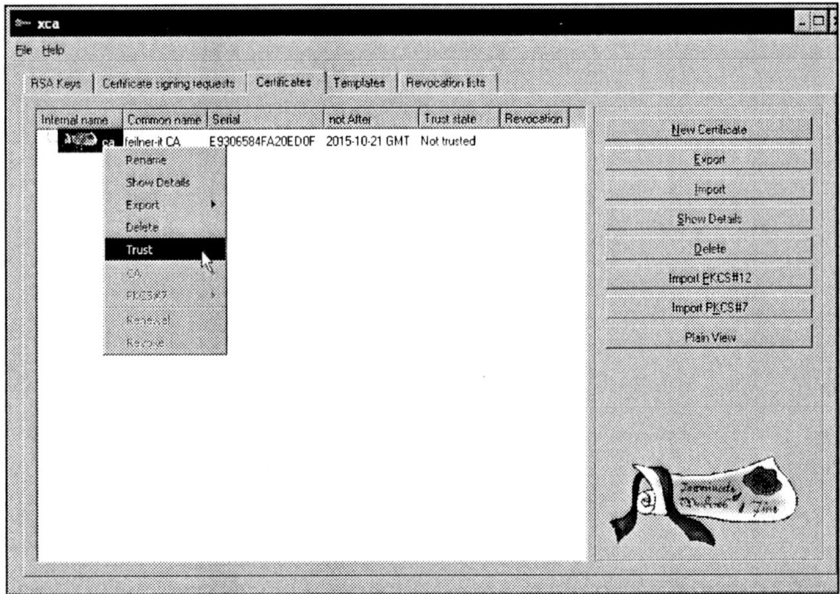


Another pop-up window is displayed, where we have to select Always trust this certificate and click on OK.

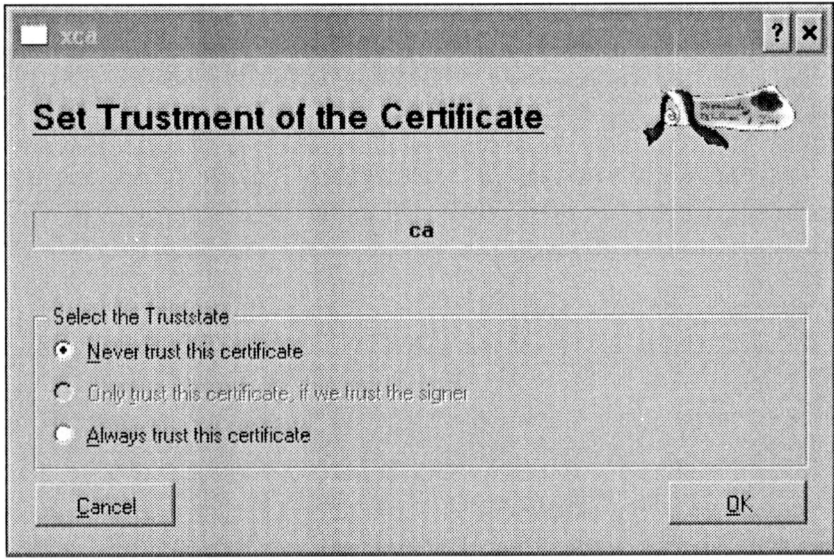


Before we can sign keys and client certificates using this CA certificate, we have to import the CA key. Switch to the RSA Keys tab and open the context menu with a right click of the mouse.

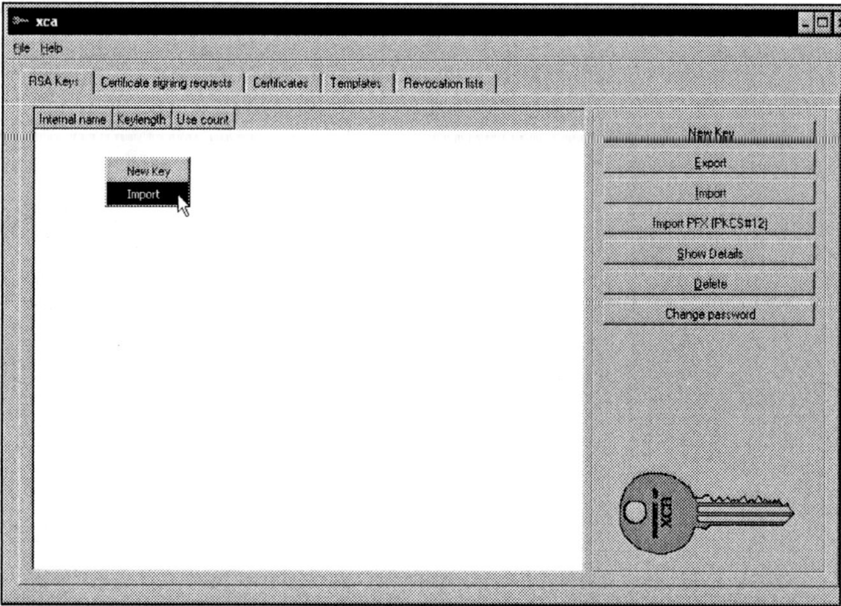

Select Import from this list, and choose the `ca.key` in the Import RSA key dialog. We now see the key imported to xca and displayed with a key symbol and its statistical features:

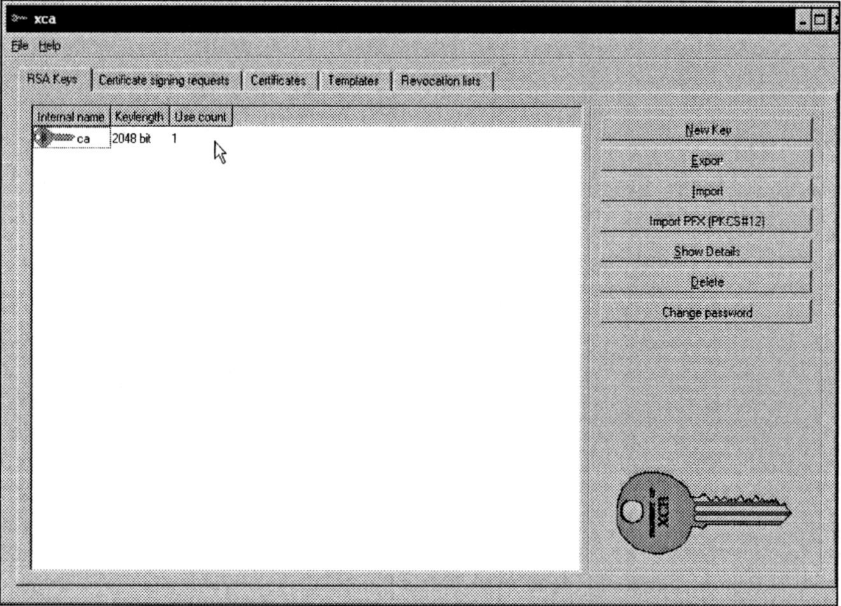

# Creating and Signing a New Server/Client Certificate

Now let's create a new certificate for a VPN client. Switch to the Certificates tab and select the New Certificate entry from the context menu or click on the button of the same name. A Certificate Wizard guiding us is started. You should read the information carefully before continuing.

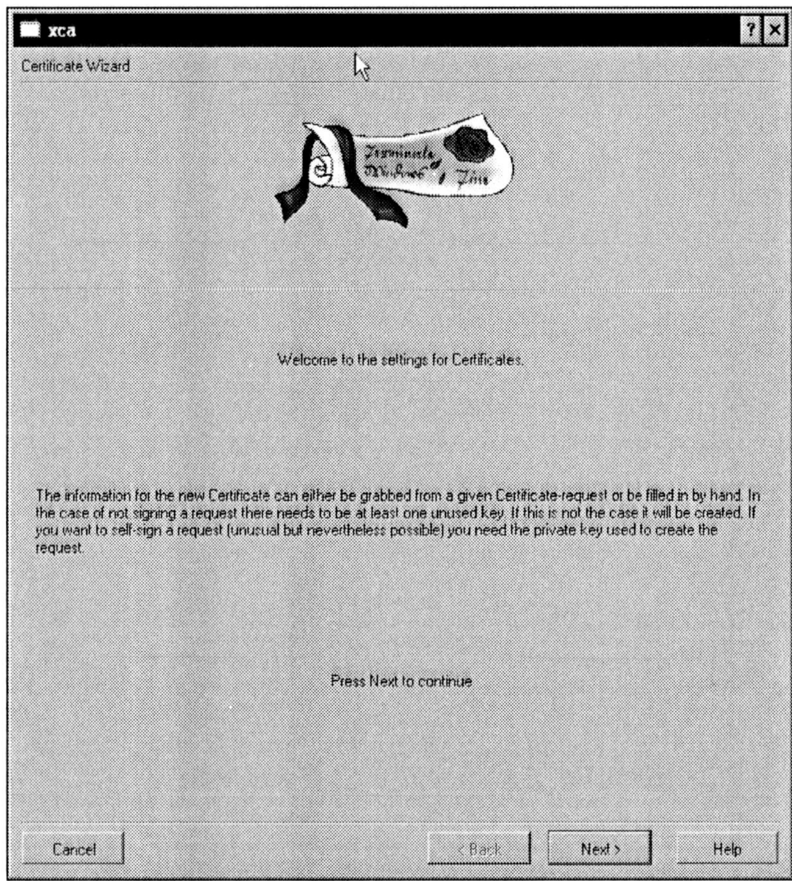


Click on the Next button to proceed with creating the certificate. In the following dialog, you can choose from templates for the certificate to be created (you can manage them with the Template tab in xca's main window), but the important selection you have to make is choosing the certificate you want to use for signing. Select the certificate you imported in the drop-down menu Use this Certificate for signing.

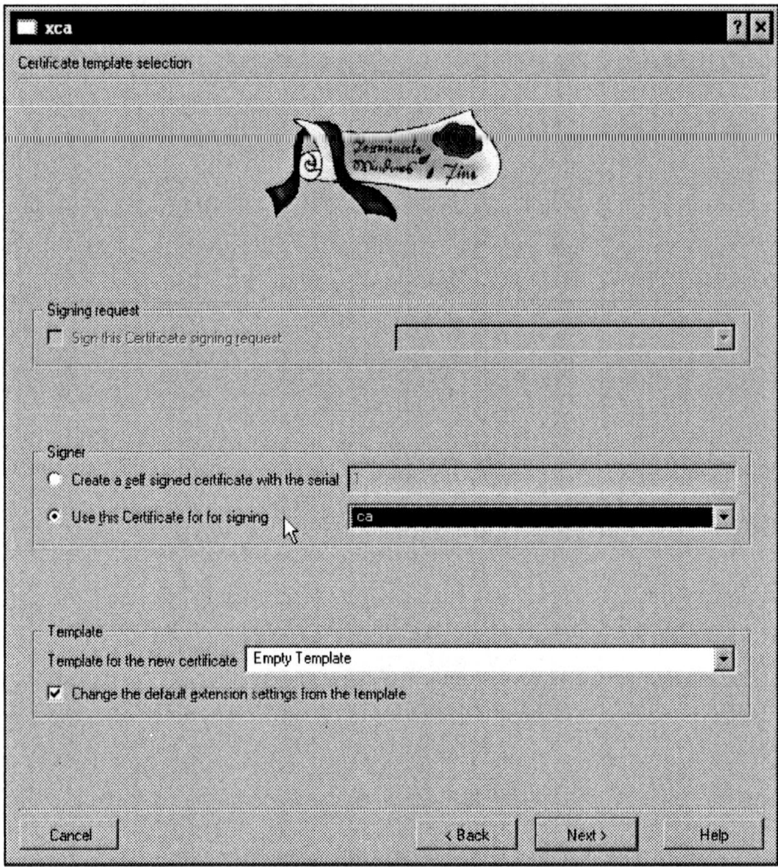


Click on the **Next** button to proceed. You are presented a window where you can choose the certificate name and key length. You should choose a distinguishing name and a key length longer than the default 1024 bit. 2048 bit should be OK; today's paranoid people will be content with 4096 bit.

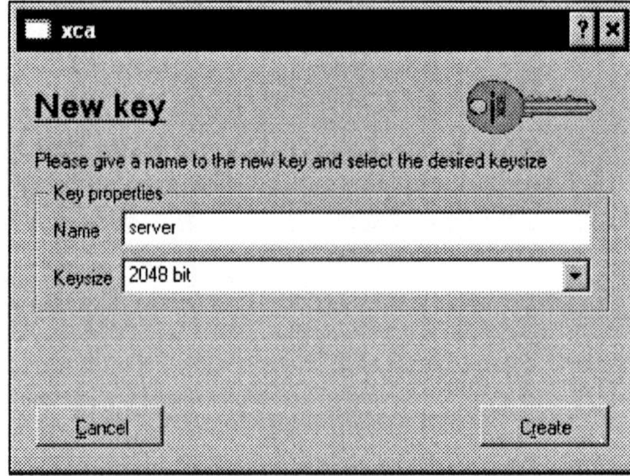

Click on Create to have the key calculated. In the next window there is some work to be done:

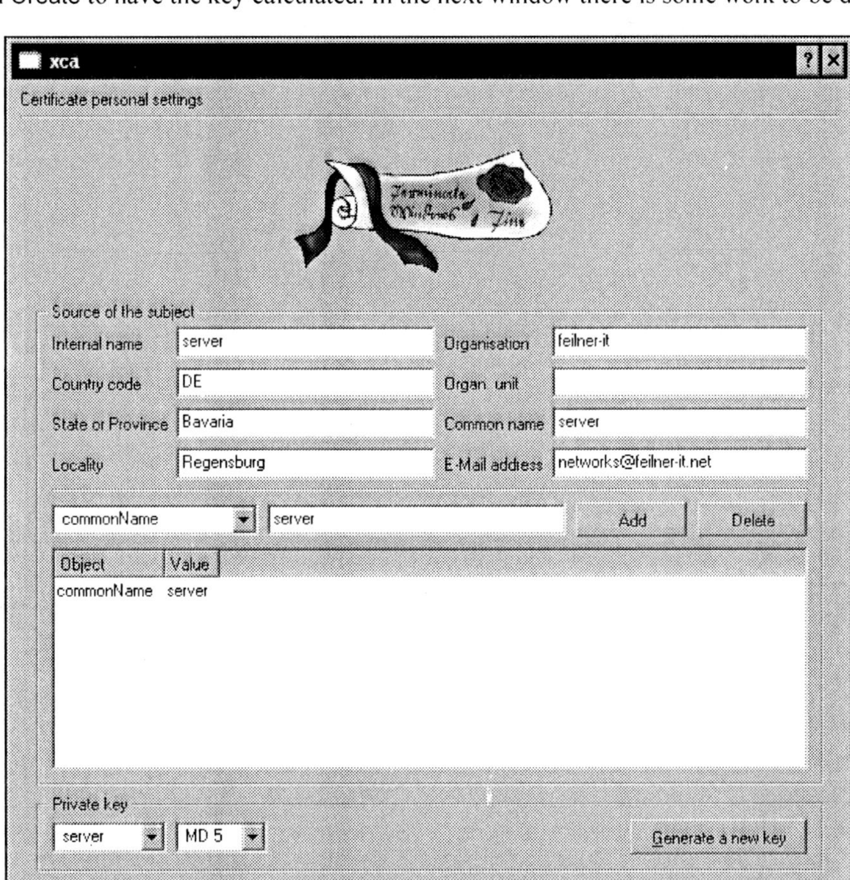


Here we can enter the data that `easy-rsa` has also asked us for. xca templates can make this a lot more comfortable. You know by now, that a very important part of this data is the field commonName, which can be used to distinguish VPN clients later. You should choose a name useful to distinguish your VPN clients in this field. Click on Next to proceed.

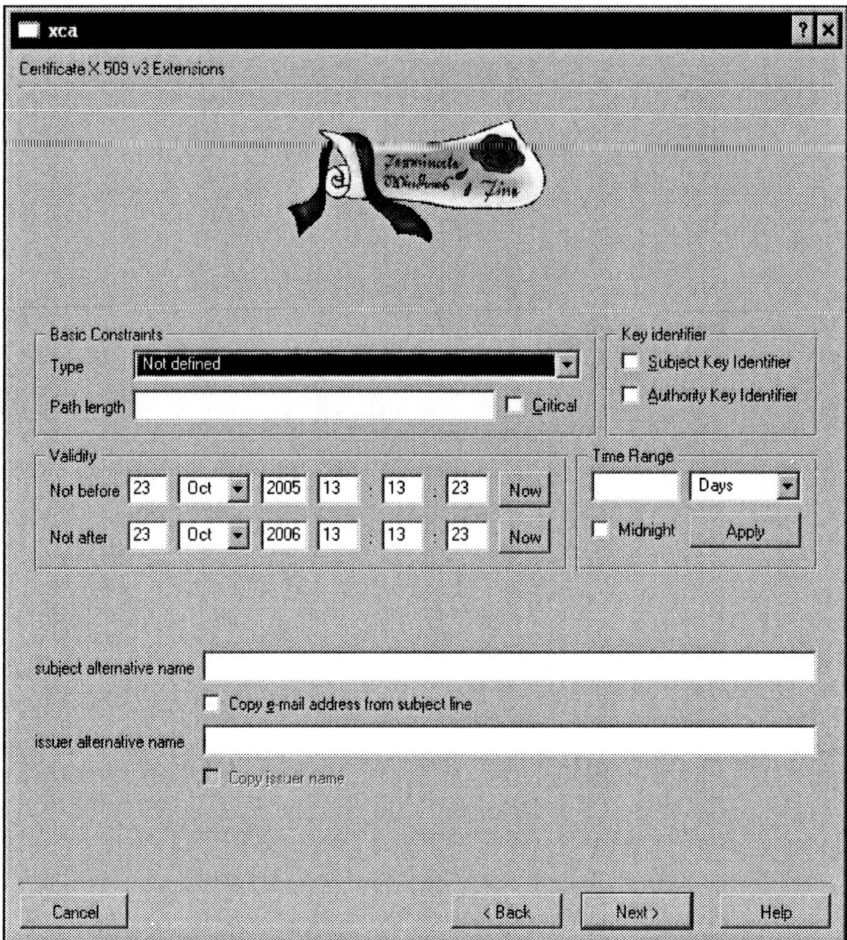


In this window another very important parameter of certificates can be set; the period of validity. If you set these values, don't forget to immediately add a reminder to your groupware or calendar software to remind you: "Mr. X will call tomorrow because his VPN doesn't work." Select reasonable values and click on **Next**.

The next two dialogs can be used to define the usage purpose of the certificates (and Netscape extensions). Normally, you can just leave the standard and proceed by clicking on the **Next** button. However, if you run into problems with "wrong certificate purpose" or get similar error messages, this might be the place to try some changes.

Finally, xca will show you again the values you entered for your certificate and its subject and issuer information.

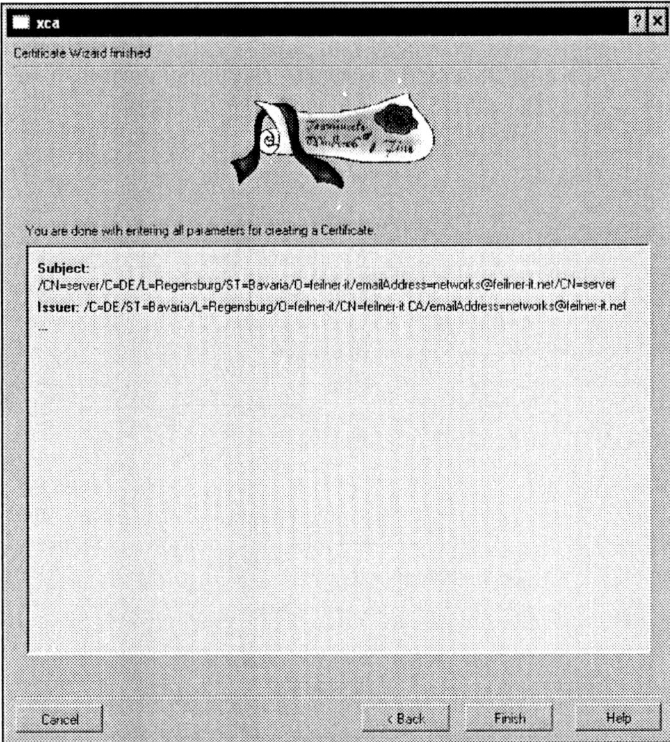


The certificate has been successfully created. Click on the **Finish** button to return to xca's main menu. Have a look at the **Certificates** tab:

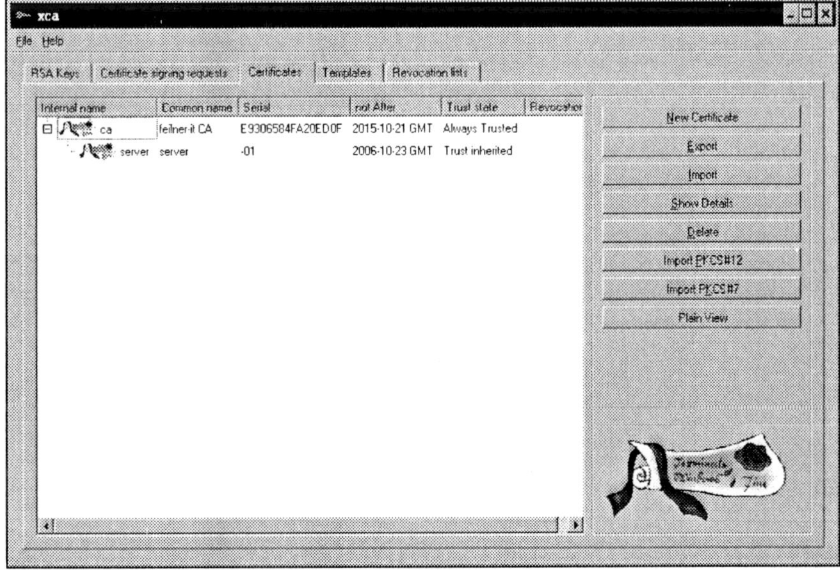

There is a new entry below our CA certificate, with the name of the certificate we created and statistical data. And in the RSA Keys section we can find a key for this certificate. The context menus of the RSA Keys and Certificates sections have entries that allow us to export the keys and certificates to directories from where we can copy them to our VPN servers and clients.

Of course we have to repeat these steps for every new certificate we want to create. Again, don't forget to use distinguishing names. That's all—isn't that easy?

> **PKI** management with xca is easy: Import the CA's CA Certificate and declare it as trusted. Then import the CA key and start the certificate generation. Don't forget to use the right CA certificate and an appropriate common name for the certificate. Again, use the context menus to export the keys and certificates.

## Revoking Certificates with xca

The context menu of a certificate in xca's Certificates tab offers an entry that is called Revoke. By clicking on this entry, a certificate is immediately made invalid. If we create a revoke list and put this list on our VPN server, with this list (and a suitable configuration), a client trying to connect with this certificate will not be granted access.

Select a certificate you have created in xca and click on the entry Revoke in its right-click context menu.

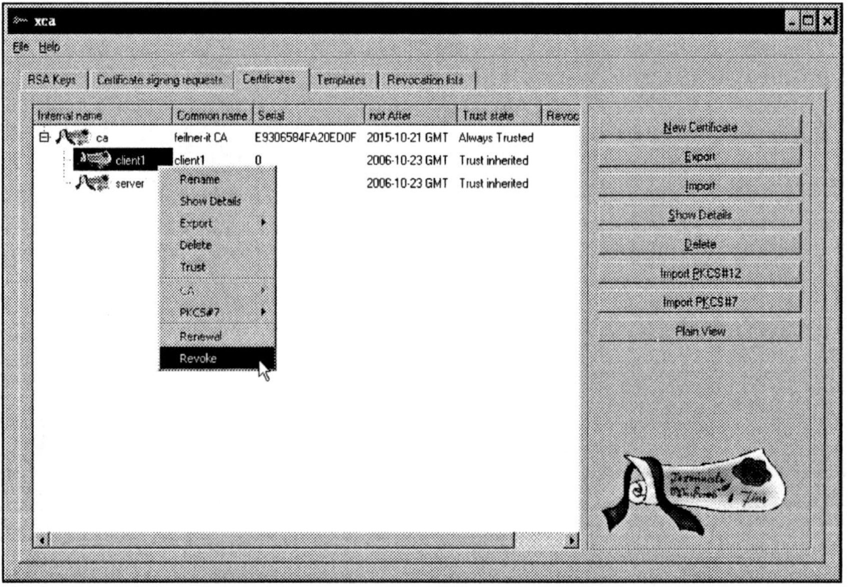


Then right-click on the CA certificate and select the entry CA | Generate CRL to create a certificate revocation list (CRL).

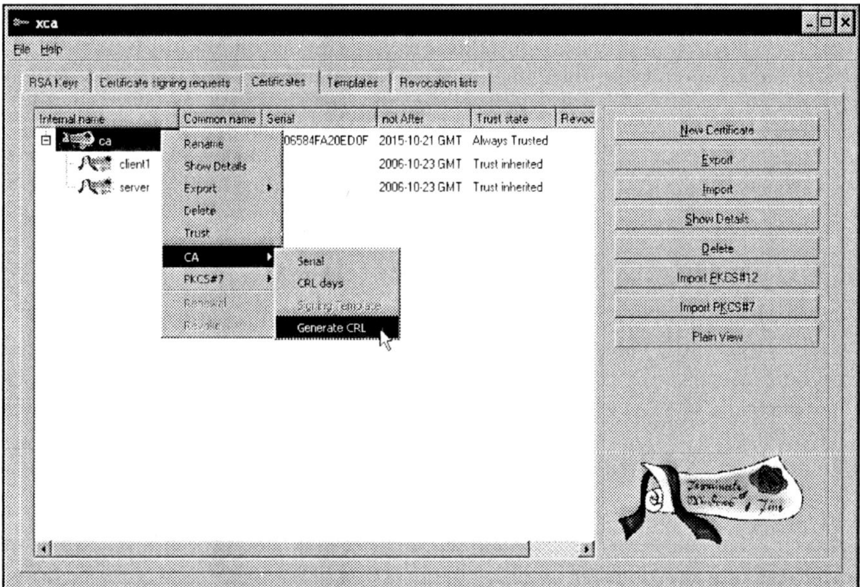


Now switch to the Revocation lists tab and double-click on the newly generated revocation list to show the details. Activate the Revocation list tab in the details view to see the revoked certificates in this list.

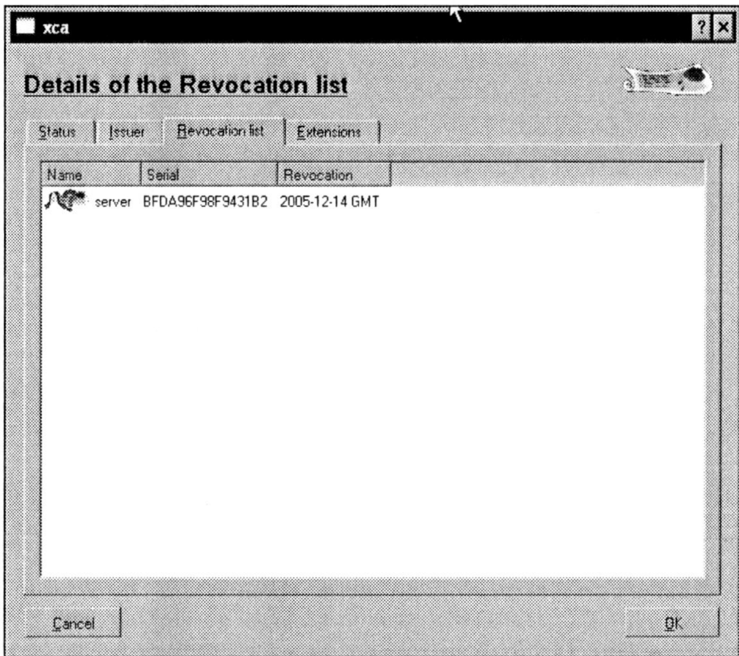

Close this dialog by clicking on OK. We can now export this list to the VPN server, using the context menu entry Export | PEM in the right-click menu of the revocation list. Copy this file to the VPN server and add an appropriate entry like `crl-verify <filename>` to your configuration.

Create some certificates and keys, export them to your VPN servers and clients and revoke them—some hours of training is very helpful to get a good feeling here. Especially when combined with a high level of verbosity in the OpenVPN configuration you will learn a lot about certificates.

# Using TinyCA2 to Manage Certificates

TinyCA2 is a very handy tool to accomplish certificate management. It provides extended functions and the possibility to influence the behavior of OpenSSL itself. TinyCA2 is available for OpenSuSE on online repositories; other distributions must look on `http://tinyca.sm-zone.net/` for appropriate packages or source code. On OpenSuSE, TinyCA2 can easily be installed using YaST. I also read about a MAC port on `http://tinyca2.darwinports.com/`, so there should be a version for almost every UNIX/Linux system.

TinyCA2 can be used to create a CA and to import and export CAs, certificates, keys, and revocation lists. It can manage several CAs and will offer the choice of which CA to load on startup, if several CAs are configured.

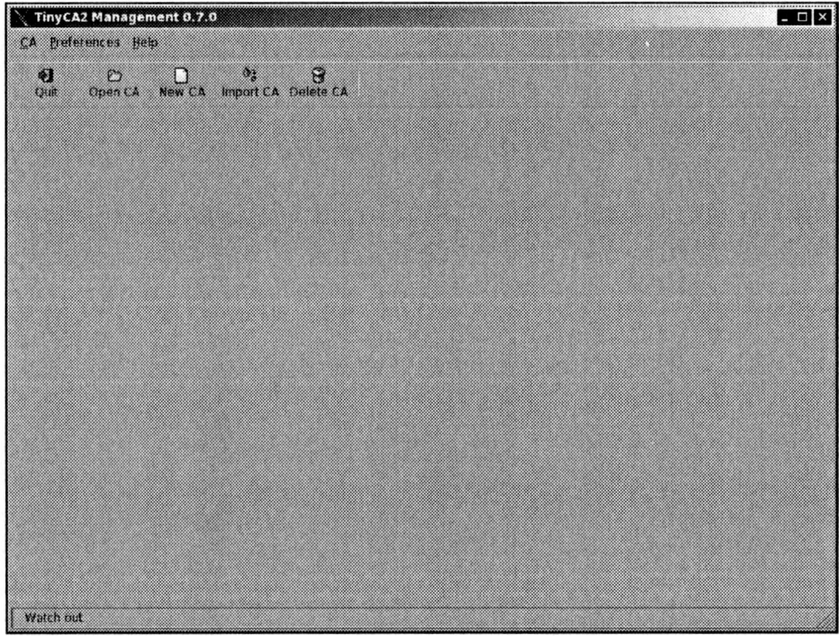


## Importing Our CA

After installation, start TinyCA2 from SuSE's main menu. Select Utilities | Security | tool to manage a Certificate Authority (TinyCA2). TinyCA2 is started and displays an empty window. The icons in the tool bar offer several possibilities:

- Open CA: Open an existing CA—that is a CA that has previously been imported to TinyCA2
- New CA: Create a completely new CAN
- Import CA: Import a CA (like those we created with `easy-rsa`) into TinyCA2

Click on the Import CA icon to import the previously created CA. The Import CA dialog is displayed:

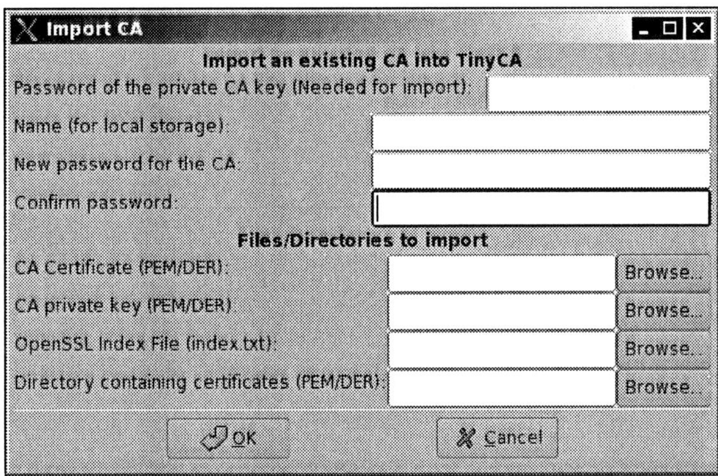


Here we must enter the password, location, and filename of the CA certificate and key file. TinyCA2 offers extended possibilities like changing the password for the CA right here or importing the SSL index file. However, entering password, certificate file, and key are enough to import the CA. Click on OK to start the import.

## Using TinyCA2 for CA Administration

If you have several CAs to administer, TinyCA2 will present the following window on startup. This window is also displayed when you select the Open CA icon.

Once you have loaded, created, or imported a CA, the main window of TinyCA2 will be much richer with icons, menus, and features. TinyCA2 offers a lot of details, information boxes, and history functions that let us manage our certificates and keys on a very reliable and controllable base.

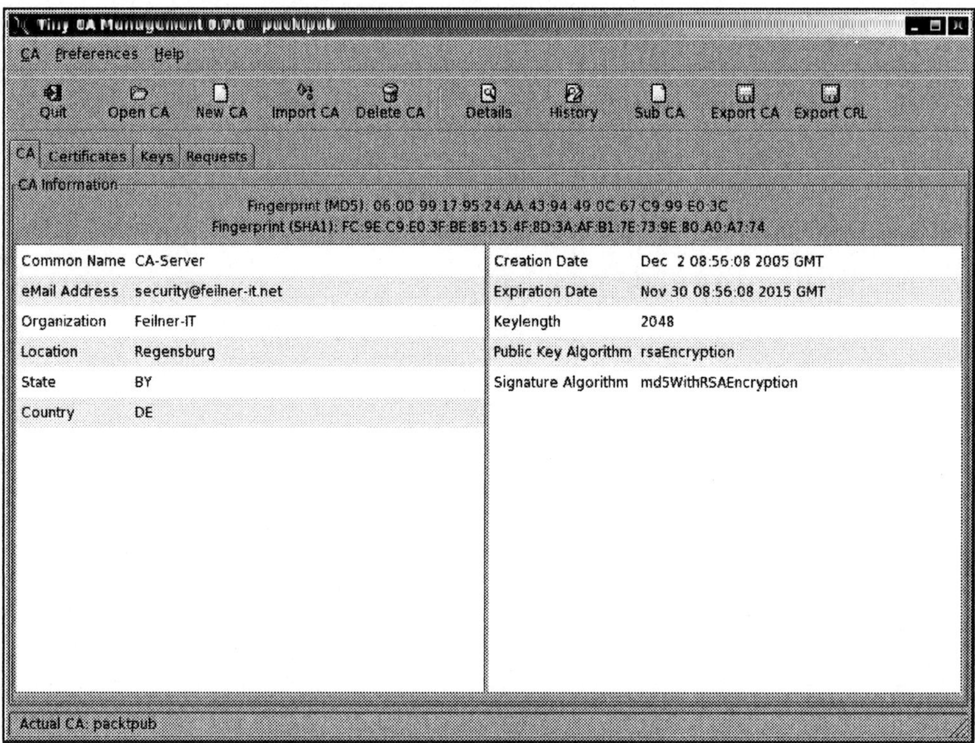


Like xca, TinyCA2 also presents some tabs in its main window, and a lot of work is done by selecting entries from context menus. The **CA** tab shows some information on the CA itself, the **Certificates** and **Keys** tabs list the existing certificates and keys for this CA, and the **Requests** tab is needed to create and sign new certificates and keys.

## Creating New Certificates and Keys

If we want to create and sign a new certificate for our CA with TinyCA2, we have to create a key signing request first. Change to the **Requests** tab, right-click, and select **New Request** from the context menu. The following window appears:

Create Request

Create a new Certificate Request

Common Name (eg, your Name, your eMail Address or the Servers Name)

eMail Address:

Password (protect your private Key):

Password (confirmation):

Country Name (2 letter code): DE

State or Province Name: BY

Locality Name (eg. city): Regensburg

Organization Name (eg. company): Feilner-IT

Organizational Unit Name (eg. section):

Keylength: 1024 2048 4096

Digest: MD5 SHA1 MD2 MDC2 MD4

Algorithm: RSA DSA

OK Cancel

I don't think that you need an explanation for the fields in this window. They are the same as in the information we provided for easy-rsa and xca on certificate generation. However, we have to make sure that an appropriate key size is selected and that the Common Name is distinguishable. Click on OK to create the request.

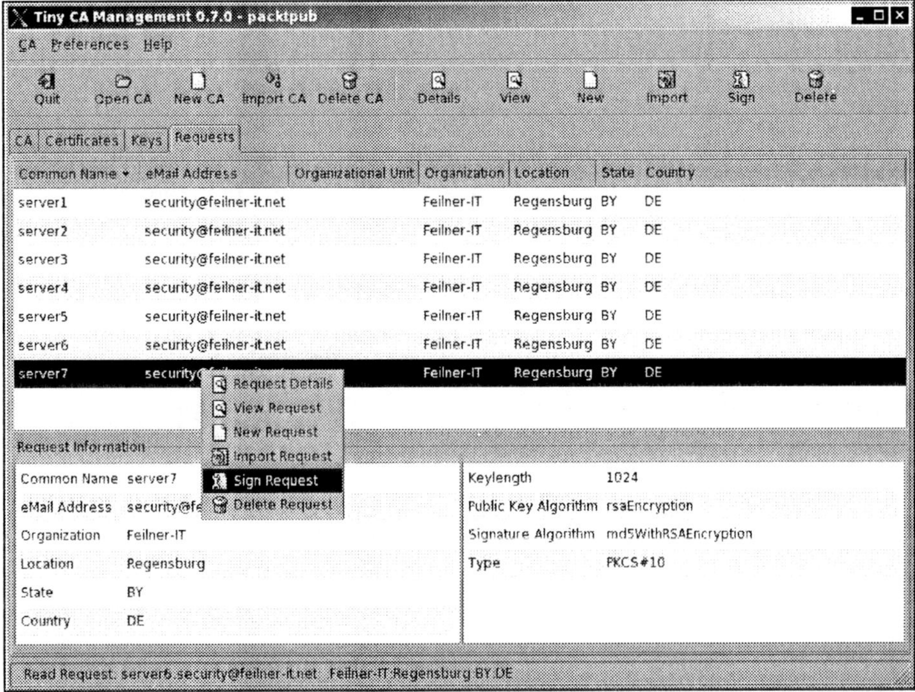

In the previous example we see a CA with many certificates and requests. Right-click on your newly generated request, and select the menu entry **Sign Request** to sign it using the active CA's certificate. Another small menu appears, asking you whether the request will be signed as a server or a client. This is for an example purpose that we have talked about on the xca pages. For a TLS server's certificate, choose **Sign Request (Server)**; for all clients, please choose **Sign Request (Client)**.

Now we are asked to enter the CA's password to sign the request:

Enter your password and check again, if the validity is suitable for your purposes and click on **OK** to confirm. After some seconds of calculating, your machine will tell you that the certificate has successfully been created. Now switch to the **Keys** section. There is a new entry for the newly created key/certificate pair, and there is also a new entry in the list of the available certificates.

## Exporting Keys and Certificates with TinyCA2

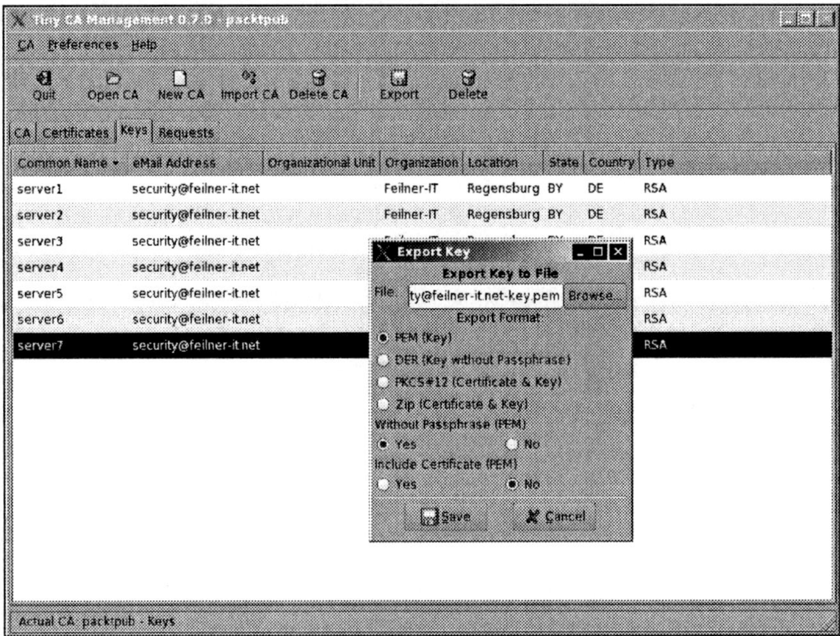

With TinyCA2 we can export the CA and the client certificate and key to a local file. TinyCA2 knows several file formats for the key/certificate pairs. In the previous screenshot, you see the default, `.pem` key files. Please note that if you do not want to enter a passphrase every time your OpenVPN tunnel is started, then you must activate the button Without Passphrase (PEM) | Yes. Otherwise, your key is password-protected, which may be considered as an extra level of security.

Enter a file name or select a directory by clicking on the button Browse and then click on the button Save. Repeat these steps for the client certificate (use the standard PEM Certificate) and the CA certificate (by clicking on the icon Export CA in the toolbar).

## Revoking Certificates with TinyCA2

Creating and exporting a CRL with TinyCA2 is very easy, too. In the Certificate tab, right-click on the certificate you want to revoke. You are prompted for the CA password and you are given the possibility to enter a reason for revocation:

Enter the CA password, select a revocation reason, and click on OK to revoke the selected certificate. Now switch to the CA tab and click on the Export CRL icon in the toolbar. Again, you have to enter the CA's password and a validity date for this CRL. Enter a file name and click on the Save button to export the CRL.

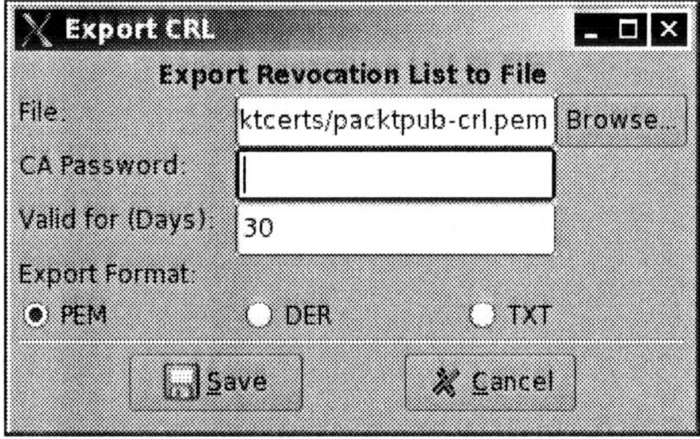

# Summary

We have created, imported, and exported CA certificates, client and server certificates and keys, in addition to revocation lists with the tools xca and TinyCA2. We have seen that there are many features TinyCA2 offers that are neither in the scope of `easy-rsa` nor available in xca. This is the reason why TinyCA2 is my favorite certificate management tool. However, all those tools use only the "toolbox" OpenSSL. If you want to read more and become a certificate professional, "man OpenSSL", then the website `http://www.openssl.org` is the place to go.

# 10

# Advanced OpenVPN Configuration

In this chapter, we will deal with several examples of advanced OpenVPN configurations such as:

- Tunneling through a proxy server like **squid**
- Scripting OpenVPN—An overview
- Authentication methods
- Using a server configuration with specific per-client configurations pushed to clients based on their certificates
- Pushing routing commands to clients
- Pushing and setting the default route through a tunnel
- Protecting clients through a firewall behind the tunnel
- Distributed compilation through VPN tunnels with **distcc**
- Automatic installation for Windows clients

Because OpenVPN offers an abundance of possibilities, some aspects of these configurations can only be covered at a basic level (like squid proxy or LDAP authentication). However, there are hints and links to Internet sites containing detailed information about these setups.

## Tunneling a Proxy Server and Protecting the Proxy

OpenVPN can use the HTTP method CONNECT to establish a tunnel between the client and its VPN server. Since this is a standard method used by most banking websites or any other security-conscious websites, most proxies and firewalls are open to such connections.

A simple OpenVPN configuration entry for use with an HTTP proxy may look like this:

```
(...)
port 443
proto tcp-client
http-proxy proxy 3128
http-proxy-retry
http-proxy-option AGENT Mozilla/4.0 (compatible; MSIE 4.01; Windows NT 5.0)
(...)
```

We are using `port 443` TCP, which will make our VPN tunnel almost invisible to local administrators. OpenVPN must furthermore know where to find the proxy server and on which port it is listening. In the aforementioned example, the name of the server is `proxy` and its port is `3128`. In addition to this, OpenVPN will try indefinitely to establish a connection and stealthily pretend to be a Mozilla browser on Windows 2000. Pretty nice, isn't it?

I consider this as one of the main advantages of OpenVPN. There are only few networks where an OpenVPN tunnel cannot be set up—don't worry about the frowning local administrators at your side!

The following table shows possible options concerning proxy configuration of OpenVPN:

| Parameter | Function |
|---|---|
| `--auto-proxy` | Tries auto-detection of proxy settings |
| `--http-proxy <IP> <port> <authfile><auth-method>` | IP and port of proxy server, optionally with proxy authentication:<br>`<authfile>` is a file containing username and password on two separate lines<br>`<auth-method>` can be `ntlm`, `basic`, or `none` |
| `--http-proxy-retry` | Retries indefinitely to connect to proxy |
| `--http-proxy-timeout <n>` | Sets proxy timeout manually to n seconds; the default is 5 (s) |
| `--http-proxy-option type <option>` | Sets user agent (browser version string) or HTTP version that is used |
| `--port` | 443 (HTTPS) is probably the most inconspicuous selection (remember to set this on both sides), but most proxies permit also port 80 (HTTP) or 21 (FTP) |
| `--socks-proxy <IP> <port>` | Uses the socks proxy on machine with `<IP> <port>` |
| `--socks-proxy-retry` | Retries indefinitely |

However, there are possible solutions to prevent OpenVPN tunnels. A secure squid proxy server configuration might for example look like this:

```
(...)
acl SSL_ports port 443 563
acl Safe_ports port 80 # http
acl Safe_ports port 21 # ftp
acl Safe_ports port 443 563 # https, snews
(...)
acl CONNECT method CONNECT
http_access allow manager localhost
http_access deny manager
http_access deny !Safe_ports
http_access deny CONNECT !SSL_ports
(...)
acl ADS_WWW_Benutzer external wb_group WWW_User
acl ADS_WWW_trusted external wb_group WWW_trusted
(...)
http_access allow WWW_User
```

```
http_access allow www_trusted
http_access allow www_trusted !Safe_ports
http_access allow www_trusted CONNECT !Safe_ports
http_access deny all
(...)
```

Squid uses access lists (acl) and access directives (http_access), which can be found in /etc/squid/squid.conf to control Internet access. In the configuration above, access lists are defined for "SSL Ports" and "Safe Ports" for HTTPS and FTP. Some lines further down in this file there are http_access directives, which explicitly allow access to SSL and safe ports for members of the user group www_trusted only. In this configuration an external authentication program, wb_group is used. wb_group is a small Perl script that enables squid to ask user information from a Microsoft Active Directory Server. On this system, Windows administrators can control the usage of HTTPS or other SSL connections through their proxy server by simply adding or removing users from the privileged group. As a side effect, only users in the group www_trusted can access https:// web pages. This may be difficult to communicate in a company, but it is definitely more secure. We have been using similar setups in recent years, and (after convincing the administrators) have only had positive experience.

# Scripting OpenVPN—An Overview

Another striking option of OpenVPN is its scripting capabilities. We can create our own scripts and have them called on changes of the connection state. This makes it easy to execute a special (e.g. Firewall) script any time a client connects or on similar occasions. There's almost no limit; I leave it up to you to imagine the possibilities.

The following table gives an overview over the possible interfaces where OpenVPN can be forced to execute arbitrary scripts:

| Option | Occurrence |
|---|---|
| --learn-address <cmd> | When the IP of a VPN partner changes |
| --ipchange <cmd> | When the IP of the server has changed |
| --client-connect <cmd> | When a client connects |
| --client-disconnect <cmd> | When a client disconnects |
| --up <cmd>, down <cmd> | After configuration (up = starting, down = stopping) of the TUN/TAP device |
| --down-pre | Before shutting down the TUN/TAP device |
| --up-restart | When tunnels are restarted, up/down scripts are also executed |

- learn-address: This option calls a command and hands over three variables: *operation*, which can be one of "add", "update", or "delete" and directly refers to the change of the client's address that has taken place, *address* containing the IP address set or deleted, and *common name*, which is again the entry from the client's certificate's subject line.

- `ipchange`: This refers to the IP address of the VPN server; the command is executed after authentication (or remote IP change).
- `client-connect` and `client-disconnect`: These call commands immediately after connection or disconnection of a VPN client. These options can only be used in OpenVPN server mode.
- `--up` and `--down`: These are probably the most interesting scripting interface options. The scripts defined here are called immediately after starting or stopping the tunnel interfaces and before an optional `--user` identity change takes place. Thus here root privileges may be available, which allow, e.g., setting routes or similar tasks.

In the manpage of OpenVPN, `http://openvpn.net/man.html`, there is a special section *Environmental Variables* listing all variables passed to commands, and the (German) website `http://www.pronix.de/pronix-991.html` shows a list of the variables that are passed to the command invoked. For non-German speakers, here is a brief English list of the variables:

| Environment Variable | Contents If DEV = TUN | Contents If DEV = TAP |
|---|---|---|
| `$1` | Name of (TUN) interface | Name of (TAP) interface |
| `$2` | MTU | MTU |
| `$3` | Link-MTU | Link-MTU |
| `$4` | Local IP of TUN interface | Local IP of TAP interface |
| `$5` | Remote IP | Netmask of TAP interface |
| `$6` | init, if called by `--up`;<br>restart if called by `--up-restart` | init, if called by `--up`;<br>restart if called by `--up-restart` |

# Using Authentication Methods

We have learned before that OpenVPN can be used with authentication based on shared secrets (static keys) and X.509 certificates. Another useful option for authentication is authentication plug-ins called with the configuration parameter `auth-user-pass-verify`, which can be used together with both methods mentioned before. For example, in a certificate-based VPN, we can use an authentication plug-in to make sure that only a user knowing the appropriate username/password combination can start the tunnel. This may be a convenient additional level of security for laptops or other road-warrior machines.

While certificates in this context tend to protect and authenticate machines rather than users, username/password combinations are useful for VPNs that are started by a human. The Windows GUI will pop up a small authentication window where the user must enter a username and password. The VPN client takes these values and sends them to the VPN server, which starts the plug-in program (as configured in `auth-user-pass-verify`) to validate the combination. If the authentication program returns an OK, authentication was successful, and the tunnel is created. The tunnel will only be established if the password is correct.

For this purpose, the following configuration parameters must be added: In the server configuration file, add `auth-user-pass-verify /path/to/your/auth/script` to your server configuration and `auth-user-pass` to your client's configuration. The following table shows the usage of these parameters:

| Parameter | Allowed options | Usage | Function |
|---|---|---|---|
| `--auth-user-pass-verify` | `<script>` `<method>` | Server configuration | Activates server's authentication and defines the name of the authentication script and the method to use for username/password handling |
| `--auth-user-pass` | `<file>` | Client configuration | Activates client's authentication and optionally defines a file where username and password are stored |

On SuSE systems there are some example scripts (like `auth_pam.pl`) provided with OpenVPN, which can be found in `/usr/share/doc/packages/openvpn/sample-scripts`. But a typical scenario for such an authentication may be a local LDAP server. LDAP is the system-independent state of the art for all modern directory services both in open-source servers and also in Microsoft's Active Directory Service. The following overview will give you some hints on how to create an authentication plug-in using your own LDAP authentication for OpenVPN.

On a Linux system with the LDAP client tools installed, the command `ldapwhoami` can be used for testing username/password pairs against an LDAP server. In the following examples the LDAP server is `10.10.10.1`, the user `mfeilner`, and the password is `correct_password`. The string `uid=mfeilner,ou=Feilner-it_Users,dc=feilner-it,dc=home` must be adapted to the settings on your LDAP server. Here is the output of the `ldapwhoami` command:

```
suse01:/var/log # ldapwhoami -x -h 10.10.10.1 -D uid=mfeilner,ou=Feilner-
it_Users,dc=feilner-it,dc=home -w correct_password
dn:uid=mfeilner,ou=Feilner-it_Users,dc=feilner-it,dc=home

suse01: # ldapwhoami -x -h 10.10.10.1 -D uid=mfeilner,ou=Feilner-
it_Users,dc=feilner-it,dc=home -w wrong_password
ldap_bind: Invalid credentials (49)
```

The first command will give a return code of "0", whereas the second command, resulting in a failed authentication returned a value of "1". Creating a little script that implements the aforementioned LDAP command and returns a 0 if authentication was successful, and a 1 if authentication has failed, is easy and I leave this up to you. An example for such an LDAP authentication plug-in script for OpenVPN can be found here: `http://www.indato.ch/openvpn/openvpn.html`.

Even though this site is in German, the LDAP script found here is documented in English. You can find it if you scroll down until the heading Optionale Authentisierung mit LDAP. An English site with an OpenVPN Auth-LDAP Plugin can be found here: `http://www.opendarwin.org/~landonf/software/openvpn-auth-ldap/`.

phpLDAPadmin is probably one of the best LDAP administration tools. If you are thinking of setting up an LDAP server (which can be used for a variety of purposes), have a look at this screenshot of phpLDAPadmin on an LDAP server with the entry `uid=mfeilner,ou=Feilner-it_Users,dc=feilner-it,dc=home`, which was used for authentication above.

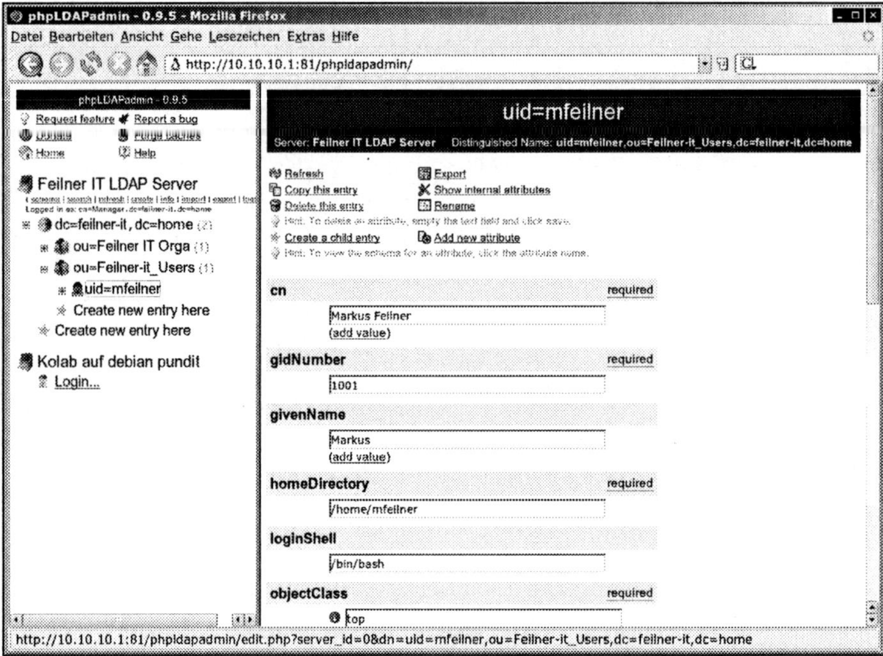


On the left is the LDAP directory tree, on the right the properties of the selected object. Here we can change e.g. the password for the OpenVPN account, create and delete accounts, and thus manage access to our VPN on the basis of the selected authentication plug-in.

# Using a Client Configuration Directory with Per-Client Configurations

Another striking feature of OpenVPN is the fact that we can have client configurations pushed through the tunnel on creation and use client-specific configurations, which are simply set by the subject line of the client's certificate. An appropriate server configuration file may look like the following:

```
port 443
dev tun0FIT
ca /etc/openvpn/certs/ca.crt
cert /etc/openvpn/certs/firewall.crt
key /etc/openvpn/certs/firewall.key
dh /etc/openvpn/certs/dh2048.pem
tls-auth /etc/openvpn/certs/ta.key 0
auth SHA1
cipher AES-256-CBC
tls-cipher DHE-RSA-AES256-SHA
server 10.179.0.0 255.255.0.0
ifconfig-pool-persist /etc/openvpn/ipp.txt
client-config-dir clients
keepalive 10 120
resolv-retry 86400
comp-lzo
```

```
status /var/log/openvpn/status.log
log /var/log/openvpn/main.log
tls-server
verb 3
```

There are three lines that are relevant in this context:

1. `server 10.179.0.0 255.255.0.0`: This tells OpenVPN on this machine to act as a server and automatically distribute IP addresses to clients connecting.
2. `ifconfig-pool-persist /etc/openvpn/ipp.txt`: This makes OpenVPN keep a list of certificate to IP relationships, so that a client connecting will (probably) always have the same IP.
3. `client-config-dir clients`: This has OpenVPN look in the directory "clients" for a client-specific configuration file when a client connects.

A client configuration file must have a name matching the `CN` in the `Subject` line of the certificate. If a client connects with a certificate containing the following subject:

```
(...)
Subject: C=DE, ST=Bayern, L=Regensburg, O=Feilner-IT,
CN=mfeilner/emailAddress=mfeilner@feilner-it.net
(...)
```

Then the server will look if the directory clients contain a configuration file named `mfeilner`. This file may contain push options like the following:

```
ifconfig-push 10.179.0.3 10.179.0.4
push "route 10.1.0.0 255.255.0.0"
```

In this scenario, this client will always have the IP address `10.179.0.3` and is told about a network (10.1.0.0) behind the tunnel. Thus, if we use different client configurations, we can control the routing and network configuration for every client. It's simple to grant access to the network by activating or deactivating a client's routing on connecting, but we must always remember that this offers no real protection, because every local administrator could also activate this routing on the client.

On the client configuration, the parameter `client` must be present. If we want to have the client redirect its default gateway through the tunnel, we simply need to add the parameter `redirect-gateway`.

Redirecting the client's default gateway is another excellent feature of OpenVPN, especially when combined with HTTP-proxy tunneling. The parameter `redirect-gateway` causes three steps:

1. A static route to the other tunnel partner is created.
2. The old default gateway is deleted.
3. A new entry for the default gateway is created (pointing to the IP address of the other tunnel endpoint).

Of course we can enter these steps manually, if we like. The `route` command will help us here:

```
debian01:~# route add 172.16.103.2 gw 172.16.247.1
debian01:~# route del default
debian01:~# route add default gw 10.179.10.2
debian01:~# route -n
Kernel IP routing table
Destination     Gateway         Genmask         Flags Metric Ref    Use Iface
```

```
172.16.103.2    172.16.247.1    255.255.255.255 UGH   0      0        0 eth0
10.179.10.2     0.0.0.0         255.255.255.255 UH    0      0        0
tunVPN0
172.16.247.0    0.0.0.0         255.255.255.0   U     0      0        0 eth0
172.16.76.0     10.179.10.2     255.255.255.0   UG    0      0        0
tunVPN0
192.168.250.0   0.0.0.0         255.255.255.0   U     0      0        0 eth1
0.0.0.0         10.179.10.2     0.0.0.0         UG    0      0        0
tunVPN0
debian01:~#
```

First, we added a static route to the VPN partner (`route add 172.16.103.2 gw 172.16.247.1`). Then we deleted the old default route (`route del default`), and as a last step we created the new default route with `route add default gw 10.179.10.2`. From this moment on, all traffic not destined to the VPN partner's public IP will be routed through the tunnel, as the output of `route -n` will show. Because the routing entries will be useless when the VPN partner's IP changes, it is a good idea to have OpenVPN set the routing for us.

The next chapter deals more detailed with interpreting routing tables.

# Individual Firewall Rules for Connecting Clients

One striking possibility OpenVPN offers is a setup where:

- An OpenVPN machine acts as a server that protects the company's network, admitting access for OpenVPN clients.
- The clients are automatically assigned IPs by the server.
- The clients are equipped with certificates, and identified and authorized by these certificates.

The scripting parameter `learn-address` in the server's OpenVPN configuration file will have the server execute a script whenever an authorized client connects to the VPN and is assigned an address. This parameter takes the full path to a script as an option:

```
learn-address /etc/openvpn/scripts/openvpnFW
```

In this example, the script `openvpnFW` will be executed each time a client is assigned an IP address and will be passed three variables by the OpenVPN server process:

1. `$1`: The action taken; this may be one of add, delete, update
2. `$2`: The IP assigned to the client connecting
3. `$3`: The common name in the subject line of the client's certificate

Add the line `learn-address /etc/openvpn/scripts/openvpnFW` to your OpenVPN server configuration file and edit the file `/etc/openvpn/scripts/openvpnFW` to be like the following. These lines will show how to make use of these parameters in a short Linux shell script:

```
#!/bin/sh
LOGFILE=
DATE=`/bin/date`
echo $DATE $1 $2 $3 >> $LOGFILE
```

This script will only export the variables passed to the logfile, including a timestamp that is added by the command `date`. Stop and start your tunnel a few times. Now let's have a look at the file `/var/log/openvpn/connections.log`:

```
Mi Feb 1 04:33:53 CET 2006 update 10.99.0.3 mfeilner
Do Feb 2 04:34:33 CET 2006 update 10.99.0.3 mfeilner
Fr Feb 3 04:34:14 CET 2006 update 10.99.0.3 mfeilner
Sa Feb 4 04:34:53 CET 2006 update 10.99.0.3 mfeilner
So Feb 5 04:34:43 CET 2006 update 10.99.0.3 mfeilner
```

This example shows my VPN client reconnecting every day. This alone might yet be an interesting feature, if you want to keep track of your users and their VPN connections. However, we can do more. Let's add some more lines to our `openvpnFW` script:

```
if [ $1 = add ]
then
/etc/openvpn/scripts/$2.FW_connect.sh
fi
if [ $1 = delete ]
then
/etc/openvpn/scripts/$2.FW_disconnect.sh
fi
```

Two simple tests are run and, depending on the content of the variable `$1`, different firewall scripts are executed. Let's express this in brief. If the first variable passed is `add`, then the script `/etc/openvpn/scripts/$2.FW_connect.sh` is run, where `$2` will be replaced by the IP of the client connecting. If for example a client `mfeilner` connects and is assigned the IP `10.99.0.3`, then the variables passed to this script `openvpnFW` will be:

```
add 10.99.0.3 mfeilner
```

And the script run will be called: `/etc/openvpn/scripts/10.99.0.3.FW_connect.sh`.

However, if the variables passed to `openvpnFW` are the following:

```
delete 10.99.0.3
```

then the script `/etc/openvpn/scripts/10.99.0.3.FW_disconnect.sh` will be executed.

I think you have already guessed that these two scripts contain firewall rules (like `iptables` statements) for the client with the certificate `mfeilner`. Even though all of this could be done within one single script, I prefer to have the tests and firewall rules split up in several scripts.

This setup can become very powerful and fairly complex. A client that has its default route set through the tunnel can be allowed selective Internet access, simply by enabling or disabling, routing or forwarding. And access to the local servers can also be easily managed: E.g. A SAP server might only be available for road warriors from 7 am to 6 pm, whereas during the night firewall rules protect the server.

# Distributed Compilation through VPN Tunnels with distcc

distcc is a compiler (or a front end to **GNU Compiler Collection** (**GCC**)) designed to split up compiling processes over many machines, which can speed up the process enormously. The **distccd** daemon has to be run on all of the systems that are to participate, then the system starting the process must be informed about the distcc hosts, and then we can start a compiling process.

On Debian systems, installation is as easy as typing `apt-get install distcc`. As the next step some parameters have to be set in `/etc/default/distcc`:

- Whether distccd should be started on boot
- A list of other distcc hosts that are allowed to connect
- The interface distcc should listen on for incoming connections

This is the file `/etc/default/distcc` on a Debian system:

```
# Defaults for distcc initscript
# sourced by /etc/init.d/distcc

#
# should distcc be started on boot?
#
# STARTDISTCC="true"

STARTDISTCC="false"

#
# Which networks/hosts should be allowed to connect to the daemon?
# You can list multiple hosts/networks separated by spaces.
# Networks have to be in CIDR notation, f.e. 192.168.1.0/24
# Hosts are represented by a single IP address
#
# ALLOWEDNETS="127.0.0.1"

ALLOWEDNETS="127.0.0.1"

#
# Which interface should distccd listen on?
# You can specify a single interface, identified by it's IP address, here.
#
# LISTENER="127.0.0.1"

LISTENER="127.0.0.1"
```

Here we will have to edit the parameters `ALLOWEDNETS` and `LISTENER` to our needs and repeat this step for every partner that is supposed to take part in the collective compilation. Then, either edit your startup files to include a system variable called `DISTCC_HOSTS` or create a configuration file `./distcc/hosts` in your home directory with a list of the other hosts that are supposed to take part in compiling. The content of this variable or file should simply be a (space-separated) list of hosts like:

```
10.179.0.1 192.168.1.4 10.179.0.3
```

I think you will already know where this is leading to: we will install OpenVPN tunnels on each machine taking part in the distcc network and then we only need to enter the IP of the tunnel machines in these files here.

That's all, now we can use distcc over the tunneled connections. Therefore the distcc daemon has to be started with /etc/init.d/disstcc start and then we can start a compiling process where we use distcc as compiler: For instance, in the directory /usr/src/linux, simply type make CC=distcc to have the selected machines in your network compile this machine's kernel together. Or have a look at the following example where OpenVPN is compiled via distcc:

```
debian01:~/openvpn-2.0.5# make CC=distcc
make  all-am
make[1]: Entering directory `/root/openvpn-2.0.5'
if distcc -DHAVE_CONFIG_H -I. -I. -I.    -I.    -g -O2 -MT mroute.o -MD -MP -MF
".deps/mroute.Tpo" -c -o mroute.o mroute.c; \
        then mv -f ".deps/mroute.Tpo" ".deps/mroute.Po"; else rm -f
".deps/mroute.Tpo"; exit 1; fi
if distcc -DHAVE_CONFIG_H -I. -I. -I.    -I.    -g -O2 -MT mss.o -MD -MP -MF
".deps/mss.Tpo" -c -o mss.o mss.c; \
        then mv -f ".deps/mss.Tpo" ".deps/mss.Po"; else rm -f ".deps/mss.Tpo";
exit 1; fi
if distcc -DHAVE_CONFIG_H -I. -I. -I.    -I.    -g -O2 -MT mtcp.o -MD -MP -MF
".deps/mtcp.Tpo" -c -o mtcp.o mtcp.c; \
        then mv -f ".deps/mtcp.Tpo" ".deps/mtcp.Po"; else rm -f
".deps/mtcp.Tpo"; exit 1; fi
(...)
```

# Ethernet Bridging with OpenVPN

On Linux, Windows XP, and Windows 2003 we can use our VPN tunnels as one big logical Ethernet network. By connecting (**bridging**) a virtual OpenVPN interface and a real Ethernet interface, we connect (bridge) the networks behind these interfaces and provide a virtual Ethernet between the hosts in the real networks, including exchange of Ethernet Frames. This feature can be useful for Windows users that will need to exchange broadcast packages through the tunnel, e.g. for network browsing, LAN parties, and more.

Setting up OpenVPN for bridging mode is simple and the same for all operating systems: We only have to make sure our OpenVPN setup is working and that we are using TAP devices. I recommend the use of TLS-server setup with clients that are automatically assigned addresses and configurations.

On Linux, you will need to install the **bridge-utils** package and follow the information on the website http://openvpn.net/bridge.html. Windows users can simply use the network settings of their operating system to activate bridging mode:

Open your Network Connections window and select (mark) the two network interfaces that you want to bridge. Then select the entry Bridge Connections from the context menu.

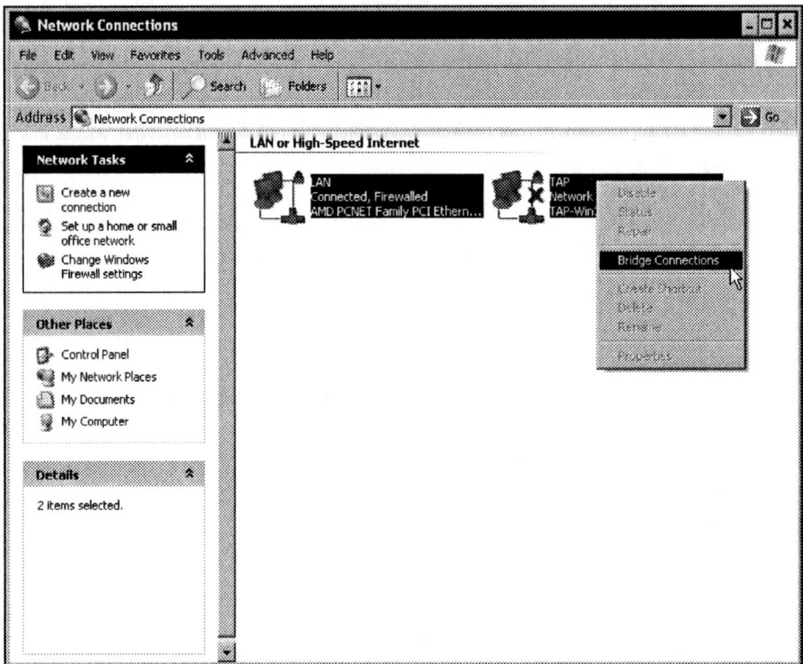


A new icon will appear, called Network Bridge, and the LAN interface will show Bridged in its name:

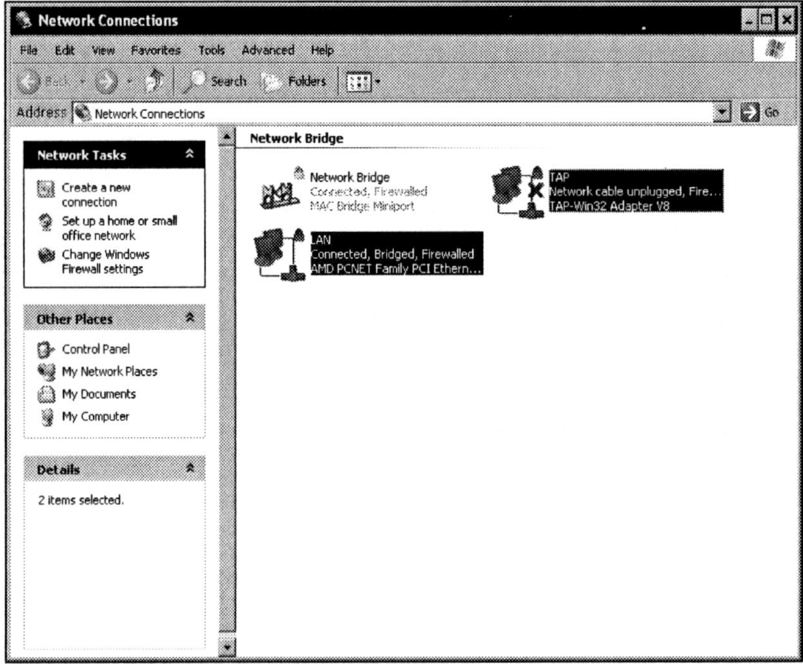

This Ethernet bridge can now be configured (almost) like any other network device. Select the entry properties from its context menu:

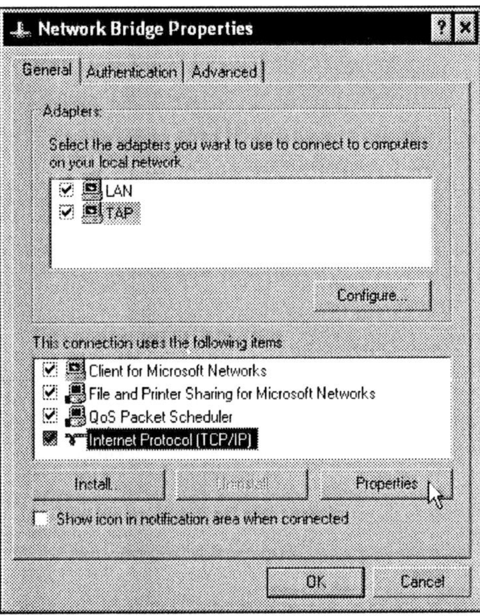


As last step we have to assign an IP to this interface or configure the interface to obtain an IP automatically, which is the default setting. Select the entry Internet Protocol (TCP/IP) from the list This connection uses the following items: and click on the button Properties to assign an IP:

Internet Protocol (TCP/IP) Properties
General
You can get IP settings assigned automatically if your network supports this capability. Otherwise, you need to ask your network administrator for the appropriate IP settings.
Obtain an IP address automatically
Use the following IP address:
IP address: 192 . 168 . 0 . 22
Subnet mask: 255 . 255 . 255 . 0
Default gateway: 192 . 168 . 0 . 1
Obtain DNS server address automatically
Use the following DNS server addresses:
Preferred DNS server: 192 . 168 . 0 . 1
Alternate DNS server: . . .
Advanced...
OK
Cancel

That's it, your Ethernet Bridge is up and running. If you run into trouble with your OpenVPN configuration, check these websites for examples and guidelines:

`http://www.pavelec.net/adam/openvpn/bridge/`

`http://openvpn.net/bridge.html`

# Automatic Installation for Windows Clients

If you have to administer a large Windows network, you will probably know the pains of having to install software on several clients. There is a convenient way to install OpenVPN (almost) automatically: The open source Windows software **Nullsoft Scriptable Install System (NSIS)** installer available from `http://www.openvpn.se/files/nsis/nsis205.exe` and documented in `http://openvpn.se/files/howto/openvpn-howto_roll_your_own_installation_package.html` creates a executable file including configuration and certificate for your client.

Simply download the NSIS installer and execute it. In most cases, you will not need to make any changes to the default values during installation, except maybe for the path. Simply click the button Next three times, agree to the license, and NSIS is installed.

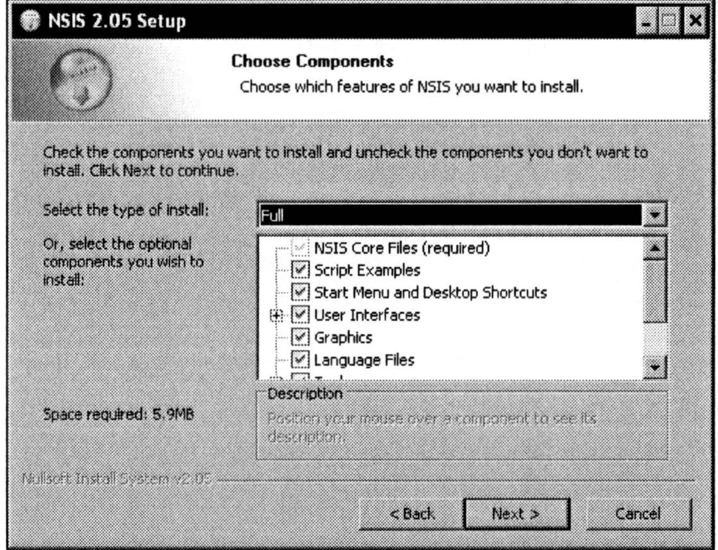

The following window shows the standard dialog of the NSIS installer providing detailed information on this tool:

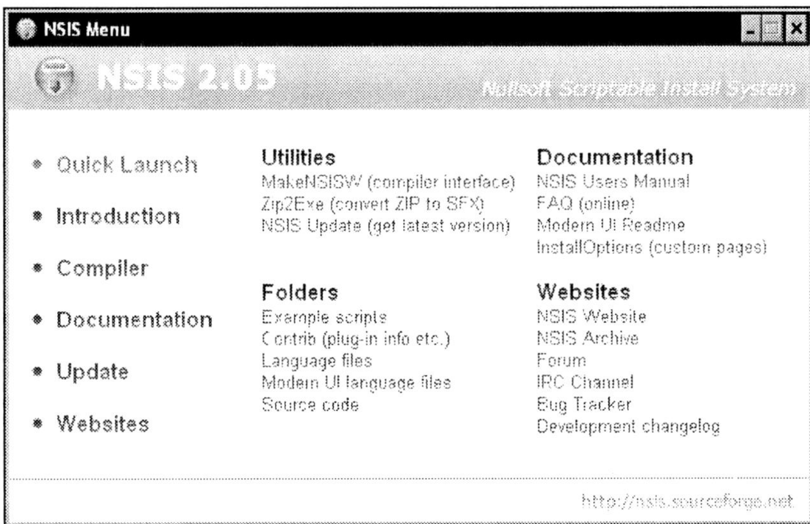


If you are interested in more information on the NSIS installer, have a look at the **Websites** link here. Your next step will be downloading and extracting the OpenVPN-GUI source code from `http://www.openvpn.se/files/install_packages_source/`.

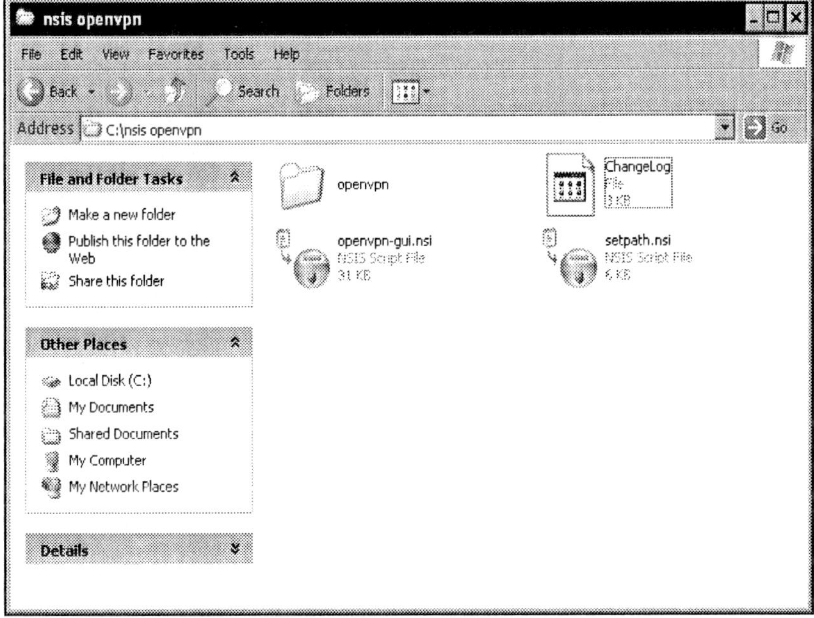

Then copy your OpenVPN configuration and certificates to the directory where you extracted the sources to and open the file `openvpn-gui.nsi` with Notepad. Here you only need to enter the name of your files and the path, if it differs from the values in the file. Search for lines containing `<File "${HOME}\config\office.ovpn">` and change this to your needs.

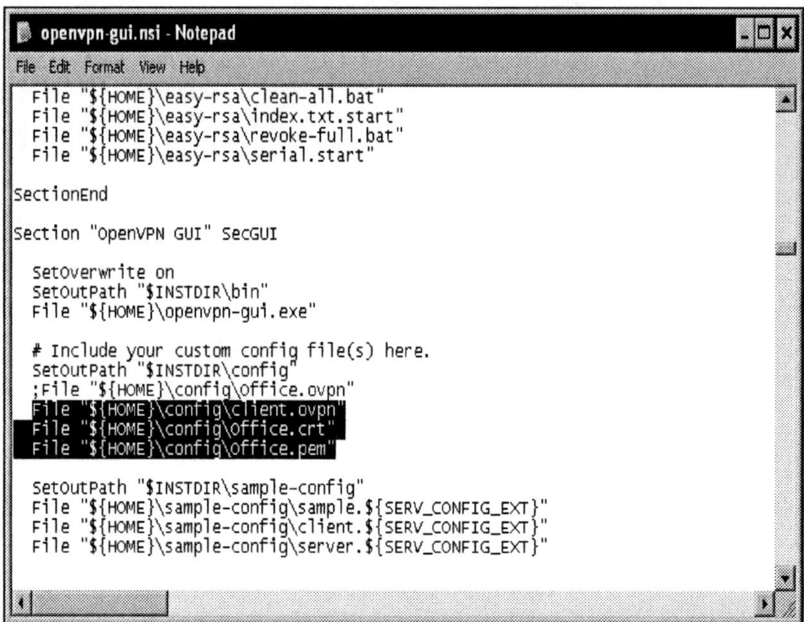

openvpn-gui.nsi - Notepad
File Edit Format View Help
File "${HOME}\easy-rsa\clean-all.bat"
File "${HOME}\easy-rsa\index.txt.start"
File "${HOME}\easy-rsa\revoke-full.bat"
File "${HOME}\easy-rsa\serial.start"
SectionEnd
Section "OpenVPN GUI" SecGUI
SetOverwrite on
SetOutPath "$INSTDIR\bin"
File "${HOME}\openvpn-gui.exe"
# Include your custom config file(s) here.
SetOutPath "$INSTDIR\config"
;File "${HOME}\config\office.ovpn"
File "${HOME}\config\client.ovpn"
File "${HOME}\config\office.crt"
File "${HOME}\config\office.pem"
SetOutPath "$INSTDIR\sample-config"
File "${HOME}\sample-config\sample.${SERV_CONFIG_EXT}"
File "${HOME}\sample-config\client.${SERV_CONFIG_EXT}"
File "${HOME}\sample-config\server.${SERV_CONFIG_EXT}"


The section *Modifying the script for your own needs* of the website `http://openvpn.se/files/howto/openvpn-howto_roll_your_own_installation_package.html` gives detailed information on possible and necessary changes for different scenarios. If you want to have configuration files deleted when OpenVPN is uninstalled, add the lines similar to the following ones:

```
Delete "$INSTDIR\config\client.ovpn"
Delete "$INSTDIR\config\client.crt"
Delete "$INSTDIR\config\client.pem"
```

As a last step we will now start the compilation progress, which is done with a simple context menu entry generated by the NSIS installer. Right-click on the file `openvpn-gui.nsi` and select the menu entry **Compile NSI Script**.

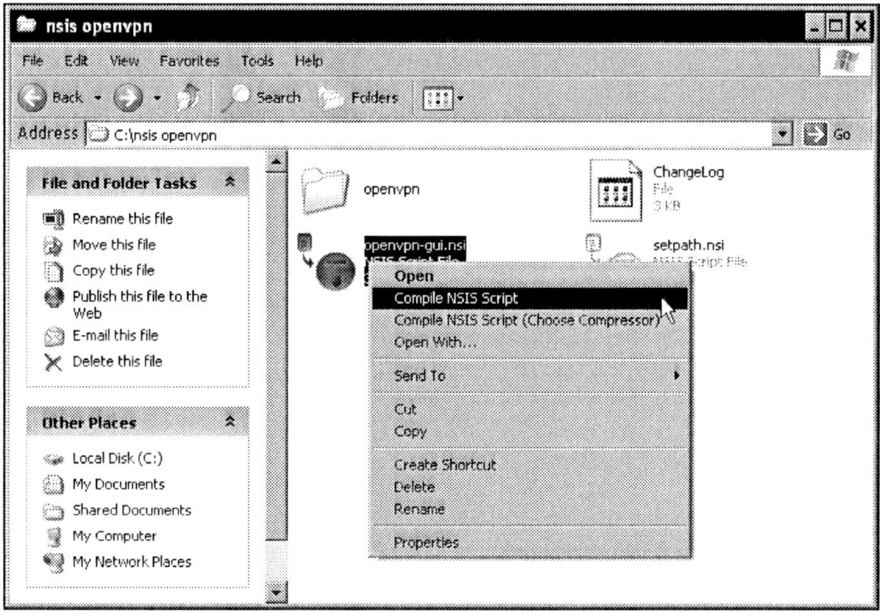


You will receive the following status window telling you about the progress. In the example below, an installer `.exe` file is created as `C:\nsis openvpn\openvpn-2.0.5-gui-1.0.3-install.exe`.

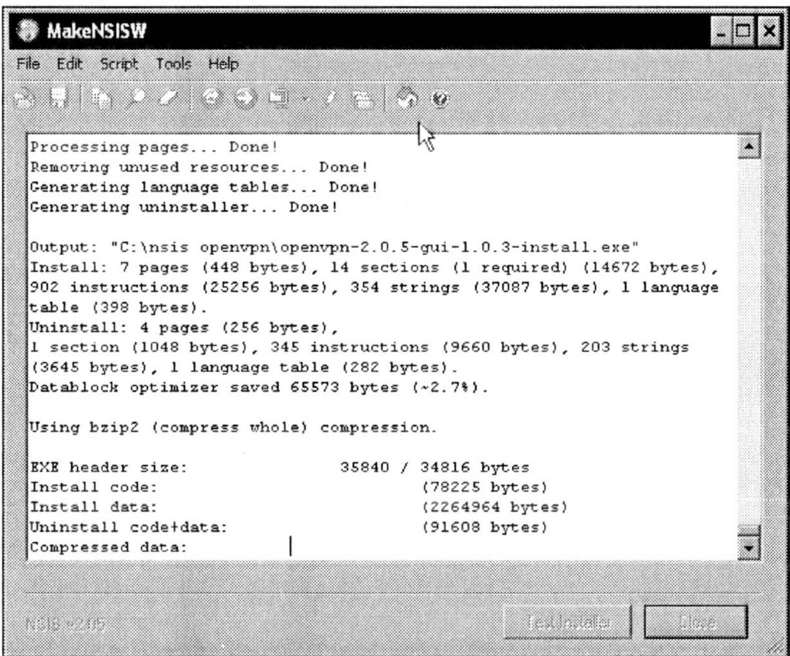

You can now transfer this `.exe` file to all clients and install them automatically with the configuration you provided. Installation works exactly as the standard installation described before.

However, there is a small problem here. We will need to change every client's certificate once; otherwise all clients would have the same certificate, which is not a really safe situation. Thus, all we have to do after having completed the steps above is:

- Transfer the `.exe` file to a client.
- Have it executed as administrator.
- Copy the client's certificate to the client.

You will need to use the same name for all certificates and configuration files on all clients, but again this is no problem, because the common name of the certificate's subject line will distinguish the clients.

# Summary

In this chapter we have discussed some typical advanced configurations for OpenVPN that showed some of its advantages. We have tunneled OpenVPN through an HTTP proxy and then we configured a squid proxy so that we could control who is allowed to do so. Then we had a closer look at the scripting interfaces OpenVPN offers, including lists of variables that are passed to the scripts by OpenVPN on invocation. One such script can be an authentication plug-in like the provided PAM authentication or better an authentication against LDAP servers. As a next step, we configured OpenVPN to use a per-client configuration based on the client's certificate, which would enable different configurations for different users connecting. This scenario can be made even more complicated when combined with per-user firewall rules being activated on the VPN server after a client connects.

`distcc`, a network-enabled compiler front end to GCC can be used together with OpenVPN tunnels to have remote machines work as a team when compiling software. And finally, we looked at automatic installation for Windows machines using the NSIS installer.

# 11

# Troubleshooting and Monitoring

In this chapter, we will learn how to use tools to debug and monitor our VPN tunnels. We will also learn how to scan and test the connectivity of a (VPN) server with standard networking tools.

## Testing the Network Connectivity

In our typical OpenVPN setup, we have connected two networks (192.168.250.0/24 and 172.16.76.0/24) via two Linux servers that are connected to the Internet via a default gateway. Between the two Linux servers is a tunnel that uses the virtual IPs 10.179.10.1 and 10.179.10.2.

In the connected local networks there are two Linux machines that we will use to test our tunnels (perhaps by conveniently accessing them remotely with Secure Shell). We will now use the tools `ifconfig`, `route`, and `ping` to show and test the network settings.

In our first step, we will check the local system's network address, default route, and if the default router is pingable. The command `ifconfig` will print statistics of all active network interfaces:

```
root@sydney:~ #ifconfig
eth0      Link encap:Ethernet  HWaddr 00:0C:29:AE:8C:D7
          inet addr:192.168.250.128  Bcast:192.168.250.255  Mask:255.255.255.0
          UP BROADCAST RUNNING MULTICAST  MTU:1500  Metric:1
          RX packets:2640 errors:0 dropped:0 overruns:0 frame:0
          TX packets:2290 errors:0 dropped:0 overruns:0 carrier:0
          collisions:0 txqueuelen:1000
          RX bytes:250738 (244.8 KiB)  TX bytes:273328 (266.9 KiB)
          Interrupt:10 Base address:0x1080

lo        Link encap:Local Loopback
          inet addr:127.0.0.1  Mask:255.0.0.0
          UP LOOPBACK RUNNING  MTU:16436  Metric:1
          RX packets:57 errors:0 dropped:0 overruns:0 frame:0
          TX packets:57 errors:0 dropped:0 overruns:0 carrier:0
          collisions:0 txqueuelen:0
          RX bytes:7907 (7.7 KiB)  TX bytes:7907 (7.7 KiB)
root@sydney:~ #
```

This system has the IP address `192.168.250.128`, and its network interface is up and running. Obviously this machine is located in Sydney, Australia.

Now let's look at its routing entries. The command `route` prints all routing entries, including the router to the Internet. A **default gateway** is a router that is supposed to handle all traffic not specified by any other routing entries. In our networks, the OpenVPN server is the only router from the internal network and is therefore configured as default gateway for the local network.

Type `route -n` to receive a numeric output of the routing table of your system. Simply typing `route` will work in most cases, but the command will try to resolve the IPs via DNS, which might take a little time.

```
root@sydney:~ #route -n
Kernel IP routing table
Destination     Gateway         Genmask         Flags Metric Ref    Use Iface
192.168.250.0   0.0.0.0         255.255.255.0   U     0      0        0 eth0
0.0.0.0         192.168.250.251 0.0.0.0         UG    0      0        0 eth0
root@sydney:~ #
```

We see a table where destinations, gateways, netmasks, and interfaces are listed. Every line is a routing entry that can be read like a real sentence. An entry `0.0.0.0` simply matches every address (source or destination, depending on the context) and is e. g. used for the default gateway.

Line three means that all traffic to the network `192.168.250.0` is sent directly to the network interface `eth0`, no matter which gateway is to be used.

Line four indicates that all the traffic to any destination will be sent over the default gateway `192.168.250.251` via interface `eth0`.

This setup is perfectly OK for a typical network client. Let's now test if the default gateway is reachable by pinging it from the client:

```
root@sydney:~ #ping 192.168.250.251
PING 192.168.250.251 (192.168.250.251): 56 data bytes
64 bytes from 192.168.250.251: icmp_seq=0 ttl=64 time=1.3 ms
64 bytes from 192.168.250.251: icmp_seq=1 ttl=64 time=0.6 ms
64 bytes from 192.168.250.251: icmp_seq=2 ttl=64 time=0.4 ms

--- 192.168.250.251 ping statistics ---
3 packets transmitted, 3 packets received, 0% packet loss
round-trip min/avg/max = 0.4/0.7/1.3 ms
root@sydney:~ #
```

It works. The default gateway (our OpenVPN server) answers the ping requests from our client. If it doesn't in your setup, check the firewall rules on this server as to whether they allow traffic from the internal network to the firewall itself. If you are unsure, it may be a good idea to temporarily stop the firewall services.

Now let's try the same on the client in the other network (obviously in Germany):

```
root@munich:~ #ifconfig
eth0      Link encap:Ethernet  HWaddr 00:0C:29:21:07:FC
          inet addr:172.16.76.128  Bcast:172.16.76.255  Mask:255.255.255.0
          UP BROADCAST RUNNING MULTICAST  MTU:1500  Metric:1
          RX packets:2399 errors:0 dropped:0 overruns:0 frame:0
          TX packets:2715 errors:0 dropped:0 overruns:0 carrier:0
          collisions:0 txqueuelen:1000
          RX bytes:345146 (337.0 KiB)  TX bytes:271839 (265.4 KiB)
          Interrupt:10 Base address:0x1080

lo        Link encap:Local Loopback
          inet addr:127.0.0.1  Mask:255.0.0.0
          UP LOOPBACK RUNNING  MTU:16436  Metric:1
          RX packets:8 errors:0 dropped:0 overruns:0 frame:0
          TX packets:8 errors:0 dropped:0 overruns:0 carrier:0
          collisions:0 txqueuelen:0
          RX bytes:772 (772.0 B)  TX bytes:772 (772.0 B)
```

```
root@munich:~ #route -n
Kernel IP routing table
Destination     Gateway         Genmask         Flags Metric Ref    Use Iface
172.16.76.0     0.0.0.0         255.255.255.0   U     0      0        0 eth0
0.0.0.0         172.16.76.251   0.0.0.0         UG    0      0        0 eth0
root@munich:~ #ping 172.16.76.251
PING 172.16.76.251 (172.16.76.251): 56 data bytes
64 bytes from 172.16.76.251: icmp_seq=0 ttl=64 time=2.0 ms
64 bytes from 172.16.76.251: icmp_seq=1 ttl=64 time=0.5 ms
64 bytes from 172.16.76.251: icmp_seq=2 ttl=64 time=0.5 ms

--- 172.16.76.251 ping statistics ---
3 packets transmitted, 3 packets received, 0% packet loss
round-trip min/avg/max = 0.5/1.0/2.0 ms
root@munich:~ #
```

Network configuration and routing are correct, and pinging the VPN server works.

> On Microsoft operating systems you will have to type `ping /t` for persistent pings, `ipconfig /all` for network data, and `route print` to receive the routing table.

# Checking Interfaces, Routing, and Connectivity on the VPN Servers

In our next step we will have a close look at the network settings on the VPN servers. We will use the same tools as above, but the output will be a little more complex:

```
opensuse01:~ # ifconfig
eth0      Protokoll:Ethernet  Hardware Adresse 00:0C:29:13:EC:48
          inet Adresse:172.16.103.2  Bcast:172.16.103.255  Maske:255.255.255.0
          inet6 Adresse: fe80::20c:29ff:fe13:ec48/64
Gültigkeitsbereich:Verbindung
          UP BROADCAST NOTRAILERS RUNNING MULTICAST  MTU:1500  Metric:1
          RX packets:2900 errors:0 dropped:0 overruns:0 frame:0
          TX packets:4790 errors:0 dropped:0 overruns:0 carrier:0
          collisions:0 Sendewarteschlangenlänge:1000
          RX bytes:759578 (741.7 Kb)  TX bytes:666545 (650.9 Kb)
          Interrupt:10 Basisadresse:0x1080

eth1      Protokoll:Ethernet  Hardware Adresse 00:0C:29:13:EC:52
          inet Adresse:172.16.76.251  Bcast:172.16.76.255  Maske:255.255.255.0
          inet6 Adresse: fe80::20c:29ff:fe13:ec52/64
Gültigkeitsbereich:Verbindung
          UP BROADCAST NOTRAILERS RUNNING MULTICAST  MTU:1500  Metric:1
          RX packets:797 errors:0 dropped:0 overruns:0 frame:0
          TX packets:421 errors:0 dropped:0 overruns:0 carrier:0
          collisions:0 Sendewarteschlangenlänge:1000
          RX bytes:77682 (75.8 Kb)  TX bytes:42404 (41.4 Kb)
          Interrupt:9 Basisadresse:0x1400

lo        Protokoll:Lokale Schleife
          inet Adresse:127.0.0.1  Maske:255.0.0.0
          inet6 Adresse: ::1/128 Gültigkeitsbereich:Maschine
          UP LOOPBACK RUNNING  MTU:16436  Metric:1
          RX packets:109 errors:0 dropped:0 overruns:0 frame:0
          TX packets:109 errors:0 dropped:0 overruns:0 carrier:0
          collisions:0 Sendewarteschlangenlänge:0
          RX bytes:8380 (8.1 Kb)  TX bytes:8380 (8.1 Kb)
```

```
tunVPN0    Protokoll:UNSPEC  Hardware Adresse 00-00-00-00-00-00-00-00-00-00-
00-00-00-00-00
           inet Adresse:10.179.10.2  P-z-P:10.179.10.1  Maske:255.255.255.255
           UP PUNKTZUPUNKT RUNNING NOARP MULTICAST  MTU:1500  Metric:1
           RX packets:1337 errors:0 dropped:0 overruns:0 frame:0
           TX packets:1547 errors:0 dropped:0 overruns:0 carrier:0
           collisions:0 Sendewarteschlangenlänge:100
           RX bytes:470725 (459.6 Kb)  TX bytes:181397 (177.1 Kb)
opensuse01:~ #
```

OK, this server seems to have to network interface cards `eth0` and `eth1` (with two networks 172.16.103.0/24 and 172.16.76.0/24 in addition to the OpenVPN tunnel network `tunVPN0` with the network address `10.179.10.2` and the point-to-point partner's IP `10.179.10.1`. How about routing?

```
opensuse01:~ # route -n
Kernel IP Routentabelle
Ziel            Router          Genmask         Flags Metric Ref    Use Iface
10.179.10.1     0.0.0.0         255.255.255.255 UH    0      0        0
tunVPN0
172.16.103.0    0.0.0.0         255.255.255.0   U     0      0        0 eth0
172.16.76.0     0.0.0.0         255.255.255.0   U     0      0        0 eth1
192.168.250.0   10.179.10.1     255.255.255.0   UG    0      0        0
tunVPN0
127.0.0.0       0.0.0.0         255.0.0.0       U     0      0        0 lo
0.0.0.0         172.16.103.1    0.0.0.0         UG    0      0        0 eth0
opensuse01:~ #
```

Routing is a little more complicated here. We have two subnets connected to `eth0` and `eth1`, and two entries for our tunnel; everything to the virtual address `10.179.10.1` is routed via the interface `tunVPN0`, likewise traffic to the subnet 192.168.250.0/24, but this is routed via the gateway `10.179.10.1`. Last but not least, the default gateway of this router has the IP `172.16.103.1`. Obviously there is another network between this firewall and the Internet.

Let's now ping the point-to-point partner of this machine. We could see from the aforementioned interface list that this machine has the virtual IP `10.179.10.2`, and the VPN partner has the IP `10.179.10.1`. If our tunnel is working, it should be possible to ping through the tunnel:

```
opensuse01:~ # ping 10.179.10.1
PING 10.179.10.1 (10.179.10.1) 56(84) bytes of data.
64 bytes from 10.179.10.1: icmp_seq=1 ttl=64 time=1.77 ms
64 bytes from 10.179.10.1: icmp_seq=2 ttl=64 time=1.50 ms
64 bytes from 10.179.10.1: icmp_seq=3 ttl=64 time=1.42 ms
64 bytes from 10.179.10.1: icmp_seq=4 ttl=64 time=1.44 ms

--- 10.179.10.1 ping statistics ---
4 packets transmitted, 4 received, 0% packet loss, time 3013ms
rtt min/avg/max/mdev = 1.425/1.535/1.770/0.141 ms
opensuse01:~ #
```

It's working. Please note that the time taken to answer a ping will be significantly higher through the tunnel than for a local or direct ping.

Now let's do the same tests the other way around. We will analyze the network and routing of the Sydney server and try to ping to Munich through the tunnel:

```
debian01:~# ifconfig
eth0       Link encap:Ethernet  HWaddr 00:0C:29:99:7B:CA
           inet addr:172.16.247.2  Bcast:172.16.247.255  Mask:255.255.255.0
           UP BROADCAST RUNNING MULTICAST  MTU:1500  Metric:1
           RX packets:7735 errors:0 dropped:0 overruns:0 frame:0
           TX packets:11012 errors:0 dropped:0 overruns:0 carrier:0
```

```
          collisions:0 txqueuelen:1000
          RX bytes:924335 (902.6 KiB)  TX bytes:1714169 (1.6 MiB)
          Interrupt:18 Base address:0x1080

eth1      Link encap:Ethernet  HWaddr 00:0C:29:99:7B:D4
          inet addr:192.168.250.251  Bcast:192.168.250.255  Mask:255.255.255.0
          UP BROADCAST RUNNING MULTICAST  MTU:1500  Metric:1
          RX packets:490 errors:0 dropped:0 overruns:0 frame:0
          TX packets:468 errors:0 dropped:0 overruns:0 carrier:0
          collisions:0 txqueuelen:1000
          RX bytes:47652 (46.5 KiB)  TX bytes:43728 (42.7 KiB)
          Interrupt:19 Base address:0x1400

lo        Link encap:Local Loopback
          inet addr:127.0.0.1  Mask:255.0.0.0
          UP LOOPBACK RUNNING  MTU:16436  Metric:1
          RX packets:0 errors:0 dropped:0 overruns:0 frame:0
          TX packets:0 errors:0 dropped:0 overruns:0 carrier:0
          collisions:0 txqueuelen:0
          RX bytes:0 (0.0 b)  TX bytes:0 (0.0 b)

tunVPN0   Link encap:UNSPEC  HWaddr 00-00-00-00-00-00-00-00-00-00-00-00-00-
00-00
          inet addr:10.179.10.1  P-t-P:10.179.10.2  Mask:255.255.255.255
          UP POINTOPOINT RUNNING NOARP MULTICAST  MTU:1500  Metric:1
          RX packets:1849 errors:0 dropped:0 overruns:0 frame:0
          TX packets:1489 errors:0 dropped:0 overruns:0 carrier:0
          collisions:0 txqueuelen:100
          RX bytes:206765 (201.9 KiB)  TX bytes:483493 (472.1 KiB)

debian01:~# route -n
Kernel IP routing table
Destination     Gateway         Genmask         Flags Metric Ref    Use Iface
10.179.10.2     0.0.0.0         255.255.255.255 UH    0      0        0
tunVPN0
172.16.247.0    0.0.0.0         255.255.255.0   U     0      0        0 eth0
172.16.76.0     10.179.10.2     255.255.255.0   UG    0      0        0
tunVPN0
192.168.250.0   0.0.0.0         255.255.255.0   U     0      0        0 eth1
0.0.0.0         172.16.247.1    0.0.0.0         UG    0      0        0 eth0
debian01:~# ping 10.179.10.1
PING 10.179.10.1 (10.179.10.1) 56(84) bytes of data.
64 bytes from 10.179.10.1: icmp_seq=1 ttl=64 time=0.221 ms
64 bytes from 10.179.10.1: icmp_seq=2 ttl=64 time=0.069 ms
64 bytes from 10.179.10.1: icmp_seq=3 ttl=64 time=0.059 ms

--- 10.179.10.1 ping statistics ---
3 packets transmitted, 3 received, 0% packet loss, time 2005ms
rtt min/avg/max/mdev = 0.059/0.116/0.221/0.074 ms
debian01:~#
```

It worked. We have now made sure that:

- The VPN servers are reachable in their local networks.
- The OpenVPN tunnel is up and running.
- The OpenVPN tunnel is working in both directions.

Let's now enter another level of testing. We will now test if the Sydney network is reachable from our VPN server in Munich—still using ICMP packets only. Furthermore, the program `traceroute` will help us follow the route the packets take:

```
opensuse01:~ # ping 192.168.250.128
PING 192.168.250.128 (192.168.250.128) 56(84) bytes of data.
64 bytes from 192.168.250.128: icmp_seq=1 ttl=63 time=1.90 ms
64 bytes from 192.168.250.128: icmp_seq=2 ttl=63 time=1.26 ms
64 bytes from 192.168.250.128: icmp_seq=3 ttl=63 time=1.57 ms

--- 192.168.250.128 ping statistics ---
3 packets transmitted, 3 received, 0% packet loss, time 2009ms
rtt min/avg/max/mdev = 1.261/1.577/1.900/0.264 ms
opensuse01:~ # traceroute -n 192.168.250.128
traceroute to 192.168.250.128 (192.168.250.128), 30 hops max, 40 byte packets
 1  10.179.10.1  1.874 ms   8.949 ms   20.241 ms
 2  192.168.250.128  24.911 ms   35.618 ms   40.988 ms
opensuse01:~ #
```

Again, pinging worked fine. This indicates correct routing on the Sydney side and on the Munich VPN server. The output of the program `traceroute` lists all servers the packets passed on their way to Sydney; they were *thrown* into the tunnel immediately and arrived at the VPN server in Sydney `10.179.10.1`, which passed them on to the local machine, which took forty milliseconds. Of course we can also "traceroute" our packets that go the other way, provided that the administrator of the Debian server has installed `traceroute` (`apt-get install traceroute`).

> On Microsoft operating systems the command `tracert` offers the same functionality as `traceroute` on Linux.

Another very handy tool is "My traceroute", or `mtr`. Called with `mtr -n 192.168.250.128`, `mtr` keeps running `traceroute -n 192.168.250.128` command until you type q or *Ctrl+C*. The output is displayed in a clear table. With this command, we can easily switch routing entries and control the effect interactively.

```
                                  My traceroute  [v0.69]
opensuse01 (0.0.0.0)(tos=0x0 psize=64 bitpattern=0x00) Fri Dec  2 17:33:29 2005
Keys:  Help   Display mode   Restart statistics   Order of fields   quit
                                            Packets               Pings
 Host                                     Loss%   Snt   Last   Avg  Best  Wrst StDev
 1. 10.179.10.1                            0.0%     9    1.3   1.4   1.2   2.0   0.3
 2. 192.168.250.128                        0.0%     8    1.8   2.3   1.6   3.2   0.6
```

# Debugging with tcpdump and IPTraf

Another very handy tool to control traffic is `tcpdump`. As a network sniffer, `tcpdump` is often used by administrators or hackers to collect the data exchanged on the network. `tcpdump` prints all traffic that passes the interface given as a parameter. The following example shows the usage of `tcpdump`. When called with the options `-n` and `-i eth1`, `tcpdump` will listen on interface `eth1` and give a numeric output (without resolving DNS):

```
debian01:~# tcpdump -n -i eth1
tcpdump: verbose output suppressed, use -v or -vv for full protocol decode
listening on eth1, link-type EN10MB (Ethernet), capture size 96 bytes
21:00:16.640142 IP 192.168.250.128 > 172.16.76.128: ICMP echo request, id
```

```
55298, seq 0, length 64
21:00:16.648116 IP 172.16.76.128 > 192.168.250.128: ICMP echo reply, id 55298,
seq 0, length 64
21:00:17.678429 IP 192.168.250.128 > 172.16.76.128: ICMP echo request, id
55298, seq 256, length 64
21:00:17.680701 IP 172.16.76.128 > 192.168.250.128: ICMP echo reply, id 55298,
seq 256, length 64
21:00:18.668565 IP 192.168.250.128 > 172.16.76.128: ICMP echo request, id
55298, seq 512, length 64
21:00:18.670722 IP 172.16.76.128 > 192.168.250.128: ICMP echo reply, id 55298,
seq 512, length 64
21:00:19.688618 IP 192.168.250.128 > 172.16.76.128: ICMP echo request, id
55298, seq 768, length 64
21:00:19.690836 IP 172.16.76.128 > 192.168.250.128: ICMP echo reply, id 55298,
seq 768, length 64
```

As we can see, there were four `ICMP echo request` messages sent from `192.168.250.128` to `172.16.76.128`. All of them were answered by the machine `172.16.76.128` with the appropriate "echo reply" message.

Now we can use `tcpdump` on every machine in the chain of routers between the two clients in order to track the ICMP packets. For example, if a firewall is blocking the ICMP messages, then no PC *behind* this firewall will receive any the requests or replies, whereas the machines *before* the firewall will do.

```
debian01:~# tcpdump -ni tunVPN0
tcpdump: WARNING: arptype 65534 not supported by libpcap - falling back to
cooked socket
tcpdump: verbose output suppressed, use -v or -vv for full protocol decode
listening on tunVPN0, link-type LINUX_SLL (Linux cooked), capture size 96
bytes
21:07:53.800707 IP 172.16.76.128 > 192.168.250.128: ICMP echo request, id
19971, seq 9472, length 64
21:07:53.801608 IP 192.168.250.128 > 172.16.76.128: ICMP echo reply, id 19971,
seq 9472, length 64
21:07:54.799266 IP 172.16.76.128 > 192.168.250.128: ICMP echo request, id
19971, seq 9728, length 64
21:07:54.800531 IP 192.168.250.128 > 172.16.76.128: ICMP echo reply, id 19971,
seq 9728, length 64
21:07:55.800302 IP 172.16.76.128 > 192.168.250.128: ICMP echo request, id
19971, seq 9984, length 64
21:07:55.801296 IP 192.168.250.128 > 172.16.76.128: ICMP echo reply, id 19971,
seq 9984, length 64
21:07:56.752248 IP 172.16.76.128 > 192.168.250.128: ICMP echo request, id
19971, seq 10240, length 64
21:07:56.752876 IP 192.168.250.128 > 172.16.76.128: ICMP echo reply, id 19971,
seq 10240, length 64

8 packets captured
16 packets received by filter
0 packets dropped by kernel
debian01:~#
```

You see, `tcpdump` runs also on the tunnel interfaces, but some features won't work with TUN or TAP interfaces. Also because the network interface will be run in promiscuous mode, `tcpdump` will need root privileges. Furthermore, the information returned will be scarce in most switched networks, where only local packets can be displayed.

Another helpful tool is IPTraf (on Debian installed with `apt-get install iptraf`). IPTraf collects and displays packets and statistical data on selected interfaces. IPTraf comes with many options, but we will only focus on its list view.

Enter `iptraf` and hit return four times. You will get a window as depicted in the following screenshot:

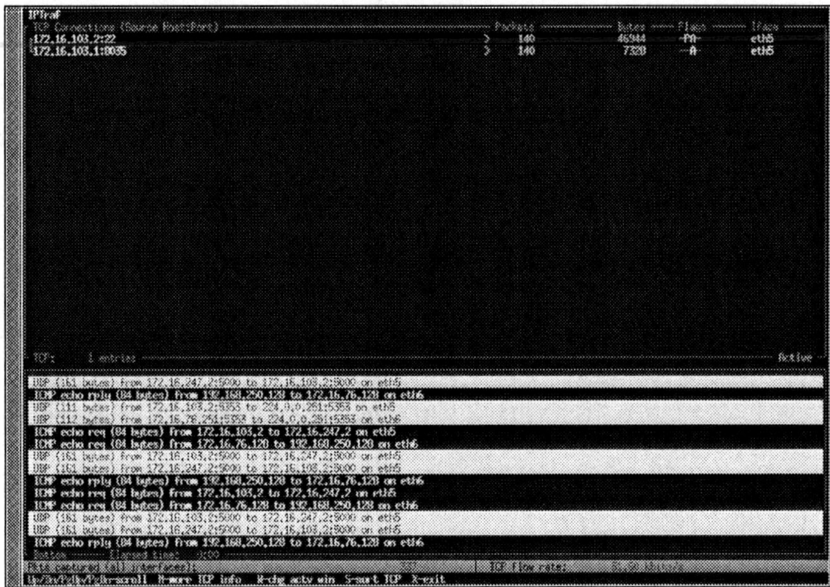

In the upper half of the window, TCP connections are displayed. UDP, ICMP, and other connections can be found in the lower half. In the example above, we can recognize an SSH session (from which IPTraf was started), ICMP packages between the Sydney and Munich client PCs, and the UDP packages encapsulating these ICMP packages.

Hit *X* twice and *Enter* once to quit IPTraf.

# Using OpenVPN Protocol and Status Files for Debugging

A very convenient method to watch tunnel traffic is setting the verbosity of OpenVPN to the fifth level. This is simply done with the entry `verb 5` in its configuration file. The following output shows an excerpt of OpenVPN's protocol file (as specified in the OpenVPN configuration file):

```
Fri Dec  9 21:05:15 2005 us=51912 Data Channel Encrypt: Cipher 'AES-256-CBC'
initialized with 256 bit key
Fri Dec  9 21:05:15 2005 us=51944 Data Channel Encrypt: Using 160 bit message
hash 'SHA1' for HMAC authentication
Fri Dec  9 21:05:15 2005 us=51962 Data Channel Decrypt: Cipher 'AES-256-CBC'
initialized with 256 bit key
Fri Dec  9 21:05:15 2005 us=52033 Data Channel Decrypt: Using 160 bit message
hash 'SHA1' for HMAC authentication
Fri Dec  9 21:05:15 2005 us=131924 Control Channel: TLSv1, cipher TLSv1/SSLv3
DHE-RSA-AES256-SHA, 2048 bit RSA
WRwrWRwrWRwrWRwrWRwrWRwrWRwrWRwrWRwrWRwrWRwrWRwrWRwrWRwrWRwrWRwrWRwrWRwrWRwrWR
wrWRwrWRwrWRwrWRwrWRwrWRwrWRwrWRwrWRwrWRwrWRwrWRwrWRwrWRwrWRwrWRwrWRwrWRwrWRwr
WRwrWRwrWRwrWRwrWRwrWRwrWRwrWRwrWRwrWRwrWRwrWRwrWRwrWRwrWRwrWRwrWRwrWRwrWRwrWR
wrWRwrWRwrWRwrW (...)
```

In the last lines we find the detailed statistics of all tunnel traffic. Upper cased letters stand for TCP or UDP datagrams on the real interface, encapsulating OpenVPN traffic, and lower case letters indicate traffic on the TUN/TAP interface. Unsurprisingly, `r` is for read and `w` is for write. Thus a successful ping command through the tunnel will always cause an entry like `WRwr` or vice versa.

Another file that our sample setup writes information to is the status file. Depending on the time period given as a parameter, OpenVPN will update the information in this file on a regular basis. In the example the file was `/var/log/openvpn/feilner-it.status`; the command `cat` can show us the content of this file:

```
debian01:~# cat /var/log/openvpn/feilner-it.status
OpenVPN STATISTICS
Updated,Fri Dec  9 21:26:53 2005
TUN/TAP read bytes,1102504
TUN/TAP write bytes,806453
TCP/UDP read bytes,1302857
TCP/UDP write bytes,1588558
Auth read bytes,808809
pre-compress bytes,55193
post-compress bytes,53110
pre-decompress bytes,1449
post-decompress bytes,2076
END
debian01:~#
```

We find detailed statistical data. If you run into problems with OpenVPN, it may be a good idea to check this file to find out if the values make sense, or if there is either too much or missing traffic on either side, for example, if it gets lost or the routing is wrong.

Depending on your system and logging setup, there may also be entries in your system protocol, like those here on this SuSE system:

```
opensuse01:~ # tail /var/log/messages
Dec  2 17:50:09 opensuse01 openvpn[11661]: Local Options String: 'V4,dev-type
tun,link-mtu 1545,tun-mtu 1500,proto UDPv4,ifconfig 10.179.11.1
10.179.11.2,comp-lzo,cipher BF-CBC,auth SHA1,keysize 128,secret'
Dec  2 17:50:09 opensuse01 openvpn[11661]: Expected Remote Options String:
'V4,dev-type tun,link-mtu 1545,tun-mtu 1500,proto UDPv4,ifconfig 10.179.11.2
10.179.11.1,comp-lzo,cipher BF-CBC,auth SHA1,keysize 128,secret'
Dec  2 17:50:09 opensuse01 openvpn[11661]: Local Options hash (VER=V4):
'59c313f6'
Dec  2 17:50:09 opensuse01 openvpn[11661]: Expected Remote Options hash
(VER=V4): '36b1f115'
Dec  2 17:50:09 opensuse01 openvpn[11661]: Output Traffic Shaping initialized
at 20000 bytes per second
Dec  2 17:50:09 opensuse01 openvpn[11674]: Socket Buffers: R=[113664->131072]
S=[113664->131072]
Dec  2 17:50:09 opensuse01 openvpn[11674]: UDPv4 link local (bound):
[undef]:5001
Dec  2 17:50:09 opensuse01 openvpn[11674]: UDPv4 link remote:
172.16.247.2:5001
```

This shows that another VPN tunnel has been created; OpenVPN is listening on UDP port 5001.

# Scanning Servers with Nmap

Nmap is a port scanner that can be used to determine whether a UDP or TCP port on a machine is open, and whether there is a server process accepting connections. Nmap can also find out if a firewall is protecting the machine scanned, and Nmap can scan whole networks. Let's scan the local client PC (which is obviously not protected by a firewall...):

```
opensuse01:~ # nmap 172.16.76.128

Starting nmap 3.81 ( http://www.insecure.org/nmap/ ) at 2005-12-02 18:02 CET
Interesting ports on localhost (172.16.76.128):
(The 1661 ports scanned but not shown below are in state: closed)
PORT    STATE SERVICE
22/tcp open  ssh
68/tcp open  dhcpclient
MAC Address: 00:0C:29:21:07:FC

Nmap finished: 1 IP address (1 host up) scanned in 1.773 seconds
```

There are two ports open on this system; port 1661 and other scanned ports are closed. If there were a firewall on this system, then scanning would not be that easy, because most firewalls detect scans and can prevent them. But there are many options to Nmap, including stealth scans, altering sender IPs, and many more—the manual page is really good.

We will now scan one of our OpenVPN servers to find out if our VPN port (5000) can be reached. The command `nmap -sU <IP> -p <Port>` will make Nmap scan only if the UDP port on the machine with the given IP address is open:

```
opensuse01:~ # nmap -sU 172.16.247.2 -p 5000

Starting nmap 3.81 ( http://www.insecure.org/nmap/ ) at 2005-12-02 18:06 CET
Note: Host seems down. If it is really up, but blocking our ping probes, try -
P0
Nmap finished: 1 IP address (0 hosts up) scanned in 2.067 seconds
opensuse01:~ # nmap -P0 -sU 172.16.247.2 -p 5000

Starting nmap 3.81 ( http://www.insecure.org/nmap/ ) at 2005-12-02 18:06 CET
Interesting ports on debian01.feilner-it.home (172.16.247.2):
PORT     STATE         SERVICE
5000/udp open|filtered UPnP

Nmap finished: 1 IP address (1 host up) scanned in 2.039 seconds
opensuse01:~ #
```

You saw how our Shorewall firewall did not reveal information about the port when we scanned it in the first try. However, Nmap already gave us a hint: add the parameter `-P0` to act even more stealthily. With this option, Nmap does not ping the hosts it scans before really scanning them. Some firewalls recognize this as a typical behavior of port scanners and block it. The second try, however revealed that the UDP port 5000 is filtered (by a firewall). This means: firewall rules may be protecting and limiting access to this port, but it is open.

> On Windows the program "Angry IP Scanner" will probably be your first choice for scanning.

# Monitoring Tools

There are many tools that provide detailed statistics on network interfaces. Two very easily installed monitoring tools with great functions are **ntop** and **Munin**.

## ntop

ntop monitors a network and may in some states be illegal because it creates detailed records of connections between IP addresses. Furthermore, it offers a nice browser GUI and does not need a running web server. `ntop` installs easily on Debian.

Enter `apt-get install ntop` and choose the interface you want to monitor. After software installation, type `ntop -A`, and enter an administrator password for ntop's admin account. Now type `/etc/init.d/ntop start` and point a browser to the `http://IP:3000` of this system (ntop is running on port 3000). You will get a feature-rich window with a growing amount of information, especially if ntop has been for running some time:

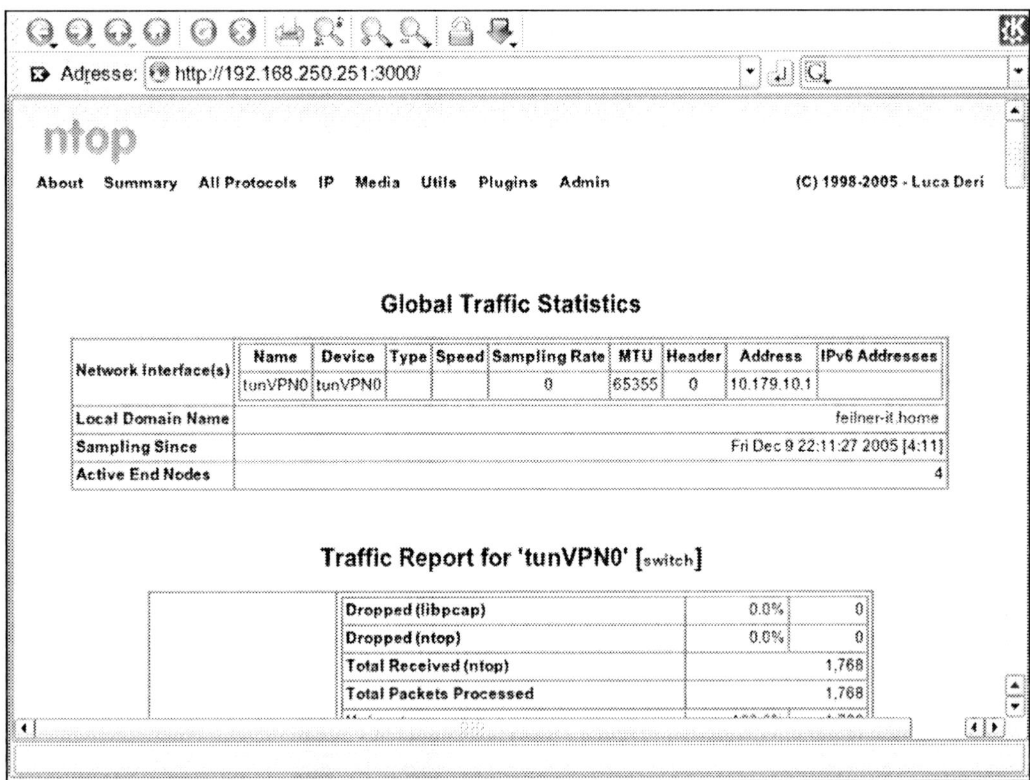


ntop offers many possibilities. We can save the data to a database, access to a database can be secured and monitored, interfaces can be switched online, and many more possibilities.

# Munin

Another helpful statistic tool is Munin. Munin consists of a client and a server process that collect data that is provided from an almost arbitrary source on Linux (or even Windows) systems. The example below shows the standard Munin interface after installation as documented on `http://munin.sf.net`. Unfortunately, Munin needs a web server like Apache, but apart from this, the installation is very easy. Munin is configured from files in `/etc/munin/`, and makes use of a great number of plug-ins; even more can be downloaded.

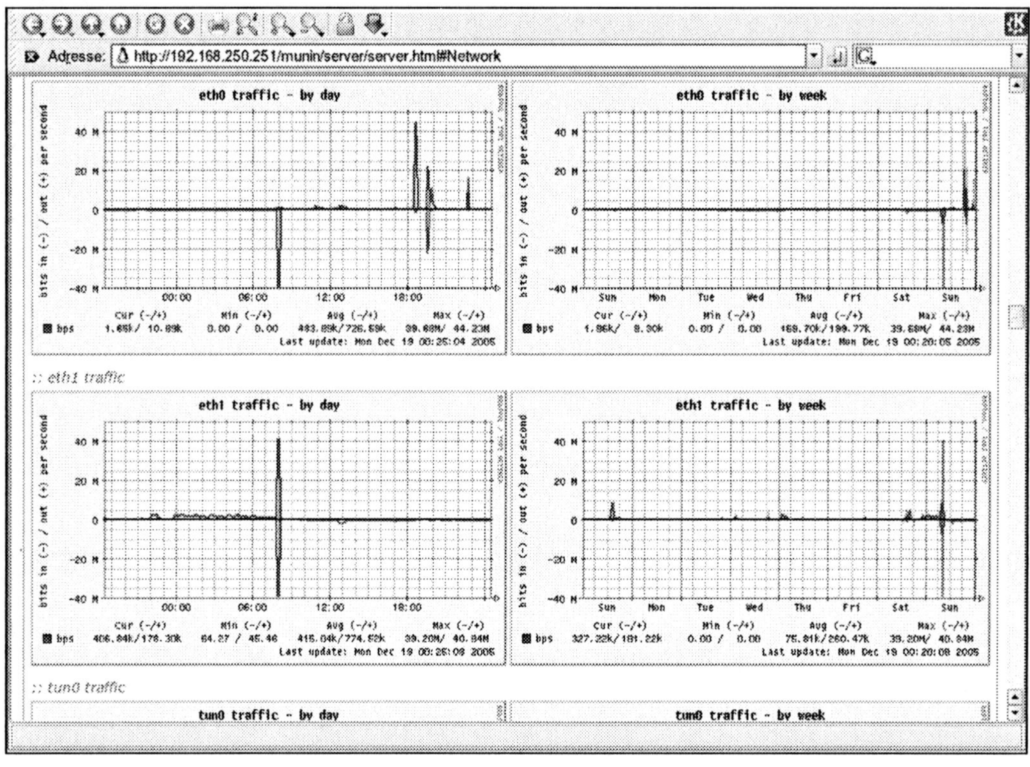


Since there are only a few requirements for a Munin plug-in, we can easily create our own OpenVPN monitoring plug-in. Such a plug-in must be executable, and return data in the format of:

```
router:/usr/share/munin/plugins # /etc/munin/plugins/if_eth0
down.value 1777836059
up.value 94615124
router:/usr/share/munin/plugins #
```

As an example, on `http://rodolphe.quiedeville.org/hack/openvpn` there is a simple plug-in that reports the number of users connected to an OpenVPN server. I leave it up to you to imagine the possibilities of such plug-ins when combined with `samba`, `iptables`, OpenVPN, and more. Just think of the OpenVPN status file and the information it provides.

## Hints to Other Tools

There is an abundance of networking tools concerning monitoring, sniffing, and scanning. Two of my favorites are Cacti and Nagios. Cacti is a monitoring tool similar to Munin, but it seems more powerful. Nagios is a tool designed to monitor machines and services.

With Nagios you can not only determine if a server is still answering pings, but can also check for services by accessing them (using e.g. the `samba` or HTTP protocols) and trigger actions when the service is not available. You can have your Nagios machine send you an SMS if your OpenVPN tunnel is down, or if the management interface is not reacting.

## Summary

In this chapter we have learned how to check our OpenVPN and networking setup step-by-step using standard Linux tools and evaluating their output. With tools like `ifconfig`, `ping`, `traceroute`, and `mtr`, we could analyze the flow of datagrams between the VPN servers and the connected networks. Programs like `tcpdump`, IPTraf, ntop, and Munin will give us detailed information about the current traffic or statistical breakdowns of it. The first place to look for troubleshooting should always be the log file of OpenVPN itself—especially at a higher level of verbosity.

# Internet Resources

## VPN Basics

The baseline protection manual of the German BSI:

http://www.bsi.bund.de/english/gshb/index.htm.

http://www.bsi.bund.de/english/.

Handbook of Information Security Management:

http://www.cccure.org/Documents/HISM/ewtoc.html.

IT Baseline Protection as published by the German BSI (but in English):

http://www.bsi.bund.de/english/gshb/index.htm.

http://www.bsi.bund.de/english/.

The IT-Sec Handbook—concise security hints:

http://www.cccure.org/Documents/HISM/ewtoc.html.

Wikipedia articles are good to start with and contain lots of interesting links:

http://en.wikipedia.org/wiki/Symmetric_encryption.

http://en.wikipedia.org/wiki/Asymmetric_encryption.

http://en.wikipedia.org/wiki/Cryptography.

http://en.wikipedia.org/wiki/Secure_Sockets_Layer.

http://en.wikipedia.org/wiki/Public_key_certificate.

Windows Security and SSL:

http://www.windowsecurity.com/articles/Secure_Socket_Layer.html.

The TLS protocol as specified by the IETF:

http://www.ietf.org/rfc/rfc2246.txt.

A concise but easy explanation of the OSI model can be found in the Wikipedia:

http://en.wikipedia.org/wiki/OSI_model.

A very good overview on Layer 2 Forwarding (L2F) can be found here:

http://www.javvin.com/protocolL2F.html.

The Internet Engineering Task Force details can be found at:

http://www.ietf.org.

Read the IPsec article in Wikipedia:

http://en.wikipedia.org/wiki/IPsec.

The Linux IPsec Howto:

http://www.ipsec-howto.org/t1.html.

An example for a TLS/SSL web-based SSL/TLS VPN solution:

http://sourceforge.net/projects/sslexplorer/.

http://3sp.com/showSslExplorer.do.

## OpenVPN Resources

An interview with James Yonan on Linuxsecurity.com:

http://www.linuxsecurity.com/content/view/117363/49/.

Community: The project website of OpenVPN

http://openvpn.net/.

OpenVPN changelog and release notes:

http://openvpn.net/changelog.html.

http://openvpn.net/relnotes.html.

Shorewall Firewall:

http://www.shorewall.net/OPENVPN.html.

http://home.arcor.de/u.altinkaynak/openvpn.html.

OpenVPN forum:

http://www.vpnforum.de/.

The mailing lists:

http://openvpn.net/mail.html.

The SSL/TLS Cryptographic Libraries website:

http://www.openssl.org/.

The website of the Transport Layer Security Charter by the TLS Working Group:

`http://www.ietf.org/html.charters/tls-charter.html.`

The universal TUN/TAP driver:

`http://vtun.sourceforge.net/tun/.`

Installing the OpenVPN LZO project:

`http://www.oberhumer.com/opensource/lzo/.`

For Microsoft Windows operating systems you have to download the binary `.exe` file from:

`http://openvpn.net/download.html.`

Or the package containing a graphical user interface from:

`http://openvpn.se/.`

Daily (unstable!) snapshots of OpenVPN Source Code:

`http://sourceforge.net/cvs/?group_id=48978.`

Mac Tool:

`http://www.tunnelblick.net/README.txt.`

Detailed installation instructions for Mac OS 10.3:

`http://www.helsinki.fi/atk/english/hy-ppp/hy-vpn/hy-vpn-mac.html.`

Homepage of the Tunnelblick OpenVPN GUI for Macintosh:

`http://www.tunnelblick.net/.`

Open SUSE Support Database:

`http://en.opensuse.org/SDB:SDB.`

Novell's SuSE site:

`http://www.novell.com/linux/suse/.`

Redhat:

`www.redhat.org.`

`www.fedora.org.`

Redhat (Fedora frequently asked questions):

`http://www.fedorafaq.org/.`

Yum:

`http://linux.duke.edu/projects/yum/.`

Suitable configurations file for yum:

`http://www.fedorafaq.org/samples/yum.conf.`

OpenVPN Fedora RPMs:

`http://dag.wieers.com/packages/openvpn/`.

OpenVPN SuSE RPMs:

`ftp://ftp.suse.com/`.

Debian: A detailed Howto on configuring one of your HTTP or FTP servers to act as a Debian repository can be found here:

`http://www.debian.org/doc/manuals/repository-howto/repository-howto.en.html`.

The Debian New Maintainers' Guide—create Debian packages:

`http://www.debian.org/doc/manuals/maint-guide/index.en.html`.

Detailed information about the Debian packages for OpenVPN can be found at:

`http://packages.debian.org/stable/net/openvpn`.

Carpaltunnel is a script to manage tunnels and their certificates. The Debian package can be found here:

`http://packages.debian.org/stable/net/carpaltunnel`.

BSD:

`http://blog.innerewut.de/articles/2005/07/04/openvpn-2-0-on-openbsd`.

`http://blog.innerewut.de/articles/2005/07/08/improving-openvpn-s-security`.

FreeBSD:

`http://www.freshports.org/security/openvpn/`.

`http://openvpn.net/wiki/Platforms:FreeBSD`.

NetBSD:

`http://pkgsrc.se/net/openvpn`.

OpenBSD:

`http://software.newsforge.com/software/05/11/21/175249.shtml?tid=92&tid=78`.

`http://www50.brinkster.com/dachee/OpenVPN.htm`.

Ports:

`http://openvpn.net/ports.html`.

Kernel compilation Howto:

`www.linuxhaven.de/dlhp/HOWTO/DE-Kernel-HOWTO.html`.

`http://www.digitalhermit.com/linux/Kernel-Build-HOWTO.html`.

Kernel sources:

`http://www.kernel.org/`.

OpenVPN and Debian:

`http://www.debian-administration.org/articles/35`.

OpenVPN and SuSE:

`http://freifunk.net/wiki/OpenVPN` (German).

`http://sarwiki.informatik.hu-berlin.de/OpenVPN_(deutsch)` (German).

OpenVPN and Redhat:

`http://mia.ece.uic.edu/~papers/volans/openvpn.html`.

Installing OpenVPN Devices run by OpenWrt:

`http://martybugs.net/wireless/openwrt/openvpn.cgi`.

# Configuration

Information on the init system of Debian systems:

`http://www.debian.org/doc/debian-policy/ch-opersys.html#s-sysvinit`.

Troubleshooting connection problems on Windows:

`http://www.helsinki.fi/atk/english/hy-ppp/hy-vpn/win_trouble.html`.

WinSCP—an SSH/SCP client for Windows:

`http://winscp.net/ - Freeware SFTP and SCP client for Windows`.

The dos2unix converter:

`http://www.megaloman.com/~hany/software/hd2u/ - Hany's Dos2Unix convertor`.

Detailed information about the Diffie-Hellman key exchange algorithm:

`http://www.rsasecurity.com/rsalabs/node.asp?id=2248`.

The Network Time Protocol:

`http://www.ntp.org/`.

Public Key Infrastructure (X.509) Working Group:

`http://www.ietf.org/html.charters/pkix-charter.html`.

Wikipedia on X509 certificates:

`http://en.wikipedia.org/wiki/X509`.

Information on a PKI using OpenSSL:

`http://www.rajeevnet.com/crypto/ca/ca-paper.html`.

Online manual page of the stable version of OpenVPN:

`http://openvpn.net/man.html`.

Online manual page of the unstable version:

`http://openvpn.net/man-beta.html`.

The Webmin project website:

`http://www.webmin.com`.

Development version of Webmin (new Shorewall module):

`http://webmin.com/devel.html`.

Shoreline Firewall (Shorewall) project:

`http://www.shorewall.net/`.

Linux `iptables` Howto:

`http://www.linuxguruz.com/iptables/howto/`.

Hardening OpenVPN security:

`http://openvpn.net/howto.html#security`.

XCA SourceForge project website:

`http://sourceforge.net/projects/xca`.

OpenCA Research and Development Labs:

`http://www.openca.org/`.

The TinyCA project:

`http://tinyca.sm-zone.net/`.

A Guide to basic RSA Key Management:

`http://openvpn.net/easyrsa.html`.

Certificate management and installation with OpenSSL:

`http://www.gagravarr.org/writing/openssl-certs/`.

Securing `distcc` with `chroot` and OpenVPN:

`http://www.northernsecurity.net/articles/distcc.html`.

NSIS software installer for Windows:

`http://nsis.sourceforge.net/Main_Page`.

How to roll your own OpenVPN Windows installation package:

`http://openvpn.se/files/howto/openvpn-howto_roll_your_own_installation_package.html`.

Connecting to an OpenVPN server via an HTTP proxy:

`http://openvpn.net/howto.html#http.`

Pushing DHCP options to clients:

`http://openvpn.net/howto.html#dhcp.`

Routing all client traffic (including web traffic) through the VPN:

`http://openvpn.net/howto.html#redirect.`

## Scripts and More

Environmental variables (German) for OpenVPN:

`http://www.pronix.de/pronix-991.html.`

Distributed compiling with `distcc`:

`http://distcc.samba.org/.`

`http://www.debian-administration.org/articles/157.`

Bridging Howtos:

`http://openvpn.net/bridge.html.`

`http://www.pavelec.net/adam/openvpn/bridge/.`

Information for automatic installation:

`http://www.openvpn.se/files/nsis/nsis205.exe.`

`http://openvpn.se/files/howto/openvpn-howto_roll_your_own_installation_package.html.`

`http://www.openvpn.se/files/install_packages_source/.`

## Network Tools

My traceroute (mtr):

`http://www.bitwizard.nl/mtr/index.html.`

tcpdump:

`http://www.tcpdump.org/.`

Windump: tcpdump for Windows:

`http://www.winpcap.org/windump/.`

IPTraf:

`http://iptraf.seul.org/.`

Angry IP Scanner (Windows):

`http://www.angryziber.com/ipscan/`.

Nmap:

`http://www.insecure.org/nmap/index.html`.

ntop:

`http://www.ntop.org/ntop.html`.

Munin monitoring server:

`http://munin.projects.linpro.no/`.

Nagios:

`http://www.nagios.org/`.

Cacti:

`http://www.cacti.net/`.

## Howtos

The Linux file server Howto (includes networking basics and troubleshooting):

`http://linux.vyrax.com/`.

IPTraf:

`http://iptraf.seul.org/2.7/manual.html`.

Monitoring with tcpdump:

`http://www-iepm.slac.stanford.edu/monitoring/passive/tcpdump.html`.

TCP/IP and tcpdump, pocket reference guide:

`http://www.sans.org/resources/tcpip.pdf`.

Wikipedia on tcpdump:

`http://en.wikipedia.org/wiki/Tcpdump`.

Understanding traceroute and ping results:

`http://www.visualware.com/resources/tutorials/tracert.html`.

A short Nmap Howto:

`http://www.tldp.org/LDP/LG/issue56/flechtner.html`.

Munin Howto for Debian:

`http://www.debian-administration.org/articles/229`.

Howto on writing your own Munin plug-ins:

`http://munin.projects.linpro.no/wiki/HowToWritePlugins`.

# Openvpn GUIs

OpenVPN GUI for Windows:

`http://openvpn.se/`.

OpenVPN GUI for Linux, written in Gambas:

`http://www.linprofs.com/modules/news/article.php?storyid=8`.

OpenVPN-Admin, a multi-platform OpenVPN GUI:

`http://sourceforge.net/projects/openvpnadmin/`.

KVpnc, a KDE VPN GUI for Cisco, IPSec, PPTP, and OpenVPN:

`http://home.gna.org/kvpnc/en/index.html`.

OpenVPN control, a graphical management interface:

`http://sourceforge.net/project/showfiles.php?group_id=152302`.

Tunnelblick—a GUI for MacOS X:

`http://www.tunnelblick.net/`.

A promising OpenVPN Webmin module:

`http://www.openit.it/index.php/openit_en/soluzioni_gpl/openvpnadmin`.

# Index

## A



## B



## C

## O



## P

# R



# S

## T



## U



## V

Printed in the United States
49671LVS00002B/49-128

9 781904 811855